LEADERSHIP

To my mentors:

Fred Fiedler ("Write so your work passes the 'after dinner' test"), and Joe Litterer (Question: "What's the good word on my dissertation progress?" Answer: "You're inching along.")

LEADERSHIP

A New Synthesis

James G. Hunt

SAGE PUBLICATIONS
The International Professional Publishers
Newbury Park   London   New Delhi

For information address:

SAGE Publications, Inc.
2455 Teller Road
Newbury Park, California 91320

SAGE Publications Ltd.
6 Bonhill Street
London EC2A 4PU
United Kingdom

SAGE Publications India Pvt. Ltd.
M-32 Market
Greater Kailash I
New Delhi 110 048 India

Printed in the United States of America

Library of Congress Cataloging-in-Publication Data

Hunt, James, G., 1932-
    Leadership : a new synthesis / J.G. Hunt.
        p.   cm.
    Includes bibliographical references and index.
    ISBN 0-8039-3767-9. — ISBN 0-8039-3768-7 (pbk.)
    1. Leadership. I. Title.
HD57.7.H87 1991
303.3'4—dc20   91-93242
                                                                    CIP

92 93 94 15 14 13 12 11 10 9 8 7 6 5 4 3 2

Sage Production Editor: Astrid Virding

Contents

Acknowledgments

In terms of acknowledgments, I would like to start with T. Owen Jacobs of the Army Research Institute, and with those who reviewed substantial portions of the manuscript. "Jake" influenced my thinking greatly on this project and provided me with hard-to-find reference materials. Kimberly Boal, Rao Korukonda, Phillip Lewis, James McElroy, Arja Ropo, Marshall Sashkin, and Leonard Wong are those who reviewed much of the manuscript in various stages.

In addition to the stalwart, patient, and prompt reviewers just mentioned, there were a number of people who reviewed specific chapters and provided expert advice. These were: Richard Barton, Gail Futoran, Roy Howell, Shelby Hunt, Linda Krefting, T. K. Peng, Mark Peterson, Eero Ropo, Grant Savage, and Alex Stewart.

Besides all those who reviewed various portions of the manuscript, I want to recognize those who reviewed the prospectus. In addition to some anonymous reviewers these included: Larry Austin, Urs Gattiker, Mark Peterson, and Robert Phillips.

All of the previously mentioned people have helped me more than they know.

I was fortunate to obtain a semester's faculty development leave from Texas Tech and am thankful to those who made that possible. Carlton Whitehead, the Area Coordinator of Management (department chair), provided both necessary area moral support and area resources to complete the project. An important part of those resources consisted of typing, which was ably provided by Francis Pinkerton and her competent student work-study assistants, Andrea Bullock, Chrene Johnson, Devona Smith, and Deanna Stewart. Amber Ferguson was also helpful when the final typing crunch came to meet the publisher's deadline. Library work and other help as well was provided by Joan Rivera and Matthew Yoder, my research assistants. Robert Phillips provided additional support by making available a College of Business

Administration Small Research Grant to pay for typing help and related matters.

My wife Donna provided a stress-free "organizational culture" at home where I did my writing. She also pitched in to help with the final typing crunch. My home culture, along with the encouraging one in Tech's College of Business Administration and Area of Management, were useful facilitators in addition to the college's and area's physical support. Finally, I would like to acknowledge the people at Sage and especially Sage's Ann West, who provided the right mix of carrot and stick in seeing me through this project.

As always, in spite of all the previously mentioned help, any errors remain mine.

—James G. (Jerry) Hunt
Lubbock, Texas

1 First Things First

- Focus of the Book
- Organization of the Book
- Audience
- A Personal Word

Once I was active in the leadership field. Then I left it for about ten years.
When I returned it was as if I had been gone only ten minutes.

—unknown leadership scholar

The heresy that I propose is that the concept of leadership itself has
outlived its usefulness. Hence, I suggest that we abandon leadership in
favor of some other more fruitful way of cutting up the theoretical pie.

—John B. Minner
(quoted in Hunt & Larson, 1975, p. 200)

The literature regarding . . . leadership is paradoxical: Popular thinking
. . . emphasizes the importance of . . . leadership in establishing excellent
organizations, but many academic publications assert that leadership is
inconsequential.

—David B. Day and Robert G. Lord (1988, p. 453)

I believe there are two kinds of people in this world—those who read
prefaces and those who don't. I also believe that there are many more
who don't than who do—thus, with the exception of the acknowledgments, I have combined traditional preface and introductory material
into this chapter. (Of course, I have not dealt with those who read
neither prefaces nor introductions.)

FOCUS OF THE BOOK

The opening quotes about staleness, lack of usefulness, and even
whether leadership makes a difference or not remind us of the state of
the leadership field not so very long ago. Since that time, there has been

1

a dramatic increase in interest with a far wider group of people involved in serious study of the area. Indeed, this increase in interest means that things are moving so rapidly that unless we run extremely fast we are in danger of falling behind in terms of what is happening in the field today. I try both to "run fast" and to avoid Calvin's dilemma by proposing a new leadership synthesis that provides the base for an expansion in the way we think about both leadership knowledge content and leadership knowledge orientation (i.e., how we gain, use, and assess leadership knowledge).

The knowledge-content aspect of the proposed synthesis involves going beyond the overwhelming majority of leadership studies that view leadership as simply face-to-face influence at the bottom of the organization. In terms of sheer numbers, I am saying, then, that of the estimated more than 10,000 leadership studies (see Yukl, 1989), almost all have been done at the bottom of the organization! Even so, many people have felt that there must be differing leadership requirements by organizational level, and that top-level leadership must be different in important ways from that of bottom-level leaders. Thus today there is increasing interest in the study of leadership at the chief executive officer (CEO) level as well as at other levels in the organization. However, such work has not tended to be very systematic and mostly has not had much of a conceptual base.

With these things in mind, the knowledge-content component of the synthesis includes a comprehensive conceptual framework that can be used for the systematic investigation of leadership at multiple organization levels, across organizations. Accompanying this multilevel focus is a virtually inseparable emphasis on various temporal aspects, including differences by organizational level and a stress on dynamic changes across time. Just as the overwhelming majority of leadership studies have been lower level and face-to-face, most also have neglected time or treated it only in passing. Unlike these studies, the multilevel approach here gives time the emphasis it deserves. It does so by recognizing time explicitly rather than neglecting it or treating it as an afterthought.

The way in which we obtain, use, and evaluate such knowledge content is the second (or knowledge orientation) aspect of the synthesis. Here I develop a framework that looks at underlying leadership reality assumptions, along with the specific purposes, the specific way in which leadership is defined, and the specific stakeholders involved. Although I devote Chapter 4 to this framework, for now let's try to provide some preliminary understanding. People interested in leadership knowledge have certain assumptions about how they really can "know the reality" of leadership. Is it something "out there" and "real," akin to physical science phenomena? Or instead, is it something that they see as largely the product of their minds? These assumptions will have an impact on the way these individuals go about attaining, using, and evaluating leadership knowledge.

For example, if they believe leadership is something out there and real, they may try to measure it through such devices as a questionnaire or a systematic observational system and try to draw generalizations. If they believe it is more a product of their minds, they are more likely to rely on their personal feelings and reactions.

These basic assumptions are seen as a core aspect of people's leadership knowledge orientation.[1] Joining these assumptions as part of this orientation are three other aspects. First are the purposes for which the leadership knowledge is to be used. Second is how broadly or narrowly these purposes define the leadership concept. Finally, the stakeholders (e.g., supervisors, publishing outlets) involved with the knowledge are a part of this leadership knowledge orientation.

Let's consider a leadership researcher, a leadership consultant, and a leadership practitioner. The three parties may or may not have similar basic assumptions about the reality we call leadership. At the same time, it's quite likely that their purposes for obtaining the knowledge, their ways of defining leadership, and the stakeholders of relevance to them will be different. In turn, these differences will influence the ways they attain leadership knowledge and their use of what we mean by the knowledge orientation component of the new leadership synthesis.

I'm advocating a pragmatic perspective concerning leadership knowledge orientation. Indeed, I'll go further and argue that without such pragmatism we can't fully realize the potential of the multilevel model. Thus a pragmatic view of both knowledge content and knowledge orientation go hand-in-hand. As we shall see, such pragmatism is not typical of current mainstream leadership approaches. Not only do they overconcentrate on the bottom reaches of the organization, but they operate from a restricted knowledge orientation.

This, then, is the thrust of the book—an emphasis on a new synthesis and an expanded view of leadership based on an open-minded approach to leadership knowledge content and leadership knowledge orientation. This view is largely consistent with conceptual or empirical work I've done, individually or collaboratively, over many years. As we shall see, some of that work has emphasized multiple levels and much has focused on environmental and organizational factors. Here I attempt to integrate and extend these directions. I also should note, however, that until quite recently that work followed the narrow knowledge orientation perspective that is characteristic of mainstream leadership approaches. So, in this regard, the perspective in this book reflects a major change in my thinking.

Let's look at a few of the many implications of the new synthesis here to show how it differs from more traditional emphases. Perhaps the key implication is that at the top, leadership becomes organizational in nature. Thus the previously mentioned environment and organizational factors become extremely important. Instead of thinking of leadership as narrow, face-to-face interaction, I am concerned here with such things as the impact of mission definition, strategy setting, and organizational design on those deep within the organization's bowels. In other words, not only are there direct effects, but also indirect second- and even third-order effects felt far down in the organization. The multiple-level aspect means that this approach is not only concerned with these kinds of things at the strategic level of the organization but also with corresponding, though narrower (what I later term *cascading*), aspects as we move down the hierarchy.

A second implication considers the differences in complexity and time emphasis expected at the different levels, and the way that we view various aspects of effectiveness at each level. Still another implication concerns the focus on organizational and individual transformation and change that is suggested by the temporal emphasis in this broadened view.

Finally, the broadened knowledge orientation has implications for the way we come to understand and explore the reality we call leadership. Consultants and practitioners will tend to have a different knowledge orientation than academic researchers. These parties typically will obtain, use, and evaluate leadership differently.

Essentially what all of this means is that after reading this book one should have a considerably expanded view of leadership. The opening quotes will no longer be true—if they ever were. There are clearly new developments taking place, the leadership concept has not lost its usefulness, and the reader will have a better idea when and where leadership is consequential and when and where it's not.

ORGANIZATION OF THE BOOK

The three chapters of Part I emphasize the knowledge content and knowledge orientation aspects of the proposed leadership synthesis. Chapter 2 focuses on a quick review of the literature on multiple-level leadership and discussion of some core concepts. Chapter 3 goes beyond these core concepts to provide what I call the *extended multiple-level leadership* model, incorporating a wide range of thinking. Finally, Chapter 4 addresses knowledge orientation aspects by developing a leadership knowledge-orientation framework. There I discuss underlying leadership reality assumptions and the purposes, definitions, and stakeholders involved in this knowledge orientation.

Part II then explores, in more detail, the issues presented in Part I. Its seven chapters look at separate components of the extended model and incorporate treatment of important knowledge orientation aspects as a part of the knowledge content discussion of these components. Chapter 5 examines the external environment and societal culture and the nature and importance of leader critical tasks. Chapter 6 first considers a range of leader background variables, such as education and experience. Then it explores predisposition to lead and related preference aspects of the model's individual capability cluster. Later chapters then consider additional aspects of leadership capabilities: Chapter 7 examines cognitive complexity and various social-cognition aspects; Chapter 8 looks at transactionally oriented leadership skills; and Chapter 9 discusses transformationally oriented leadership skills. Chapter 10 focuses on organizational culture as a linkage for various aspects of the model. Chapter 11 concludes Part II by examining the model's long- and short-term leadership development implications.

Finally, Chapter 12 concludes the book by focusing on where we've been and areas for further development, including additional treatment of temporal aspects and the extended model in a dynamic setting.

AUDIENCE

The book is directed toward those interested in the scholarly study of leadership, be they scholars, practitioners, consultants, or students. The word *scholarly* is important, however; the book is not a "quick read" on a cold winter's night. Nor is it loaded with anecdotal how-tos, even though it does include relevant examples. Although it isn't a text in the traditional sense of the term, it can be used as one if it is supplemented. Alternatively, it can be used as a supplement to other material to stimulate additional thinking and emphasize differing views.

In terms of leadership orientations, for openers, the book should appeal to those with a mainstream or traditional leadership bent, such as organizational behavior scholars and industrial/organizational psychologists. They may or may not agree with its perspective but should find its topic and literature coverage of interest. Along with these "mainstreamers," the book should be of interest to those, in such areas as educational and public administration, who are interested in leadership. They typically have a very different perspective than those with organizational behavior or I/O psychology backgrounds.

Given its combined organizational and cognitive direction and its emphasis on a broad knowledge orientation, the book also should appeal to those who typically do *not* have an interest in leadership because they see it as too narrow. Such a broad perspective seems to be especially prevalent outside the United States (see Hunt, Sekaran, & Schriesheim, 1982; Hunt, Hosking, Schriesheim, & Stewart, 1984). Hence the book should have greater than usual appeal to Europeans and others with this broader view. Finally, its top-level findings draw heavily on the strategic management literature. Thus the book should be suitable for those from the strategic management area, particularly individuals with a strategic management process or strategic leadership focus.

A PERSONAL WORD

This book has stretched me! I wrote it because I wanted to broaden people's thinking—yours and mine. That drew me into a wide range of literature outside that traditionally covered in leadership (e.g., philosophy of science, systems theory, simulation, dynamic analysis). Much of this literature is scattered across various sources that are not always easily available to those studying leadership. For instance, I include a number of military sources, not all of them published, as well as some foreign literature. Essentially, in addition to whatever direct contribution the book makes toward a new synthesis, I want it to be a sourcebook for a range of relevant literature. These sources and their topics should be useful to those who are serious students of leadership even if they do not have a direct interest in the model of leadership that is developed. The sources are relevant for the current study of leadership from many perspectives.

I also should note that, wherever possible, I tried to find summary treatments of materials such as textbooks, review articles and chapters, and so on. In many cases, these may not go into the depth desired by an expert in the area but themselves usually do include extensive reference lists. Wherever appropriate, I also cover references that will provide additional insight for readers even though sometimes I can do no more than mention them in my coverage. Also, some sources came along too late in the writing process for me to do more than mention them briefly.

Because of the breadth and stretching, I often found myself in areas of specialization outside my expertise. It's possible that experts in these fields might conclude that I haven't included the most comprehensive, up-to-date works or that my interpretations aren't completely accurate. If that happens, I invite them to clarify my misinterpretations and strengthen the formulations where necessary. If this occurs, we'll all be the better for it.

The level of treatment of each of the topics was also of concern to me in writing for the broad intended audience just mentioned. For example, the treatment of organization theory concepts could be both too elementary and too detailed for those with OT backgrounds. However, this level would be necessary for those with a cognitive science background (and vice versa, of course). I tried to strike a reasonable balance; although, this has been clearly a judgment call.

Finally, I should mention that I have tried to provide an historical perspective. I haven't used a separate chapter or chapter section for historical developments, but I have tried to refer to earlier work as appropriate. This is consistent with my view that too often we reinvent the wheel or get excited about old wine in new bottles. Although there may be nothing wrong with this excitement, we should at least recognize its origins.

This book has been both rewarding and frustrating for me—although, happily, more the former than the latter. In that, it is much like the experience of building a new house. I hope you, too, find the book rewarding and that your frustrations are few. Let's now move into Part I and Chapter 2, where I begin the focus on the knowledge content aspect of leadership synthesis. There I examine the core concepts that lay the groundwork for the extended multiple level model.

NOTE

1. Such assumptions are receiving increasing attention in the managerial and marketing literature as well as in the behavioral sciences in general (see Burrell & Morgan, 1979; S. D. Hunt, 1991).

Part I

Leadership Knowledge Content and Knowledge Orientation

This part illustrates the knowledge content component of the new synthesis by developing an extended multiple-level leadership model. It illustrates the knowledge orientation component by developing a framework focusing on knowledge orientation assumptions, purposes, definitions, and stakeholders.

- Chapter 2: Core Concepts for a Multiorganizational Level Leadership Model
- Chapter 3: The Extended Multilevel Leadership Model
- Chapter 4: Leadership Knowledge Orientation Aspects

2 Core Concepts for a Multiorganizational Level Leadership Model

- **Organizational-Level Leadership Literature**
- **Development of Core Concepts**
  - *Levels and Domains*
  - *Leader Cognitive Complexity (Cognitive Power)*
- **Some Key Issues Involved in the Core Concepts**
- **Genotypic Versus Phenotypic Considerations**
- **Concluding Commentary**

> You cannot make a crab walk straight.
>
> —Aristophanes, Athenian comic playwright
> (quoted in Eigen & Siegel, 1989, p. 486)

> All of these [sensors and procedures] reinforce the chain of command, and reinforce this business of each having his own job at a particular level. All of these play different roles at different levels. As you progress up the ranks, you have to understand that the roles change.
>
> —Unidentified four-star general
> (quoted in U. S. Army War College, 1988, p. 23)

> Genius must be born, and can never be taught.
>
> —John Dryden, English poet
> (quoted in Eigen & Siegel, 1989, p. 490)

In this chapter I turn to the knowledge-content aspect of the leadership synthesis emphasized in Chapter 1. I am interested in developing a richer picture of the leadership phenomenon by systematically moving beyond an exclusive emphasis on lower-level, face-to-face leadership. I start by reviewing literature (limited as it is) that slices leadership vertically and looks at its organizational-level aspects.

11

ORGANIZATIONAL-LEVEL
LEADERSHIP LITERATURE

Even though the preponderance of leadership research and leadership models concentrate on face-to-face leadership at lower organizational levels, some people have shown a simultaneous interest in possible different leadership requirements by level. This consideration goes back fifty years, or more (see Barnard, 1938; Holden, Fish & Smith, 1941). The interest is reflected in descriptive literature which tends to differentiate on the basis of the broadness of duties or functions and the time frame within which results are fed back (e.g., Barnard, 1938; Holden et al., 1941; Litterer, 1973; Miles, 1949; Parsons, 1960; Pfiffner & Sherwood, 1960). A frequent direction of this early work is to divide the organization into three or four hierarchical "zones," "layers," or something similar, and argue that requirements are similar within zones but differ qualitatively between zones. We also see similar arguments by those such as Simon (1977) and in organization theory books (e.g., Osborn, Hunt, & Jauch, 1980).

The embodiment of such work was the systems model developed by Daniel Katz and Robert Kahn (1966, 1978). This model is widely cited and is arguably the most conceptually elegant of these frameworks. Its authors contend that three basic types of leadership occur in organizational hierarchies:

(1) *Origination of structure (origination)*—introduction of structural change or policy formulation

(2) *Interpolation of structure (interpolation)*—piecing out the incompleteness of existing formal structure via implementation of policies to deal with immediate problems

(3) *Applying existing structure (administration)*—using structure formally provided to keep the organization moving and in effective operation, or in other words, the routine application of prescribed remedies for predicted problems.

Katz and Kahn assume that the amount of freedom or discretion to supplement existing structure decreases as we look down the hierarchy, and that the freedom to originate and substantially alter organizational structure is less at the intermediate than at the top levels. They also suggest some very general leadership abilities and skills, which they see as necessary to deal with these differing hierarchical requirements, and make the point that skills appropriate at one level may be inappropriate or even dysfunctional at another. Although the Katz and Kahn framework has not been subjected to empirical testing per se, the kind of thinking involved in it has had a strong influence on the stratified-systems approach to be described shortly.

Along with the stratified-systems framework, there have been some other directions that provide additional perspective. Hunt (1984a, 1984b, 1985) touches on these, but let's consider them here. First, there have been large numbers of piecemeal studies examining some aspect of leadership by hierarchical level. Often these have very little, if any, conceptual justification other than the implicit premise that something about organizational level should make a difference (see Yukl, 1989, for a recent review conveying the tenor of this kind of work). The studies do not advance our knowledge much and, if anything, point out our woeful lack of knowledge. However, they do show the undying intuitive feeling that, somehow, organizational level must be an important leadership contingency.

Second, work by Robert Katz (1955) and Floyd Mann (1965) has been influential in arguing for differences in three required leadership skills by level. The skills are *technical* (performing technical activities), *human* (understanding and motivating individuals and groups), and *conceptual* (coordinating/integrating organizational activities toward a common objective). Both Mann and Katz contend that the mix of these skills will differ by level, with the importance of technical skill decreasing by level while conceptual skill becomes increasingly important. Katz's work does not use data, whereas Mann's is empirical with a very general conceptual base, not inconsistent with that of Daniel Katz and Robert Kahn (1966, 1978). We return to this skill-mix notion later in the book.

Third, Mintzberg's (1973/1980) classic study of CEOs contains a number of propositions about variations in managerial work content and role by organization level (higher and lower, or top versus other levels), as well as environment, person, and situational variables. These aspects of his widely cited research are not typically mentioned, perhaps because he studied top-level CEOs. His propositions address not only role differences by level (based on his well known 10-role framework) but differences in such notions as hours worked, time spent in various activities, fragmentation of work, and so on. His book has served as the genesis for a few empirical studies in the late 1970s and early 1980s. These studies attempted to use questionnaires to measure his observationally derived roles; some of them also examined the skill-mix notion discussed above. The studies are interesting and I return to some of them later. Basically, however, like other such work, they tend to show inconsistent results and do not add much to our conceptual understanding (see Alexander, 1979; McCall & Segrist, 1980; Paolillo, 1981; Pavett & Lau, 1983).

Fourth, a military monograph attempted to combine aspects of some of the above work with extensions of leader behavior typologies available when the monograph was written (Clement & Ayers, 1976). The authors proposed an organization-level/leadership-dimension matrix to predict the importance of different leadership dimensions at five different organizational levels. Although there was no attempt at empirical verification, the monograph is noteworthy for its multiple-organizational-level conceptual thrust.

Fifth, some recent works that have developed leadership typologies (see Chapter 8) also have considered organizational level to a greater or lesser extent (see Boyatzis, 1982; Luthans, Hodgetts, & Rosenkrantz, 1988; Luthans, Rosenkrantz, & Hennessey, 1985; Quinn, 1988). Again, however, there is not a very strong conceptual base for level differences.

Finally, a literature review from nearly a quarter of a century ago focused on a number of important aspects concerning multiple-level leadership (Nealy & Fiedler, 1968):

• What is the meaning of organizational level and how should it be measured?
• Many leadership positions involve multiple or split roles. Multiple roles involve operating simultaneously at more than one organizational level (e.g., an executive vice president who also is involved in the first-level leadership of immediate subordinates). Split roles involve two individuals jointly performing one set of functions (e.g., chief and her deputy or store manager and assistant store manager, where the deputy and assistant operate in the name of the superior; see Osborn, Hunt, & Skaret, 1977; Stewart, 1982a).
• Person-oriented (career-progression) approach versus a function-oriented approach: The former implicitly assumes higher-level leadership success can be predicted from that at lower levels (i.e., focuses on the leader as a person). The latter focuses on leadership as a process within the organization and asks what system of leadership functions is necessary for organizational as opposed to personal success.
• Various kinds of leader similarities and differences by organizational level (e.g., satisfaction, importance of different job aspects, behavior).

• Relative impact of lower- and upper-level leaders on employee-level outcomes and the importance of congruence or noncongruence of leader characteristics at these levels in terms of employee-level outcomes (see Hunt, 1971; Hunt & Liebscher, 1971; Hunt, Hill, & Reaser, 1973; Osborn & Hunt, 1974a).

DEVELOPMENT OF CORE CONCEPTS

Coincidental with much of the previously cited literature has been work by Elliott Jaques that has evolved into stratified-systems theory (SST; see Jacobs & Jaques, 1987; Jaques, 1976, 1989). Just as SST builds on many ideas set forth in the Katz and Kahn (1966, 1978) framework, it provides core concepts useful in developing the extended multilevel leadership model in Chapter 3. Both Katz and Kahn and SST use open-systems notions, and both conceptualize different and increasingly complex leadership requirements as we move higher in the organization. Furthermore, there are break points in each where the requirements become qualitatively different.

Essentially, the stratified-systems framework suggests a general model of organizational functioning such that there are increasingly complex critical tasks or requirements at each organizational level and that effective leaders address these tasks. The increasing task complexity is a function of the uncertainties created by the necessity to deal with a more encompassing and more turbulent environment as a leader moves up the hierarchy. Jaques contends that higher-level leaders must themselves possess increasing levels of cognitive complexity (built on top of that operating at lower organizational levels) to deal with the increasingly more demanding critical tasks as they move up the organizational hierarchy.

Thus, consistent with Ashby's (1952) law of requisite variety, the stratified-systems perspective argues that complexity in the leader must be consistent with that in the organization. Therefore, as the task becomes more complex, so must the leader's cognitive complexity develop to provide an appropriate "match." Let's now examine this notion of increasing organizational task complexity more specifically within the context of levels and domains, then consider the leader's cognitive complexity in view of these organizational aspects.

Levels and Domains

The basic stratified-systems approach argues that the maximum number of organizational levels needed in any organization to which it is applied will not be more than seven. These seven levels are grouped into three domains—systems leadership, organizational leadership, and direct leadership. The grouping is based on Jaques's measure of task complexity at each level, termed *time span of discretion* of the leader's critical tasks. This is the longest of the maximum target completion times for critical tasks of the leader at each hierarchical level (see Jacobs & Jaques, 1987; Jaques, 1989). Table 2.1 summarizes these points.

Notice the relationship of the domains in the table to the origination, interpolation, and administration concepts of Katz and Kahn, and the zone or layer ideas of others mentioned earlier. Of course, as the table shows, these domains have greater differentiation of function internally, and more specific reference to organization structures and correspondingly differentiated tasks, when compared to the earlier approaches.

In terms of systems and subsystems,[1] it is argued that only at level V and higher is there an open system in the full sense of the term (the level of the full-scale, profit and loss account-trading subsidiaries of large corporations). The levels below level V (i.e., I through IV) are all considered to be subsystems, contained within the boundary conditions established by level V. Each subsystem is increasingly constrained as one moves down the organization, and these constraints decrease openness as they increase rationality. When work at these levels does impact with the total system's environment, it is within system rules and regulations that limit the environment within which the subsystem may operate and the subsystem's options within that environment.

At the very top, those leaders at levels VI and VII operate within the relatively unbounded environment (the strategic levels of functioning). Leaders at these levels are concerned with the establishment and modification of level V systems, overseeing and providing resources for these systems and sustaining conditions within the external environment favorable for the systems (Jacobs & Jaques, 1987; Jaques, 1989).

Leader Cognitive Complexity (Cognitive Power)

I've summarized briefly the organizational side of complexity—essentially that required of a leader at any of the levels beyond the

Table 2.1
Domains and Levels in Jaques & Jacobs's Stratified-Systems Approach

Time Span	Level	Domain
		Systems
20 years and up	VII Corporation	• Operate in nearly unbounded world environment
		• Identify and develop consensus on futures
*10-20 years	VI Group	• Build resource base to create whole systems to function in environment; influence environment to be receptive
		• Creates organizational culture consistent with societal culture and with organizational mission/ goal/ strategies/policies, etc.
		Organizational
5-10 years	V Company	• Level V leaders operate bounded open systems fom systems domain
*2-5 years	IV Division (General Management)	• Level IV leaders assist in managing adaptation of such systems
		− fine tune processes and subcultures, oversee subsystems.
		Direct Production
1-2 years	III Department	• Within context/boundaries of larger system, run
		− face-to-face mutual recognition/knowledge subsystems
3 months and less-1 year	II Section	− groups with differentiated functions interdependent with others
	I Shop Floor (Direct Employee)	

Note: *Considered to involve especially big jumps from the previous level, thus they are in the next domain
Source: Based on Jacobs & Jaques (1987, p. 16).

employee shop floor (level I). A second core notion is involved with the other side of the equation—the cognitive complexity (or what Jaques also terms *cognitive power*) required of leaders to deal with the earlier-mentioned organizational task complexity requirements.

For Jaques, cognitive processes are those mental processes used to take information, pick it over, play with it, analyze it, put it together, reorganize it, judge and reason with it, make conclusions, plans, and decisions, and take action. Cognitive power is defined as the maximum

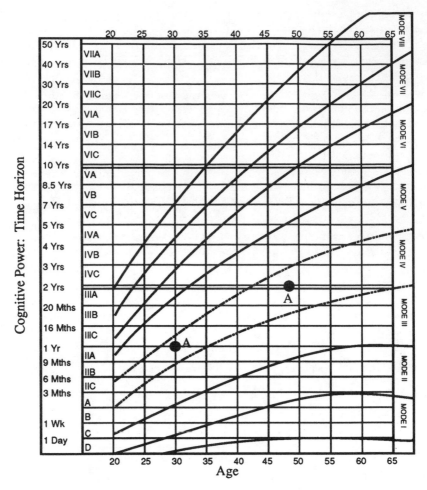

Figure 2.1. Maturation Modes, Age, Organizational Time Span, and Individual
Cognitive Power

Source: Adapted from Jaques (1989). Used with permission.

scale and complexity of the world that one is able to pattern and
construe, including the amount and complexity of information that must
be processed in doing so (Jaques, 1989, p. 33). It is the raw mental
power enabling a person to sustain increasingly complex decision
processes. As the leader's critical tasks become more complex, this

complexity needs to be matched by increasing leader cognitive complexity or cognitive power. Jaques measures cognitive power in terms of an individual's *time horizon* (the maximum time span at which an individual is capable of working at a given point in his or her life, or the person's working capacity).

Jaques (1986, 1989) approaches the just-mentioned organizational and individual leader match in a very specific way. Based on tracking careers of individuals over a number of years, he plots a series of "maturation bands" or modes, with a person's age on the horizontal axis and organizational levels with their accompanying time span of discretion and required individual cognitive-power time horizon (working capacity) in years on the vertical axis (see Figure 2.1). The organizational levels and time spans (D through VIIA in the figure) correspond to those previously discussed under levels and domains, except that there are more specific subdivisions within them (A, B, C, and so on).

The figure shows eight modes (I through VIII), which become progressively steeper as people move up the organization hierarchy. Jaques argues that any given individual can be located within a cognitive-power maturation mode at any given age. Each person's cognitive power will increase with age in a predictable way within that individual's maturation mode.

As an example, let's look at point A in the figure. Here we see a 30-year old, in the mode IV band, with a current potential working capacity at the top of organizational level II (one year) who is likely to have the potential to move through level III and into the bottom of a level IV (two years) position in about 19 years, at the age of approximately 49.

In the 1970s, Gillian Stamp (1978) developed a procedure called the Career Path Appreciation (CPA) technique to help place individuals in the above framework. The CPA is an assessment interview, built around three components, and lasts two hours or more. The components are Bruner's (1966) card-sorting task, a comprehensive work history, and a set of phrase cards, sorted as to preference and then discussed by the assessees (Jacobs & Jaques, 1990; Stamp, 1988).

The approach is used to tap both a person's current time horizon and the dynamic strategies the individual uses for problem solving. It also places people at high, medium, or low points within levels and maturation modes. Stamp concludes that all individuals express their currently matured time horizon in their work while indicating their awareness of their potential maturation modes and time horizons. Thus those who are high in cognitive power readily understand the world in long time horizons, even though they are not yet mature enough to work at that level of time extension (Jaques, 1986).

If this sounds like a complicated procedure, requiring a high level of assessor skills, that is correct. It's estimated that the assessors must be at Jaques's current level IV or higher to do a good job administering and interpreting the CPA (Jacobs & Jacques, 1990).

Let's close this section by emphasizing several points (see Jaques, 1989). First, the higher a person's maturation mode or cognitive power, the faster is the rate of maturation and the longer in life it continues (indeed, at high levels it is argued to continue past retirement and until the person dies). Second, an individual's location within a given maturation mode is gender and background blind and says nothing about social groupings of people. Third, it is contended that although a person develops cognitive power over a lifetime, it is done regardless of education and experience. The maturation process will override all but catastrophic events befalling the individual, despite socioeconomic opportunities or deprivation. Finally, it is argued that there is no consistent relationship with traditional intelligence measures—in other words, we are not just talking about smart executives in a new guise.

SOME KEY ISSUES INVOLVED IN THE CORE CONCEPTS

At this point it's appropriate to reiterate and sharpen the earlier arguments concerning the SST core concepts just discussed:

- They are logical extensions of the kind of work summarized earlier in the chapter.
- They direct attention to the hierarchical aspects of leadership as opposed to a lower-level, face-to-face orientation. Hence, they reflect the knowledge-content component of leadership synthesis.
- With suitable modifications they lay the groundwork for our extended multilevel leadership model, developed in the next chapter. For us to utilize the full potential of these core concepts in our movement toward leadership synthesis, we need to deal with some of the core concepts' key issues and a number of their implications.

These key issues are concerned with the determinism and narrowness of the core concepts just discussed. In terms of *determinism*, we are first confronted with the tight tie between the organization's time span of discretion at each level and the maturational modes reflecting cognitive power shown in Figure 2.1. As it stands, the approach, with its use of the CPA technique, locks the organizational (time span) and individual (cognitive-power time horizon maturational modes) components together, as in the figure. As such, it does not explicitly utilize or deal with the separate stream of cognitive complexity literature developed by others (see especially Streufert & Nogami, 1989; Streufert & Streufert, 1978; Streufert & Swezey, 1986).

This cognitive complexity focuses on cognitive complexity at both the organizational and personal levels with an emphasis on the processes of differentiation and integration. Although I will discuss these in detail later, for now we can think of *differentiation* as the separation of cognitions or structures, and *integration* as their combination (see Wegner & Vallacher, 1977). Cognitively complex individuals are able both to differentiate and to integrate more elements than are less complex persons. Explicit recognition of this and related literature would allow for separate treatment of the match between increasingly complex organizational tasks by level and the individual cognitive complexity required.

A second aspect of determinism is Jaques's (1989) contention, illustrated in Figure 2.1, that a person develops over a lifetime within a cognitive power mode but basically cannot move to a higher-level one. If true, this would be a variation of the born-leader argument—in spite of developmental efforts, only those with the innate appropriate cognitive mode can function satisfactorily at the top. This new version of the born-leader argument needs careful examination and for now, at least, should remain an open question.

A third aspect of determinism—flexibility, determinism's flip side— is highlighted in management simulation work (see Streufert & Nogami, 1989; Streufert & Swezey, 1986). The argument is that managers frequently function under conditions where dynamic plans and actions call for a rapid succession of sequential decisions, or where long-range plans are not appropriate because of uncertainty and rapid change. Such conditions are especially important in time-compressed management simulations, and flexibility in dealing with them is argued to be representative of successful managers (Streufert & Swezey, 1986). To the extent that such flexibility requirements are generally true, they raise a question about the adequacy of time span of discretion as the sole measure of organizational-level requirements.

A fourth aspect of determinism focuses on "method-boundness." It is the same issue that has plagued Herzberg's well-known, two factor motivation research (for a review of the argument, see Pinder, 1984). In a nutshell, any approach that is dependent on a single method to obtain predicted results is suspect. Thus we do not want to restrict ourselves solely to the strict conceptualization and measurement outlined above.

A fifth concern that some might argue illustrates both narrowness and determinism is that what we have is nothing more than a trait-contingency model of leadership. The trait is individual cognitive complexity, which serves to moderate the relationship between an increasingly longer hierarchical time span of discretion and various outcomes. Put this way, the statement suggests a narrow, deterministic model. However, as we shall see, this general notion lays the base for a much broader and more flexible interpretation as reflected in Chapter 3.

A sixth concern, related to narrowness, is to what extent time span of discretion picks up various aspects of organizational differentiation. For example, to what extent does it reflect organizations in different industries, or to what degree does it pick up differences within the organizations? Jaques and associates' writings implicitly argue that it reflects these kinds of differences, and well it may. However, we need more explicit examination of this question. Also, to what extent does time span of discretion (operationalized in terms of the longest of the target completion times for the leader's critical tasks) deal with ambiguity or flexibility of feedback? Although long-term feedback is inherently more ambiguous than short-term feedback, nevertheless time is not likely to be the sole determinant of such ambiguity. These questions, as well as the flexibility concern above, raise both determinism and breadth questions about time span of discretion as *the* measure of organizational task complexity. They suggest the importance of future empirical work and being sensitive to possible additional measures of organizational task complexity.

Other issues undoubtedly have occurred to you as you have read this chapter. However, those above convey the tenor of the kinds of issues that I try to deal with as I use these core concepts as a base for the extended multilevel model of Chapter 3.

GENOTYPIC VERSUS
PHENOTYPIC CONSIDERATIONS

Another important consideration for us that is implicit in Jaques and associates' work involves genotypic versus phenotypic aspects. These terms came from genetics (see Hartl, 1981; Silverstein & Silverstein, 1980). Applied in the present context, one can argue that organization level is simply the surface manifestation or outward appearance of some more basic underlying phenomenon, such as critical task complexity. In other words, level is the *phenotypic* manifestation of the underlying *genotypic* phenomenon of task complexity (see Misumi & Peterson, 1985, chapter 1, for a related notion). The development of a genotypic framework allows cross-organizational comparisons and can enhance conceptual development.

A major problem with the organizational-level literature reviewed at the beginning of the chapter—and one particularly emphasized by Nealey and Fiedler (1968)—is that it's difficult to compare levels from one study to another. We have no way of knowing whether, say, the third level (using a phenotypic description) in one organization is the same as the third level in another (e.g., GM versus Bank of America, or GM versus Toyota). However, if we use a genotypic notion such as task complexity, we can readily compare across organizations. Jaques and associates' work and the extended model use such a genotypic concept in combination with the genotypic individual cognitive-complexity notion in examining the hierarchical aspects of leadership. The use of a similar underlying genotypic complexity notion at both organizational and individual levels also is useful in tying together individualist and structuralist perspectives. In addition, this genotypic emphasis is consistent with recent arguments by Osigweh (1989) that we should be concerned with concepts that "travel"; in other words, the concept is defined in such a way that it will allow generalization across a range of situations.

CONCLUDING COMMENTARY

In this chapter I've shown the long-term interest in looking at leadership at different organizational levels. In spite of such interest, virtually all of the empirical literature lacks much conceptual thrust. This is in spite of some very suggestive theoretical aspects discussed by various people over the past 50 years or so. The work of Katz and Kahn has essentially summarized many of these earlier ideas and serves as the forerunner of the stratified-systems notions of Elliott Jaques and his associates, introduced in this chapter. At the heart of such a conceptualization is the genotypic notion that we must try to get beyond the phenotypic (surface) notion of organizational level and develop some kind of underlying concept that will allow generalization across samples.

Core aspects of Jaques's stratified systems approach emphasize critical task complexity measured by time span of discretion of the leader's critical tasks encompassed within organizational domains and levels. Increasingly long time spans for task feedback for leaders higher up in the hierarchy call for increasing cognitive power or complexity on the part of a leader. This cognitive complexity, in turn, is argued to be reflected in a series of cognitive-power modes, tied into a series of organizational levels.

These core concepts, though possessing some deterministic and narrow aspects, can with sufficient elaboration and expansion form the basis for the extended multilevel model in the next chapter. That model can help move our leadership thinking beyond simple face-to-face interactions at lower levels and toward a much broader view encompassing the organization at all levels and emphasizing the importance of temporal aspects. Furthermore, this perspective represents the knowledge-content component of leadership synthesis as discussed earlier and joins the knowledge-orientation component developed in Chapter 4. Let's now develop that new synthesis further by turning to the extended multilevel model in Chapter 3. I then explore details of the model's components throughout Part II of the book.

NOTE

1. The term "subsystem" is used often and not always consistently throughout this book. However, the context typically clarifies the meaning, if it is not otherwise provided.

3 The Extended Multilevel Leadership Model

- **The Extended Model and Its Components**
  Systems Leadership Domain
  Organizational Leadership Domain
  Direct Leadership Domain
- **Discretion, Indirect Effects, and Leadership Teams**
- **Relation to Strategic Leadership Approaches**
- **The Model and Empirical Explorations**
- **Concluding Commentary**

We have begun to understand that we must, from the outset, look at the whole system and fit the pieces together, rather than look at the pieces and fit them to the system. . . . Because it is easier to manage the "each's," and the day to day problems drive you to manage the "each's." But you have to be careful and set time aside to manage the whole.

—Unidentified four-star general
(quoted in U.S. Army War College, 1988, p. 53)

It took me awhile to realize that being involved in the totality of the military of this country meant that my interest was just about everything, everywhere, all the time. This awareness is absolutely crucial.

—Unidentified four-star general
(quoted in U.S. Army War College, 1988, p. 55)

The Hall was the place where the great Lord used to eat. . . He ate not in private, except in time of sickness. . . . Nay, the King himself used to eat in the Hall, and his lords sat with him, and then he understood men.

—John Selden, English statesman
(quoted in Eigen & Siegel, 1989, p. 228)

Now that Chapter 2 has covered the genotypic organizational task complexity and individual cognitive complexity core notions, we can

25

develop the extended multiorganizational-level leadership model. I will use the core notions as the basis for this model but will open up their conceptualization and measurement. I mean this opening up both to deal with the kinds of narrowness and determinism issues in Chapter 2 and to encourage the kind of wide-ranging work indicated in Chapter 1. Thus I intend the synthesis provided by the model to broaden the ways in which we think about and approach leadership.

More especially, the intent of the extended multilevel leadership model is to:

* provide an integrating framework for the wide range of literature relevant to a multilevel, systems-orientated leadership perspective that emphasizes temporal aspects;
* focus on key multilevel leadership components and expected interrelationships among these; and
* encourage a wide-ranging knowledge-orientation perspective in exploring the various aspects of the model.

Both to use the core stratified-systems notions discussed in the previous chapter and to deal with charges of their narrowness and determinism, I will first break apart the tight tie between organizational task complexity and leader complexity as illustrated in Chapter 2. First, although it still argues for a fit between these genotypic notions, the extended model treats them separately. Second, the model emphasizes a number of additional leader capability and organizational complexity aspects. Third, within its multilevel systems framework, the model focuses on such important concepts as environment, charisma, societal and organizational culture, and various aspects of effectiveness.[1]

As a final point I should reiterate that the model systematically unfolds around the core concept domain and time span notions. Essentially, these assume a form of hierarchical bureaucracy. The final unfolding of the model in the book's concluding Chapter 12 examines this assumption in the light of sociotechnical systems (see Pasmore, 1988) and other basically flat, "new-wave" organization approaches, and extends the multiple-level perspective still further. That chapter also addresses a number of other issues, including an extended treatment of time and temporal concerns.

THE EXTENDED MODEL
AND ITS COMPONENTS

Based on the previous discussion, Figure 3.1 summarizes the extended multiple-organizational-level leadership model. For simplicity, the figure does not show all the direct relationships, nor does it show feedback loops or arrowheads, although all are part of the systems-oriented model. The figure also serves as the organizing framework for Part II of the book—starting with environment and societal culture, and leader critical tasks, and then moving to individual capability variables, and organizational culture and effectiveness at the various organizational domains and levels.

Systems Leadership Domain

External Environment and Societal Culture/Values

Here, the focus is on the immensely complex environment and societal-culture/values forces facing leaders at the very highest levels. These are leaders of huge multinationals, very high-level political leaders, three- and four-star army generals, and the like. These people must engage in such activities as interfacing across different societal cultures, coordinating organizational systems across these different cultures, and interacting with high-level political officials (see U.S. Army War College, 1988). There are a number of systematic treatments of both environment and societal cultures available in the literature, and these are discussed in Chapter 5 (e.g., Daft, 1989; Osborn, Hunt, & Jauch, 1980).

Leader-Critical Tasks

These are the tasks that form the major responsibilities of systems leaders and are discussed in Chapter 5. I've captured their general elements in Figure 3.1. These elements are suggested in such literature as U.S. Army War College (1988), Jacobs and Jaques (1987), and U.S. Army Research Institute (1989), as well as in other management and organization books. Goal and mission and strategy/policy development are conceptualized similarly to such works as Daft (1989) and Glueck

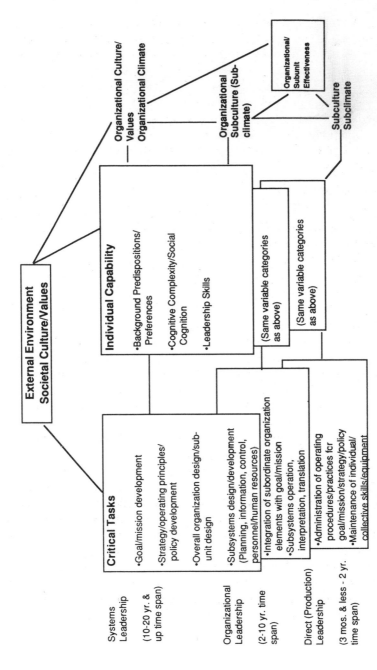

Figure 3.1. Extended Multiple-Organizational-Level Leadership Model
Note: For simplicity, some direct relationships, feedback, and arrowheads are not shown.

and Jauch (1984). Overall and subunit organizational design connotes the anatomy of vertical and lateral authority and accountability relationships. It provides the basis for departmentation and the design of the kinds of process and procedural subsystems shown in the figure (see U.S. Army Research Institute, 1989; U.S. Army War College, 1988). Such process subsystems are used to specify procedures and routines and enable recognition of and serve leaders in decision/problem-solving functions (U.S. Army War College, 1988, p. 34). For now, it's sufficient simply to recognize that the subsystems titles in the figure convey the essence of their functions.

Individual Capabilities

Turning now to the leader individual capability cluster shown in Figure 3.1, let's start with the individual background and predispositions/preferences component. This component is the subject of Chapter 6. Individual background variables consist of such aspects as family and childhood experiences, educational and work experience, age, and the like. They have been widely treated in the organizational and strategic management literatures and are especially important when considering leader development, discussed in Chapter 11.

Leader predispositions are concerned with the predisposition or desire to want to be a leader. Simply having appropriate abilities, skills, and opportunities is not sufficient—the individual must be motivated to want to be a leader. In the extended model, this predisposition is reflected in terms of the need for socially oriented (i.e., directed toward others rather than oneself) power and a feeling of competency or efficacy in exerting this power and assuming a leadership role (see Sashkin & Burke, 1990; Wood & Bandura, 1989).

Besides predispositions and efficacy, the preferences component of the individual capability cluster is quite important. It focuses on value and ideology preferences and cognitive or intellectual style preferences (what are individuals' preferred styles of gathering and processing information)? Earlier, values were referred to on a collective basis as part of societal culture. Here they refer to those preferences held by individual leaders and their top-level teams. As we shall see throughout the book and especially in Chapter 6, value preferences are considered to play an important part in leader functioning and are expected to have linkages to a number of other aspects of the extended model.

The cognitive or intellectual style-preference component is considered to be an important accompaniment to the model's emphasis on cognitive complexity. The most widely known measure of cognitive style is the Myers-Briggs Type Indicator (Myers & McCaulley, 1985). However, there are many others, as we shall see in Chapter 6. Besides its potential usefulness for tapping modes of thinking involved in information processing at different organizational levels, there are those who suggest that cognitive style may be useful in revealing developmental inclinations of leaders to construct the kinds of complex thinking modes required at higher organizational levels (see Jacobs & Jaques, 1990). Findings bearing on this suggestion, along with many other aspects with potential relevance to the extended multilevel model, are summarized in Chapter 6.

The second component of the leader capability cluster in the figure is concerned with complexity. As a core concept of the stratified-systems approach in Chapter 2, I showed this to consist of an individual's cognitive power and emphasized time horizon (the maximum time span at which an individual is capable of working at a given point in his or her life). The Career Path Appreciation (CPA) technique was used to link this with organizational task complexity in terms of time span of discretion (see Stamp, 1988). In the extended model, I open up this concept to reflect the extensively developed differentiation and integration notions (see Streufert & Nogami, 1989; Streufert & Streufert, 1978; Streufert & Swezey, 1986).

Especially important is the notion of a cognitive map that reflects the various aspects of an individual's frame of reference (see Jacobs & Jaques, 1987; Quinn, 1988), belief structure (e.g., Walsh, 1988), and the like. A frequently used simplified version of a cognitive map called a "cause map" typically contains a person's ends, means, conflicts, and content for decision making—it shows the means/end beliefs necessary to the development of plans and the initiation of behaviors directed to desired ends (Axelrod, 1976; Bougan, 1983). These means/ends allow for the inclusion of time horizon and Weick and Bougan (1986) argue that cognitive maps can tap cognitive complexity, via differentiation and integration to be measured from elements of the map. In the systems leadership domain, they are especially important in tracing strategy/policy implications across time (see Hall, 1984). They are discussed in more detail in Chapter 7.

Cognitive maps also are a part of the broader social-cognition aspects of the extended model. These focus on cognitive processes and emphasize, especially, cognitive schemas (knowledge structures), attributions, and implicit leadership theories (see Fiske & Taylor, 1984; Lord & Maher, 1989a). Again, see Chapter 7 for details.

The final component of the leader capability cluster is concerned with leadership behavior and skills. I include here concepts variously termed skills, behaviors, roles, or competencies, depending upon the literature base (e.g., Boyatzis, 1982; R. L. Katz, 1955; Mintzberg, 1973/ 1980; Quinn, 1988). A number of recent leadership typologies have been developed that are important for the extended model. These typologies are split into two chapters, with Chapter 8 covering those that are transactionally oriented (broad range of "traditional" leadership/managerial aspects) and Chapter 9 focusing on more transformationally oriented ones (transformational, charismatic, or visionary in nature; e.g., Conger & Kanungo, 1988).

Organizational Culture/Values

So much for the systems leadership domain individual capability cluster. Figure 3.1 next shows organizational culture/values and organizational climate, which are treated in detail in Chapter 10. Organizational culture is derived from societal culture and has developed a burgeoning literature of its own over the last few years. As I show in Chapter 10, organizational culture (especially in combination with organizational climate) is considered to be particularly important in linking together critical tasks, subcultures, and various facets of effectiveness up and down the organization. Also, as Chapter 10 makes abundantly clear, there are a number of different conceptions of organizational culture. These are intertwined with the kinds of basic assumptions about the nature of reality and its measurement in Chapter 4. They also are intertwined with the depth with which culture is conceived (e.g., a surface-level manifestation, suggested by such artifacts as jargon or dress code, versus a level of basic underlying assumptions that are very difficult to surface).

For now, we can think in terms of a comprehensive view of organizational culture that includes shared beliefs, values, underlying assumptions, and patterns of behaviors. The common thread in any definition or description of organizational culture is *shared*; the assumptions, values, and so forth must be shared to a greater or lesser extent by organizational members.

Chapter 10 links organizational culture and organizational climate together by arguing that climate is the message provided by organizational policies, practices, rewards, and so on (the "what happens around here"); whereas culture reflects the underlying values or assumptions that are the basis for these (the "why things happen the way they do"; see Schneider & Renttsch, 1988). Thus the two function together. Although Figure 3.1 shows organizational culture to have linkages with the individual capability cluster in general, the literature reviewed in Chapter 10 suggests especially strong links with charismatic and related transformational/visionary leadership skills. These skills are considered to be crucial in the creation and transmission of organizational culture (e.g., Sashkin & Fulmer, 1988) or what some (see Smircich & Morgan, 1982) describe as the "creation of meaning." This thinking is captured in a well-known quote from Edgar Schein (1985) where he argues that perhaps "the *only thing of real importance that leaders do is to create and manage culture*" (p. 2, emphasis in original). These kinds of skills are expected to be especially important in the systems leadership domain.

Organizational Effectiveness

Finally, at the systems levels, the figure shows organizational effectiveness to be linked to the previously mentioned clusters. At the systems leadership levels, the range of effectiveness criteria refers to the entire organization as a system. Key aspects to keep in mind in dealing with organizational effectiveness are discussed in Chapter 5.

Organizational Leadership Domain

Given the just-completed discussion of the key aspects of the systems leadership domain, let's turn now to the organizational leadership domain shown in Figure 3.1. In so doing we need to recognize:

- There is an organizational time span of discretion of 2 to 5 years and 5 to 10 years, respectively, for levels IV and V.
- There is an emphasis on the bounded open systems established higher up.
- A typical level V leader would head a strategic business unit (SBU) or equivalent (see Glueck & Jauch, 1984, for an SBU discussion).

Leader-Critical Tasks

As with higher-level systems domain leadership, there is a heavy emphasis on subsystems or their equivalent and their linkages with goals, missions, strategies, and the like (see Figure 3.1). However, whereas before the primary emphasis was on the design of these elements as a part of the overall design of the organization as a system, now I emphasize their operation, interpretation, and translation and their linkage with lower-level equivalents (see U.S. Army War College, 1988). Both here and when considering systems domain leadership, it's useful to think in terms of teams. In the organizational leadership domain there is likely to be very heavy staff team involvement in dealing with the domain's critical tasks. Essentially, in this domain the intent is to make operational, here and for those below, the higher-level systems design, based on goals, strategies, and so forth.

Individual Capability

In comparing this cluster with that in the systems leadership domain, we anticipate reduced domain critical task complexity and shorter time span of discretion to call for a lower level of leader cognitive complexity. We expect the needed cognitive maps to be simpler than those above. In terms of their similarity, one argument is that they may just be simplified versions of those at higher levels. However, Teulings (1986) argues that there are different underlying logics operating at different hierarchical levels. To the extent that this is true, the maps would not only be simpler but different in other ways as well. The considerations are similar in the preference and leadership skill components in the individual capability cluster. Given the recognition of decreasing complexity relative to that at higher levels, then the question is how similar or different these various components need to be to provide the necessary degree of consistency with those for people at higher levels. This question is related to some of the issues raised in the Nealey and Fiedler (1968) review, summarized in the previous chapter.

Organizational Subculture/Subclimate

Here I conceptualize organizational subculture and subclimate as lower-level analogues to the broader systems domain culture/climate cluster. Figure 3.1 shows the most important hypothesized linkages between subculture/subclimate in this domain and other clusters in the extended model.

Effectiveness

Here, the whole range of issues relevant for higher-level organizational effectiveness also is relevant but the unit of analysis is different (for more detail, see Chapters 5 and 12). The unit of analysis shifts to the levels included in the organizational leadership domain and must be consistent with other aspects of the domain.

Direct Leadership Domain

Turning now to the direct (production) leadership domain, Figure 3.1 shows a span of discretion at levels II and III ranging from three months or less to one year, and from one to two years.

Leader Critical Tasks

Operating procedures and practices (standard operating procedures, or SOPs) are a way of operationalizing the higher-level subsystems interpretation, translation, and operation in this domain. Maintenance of these subsystems as a critical task is consistent with this discussion (see Figure 3.1). The critical tasks are relatively concrete and specific compared with those higher up. In addition to their linkage to individual capabilities within the direct leadership domain, the figure shows these tasks to be linked to their higher-level counterparts and organizational subculture/subclimate in the organizational domain.

Individual Capability

Given the reduction in organizational critical task complexity, we expect a corresponding decrease in the leader cognitive complexity called for. As in the organizational leadership domain, with this decrease in complexity we anticipate simpler leader cognitive maps subject to the consistency question raised earlier. Leadership skills should place a premium on those traditionally emphasized for lower-level, face-to-face kinds of leadership. Thus traditionally emphasized supportive, task-oriented and related dimensions, as well as technical expertise, are expected to be especially important. Their exact emphasis and scope depend on situational contingencies within this domain as well as their linkages with higher-level domain clusters. As I point out in Chapter 1 and elsewhere in the book, it is within this direct leadership domain that most of the mainstream leadership models and leadership research in general have focused.

Direct Leadership Subculture/Subclimate

Again, we expect a lower-level analogue to the organizational culture and climate and subculture/subclimate in the higher-level domains. Some have argued that, at these lower levels, cohesion may be interpreted as similar to these subculture/subclimate components (see Jacobs, Clement, Rigby, & Jaques, 1985). Conceptualization, measurement, and empirical work ultimately will determine how similar the concepts are. For now, Figure 3.1 shows these as the direct leadership domain subculture/subclimate and also shows the major expected linkages with other parts of the extended model.

Effectiveness

As with the higher-level domains, Figure 3.1 shows effectiveness to be important in this domain. It can be either a group or individual concept, depending on the specific questions of interest. Regardless of whether we treat it as a group or individual concept, the unit of analysis is narrower than at higher levels and needs to reflect the kinds of considerations treated in Chapter 12. The kinds of effectiveness issues discussed in Chapter 5 also are as relevant here as in the higher-level domains (e.g., time, differing criteria).

DISCRETION, INDIRECT EFFECTS AND LEADERSHIP TEAMS

In addition to the previous discussion, we need to consider three more notions important in the extended model and implicit in Figure 3.1. These are discretion, indirect effects, and leadership teams.

Discretion

I hypothesize that leadership discretion (latitude for action; Hambrick & Finklestein, 1987; Hunt, Osborn, & Martin, 1981; Jacobs & Jaques, 1987) increases at higher levels in the hierarchy and is influenced by environmental, organizational, and individual capability variables (see Hambrick & Finkelstein, 1987). In other words, as a leader's critical task complexity increases, his or her amount of discretion is expected to increase as well. Indeed, recall that Jaques's time span of discretion notion suggests such a relationship. Discretion as a concept is receiving increasing importance in the literature, as implied by the references previously cited, and is treated at various places throughout this book. Thus discretion provides one more potential linkage between the extended model and other recent work. It is also possible to relate it to the "substitutes for leadership" approach of Kerr and Jermier (1978), touched on in Chapter 4. "Substitutes" can enhance the leader's choices or discretion, whereas "neutralizers" serve as constraints and inhibit such discretion (see Yukl, 1989).

Indirect Effects

A key concept emphasized in the extended model is that of indirect effects (mentioned in Chapter 1), in addition to the more familiar direct effects. Consideration of indirect (higher order) as well as direct (first order) relationships allows us to move away from strict emphasis on face-to-face effects. Indeed, as mentioned in Chapter 4, a frequently used leadership definition regards *leadership* as essentially influence in a face-to-face situation (see, e.g., Bass, 1981; Yukl, 1989). As I have argued earlier, and as the extended multilevel model emphasizes, a more comprehensive view of leadership is not limited merely to such face-to-face influence.

An example of face-to-face direct leadership effects is where the leader is seen as leading considerately, and this contributes to greater subordinate satisfaction. Or, in a situational contingency mode, the leader is seen as considerate, and under the contingency where the subordinate has a boring job, this consideration leads to greater satisfaction than under the contingency where the job is challenging.

However, if we consider indirect as well as direct effects, we are not limited to a face-to-face definition of leadership influence. As an example, we can think of the impact of selected organizational design characteristics by top leaders in the systems leadership domain on organizational subculture/subclimate in the direct leadership domain. Although organizational design characteristics may have a direct impact on organizational effectiveness (especially if considered in conjunction with environment and technology as contingencies), their impact on direct leadership domain subculture/subclimate would be indirect.

In other words, the impact would be expected to operate through one or more variables at the systems and organizational domains to influence the direct leadership domain subculture/subclimate. Nevertheless, the effect could be quite strong; indeed, it might be stronger than lower-level direct leadership effects. Another example is where top-level strategies and policies influence organization culture and values, which in turn influence lower-level subculture/subclimate, which then influences the way in which critical tasks are operationalized at the bottom, which influences morale at the lowest level. A couple of examples from earlier literature illustrating this kind of notion are provided by Hunt (1971) and especially Hunt, Osborn, and Larson (1975).

Indeed, based on a broad conception of various aspects of leader cognitive complexity and some arguments in Jaques (1989), we can hypothesize that higher-level, more cognitively complex leaders are able to think in such more abstract, indirect-effects terms. That is, their complexity allows them to anticipate from given actions not just possible direct effects but second- and even higher-order indirect effects deep within the organization.

Leadership Teams

For simplicity, the labels in the model and much of the discussion in the book are phrased in such terms as "the leader." However, as the literature makes abundantly clear, especially at the upper organizational levels, we are talking about leadership teams. Mintzberg (1973/1980) and Baliga and Hunt (1988) use the term *strategic apex,* Hambrick and Mason (1984) refer to *upper echelon,* and Jaques (1989) uses the label *collegium.* Osborn (1985) and Osborn, Morris, and O'Connor (1984) discuss the "patterning of activity" where the patterning is done by various leadership collectivities. Finally, Gupta (1988) generates a series of hypotheses based on "executive teams."

Thus it is important to keep this team concept in mind in digesting the content of this book. Indeed, frequently I make specific reference to various aspects of leadership teams. However, even when the book is not that explicit, the team aspects should be kept in mind.

RELATION TO
STRATEGIC LEADERSHIP APPROACHES

I've pointed out here and earlier where this model fits vis-à-vis other hierarchical approaches and the mainstream leadership literature.

However, there is an increasingly large group of people involved with strategic leadership and related work. Where might these approaches fit relative to the extended model?

Generally, these studies tend to focus on the very top level or levels (e.g., Day & Lord, 1988; Hambrick & Brandon, 1988; Hambrick & Finkelstein, 1987; Hambrick & Mason, 1984; Jackofsky & Slocum, 1988; Romanelli & Tushman, 1988). Sometimes they focus on a different group of leaders such as "general managers" (e.g., Kotter, 1982a). Or, less frequently, there is work such as Mintzberg's (1973/1980), which although emphasizing the strategic leadership level also has some discussion related to lower levels (although the latter are not the major focus). Essentially, these approaches do not provide a systematic framework for differentiating leadership at different levels, although they are very useful in terms of upper-level leadership notions.

I incorporate these notions, as they become relevant, as the model unfolds throughout the book. For example, I emphasize from the above literature such aspects as societal culture and values; leadership roles; organizational life cycles; leader discretion; strategic vision; leader schemas; leader information processing; leader background factors; direct and indirect effects; and organizational culture and climate. Basically, I see this work as enriching the extended model with a range of important concepts, but having a narrower focus than does the perspective here.

A final work came to my attention in manuscript form so late in the process of writing this book that I can do no more than touch on it. It is a comprehensive treatment of leadership from a social-cognitive perspective (Lord & Maher, in press). It emphasizes top-level leadership and its relation to lower-level leadership in ways both similar and different from emphases in the extended model presented herein. For example, both books deal with social cognition, discretion, direct and indirect effects, organizational culture, leadership behaviors, and organizational effectiveness. However, the specific treatments of these topics generally are quite different. Some, but not all, of the essence of the Lord and Maher (in press) book is conveyed in the Day and Lord (1988) article referenced above—but the book is more comprehensive. Without pretending to be systematic, I reference the Lord and Maher book in the context of various aspects of the extended model and invite those interested to read their book.

THE MODEL AND
EMPIRICAL EXPLORATIONS

The systems focus of the model emphasizes a holistic approach to its systematic exploration. In other words, because everything is related to everything else, we need to examine all aspects of the model together and check for feedback loops and other systems notions in exploring relationships among the model's many aspects (see Seiler, 1967). Of course, this is difficult if not impossible to do given our present state of knowledge development. In Chapter 12, I examine this point from two perspectives—simulation and structural equation modeling—that appear to deal partially with some of the issues involved in more holistic analyses.

In the absence of such holistic development, I devote a section near each chapter's end to a number of the more important expected linkages between and among the components in question and other aspects of the model. Figure 3.1 and its counterparts in the various chapters are suggestive of these, but the linkages are discussed in much more detail in these sections. Of course, we must keep in mind that these have been isolated from the rest of the model. We do not really know how the isolated relationships would compare with what would be revealed if we were able to consider them as part of a holistic exploration of the model. In developing the discussion of these linkages, I first thought about using a series of propositions. However, I finally decided that they might be too restrictive and would not follow the holistic spirit as well as the broader treatment of linkages.

CONCLUDING COMMENTARY

The core organizational task complexity and individual leader cognitive complexity concepts discussed in the previous chapter form the basis for the extended multilevel leadership model developed here. This model opens up the conceptualization and measurement of these core concepts to deal with issues of narrowness and determinism and to provide an integrating framework for a wide range of leadership literature. The intent of this model is to emphasize both vertical and temporal aspects of leadership and thus to broaden our view of the phenomenon—that is, to encourage a leadership synthesis that goes beyond horizontal face-to-face interaction at the bottom of the organization.

At the same time, the extended model also recognizes the knowledge-orientation component of leadership synthesis emphasized in Chapter 1 and handled in depth in Chapter 4. Thus the model encourages ecumenicalism (or what Chapter 4 calls a critical pluralism) in gaining, using, and assessing this broadened leadership knowledge. Consistent with the previous discussion, each of the extended model's components is treated in a separate chapter that incorporates a wide range of literature and uses categories that invite the inclusion of concepts in place of or in addition to those components. Consequently a range of work relating to each category is dealt with and the door is left open for others to relate their ongoing work to that in the extended model. In other words, I hope that as many people as possible will get involved with this expanded way of dealing with leadership and enhance the leadership knowledge base over time.

Before moving into a more detailed discussion of the extended model's components, we need to elaborate on the knowledge-orientation aspect of the synthesis, mentioned above. For this, turn to Chapter 4.

NOTE

1. In fairness, I should recognize that Jaques and his associates also have begun to broaden the core concepts in Chapter 2. I include that broadened thinking as part of the expansive literature used to develop the extended model.

4 Leadership Knowledge Orientation Aspects

- **Seeing and Knowing Leadership Reality**
- **A Leadership Knowledge Orientation Framework**
  Assumptions
  Purposes
  Definitions
  Leadership Stakeholders
  Outcomes
  Interrelations
- **Assumptions and Critical Pluralism Revisited**
- **Assumptions and Single/Double-Loop Learning**
- **Concluding Commentary**

I would like to stress my belief that the study of leadership has yielded a number of empirically supported generalizations and a number of promising theories. I am optimistic about the future. I see promise and progress in leadership research and theory.

—Robert House (1988a, p. 260)

The desire to . . . evaluate scientific progress in leadership and management research takes on a different meaning within an epistemology that acknowledges explicitly the social and subjective processes of interpretation when observing reality. This alternative . . . is based upon a fundamental dissatisfaction with and realization of the untenable root assumptions upon which the empiricist position is based.

[New leadership knowledge] does not imply a search for new variables and new relationships among "facts" delivered by an observer independent and value free—that is, objective leadership reality. Rather it implies a search involving a systematic questioning of the processes by which we see and know.

—H. Peter Dachler (1988, p. 265)

If you are shot with a magic bullet, you are just as dead whether or not the bullet is "real" to you.

—Richard N. Osborn (personal communication, 1979)

Earlier I discussed leadership synthesis in terms of knowledge content and knowledge orientation aspects. I emphasized the knowledge content component in the discussion of the extended multiple-level model in the previous chapter. There, and in the opening chapter, the extended view of leadership provided by the model's multiple-organizational-level, systems-orientation focus was contrasted with a more typical bottom-level horizontal emphasis limited to face-to-face interactions.

In the present chapter I examine the knowledge orientation aspect of leadership synthesis. To do justice to the wide-ranging kinds of questions suggested by the extended multiple-level leadership model, we must approach knowledge acquisition, use, and assessment in an equally wide-ranging, pragmatic manner. This is the orientation of this chapter.

SEEING AND KNOWING
LEADERSHIP REALITY

The chapter-opening quotes show dramatically the difference in underlying assumptions about how we see and know reality in leadership knowledge. In the opening salvo between House and Dachler, House essentially accepts the underlying assumptions of the traditional science or objectivist view that leadership is "real," can be measured in a relatively objective manner, and has generalizable and lawlike relationships waiting to be discovered. In sharp contrast, Dachler questions such presuppositions when applied to concepts like leadership and argues that the subjective assumptions of the observer will determine what is found and how it is interpreted. In this, he represents what we can call a subjectivist or interpretist perspective.[1] These contrasting positions reflect markedly different presumptions about the social world and the way in which it is appropriate to investigate it.

More formally, each differs in forms of *ontology*—assumptions about the very essence of the phenomenon under investigation. Is the "reality" to be investigated external to the individual—imposing itself on individual consciousness from outside—or the product of individual consciousness? Is reality objective, or the product of a person's mind? Related to ontological assumptions are those involving *epistemology*. How might we begin to understand the world and communicate this knowledge to others? For example, do we identify and transmit knowledge in hard and real forms? Or, instead, is "knowledge" softer, more subjective, or perhaps even spiritual or transcendental, based on insights of a unique and essentially personal nature (see Burrell & Morgan, 1979)?

A LEADERSHIP KNOWLEDGE ORIENTATION FRAMEWORK

We can see the basic ontological and epistemological assumptions, along with those concerning human nature, as core notions in gaining, using, and assessing leadership knowledge (the knowledge-orientation aspect of leadership synthesis). In Chapter 1 I argued that at a less abstract level, we could think also of leadership knowledge as being influenced by its purpose and definition and the stakeholders involved. I've summarized these aspects in the knowledge orientation model shown in Figure 4.1. The figure indicates that all these components are interrelated and serve to influence the gaining, using, and assessing of leadership knowledge. Let's look at each of these elements in turn, starting with assumptions.

Assumptions

Based on the work of Morgan and Smircich (1980), I begin the discussion of assumptions by thinking of them on an objectivist-subjectivist continuum as summarized in Table 4.1. The table shows six different positions, which expand on the earlier mentioned ontological, human nature, and epistemological assumptions. It also shows some summary descriptions and some example research approaches representative of each of the positions. Without going into detail, I intend these positions to convey the essence of the extreme objectivist-subjectivist views, and varying positions in between, as applied to leadership.[2] The continuum reflects leadership researchers' (and other users') views of the world and their assumptions (often implicit and taken for granted) that shape the kinds of questions asked and help define the research strategy adopted (see Pondy, Frost, Morgan, & Dandridge, 1983).

Let's take a closer look at the six positions shown in the table. In the extreme *objectivist, machine* position on the left-hand side of the continuum, we see a quest for systematic laws to explain and predict an orderly "real" world and thus to construct a rationalistic science. The *organism* position extends the static machine position by focusing

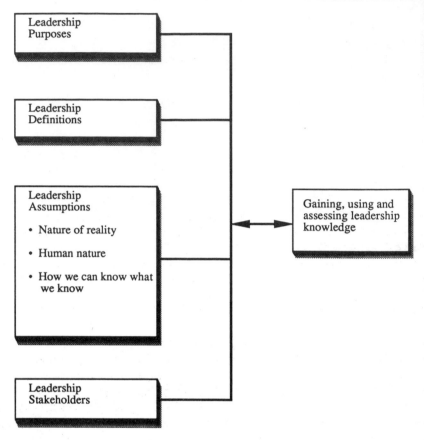

Figure 4.1. Leadership Knowledge-Orientation Framework

on the social world as an evolving process, still concrete but constantly changing in detailed form. Relations between individuals and
the environment express an activity pattern necessary for the survival
and well-being of the individuals and even the organization itself.
Evolution of these patterns over time becomes important. Leaders and
followers have moved from simple responders to adapters (Morgan &
Smircich, 1980).

The *hologram, cybernetics, brain* position is indeed a holistic one
where a change in the appropriate pattern and balance in any one part
will affect the whole, initiating patterns of adjustment and readjustment

Table 4.1
A Continuum of Basic Ontological, Human Nature, and Epistemological Assumptions and Example Research Approaches to Leadership

	Objectivist Approaches to Leadership					*Subjectivist Approaches to Leadership*
Core Ontological (nature of reality) Assumptions	reality as concrete structure	reality as concrete process	reality as contextual field of information	reality as realm of symbolic discourse	reality as social construction	reality as projection of human imagination
Metaphors and Brief Descriptions	*machine*	*organism*	*hologram, cybernetics, brain*	*theater, drama, culture*	*language game, sense-making, text*	*transcendental*
	• Leader/follower (LF) actions follow laws which make them routinized, reliable, and predictable; LF's respond predictably	• LF actions play certain roles and functions in the continuation and operation of the organizational system of which they are part. • Organizations, as systems, are continually evolving because of external context (environment) and LF actions influence system equilibrium	• LF actions provide information about the context which allows contextual and LF interrelations to be mutually regulated. • The whole is stored in all the parts and there is autopoesis: self-production through circular interaction patterns; environment and system are one.	• By framing contexts and manipulating symbolic actions, LFs manage organizational culture, interpersonal impressions, and meanings associated with organizational events and relationships.	• Organizational events/situations created and made sense of through LF rule-governed symbolic actions. Many different language games can be played; many realities, with multiple levels, exist. • When creating and sustaining organizational reality, LFs not only *use* but *are* symbols.	• LF social (phenomenological) world and "reality" is projection of individual consciousness; may be accessible only through phenomenological modes of insight. • Consciousness

(continued)

Table 4.1. Continued

Human Nature Assumptions	LFs as responders	LFs as adaptors	LFs as information processes	LFs as actors, symbol users	LFs as social constructors, symbol creators	LFs as pure spirit, consciousness, being
Epistemological Stance (How can we know what we know?)	• Construct a rationalistic, objectivist science that emphasizes networks of causal laws and resulting rule-governed relationships	• Study systems, process, and change. • Monitor leadership process and/or ways by which it changes over time in relation to internal and external context/ecology (system and environment).	• Map contexts so understand how leadership and context mutually evolve over time.	• Understand LF patterns of symbolic discourse where symbolic actions *used* to shape and to make meaningful their social reality.	• Understand processes by which LFs *create* and *sustain* social reality—make symbolic sense of situations and share organizational realities.	• Obtain LF phenomenological insight, revelation
Knowledge Generated	• Systematic laws to explain and predict LF actions and their impact.	• Emphasizes impact of context on organization and LFs.	• Emphasizes mutual causality (causes cause causes to cause causes; Wilden, 1980) linking LFs and organizational contexts through causal loops.	• Emphasizes typologies of symbolic actions and insight about general nature of organizational reality.	• Emphasizes understanding of processes LFs use to create specific organizational realities.	• Emphasizes contents of LF conscious phenomena (objective or subjective) or consciousness itself.
Example Research Approaches	Laboratory experiments, surveys, etc. (see Kerlinger, 1973).	Historical analysis (see Wren, 1986), ecological organizational studies (e.g., Aldrich, 1979)	Contextual analysis (see Morgan, 1986; Masuch, 1985; Smith, 1984)	Symbolic interactions, dramaturgy (see Morris, 1977; Wexler, 1983).	Semiotics, ethnomethodology (see Agar, 1986; Manning, 1987)	Exploration of pure subjectivity

Source: Based on Morgan (1986), Morgan & Smircich (1980), and Pondy, Frost, Morgan, & Dandridge (1983).

capable of changing the whole. As Wilden (1980) expresses it, "causes cause causes to cause causes" (p. 39). We can view leaders and followers as information processors. In other words, the ways in which they deal with information affect changes in the field as a whole. There is a pattern of learning and mutual adjustment between individuals and the context, termed *autopoesis* (see Maturana & Varela, 1980; Morgan, 1986; Morgan & Smircich, 1980; K. K. Smith, 1984). Particularly interesting here are counterintuitive "vicious circle" notions where actions taken to deal with a problem in one component of a system have a dysfunctional impact on another aspect and generate a series of progressively more dysfunctional "vicious circles" (see Masuch, 1985; Morgan, 1986).

The *theater, drama, culture* position sees leaders and followers as actors, using symbols to interpret and enact a meaningful relationship with their world. They become actors who can use symbols to modify their roles, which they play as if they were on life's stage. The Reagan presidency, as described in a sophisticated journalistic treatment by H. Smith (1988), is an excellent case in point.

The *language game, sense-making, text* position defines reality as a social construction. The world in which leaders and followers operate has no concrete status—it is strictly a symbolic construction. Symbols can create shared realities with others but these are fleeting and confined to those moments when they are actively constructed and sustained. Leaders and followers are assumed to create symbols and to create their own reality. Some aspects of the Reagan presidency are also applicable here (see H. Smith, 1988).

The final *reality as a projection of human imagination* position anchors the extreme subjectivist end of the continuum. Here the social world and its "reality" are projections of individual consciousness. They are acts of creative imagination and essentially assume that an individual's mind is that person's world; sometimes this is described as *solipsism*. Leaders and followers are seen as transcendental beings who shape the world within the realm of their own immediate experience. The more extreme treatments of phenomenology fit the description just given (see Stewart & Mickunas, 1974).

The summary descriptions in the table show the differing ontological/epistemological and human nature assumptions underlying each of the positions. Furthermore, when we realize that many of these assumptions are hidden and taken for granted, it is no wonder that there is controversy concerning what is really "known" about leadership and how best to go about gaining, using, and assessing leadership knowledge.

Illustrative Research Approaches

Now let's look at the illustrative research approaches in Table 4.1. They should help to convey further the tenor of the various positions; I provide more detailed treatment of some of these as needed in future chapters. I describe these as "illustrative" because there are other approaches not shown and the ones that are shown often are used for more than one position on the continuum. Also, there are differences in research techniques *within* these approaches. Perhaps reflecting my own objectivist training and bias, I assume that most readers are likely to be at least somewhat familiar with the approaches listed under the machine and organism positions. Thus I emphasize the cybernetics, theater, and language positions. And although I provide a reference in the table for an example research approach illustrating phenomenology and the transcendental position, I do no more than that. That's because it is hard to do it justice without a more detailed discussion than I have space to provide, and because I assume it is so extreme that most people will not identify with it, at least not in a leadership context. For those who are interested, I recommend Sanders (1982).

Starting with cybernetics, the key point in conducting research is to recognize the earlier discussion and the hologram and "causes cause causes to cause causes" notion. Morgan (1986) describes an approach labeled *contextual analysis* based on the arguments of Maruyama (1963), among others. Essentially, contextual analysis reflects nonlinear, holistic ways of thinking that are particularly important in the systems-oriented extended model developed in the previous chapter; loops, rather than lines, are emphasized (see Masuch, 1985). In the organism metaphor, structural equation modeling (e.g., Hughes, Price, & Marrs, 1986) might be one method used to show complex causal relations in terms of linearity. In contrast, the cybernetic analyses emphasize loops and circular relations, rather than lines (Morgan, 1986, p. 247).

In terms of leadership, we would be looking for the patterns of relations among leaders, followers, and various aspects of the context within which they operate, recognizing that a change in one part of the system would change other parts of the system. However, as argued in the previous chapter, for analysis sometimes we can focus on separate subsystems within the system. Masuch (1985) indicates some current limitations in doing these holistic kinds of analyses and suggests network theory (Schwartz & Sprinzen, 1984) and topological algebra (Casti, 1979) as useful, although highly technical, points of departure.

Moving from the cybernetic to the theater and language game positions in the table, one should recognize that these are bound together by their image of human beings as creating reality in interaction with others. These views aim for the discovery of the methods by which individuals make sense of their world, create order where none is inherent, and organize their routine activities. The views question the more objectivist notions characteristic of the left-hand positions on the continuum, and tend to use approaches different from those of the natural sciences (see Morris, 1977).

Bearing in mind that there are sometimes substantial differences *within* each of the research strategy streams illustrating these metaphors, let's look at some symbolic interaction, ethnomethodology, semiotic, and dramaturgy illustrations. We can embed these within a more general ethnographic study of presidential leadership in a small Roman Catholic liberal-arts college (Tierney, 1988). The study was conducted over a recent one-year period that turned out to be a year of crisis within the college. In contrast to studies that view leaders in narrowly abstracted settings or in terms of placing them on a hierarchical scale of ability to affect change, the ethnographic focus of this research had a different thrust. It emphasized how the participants viewed their world, and within that world how leadership was seen to exist. The study involved Tierney as the ethnographic observer who sought to understand leadership by observing how events happened, how those involved used symbols, and by viewing the participants as being embedded within their organizational culture. Tierney used evidence from formal meetings, interviews, informal observations, and analyses of presidential communications.

The crisis situation was reflected in the "we-they" atmosphere conveyed by the participants. Leadership was seen by the researcher as a matrix of relationships influenced by a wide variety of practices, rather than as a list of identifiable traits. Time, space, and communication were three key reference points for helping to interpret the matrix of relationships.

The time reference point was reflected primarily in terms of the college's historical context and the web of interconnected relationships that existed within the college before the current participants entered the scene. The space reference point emphasized both private and public space, including interpretation of physical gestures, an individual's regular bypassing of a building to avoid the administrative vice president, the president's emphasis on her office as "her space" as contrasted with the previous president's use of the entire campus as her space, and so forth. Communication was viewed as a process where people formed meanings about the participants' language, and symbols were analyzed in terms of their significance for leadership.

This study is a good example of one with an ethnomethodological emphasis (e.g., Fetterman, 1989)—recognizing, of course, that there are many different variations within this general approach. Lyman and Scott (1970) see ethnomethodology as the study of procedures used by everyday people in an attempt to cope meaningfully with their world. It is concerned with how everyday meaning structures are made and sustained as meaningful (Zimmerman & Wilson, 1973). Ethnomethodology focuses on those things that are so taken for granted that they are scarcely noted by the participants.

Even with the variations within both ethnomethodology and the symbolic interactions approach indicated in Table 4.1, there are underlying similarities. For example, symbolic interaction is concerned with mutual responses to and interpretations of symbols, gestures, and behaviors of those in a given setting. Because of symbolic interaction, human group life becomes an ongoing process in which individuals fit their actions to those of others (Morris, 1977). As such, both it and ethnomethodology go beyond the simpler nonsymbolic stimulus responses involved in the more objectivist emphases shown in Table 4.1.

Perhaps the biggest difference between symbolic interaction and ethnomethodology is that those emphasizing the former try to distance themselves from the participants, whereas ethnomethodologists believe that they must "go native" and "live within" the setting they are attempting to understand. The latter attempts to balance what is immediate and what is reflective. Thus Tierney spent a year as a part of the college that he was trying to understand. Unlike the more objectivist approaches, there is no attempt to distance the researcher from those researched. In other words, the researcher is also the instrument.

Tierney (1988) also emphasized some aspects of semiotics (Table 4.1) in the communications reference point in his study. *Semiotics* is the study of signs and what they mean. It is concerned with the process by which words, events, objects, and behaviors carry meaning for individuals, as well as the content conveyed (see Barley, 1983; Manning, 1987). Tierney was especially interested in these semiotic aspects as a means of helping to interpret the we-they split that he encountered between the president and various administrators and faculty members. More extended and formalized illustrations of various aspects of semiotics as a research strategy are covered by Manning (1987) in his study of police work and Barley (1983) in his study of funeral directors. In a different vein, Calas and Smircich (1988) show the use of semiotics in analyzing scholarly journal articles as representations of the work of leadership scholars.

Tierney (1988) also touches on the dramaturgy approach shown in Table 4.1 in interpreting some of his findings. This approach emphasizes symbols in terms of theatrical metaphors to capture the "how" of symbolizing (see Brisset & Edgley, 1975). Participants' behaviors are interpreted as if they were performing in a theater. The participant is seen as an actor with an emphasis on symbolism to project an image and direct and shape the "character" the audience is to perceive (see Goffman, 1974; Morris, 1977; Wexler, 1983).

Essentially, Tierney's work is a good exemplar of what Geertz (1973) calls "thick" description (in contrast to the "thin" description of surveys, and the like) and what Glaser and Strauss (1967) term "grounded theory." Grounded theory essentially involves using ongoing data to refine and extend interpretations continually. Tierney's study embodies subjectivist assumptions and illustrates well the role of the researcher in this kind of work. Finally, as I have shown, it serves as a vehicle to illustrate a range of subjectivist-oriented research approaches used within a leadership setting.

Objectivist/Subjectivist Positions and Traditional Leadership Approaches

Now that we've looked at the flavor of the objectivist-subjectivist assumptions, let's briefly return to Dachler's chapter-opening point that subjectivist leadership perspectives largely have been neglected. In other words, to what extent are traditional or mainstream leadership approaches biased toward objectivist assumptions and research approaches?

In addressing this question, I will *not* review each of the various traditional leadership approaches[3]—Bass (1990), Yukl (1989), and Hunt (1984a), among others, review this literature. In looking over this literature and these approaches, I conclude that all of the latter fit within the machine and organism positions in Table 4.1. These models typically are either situational contingency ones with independent, moderator, and dependent variables, or with independent and dependent variables. Processes and internal states of leaders and followers most often are treated in black-box fashion. Sometimes, intervening variables are indicated. However, even where this is the case, these usually are not empirically investigated. Basically, I am arguing that the approaches, as constituted, emphasize the objectivist positions on the left-hand side of the table. However, if intervening variables were emphasized more, the approaches would have the potential to be treated in a less objectivist fashion.

So much for the mainstream leadership literature. What about other leadership literature? Here we can identify some directions, although not all of these are specific models or theories per se. There is work focusing on such areas as subordinate attributions concerning leaders (e.g., Calder, 1977) and leader attributions concerning subordinates (e.g., Mitchell, Green, & Wood, 1981); leaders as information processors (e.g., Hunt, Baliga, & Peterson, 1988; Lord, 1985; Smith & Peterson, 1988); and leadership as a "romantic" or symbolic concept used to explain complex cause-effect relationships after the fact (Meindl, Ehrlich, & Dukerich, 1985; Pfeffer, 1981). All of these are discussed in more detail later in the book. For now, I will say simply that these move us toward the more subjectivist positions.

I conclude from all this that, in terms of traditional theories (even including much of the recent charismatic work), Dachler is right: They are extremely objectivist in nature. Some other work—especially some, though not all, that is currently emerging—tends to reflect more subjectivist orientations.

Critical Pluralism

At the continuum extremes in Table 4.1, assumptions are so different that they cannot be reconciled and it is easy to get into the kind of controversy illustrated in the chapter-opening quotes. In terms of the knowledge orientation aspect of the new leadership synthesis, each extreme is too restrictive. What comes to mind immediately, then, is some sort of compromise position that allows us to embrace both positions—to accept the "best" of both objectivist and subjectivist orientations. However, we must be careful lest we be trapped into the "relativist" position, as explained below.

Essentially, relativists say that "anything goes." Carried to an extreme, relativists would argue that they would as soon have their illness treated by a witch doctor as by a scientifically trained doctor of medicine. This is because relativists argue that the differences in underlying assumptions between traditional science and extreme subjectivism are so great that results obtained from the two approaches cannot be compared—what the philosopher of science Kuhn (1962) called "incommensurability." Thus, for them, one perspective necessarily is as good as another. This argument leads to a catch-22 situation: If the approaches are so different that they cannot be compared, then it is irrational to arrive at this conclusion by comparing them in order to derive the conclusion. If they cannot be compared, then how can one make the comparison to determine that they are not comparable (see S. D. Hunt, 1989, 1991)?

Another argument sometimes given for relativism is that it implies tolerance of opposing views. However, to argue that a person cannot compare is not to argue for tolerance. Instead it implies epistemological anarchy. An analogy is political anarchism, which certainly does not imply a tolerant, pluralistic democracy but instead a state of disarray (see S. D. Hunt, 1991).

Is there no solution, then? Are we prisoners of our underlying knowledge assumptions? Fortunately not! Shelby Hunt (1990) argues that the "rapprochement between science and politics" (Holbrook, 1989, p. 4) is to embrace "critical pluralism." The *critical* in the label indicates that critical pluralism embraces a tolerant, nonjudgmental view although it is harshly critical of both dogmatic objectivists and subjectivists. However, whatever perspective a person takes must be capable of having its results critically compared with those of another perspective. This comparison feature is the crucial difference between critical pluralism and relativism (see S. D. Hunt, 1990).

How might such a comparison be done? Hirschman (1986) proposes a set of criteria for evaluation of subjectivist findings. At first glance, Hirschman's criteria appear to be different from those used for traditional science. However, careful study shows a high degree of consistency between the two criterion sets. Shelby Hunt (1989) also proposes some possible criteria, as do Wallendorf and Belk (1989) and Yin (1989) as well, on a more limited basis.

Although the comparison issue is far from settled, it is drawing increasing attention. Proponents in the marketing literature are advocating triangulation across different sources, methods, and researchers (Wallendorf & Belk, 1989). In the management literature we are now beginning to see very active work in this area as well. For example, one set of researchers sees themselves as objectivists "who recognize and try to atone for that approach; soft-nosed logical positivism maybe"

(Miles & Huberman, 1984, p. 19).[4] In their book-length treatment, Miles and Huberman use such objectivist notions as validity and reliability and infer causal models, all done visually with a minimal use of quantitative data. Their treatment essentially takes rich observational (qualitative) findings and tries to systematize their analysis in a way analogous to those developed for objectivist data.

Kirk and Miller (1986) emphasize a similar but narrower approach by focusing on establishing a "scientific objectivity" in terms of reliability and validity in ethnographic research. Fielding and Fielding (1986) are concerned with several kinds of triangulations linking different kinds of subjectivist research as well as subjectivist and objectivist research.

Finally, Noblit and Hare (1988) pursue a quite different but very interesting direction. Rather than trying to reconcile subjectivist work using largely objectivist standards, these authors argue for synthesizing subjectivist studies on their own terms. That is, they use a subjectivist approach to providing a synthesis of subjectivist studies. They contend that the "soft-nosed positivist" approaches are involved with "bureaucratization" of data analysis (Marshall, 1985). Instead they argue that synthesis within subjectivist studies "should be as interpretive as any ethnographic account" (Noblit & Hare, 1988, p. 11).

Critical Pluralism and Public/Private Approaches

Typically the data collection and data analysis aspects of various research approaches are consistent (e.g., data collected by structured questionnaires usually are analyzed using structured statistical technologies). However, Pondy and Rousseau (1980) and Rousseau (in press) argue that for those who are flexibly inclined (in our case, critical pluralists), this consistency need not be the case.

Public methods can be specified in advance of implementation, are consistently observable by others, and are replicable across subjects, sites, and sets of data. They are relatively objectivist in nature. In contrast, private methods are specific to the researcher and involve cognitions, judgments, and experiences that can be only indirectly communicated to others. They are relatively subjectivist in nature (see Rousseau, in press). Following our discussion above, a typical approach would use the same method—either public or private—for both data collection and data analysis. However, Pondy and Rousseau (1980) instead promote flexibility by using a four-celled matrix providing for:

- (both public) standardized data collection and statistical data analysis
- (both private) impressionistic data collection and interpretist data analysis
- (public/private) standardized data collection and private, interpretist data analysis
- (private/public) impressionistic data collection and public statistical data analysis

A four-celled approach such as this is made to order for critical pluralists examining the kinds of questions suggested by the extended multilevel model. It allows for both exploration of new topics and rigorous analyses in spite of lack of clearly specified a priori constructs (Rousseau, in press).

Summary

All of the previously mentioned examples of both research approaches and cumulation of leadership data add to our knowledge, and are consistent with a strongly held critical pluralism orientation. Let's now reinforce that orientation by turning to the leadership purposes portion of Figure 4.1.

Purposes

An example of leadership purposes might involve using leadership knowledge to predict performance as contrasted with developing a model to improve leadership skills. Clearly the purposes are different and the knowledge gained, used, and evaluated should be considered with the different purposes in mind. This emphasis on different purposes seems so obvious as to need no discussion, yet such purposes have been given insufficient attention in the literature. This lack of attention is in spite of earlier pleas by those such as Campbell (1977), Karmel (1978), Pfeffer (1977), and most recently by Yukl (1989) and the emphases on axiology (purpose) in the philosophy of science literature (see S. D. Hunt, 1991). In this section I look at leadership purposes from a variety of perspectives.

I start this broad-ranging discussion with a description by some organizational behavior professors of their entrance into a brand-new work situation. They do not tell us whether this was taking a job in a new university setting or in a different type of organization. Nevertheless, they talk not only in terms of trying to make sense of their feelings of uncertainty, confusion, and perceived lack of order in this situation but also in terms of "survival." As organizational behavior scholars, they were used to doing research that had them *looking as an outside researcher at the research setting*. In the present situation, they were intimately involved. In addition to survival, critical outcomes became gaining knowledge, such as the nature of the organization; how the system worked; how to avoid undesirable outcomes; and what the critical language was.

These researchers labeled this the "inside mode of inquiry" (Evered & Louis, 1981). It is subjectivist in nature and is similar to our description of ethnography, except that it is far more personal because the subjects are also the researchers. The purpose is quite different from an "outside," objectivist approach that tends to emphasize the role of "detached 'value-free,' external observer scientists" (Evered & Louis, 1981, p. 386). In terms of purpose, these researchers' knowledge, acquired in an inside mode, was exactly what they said they needed to deal with their ultimate aim of organizational survival. This inside/outside dichotomy is very similar to that between emic and etic research. Emic research is that which takes the native frame of reference. Etic research takes the view of the researcher (see Harris, 1976). I discuss emic and etic further in Chapter 10.

Next, we should recognize that some philosophy of science scholars have been explicit about the importance of purpose. The well-known philosopher Habermas, for example, talks of three different interests or purposes—*technical, practical,* and *emancipatory* (Stablein & Nord, 1985). The first calls for studying leadership as an objectified process or concept (essentially a traditional science perspective). The practical purpose emphasizes understanding meaning in a specific situation so that a decision can be made that leads to action—the goal is understanding a specific decision, not developing a generalizable rule. The emancipatory purpose is to increase the level of human autonomy and responsibility. Here again, the knowledge needed is quite different than for the other two purposes.

Third, a synthesis from Campbell (1977), Smith and Peterson (1988), and Peterson (personal communication, 1989) suggests seven specific leadership purposes. Prediction, retrospective explanations to justify past actions, and leadership as an action lever to change aspects of an organization are three of these that convey the essence of all seven.

Finally, we can think of context-specific versus context-free knowledge purposes proposed by Blair and Hunt (1986) and the impact of these on the differing emphases of leadership knowledge considered appropriate. The former focuses on phenomena embedded within a specific organizational context or type of organization (health care, public sector, etc.). In contrast, context-free knowledge emphasizes phenomena free of the specific organizational context in which the phenomena are encountered.[5]

Those with a context-free purpose in mind are interested in leadership and related variables wherever they are found, regardless of organizational context. However, for a person with a context-specific purpose, the type of organization is a constant and the interest is in the operation of leadership within that specific context. Blair and Hunt (1986) discuss many different issues accompanying these orientations. A couple of differences relevant for us are that they tend to emphasize different literature bases and that those with a context-free orientation tend to focus on relatively few variables across many organizations, whereas a context-specific emphasis tends to focus on many variables applied to one kind of organization. Interestingly, Blair and Hunt don't see these orientations as linked to objectivist-subjectivist orientations; each can have either a subjectivist or objectivist orientation.

Definitions

In addition to the just-discussed leadership knowledge assumptions and purposes aspects of Figure 4.1, the nature of the leadership definition is an important additional influence on the specific kind of leadership knowledge needed. Let's touch on the definitional issue and invite those who wish to consider definitions in more detail to check Bass (1990) or Yukl (1989). A common thread among many leadership definitions is interpersonal influence—a person obeys or responds in other ways because of something another person does. Some would contend that this interpersonal influence must be exercised face-to-face. Indeed, as I've indicated, the previously mentioned emphasis on lower-level leadership studies tends to be oriented toward such face-to-face or direct influence. Clearly that definition has different knowledge implications than the multilevel one emphasized in this book, which among other things considers the indirect impact of higher-level leaders on what occurs at the bottom of the organization.

Another key definitional aspect is the extent to which leadership is seen as similar to or different from management. In a few cases (e.g., Hersey & Blanchard, 1988, p. 5) leadership is seen as broader than management. In other cases, leadership and management are not differentiated; a manager is by definition the same as a leader. In still other cases, a role perspective is taken and leadership is seen as one of the many roles of a manager (e.g., Mintzberg, 1973/1980); even though some, such as Mintzberg, argue that leadership is needed in carrying out many of the other managerial roles. Zaleznik (1977), Bennis and Nanus (1985), Schneider (1989), Kotter (1990), and Korukonda and Hunt (1987), among others, sharply differentiate between the leadership function and the managerial function or go so far as to call some people leaders and others managers.

It can also make a difference in studying leadership if we define leadership in terms of a process or a property (see Jago, 1982). In the former the emphasis tends to be on leadership actions and processes as opposed to individuals. In the latter, the focus is more likely to be on aspects of one or more individuals regardless of whether they are in a formal managerial role or not (see Jacobs & Jaques, 1987).

Finally, one definition of leadership, different from any of the ones just discussed, sees it as the management of meaning—"the process whereby one or more individuals succeeds in attempting to frame and define the reality of others" (Smircich & Morgan, 1982, p. 258). This definition is consistent with subjectivist orientations and, again, implies different knowledge implications than the other definitions considered.

In summary, the widely varying kinds of definitions discussed above need to be kept in mind when assessing, using, and evaluating leadership knowledge. So, too, do the leadership stakeholders shown in Figure 4.1. Let's examine the latter in more detail.

Leadership Stakeholders

We can think of leadership stakeholders as those people or entities involved with various aspects of leadership knowledge orientation. In addition to the researcher (or individual conducting the study), they may involve the subjects or those providing the data and the users of the output. Put even more specifically, we are talking about such stakeholders as publication outlets, research support agencies, students, fellow researchers, various kinds of managers, consultants, those with sites for conducting research, and even social movement groups (see Peterson & Smith, 1988).

Each of these stakeholders is likely to be quite different in terms of interests, orientations, and the like. For instance, research support agencies are likely to have quite different concerns and interests than students. And different yet would be the concerns of social movement groups. Thus we can expect them to gain, use, and assess leadership knowledge differently. Particularly interesting and important are differences in concerns between managers and researchers. Such differences are discussed in detail by those such as Shrivastava and Mitroff (1984) and McGuire (1986).

Outcomes

In terms of outcomes, Figure 4.1 simply makes explicit the point that assumptions, purposes, definitions, and stakeholders influence knowledge orientation outcomes involved in gaining, using, and assessing leadership knowledge.

Interrelations

The figure and our intuition tells us that the components of our knowledge orientation model in the figure are related to each other. I have assumed moderate to substantial linkage but enough difference, at least heuristically, to justify the components just discussed.

For openers, we can think of interrelations between assumptions and purposes. One particular example, in terms of the extended multilevel model, concerns dealing with organizational culture. In Chapter 10 I use a "peeled onion" perspective concerning culture. There, following recent scholars such as Schein (1985), Ott (1989), and Rousseau (in press), I argue that there are different "layers" of culture, with each one getting closer and closer to the core notion involving organizational members' shared basic assumptions about such things as the nature of reality, time, and the like. These are assumed to be taken for granted and so deep-seated that only highly subjectivist approaches are appropriate to get at them. However, as we move out from the core of the onion, each of the cultural layers peeled away becomes progressively less deeply embedded inside the consciousness of the members and thus more readily accessible (indeed, the outermost layers consist of behaviors and visible artifacts; see Chapter 10 for more details).

In terms of interrelationships, it can be argued that some purposes require more deep-seated assumptions than others about culture and how to tap it. For a large-scale survey, we may be satisfied with tapping culture at the values level, with a questionnaire that calls for a different and less subjectivist set of assumptions than would trying to tap organizational members' core basic assumptions. However, for other purposes, we may not be satisfied unless we can get at these basic assumptions using a more subjectivist research approach.

We also might consider assumptions and purposes interrelationships in terms of the inside/outside mode of inquiry discussed earlier. If our inside purpose is for ultimate survival in the organization, then, like the example set of organizational behavior professors, we are likely to make subjectivist assumptions and to utilize more subjectivist research approaches. Lawlike relationships and questionnaires will tend to be of little use.

It's also true that sometimes knowing who the leadership stakeholders are will define the purpose. For instance, in the inside/outside case, the stakeholders may be defined as new organizational participants. As shown, the knowledge orientation purpose of these participants was coping and survival. In most instances, that probably would be the basic purpose of those new to the organization. Thus, here as probably often is the case, it's possible from knowing the stakeholders' roles to define the stakeholders' purposes, and vice versa in other instances.

In terms of the latter, if we knew the purposes were, for example, to prepare a research proposal to conduct a scholarly leadership study, we could assume with some certainty that the key stakeholders would be the funding agency and key people in the organization to be included in the study. I'm sure readers can provide examples of many other possible interrelations. What all this means is that the previously discussed assumptions, purposes, definitions, and stakeholders and their interrelations all have a bearing on how we obtain, use, and evaluate leadership knowledge—that is, our knowledge orientation.

ASSUMPTIONS AND
CRITICAL PLURALISM REVISITED

I've emphasized underlying knowledge assumptions as the key aspect of the knowledge orientation framework in Figure 4.1, and deep down I believe this to be true. However, we virtually all know of people, who at least explicitly, do not seem concerned with underlying assumptions. In that sense, they are like leaders who operate from schemas (essentially knowledge structures) without necessarily knowing or caring about the assumptions underlying the schemas (I consider these leadership schemas in Chapter 7, but the arguments apply equally to leadership researchers). Thus we see some researchers who use whatever research methodology "works" (i.e., who emphasize purpose) without explicitly considering underlying assumptions. At the risk of adding still another term to what has become a philosophy of science terminology jungle, we might call these people "assumptions agnostics."

We can ask whether assumptions really matter, if a person is flexible on methodologies. Certainly assumptions can help in defending an individual's results from attacks by those with strong philosophy of science backgrounds. They also are especially important in fairly assessing leadership knowledge. My contention is that many of the not-uncommon attacks on others' work frequently are influenced strongly by these taken-for-granted assumptions, if not the awareness of the purpose, definition, and stakeholder aspects of the knowledge orientation framework. Finally, returning to schemas, it can be argued that concern with assumptions flavors the whole way we think about the research process that goes far beyond an objectivist using a subjectivist method. Tierney's (1988) earlier-described ethnographical study of a college president is a case in point. The researcher's entire orientation to this study was different, in all the ways mentioned previously, than would be the orientation of a researcher conducting a more objectivist study.

Essentially, then, I am reinforcing my earlier argument about the importance of assumptions as a key part of our knowledge orientation framework. I also want to reinforce the importance of critical pluralism and avoiding the objectivist-subjectivist extremes in dealing with these assumptions. Critical pluralism is important if we are to have the knowledge orientation flexibility to accompany the broadened knowledge content flexibility of the extended multilevel leadership model.

I close this section by noting that interested readers might gain additional perspectives on some of the points previously mentioned by considering the selections in Hunt, Hosking, Schriesheim, and Stewart (1984) and Hunt, Baliga, Dachler, and Schriesheim (1988). These provide a number of insights from European and North American scholars.

ASSUMPTIONS AND
SINGLE/DOUBLE-LOOP LEARNING

Given this emphasis on the importance of underlying knowledge assumptions and critical pluralism, let's ask how easy it might be to become a critical pluralist if one wanted to. Is simply being sensitized to the importance of underlying assumptions and wanting to be a critical pluralist enough? Argyris (1976) would argue no and would contend that mere sensitization, although useful, does not go far enough.

Essentially the argument is that we need "double-loop" learning but tend to think in "single-loop" terms. Single-loop learning allows a person to detect and correct error in relation to a set of operating norms (Morgan, 1986); an example is a household thermostat. In contrast, the double-loop system does everything that the single-loop system does and takes a "double look" at the existing situation by questioning the operating norms (Morgan, 1986). It is as if the thermostat can now not only detect deviations but also decide what the temperature setting *should* be.

In the present context, single-loop learning would take place where leadership scholars critique each other's work to improve it and enhance scientific understanding. Indeed, such critique is a key tenet of traditional science and of objectivist research strategies. However, the incorporation of subjectivist perspectives calls for double-loop learning on the part of these objectivist researchers. Argyris and his colleague Schön (e.g., Argyris, 1979, 1982, 1984; Argyris & Schön, 1978) have argued that there are a number of factors that inhibit double-loop learning. To understand the argument better, let's look at what Argyris calls *espoused theories of action* and *theories-in-use*.

Espoused theories are what people say they do, and theories-in-use are what they actually do (see Argyris, 1979). However, these theories are more than simply the difference between saying and doing. "People espouse theories that they use to design and manage their actions, of which they are unaware" (Argyris, 1984, p. 52). The key point is that this inconsistency is not just the difference between behaving differently from the espoused theory. Rather, a basic change in the underlying assumptions is necessary. In other words, people need to make their theories-in-use consistent with their espoused theories. However, changing the necessary underlying assumptions is particularly difficult because the underlying assumptions are defensive and self-sealing, and the system is a single-loop one.

Put another way, a basic characteristic of individuals is that they tend to be unaware of their theories-in-use (but not their espoused theories). Embedded in their theories-in-use are propositions to keep them unaware, and the people around them are programmed not to inform them of the incongruities. The people around them may be aware or unaware of the point just mentioned, but they also are programmed with the same theory-in-use; hence they cannot confront the lack of valid feedback. Finally, if the behavior is skillful, the program underlying it is tacit and hence not consciously available to the individuals. Thus the individuals tend not to receive the double-loop feedback necessary to change the assumptions (see Argyris, 1979).

In terms of leadership scholars, I argue that, like everyone else, they tend to operate in a single-loop mode. Both objectivists and subjectivists are influenced by their previous training and experience. For many of these people, Argyris would contend that intervention is needed to develop a double-loop mode, which as I argued earlier is necessary to really be a critical pluralist.

A similar intervention argument is made by Maruyama (1974) as cited by Pondy and Boje (1976). Maruyama proposes a three-phase intervention approach. The first phase makes each party aware that the other party uses different assumptions and different logics. Each individual is helped to identify and articulate those assumptions on which his or her thinking rests. In the second phase, each party attempts to put aside his or her own assumptions and tries to think in terms of the other party's assumptions, so that he or she can have the same sense of subjective experience.

The final phase involves each party helping the other to see into his or her own assumptions. As an example, a person with a holistic emphasis might help a language game-oriented individual see the world from the holistic view. But to do this the holist must understand the language game orientation well enough to be aware of where the blinders are and how to help the language game person remove them (see Pondy & Boje, 1976).

These phases are much easier to discuss than to implement. Argyris's intervention techniques could help in their implementation. Is such implementation worth the effort? I argue that it is, if one accepts the earlier argument concerning the importance of and difficulty in changing leadership knowledge-orientation assumptions.

CONCLUDING COMMENTARY

In this chapter I have approached the knowledge orientation aspect of leadership synthesis in terms of a knowledge orientation framework. That framework considers the assumptions, purposes, definitions, and stakeholders involved in gaining, using, and evaluating leadership knowledge.

The underlying knowledge orientation assumptions part of the framework is considered particularly crucial and specifies a continuum of objectivist-subjectivist assumptions about ontology, human nature, and epistemology. Extreme objectivists and extreme subjectivists structure their knowledge realities so differently that their views cannot be reconciled. In my view, such extremes are counterproductive and what is needed instead is a critical pluralist perspective. This perspective embraces a mix of objectivist-subjectivist positions as long as one keeps in mind that the results from one position must be capable of being compared with those from another. This critical pluralist perspective not only is pragmatic in terms of assumptions but also recognizes the importance of the purposes, definitions, and stakeholders, and the interrelationships among all those elements, in the knowledge orientation.

This knowledge orientation pragmatism—the second aspect of leadership synthesis for which I have argued—is consistent with that of the first, or knowledge content, aspect of the synthesis. In other words, I've argued that to realize the potential of the extended multiorganizational-level content aspect of leadership knowledge we also must have an expanded view of the knowledge orientation aspect. The critical pluralist perspective, involving the knowledge assumptions, purposes, definitions, and stakeholders, encourages such an expanded view as we obtain the data necessary to explore the many kinds of questions suggested by the extended multilevel model.

With this dual knowledge content and orientation emphasis in mind, Part II now deals with each of the components of the expanded multilevel model in some detail. To begin, Chapter 5 covers external environment, societal culture, and the leader's critical tasks.

NOTES

1. These are representative of the numerous labels for these extreme positions and we utilize them throughout. Frequently the term *positivist* is used as synonymous with objectivist. However, Shelby Hunt (1990) shows that this is an historically inaccurate usage of the term.

2. For in-depth discussion and extensive additional references concerning the long-standing philosophy of science objectivist-subjectivist debate in the social sciences see Rosenberg (1988), Burrell and Morgan (1979), and S. D. Hunt (1990). Burrell and Morgan also develop a topology that is more extensive than the objectivist-subjectivist continuum. However, discussion of that would take this book beyond its present purpose.

3. There are at least 10 such approaches, including: transformational/transactional (Avolio & Bass, 1989); leader-member exchange (Graen & Cashman, 1975); charismatic (House, 1977); reward and punishment (Podsakoff, Todor, Grover, & Huber, 1984); trait-behavior (Yukl, 1989); leadership contingency (Fiedler & Chemers, 1974); path-goal (House & Mitchell, 1974); leadership substitutes (Kerr & Jermier, 1978); situational leadership (Hersey & Blanchard, 1988); and normative (Vroom & Jago, 1988).

4. They appear to use *logical positivism* in the sense that Shelby Hunt (1990) described earlier as inaccurate. Nevertheless, the quote captures the spirit of their thinking.

5. The key here is the difference *between* these two categories and not whatever differences might be found within them (e.g., one specific kind of hospital versus another).

Part II

Exploring the Multilevel Model

This part explores each of the components of the multiple-level leadership model and considers developmental implications and ways to enrich schema variety for leaders.

- Chapter 5: External Environment, Societal Culture, and Leader Critical Tasks
- Chapter 6: Background Factors and Preference Aspects of Individual Capability
- Chapter 7: Individual Capabilities—Cognitive Complexity and Selected Social-Cognition Aspects
- Chapter 8: Individual Capabilities—Transactionally Oriented Leadership Skills
- Chapter 9: Individual Capabilities—Transformationally Oriented Leadership Skills
- Chapter 10: Organizational Culture
- Chapter 11: Developmental Implications and Enriching Schema Variety

5 External Environment, Societal Culture, and Leader Critical Tasks

Strategic change is likely to call for different . . . techniques than continuous running of well-established [organizations]. . . If effectively done, strategic [leadership] can have even greater payoffs in rough seas than in clear sailing.

—Boris Yairtz and William H. Newman
(quoted in Eigen & Siegel, 1989, p. 439)

All of the work at this level is in concepts . . . of what should be . . . force structures for the year 2000 and beyond are being set right now and the strategic mix must be right. The decisions we make [currently] will come to fruition in 2020.

—Unidentified four-star general
(quoted in Clark & Clark, 1990, p. 289)

Use your own best judgment at all times.
—Entire contents of $1.9 billion Nordstrom Corporation
policy manual (quoted in Eigen & Siegel, 1989, p. 241)

This chapter—the first of Part II—starts the detailed examination of each of the components of the extended multilevel model. I begin by looking at external environment and societal culture.

EXTERNAL ENVIRONMENT/ SOCIETAL CULTURE

The importance of the external environment in open-systems organizational studies has increased since the earlier work of those such as Lawrence and Lorsch (1967), Emery and Trist (1973), and Terreberry (1968). It now is systematically treated in organization theory and strategic management books. Societal culture, although related, has quite a different background with roots in anthropology (see Smircich & Calas, 1987, for a discussion).

Figure 5.1 shows the role of these environmental and societal forces in terms of the extended multilevel model developed in Chapter 3. Recall that, for systems domain leaders, these forces were argued to be immensely complex and to call for interfacing with and coordinating of multinational corporations. As such, for systems domain leaders, they are predicted to have direct impact on the various aspects of the model and indirect impact in the lower domains.

How might we go about conceptualizing and measuring these forces external to the organization? I use a framework developed by Osborn, et al. (1980) for this. The framework is consistent with those discussed in such sources as Daft (1989), Robbins (1990), and Scott (1987), among others. I start by dividing the environment into two partially overlapping parts: the general environment, and the specific or task environment. The *general environment* contains those forces that influence all organizations operating within a given geographical area. The *specific environment* contains those conditions unique to one organization (or strategic constituency) or a small number of organizations.

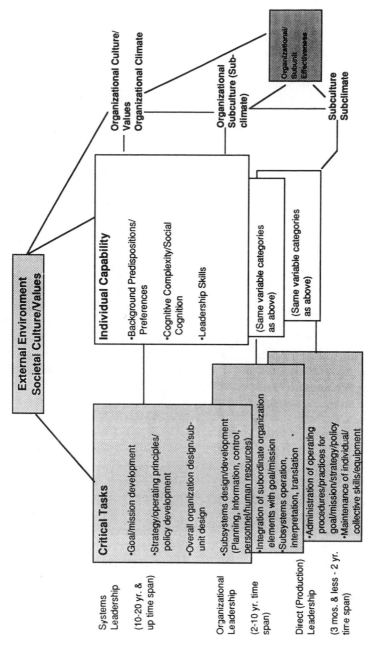

Figure 5.1. Extended Multiple-Organizational-Level Leadership Model

Note: For simplicity, some direct relationships, feedback, and arrowheads are not shown.

71

General Environment

We can expand the definition above by noting that the forces include socioeconomic, educational, legal-political and cultural aspects that operate within the specified geographical area. Political units frequently are useful for defining the perimeters here given that local, state, national, and international statistics usually are available in terms of political boundaries (e.g., various economic indicators by county, state, and so on). Census and related data provide a broad range of useful indicators for the socioeconomic, educational, and legal-political aspects of the general environment. Cultural aspects are determined differently.

Socioeconomic aspects are concerned with such things as health conditions, divorce rate, current economic level, and past and projected growth and development. Income levels, unemployment rates, retail sales, and the like are typical indicators. Representative educational indicators are literacy level, expenditures per pupil, and average number of school years completed. Some legal-political indicators are crime and crime rates, voter participation, and so forth. Osborn et al. (1980) provide a more detailed listing of possible indicators for these aspects of the general environment, as do Hunt et al. (1981).

These measures can be aggregated to provide indices of general environment richness or development, interdependence, and uncertainty. Osborn et al. (1980) argue also that these dimensions, in turn, can be combined as a measure of general environment complexity. They also cite some empirical support for the use of these general environment dimensions.

Societal Culture

Although the other aspects of the general environment are based on objective measures such as those just discussed, one way of thinking of societal culture is as the "collective mental programs of the people in an environment" (Hofstede, 1980, p. 25). It essentially taps collective values (preferences) and beliefs of a given nation or society. Here, the emphasis is on *collective* (reflected in society as a whole) as compared to individual phenomena. In other words, to what extent do people inside organizations reflect the values of society—to what extent do they share such values and what are some implications of this sharing? Though we expect individuals to reflect their society to a greater or lesser degree, we also expect each individual to possess values, beliefs, and so forth separate from those emphasized culturally. I treat such individual aspects in the value preferences section of Chapter 6.

Lammers and Hickson (1979) argue that cultural patterns have been found to influence behavior in organizations and to influence organizational forms and processes in three ways:

* Dominant societal values are reflected in the standards imposed on an organization by environmental aspects (e.g., OSHA safety regulations in the United States).
* The mental programming of organizational founders and top managers ("dominant elite"—Hambrick & Mason, 1984; "strategic apex"— Mintzberg, 1979) is imprinted in organizations from their inception.
* Members of the organization, other than those just mentioned, are influenced in various ways by such cultural mental programming.

Jackofsky and Slocum (1988) reinforce this point by developing a model of CEO behavior that includes societal culture as one of the key elements influencing CEO role behaviors. Tayeb (1988), in one of the more recent empirical reflections of earlier work, presents data showing the impact of culture on organizational structure in samples of English and Indian organizations.

Given the importance of societal culture in an organizational context, let's look at the concept in more detail. We can start by asking about underlying dimensions. Hofstede (1980) has identified a set of these that is now quite well-known and is beginning to serve as the basis for follow-up work. Using questionnaire measures, he studied the values and beliefs of over 100,000 employees in IBM plants located in 40 countries. He identified four core values, and his classification scheme has received support (e.g., Adler, 1984, 1986; Bhagat & McQuaid, 1982) as an indicator of cultural mores and beliefs. And although some (e.g., Goodstein, 1981) have criticized Hofstede's specific methodology and managerial implications, they do not question that culture influences various managerial aspects.

Hofstede identified the four core cultural dimensions of power distance (PD), uncertainty avoidance (UA), individualism versus collectivism (I-C), and masculinity versus femininity (M-F). PD is the extent to which a culture accepts the inequality of the distribution of power between two people. In high PD countries, power holders are entitled to privileges and it is expected that there will be clear and strong superior-subordinate relationships. In low PD countries there is more power equality and sharing,—and more consultative manager-subordinate relationships. UA reflects the degree to which individuals feel threatened by and try to avoid ambiguous and uncertain situations. One way that societies deal with UA is through rules and rituals. Thus high UA cultures tend to be relatively rule-bound.

I-C refers to whether a society is loosely knit, with individuals primarily responsible for themselves and their immediate families, or tightly knit with a heavy group emphasis and a sharp differentiation between in-groups and out-groups. In the latter, group rather than individual action and initiative tends to be emphasized. In high M-F countries, the dominant values are masculine in terms of assertiveness and acquisition of tangible things. There is sharp sex-role differentiation of jobs and the like.

Hofstede conducted cluster analysis of his data and derived eight clusters reflecting the 40 countries' relative standings on these dimensions. The United States was found to cluster with countries below average on PD and UA, well above average on M-F, and very high on individualism (in fact, it was the highest of all the sampled countries). Jackofsky and Slocum (1988) used published data of CEOs in five countries, each representing a different cluster, to examine the extent to which these cultural dimensions appeared to influence CEO role behaviors. For our purposes, it is enough to note that their evidence does tend to support the argument for a relationship between empirical aspects and role behaviors.

Related work has been conducted to examine cultural values from an alternative to the Western point of view. Here, a fifth dimension—Confucian dynamism—has been identified. Included in this dimension are such aspects as persistence, sense of shame, protecting "face" (see Hofstede & Bond, 1988). Other related work by Ronen and Shenkner (1985) cluster analyzed data from previously conducted studies on the basis of work goals, values, needs, and job attitudes and derived eight clusters. The United States was found most similar to Canada, New Zealand, Britain, Ireland, South Africa, and Australia and joined them in the "Anglo cluster." Tayeb (1988) used Hofstede's work for more detailed analyses in India and England and found relationships between culture and various characteristics of organizational structure. In addition, he added the cultural dimensions of trust and commitment to the earlier ones, and found that they too were important predictors.

The previously discussed findings are reinforced by earlier work reported in Osborn et al. (1980). There, values differentiated on the basis of prescientific, scientific, and postscientific patterns were dealt with and some organizational implications of contradictory value patterns (e.g., democracy versus authoritarianism) were treated. Finally, an interesting case study illustration contrasts the cultures (actually, subcultures) of two small northeastern Pennsylvania towns, Coaltown and Riverton.

The two towns are only 15 miles apart but are located in parallel valleys separated by a mountain range. Coaltown was a mining town with strong ties to the United Mine Workers, and had a history of extreme labor-management hostility. In contrast, Riverton had no coal but instead was a farming retail center. In response to aggressive recruiting, garment firms left the Northeast and relocated in both Coaltown and Riverton. Coaltown almost immediately had severe labor-management problems and all the garment firms left within three years. The situation was dramatically different in Riverton, where the firms and their managers became a part of the community (Ott, 1989). Thus we can see quite different societal cultures in each.

The previous discussion, although leaving many questions unanswered, makes it abundantly clear that societal culture has important linkages with organizational and managerial aspects. It also touches on some key research studies that are beginning to examine these relations in more detail.

Specific Environment

As mentioned earlier, the specific environment joins with the general environment to make up a second important portion of the external environment influencing organizations. It consists of the set of suppliers, distributors, government agencies and competitors with which a given organization must interact to grow and survive. Although the general environment is geographically bounded, the specific environment is not; the set with which it interacts and links itself is not limited geographically.

Whereas, with the exception of societal culture, general environment information was obtained from agencies such as the United States Bureau of the Census, descriptive characteristics of specific environment sets typically come from top management. These managers are asked to answer questionnaires asking for their perceptions covering the organizations that they selected as critical to their organization's growth and survival (see Hunt et al., 1981; Osborn et al., 1980).

In a manner similar to those for the general environment, these questionnaire responses are designed to tap richness/development, interdependence, and uncertainty. And again, results from each of these can be combined to provide a measure of specific environment complexity, and there is empirical support for this specific environmental conceptualization (see Hunt et al., 1981; Osborn et al., 1980). Consistent with strategic management and organization theory emphases on contingency theory fits (e.g., Gupta, 1988; see Chapter 12), we can speculate concerning matches between environmental complexity and the kinds of organizational complexity issues discussed throughout this book.

In closing this section, I would like to note again that the environmental framework above is one of several that might be used. I invite readers to check such sources as Daft (1989), Robbins (1990), and Scott (1987) for varied and useful treatment of the external environment literature.

CRITICAL TASKS

Turning now from external forces to leader critical tasks, I elaborate on the critical task elements mentioned earlier (see Figure 5.1). I also present some alternative ways of considering critical tasks as suggested from the literature.

To begin, I need to point out the importance of being sensitive to the differences between tasks and such individual leader capabilities as behaviors or skills. In the job analysis literature, this is the difference between job descriptions (job responsibilities, performance requirements, etc.) and job specifications (position occupant characteristics required for job performance); see Algera, 1987; Scarpello & Ledvinka, 1988; Spector, Brannick, & Coovert, 1989). As we shall see in Chapter 8, this differentiation between the requirements and the capabilities necessary to perform the requirements also has been of concern in attempting to integrate the managerial work and leadership literatures. At the extremes, it's easy to separate requirements and characteristics necessary to perform the requirements. However, in many leadership jobs it is not as easy as it first appears (e.g., is problem solving a requirement or critical task, or is it a behavior or skill necessary to perform some critical task at a higher level of abstraction?). For now it's enough to be sensitive to the just-mentioned points, which I return to in Chapter 8.

Before elaborating on the specific elements in the critical task cluster of the extended model, I will reiterate and expand the discussion of levels and domains that was touched on in Chapter 3 (see Jacobs & Jaques, 1987). This expanded discussion helps set the stage for the later treatment of leader critical tasks in this chapter.

Systems Leadership Domain

The systems domain encompasses essentially a CEO and executive vice president of a corporation with more than one independent operating subsidiary. The overall task of this domain is to develop new subordinate organizations and to condition the environment to be favorable toward them and current subsidiaries. This calls for extensive involvement at both national and worldwide levels. Domain consistencies (across levels VII and VI) are interaction with the external environment and creating critical resource masses for future ventures.

Level VII: Develop and field new subsidiaries and ensure they fit societies within which they are embedded. Open avenues for level VI leaders, validate their judgments that their subsidiaries are viable, and work with those subordinate leaders to deal with environmental scanning.

Level VI: Validate the profit and loss statements or equivalents of subsidiaries within the context of the external environment and organization as a whole. Formulate the development of objectives for the organization and subsidiaries to provide guidance for level V leaders.

Organizational Leadership Domain

This domain involves a bounded open system: a major organization or a subsidiary or division of such an organization, often termed a strategic business unit. It consists of level V and level IV leaders. Leadership domain consistencies are the need for managing organizational processes and the adaptability of the organization as a system to the environment, consistent with other systems in the environment. Typically, leaders in this domain are concerned with such things as product/service lines, technology, structuring of subunits, quantity and quality standards, and information and measurement systems. This domain is a buffer between external environmental turbulence and the rationalities at the lower levels. The domain is concerned with coordination of the actions of lower-level subunits (subsystems) and monitoring and maintaining the transactions between the whole system and the external environment.

> *Level V*: This is the highest level of general management, corresponding to the president of a full-scale independent organization or division/subsidiary of a larger organization. These leaders are responsible for vertical and horizontal integration of the total system and various strategies for the system. Here there is integration of product development, production and sales, and strategic investment decisions that could change the vertical integration of the organization. These leaders also are responsible for policies influencing level IV culture and climate.
>
> *Level IV*: This is the first level of general management. These leaders coordinate the vertical integration of several production units or their equivalent and deal with plans for achieving goals. They keep production or equivalent techniques current and recommend capital investments for technology. A central concern is whether the technology is appropriate for the transformational processes for which the leaders are accountable. These leaders also are responsible for policies influencing lower-level culture/climate.

Direct Leadership Domain

Here the superordinate operates a unit that is a bounded subsystem performing a service, product, marketing, or related function. This domain contains the core elements that achieve efficiency through rational processes (i.e., the pace is regulated or buffered to eliminate surges; see Thompson, 1967). The processes are direct and concrete and subordinates tend to work on tangible products/services. Defining tasks, setting goals, monitoring progress, and enhancing the pace of work flow are key requirements.

> *Level III*: These leaders are responsible for several subordinate managers. The work is relatively concrete but the leaders are responsible for anticipating variation in task loads over time. The central issue is consistency across levels (i.e., balancing subsystem improvements to meet current goals against improvements for future requirements).
>
> *Level II*: This is the first level of management. These leaders work through flexible use of rules, given a set of incomplete specific goals or means. They fill in the objectives and needs of each concrete situation. The

central issue is to balance individual employee development against immediate production/service requirements. These leaders have face-to-face contact with subordinate employees.

Level I: This is the immediate employee level responsible for performing production/service guided by rules and procedures at the touch-and-feel level. These people are influenced by task specifications, job descriptions, control measures, work rules and other means of standardization.

The discussion above is one way of looking at possible differences and similarities across the domains and levels indicated in the extended multilevel model. Indeed, it could be used as a base to develop a more detailed and operational listing of critical tasks at each level. Then one could use a measure such as Jaques's time span of discretion to measure organizational complexity. Recall that time span of discretion covers the longest of the target completion times of the critical tasks of a leader ("what by when"—when is the longest target completion time for the task in question?).

Jaques (1989) has recently argued for a two-step approach not dissimilar to what is discussed above. In his first step he uses time span of discretion. Then, in his second step, he advocates comparing critical tasks or projects against seven levels of complexity, where the complexity level for the task in question is determined by the highest level that is judged as describing it. These complexity levels are summarized below:

Level VII: Are there requirements for the development of worldwide strategies and the creation of business units (or their equivalent) by growth, acquisition, mergers, or joint ventures?

Level VI: Are there requirements for continual screening of a worldwide external environment to identify and influence developments with potential significance for the organization in question?

Level V: Are there requirements for a continual touch-and-feel sensing of how changes occurring anywhere in the task can impact other aspects of the organization, leading to decisions that consider the probable consequences for the whole system?

Level IV: Are there requirements for a number of interactive tasks to be undertaken and adjusted to other tasks?

Level III: Are there requirements for development of a plan that balances future requirements against current activity, and for the holding in reserve of contingency plans?

Level II: Are there requirements for the articulation and accumulation of data judged significant for the output, and for a diagnosis based on linking these data?

Level I: Are there requirements to follow an assigned plan to a goal, and to use trial and error to overcome obstacles as they are encountered?

In summary, Jaques suggests using time span of discretion in combination with the above descriptions to assess the complexity of leader critical tasks.

Explicating Critical Task Elements in the Extended Model

The previous discussion implied the importance of the specific elements shown in the critical task cluster in Figure 5.1, but it did not explicitly discuss them. Here, keeping in mind that previous discussion, I explicate these elements in more detail as a way of operationalizing critical tasks.

The critical task elements in the figure have a heavy strategy and organizational design emphasis. The essence of that emphasis is captured in the illustration below contrasting these aspects for the giant auto producers General Motors (GM) and Ford.

Both GM and Ford developed over the years into bloated and inflexible bureaucracies. Even with the many changes made by Henry Ford II, Ford's organization and culture still reflected Henry Ford I's top-down emphasis and suppression of ideas that didn't come from the top. Similarly, the ghost of Alfred Sloan walked the halls at GM. Although division managers were relatively autonomous, headquarters controlled operations through a detailed reporting system as well as through its power to allocate financial resources. Decision making required clearance from many committees, and basically the system was risk aversive.

In the early 1980s GM controlled nearly 50% of the U.S. auto market and was generating record profits; in contrast, Ford had a less than 16% market share and was losing money. With the increasing inroads of foreign competition Ford realized it needed a drastic change in strategy, organizational design, and culture. What it did was emphasize a broad-based cost-cutting effort, move aggressively to change the top-down culture, focus on listening to and working with those who made Ford products, and emphasize becoming a styling leader, rather than follower, among the three leading U.S. auto firms.

Accompanying the strategy, Ford cut layers of management, got its people more involved in production, and enhanced quality by focusing their attention on its importance. A major program was developed to increase participation, commitment, and creativity from managers and nonmanagers alike. The design staff began to emulate European styles. The results were that, by the late 1980s, Ford had reduced its break-even point by 40%, increased its market share to 22%, and seen its earnings surpass GM's for the first time in more than half a century.

GM, too, was concerned about the increasing competition and positioning itself for the future and also had a culture that was tradition bound and discouraged innovation. However, in contrast to Ford, it had huge cash reserves and the assumption that it could do no wrong. It estimated that fuel prices would rise, and that there would be shortages during the 1980s, so it decided to emphasize smaller cars and to spend some 50 billion dollars on capital investment. It emphasized a high-technology, high-volume strategy based on robots, lasers, and computers. It also continued to make most of its own parts (thus not reaping the benefits of competition among suppliers). Its executives continued to be arrogant, and attempts at reorganization simply resulted in similar-looking cars. The results were a 30% rise in the break-even point, a 15% drop in market share, and a comparative midsize-car assembly time of 41 labor hours compared to 25 for Ford (see Robbins, 1990).

Goal/Mission/Strategy

These examples illustrate vividly the goal/mission/strategy and related critical task elements in the model (Figure 5.1). At the risk of some oversimplification, we may think of goals/missions as ends and strategy as referring to a package of both means and ends. Thus goals are part of an organization's strategy. More formally, *strategy* is defined as the determination of the basic long-term mission, goals, and objectives of an organization and the adaptation of courses of action and the allocation of resources necessary for carrying out these goals (see Chandler, 1962). As we shall see, strategy can be planned ahead of time or may instead evolve as a pattern in a stream of important decisions (see Robbins, 1990, p. 122).

A complete discussion of strategy would involve many other areas, including various strategy frameworks. As an example, one recent framework classifies strategies along the four dimensions of innovations, market differentiation, breadth in terms of innovation and stability, and cost control (see D. Miller, 1986, 1987). This framework essentially is similar to one by Miles and Snow (1978) and by Porter (1980). Among other things, Miller shows the relationship between the strategy dimensions in his framework and the various kinds of organizational design structural characteristics covered below. There is a vast literature on strategy that covers details on many aspects, including those touched on above. In addition to previously cited works, I suggest such references as Certo and Peter (1988), Daft (1989), Glueck and Jauch (1984), and Quinn, Mintzberg, and James (1988).

Organizational Design

A second critical task element in Figure 5.1 is overall organizational design, which can be considered as the "wiring diagram" (U.S. Army War College, 1988) or "anatomy" (Osborn et al., 1980) of vertical and lateral authority and accountability relationships. In discussing organizational design, we can start with *contextual* variables. These are an organization's size and technology (Osborn et al., 1980). In an ongoing organization they are constant in the short run. However, given the time spans in the model, they are amenable to design changes. And even where they are constant, they serve as one limitation on an organization's structural aspects, which I discuss shortly.

Without going into detail, we can think of size in terms of the organization's total number of employees and be confident that this measure, simple as it is, is consistent with most other ways of considering organizational size (see Osborn et al., 1980; Robbins, 1990). In terms of its structural implications, we can think of size essentially as indicating an organization's scope of operations. As an organization hires more members it tends to specialize more; thus there will be increased horizontal differentiation involving the grouping together of similar functions. Activities within units will be facilitated, but there will need to be more coordination between units. The increased horizontal coordination requirements tend to lead to an emphasis on vertical differentiation to provide coordination.

At the same time, we also see a tendency toward spatial differentiation. All of these tendencies together lead to increased organizational complexity and make it more difficult for top management to supervise directly. Thus formal rules and regulations are introduced and, as the organization becomes still more complex, it tends to move away from centralization and toward decentralization. Although not without controversy, by and large, there is support for this scenario (see Osborn et al., 1980; Robbins, 1990).

However, size is but one aspect of the context influencing structure; another aspect is technology. Here, *technology* refers to the information, equipment, techniques, and processes required to transform inputs into outputs. In other words, the focus is on *how* this transformation is made. Basically, it is argued that as technology becomes more sophisticated and variable, the organization's structure must be designed to fit (see Daft, 1989; Osborn et al., 1980; Robbins, 1990; Scott, 1987). Based on the above, I contend that organizational context, in the form of size and technology, needs to be considered (along with the other aspects in Figure 5.1) when designing an organization's structure. Let's look now at that structural design in more detail.

We can identify key elements in organizational structure design (the wiring diagram) as formalization; standardization; horizontal and vertical specialization; and centralization/decentralization (see D. Miller & Dröge, 1986; Osborn et al., 1980). There is considerable literature on how these dimensions (and sometimes others) can be used in designing an organization's structure.

One gains a better intuitive feel for this by first thinking in terms of the general notion of mechanistic versus organic configurations and then considering a more sophisticated typology. Mechanistic configurations are characterized by high complexity, centralization, and formalization. They emphasize routine tasks and programmed behavior, and tend to be slow in dealing with unfamiliar situations. In contrast, organic structures are relatively adaptable and flexible and emphasize lateral, rather than vertical, communication. They also tend to stress expert-based influence (as opposed to that based on hierarchy), have loosely defined jobs and emphasize information exchange rather than top-down directives. These characteristics tend to lead to tall, narrow mechanistic structures and flat, wide organic structures (see Burns & Stalker, 1961).

This typology suggests ways in which one might fit together several of the previously mentioned components, but is oversimplified for large, complex organizations. Henry Mintzberg (1979) has developed recently a more sophisticated typology that maintains the intent of the mechanistic/organic classification. It combines many of the above elements and essentially consists of differing arrangements of five components: top management; middle management (at intermediate levels);

the technical core (those who do the basic work of the organization); the technical support staff (engineers, researchers, and analysts responsible for formal technical core planning and control); and administrative support staff (those who provide indirect services, including clerical, maintenance, and mailroom employees). Mintzberg assumes that these five components vary in size and importance depending on the external environment, strategy, and technology, and combines them into five different configerationa. As we shall see at several places later in this book, leaders tend to think in terms of organizational configurations, so a typology such as Mintzberg's should prove quite useful.

Mintzberg (1979) develops configurations in terms of the following:

- Simple structure: Small; new; entrepreneurial
- Machine bureaucracy: Large, tall, mass-production oriented; emphasis on efficiency and dealing with stable environment; large middle-management group; large technical care and support staffs (e.g., government agencies)
- Professional bureaucracy: Large support staff; flat hierarchy; many technically trained professionals (universities, hospitals, and R&D establishments are representative)
- Divisionalized bureaucracy: Extremely large, divided into product or market divisions; varying technologies, etc. depending on the divisions; headquarters with staff assistance umbrella for divisions (conglomerates are representative)
- Adhocracy: very complex, adaptable professionalized organizations such as project engineering firms; extensive division of labor; low formalization; little emphasis on hierarchy

Schermerhorn, Hunt, and Osborn (1988) discuss configuration in terms of a mechanistic "shell" with an organic technical core, and vice versa. Miner (1980) also has four differing organizational configurations, not unlike Mintzberg's.

Configurations of the kind just discussed can be useful in helping systems leaders tie together the various dimensions in a meaningful pattern. A part of this overall design also would include subunits in the form of divisions, functions, and the like.

Subsystems Design/Development

The subsystems indicated in Figure 5.1 are included by some (e.g., Jaques, 1989; U.S. Army Research Institute, 1989; U.S. Army War

College, 1988) as a part of the organizational and subunit design just discussed. Essentially, as their names imply, these subsystems are seen as emphasizing information, planning, control, and personnel/human resources processes or activities involved in organizational functioning. They are similar in many ways to the various kinds of "process" aspects developed in organization theory and organization design books (see Daft, 1989; Robey, 1986; or as discussed by Katz & Kahn, 1966, 1978). However, it is difficult to find empirical work reported on them in this literature. Although related to subunit design, these subsystem activities cut across various subunits. Thus one person or subunit may be involved in more than one subsystem.

Organizational and Direct Leadership Task Elements

As I've shown, the primary critical task emphasis in the systems domain is development of overall goals/mission/strategy/policy, and organization subunit and subsystems design for the system as a whole. Keeping in mind the discussion earlier in this chapter, as well as in Chapters 2 and 3, we can now move to the organizational and direct leadership domain critical task elements shown in Figure 5.1. These are consistent with the very general origination, interpolation, and administration notion of Katz and Kahn (1966, 1978). The primary emphasis in the organizational leadership domain is the integration of the various elements at this level with those in the systems domain and the operation, interpretation, and translation of subsystems for lower levels.

The well-known means-ends assumptions of organization and management theorists help bring this about. Here I argue essentially that at each succeeding lower level, its means of carrying out higher-level missions, strategies, organizational designs, and so forth also become its ends. Thus strategies, policies, and the like that serve as ends at lower levels become means for carrying out higher-level ends. In the process, they get more and more specific in moving down the organization until they take the form of specific operating procedures and practices with an emphasis on maintenance skills, equipment, and so forth. Put another way, there is a cascading of ends and means as we move down the organization.

Thus, going back to Ford, we can see changes in the systems-level strategic package (goals, policies, etc.) and organizational design with separate strategic packages and organization design changes as necessary for each of the divisions and subsidiaries. These lower-level elements then become both the ends at these levels and the means for accomplishing the system-level changes.

It's also meaningful to remember, once again, the importance of leadership teams within and across domains in carrying out these critical tasks. Staff teams are frequently used in addition to what I call top-level leadership collegiums, or their equivalent, at various places throughout this book.

In summary, the critical task elements summarized in Figure 5.1 are suggestive of the differences in the kinds of critical task requirements at each of the levels within each of the domains. They can provide a base for a more detailed listing of critical tasks by level, and a prediction of differences in time span of discretion along the lines specified in the extended model.

SOME ADDITIONAL CRITICAL TASK PERSPECTIVES

Another approach to dealing with the critical task complexity aspect of the extended model would be to use a variation of Stewart's demands, constraints, and choices framework (e.g., Stewart, 1982a, 1982b). This framework essentially describes managerial jobs, tasks, or work in terms of an inner core of demands, an outer boundary of constraints, and in-between area of choices.

Demands are what anyone in the job must do, that is, cannot avoid doing without invoking sanctions that would threaten continuing in the job. Some example determinants are output specifications, need for personal involvement in the organization/subunit's work, bureaucratic procedures that cannot be delegated, and relationships (contacts, expectations, and so forth).

Constraints are external and internal organizational factors that limit what the leader in question can do. Some examples are resource limitations; legal, union, and systems constraints; technological limitations; degree of output acceptance; and the extent to which the scope of the leader's organization/subunit is defined.

Choices are the opportunities that exist for those in similar jobs to do different work and to do it in different ways from other leaders. Some choices generally available include focus of attention between different job responsibilities, time spent of various kinds of contacts, and aspects of supervision emphasized. Some choices commonly available include amount and nature of delegation, and whom the leader seeks to influence. Choices sometimes available include defining the domain, sharing the task with one or more others, and the role played in leadership teams or collegiums. Technically speaking, some of the elements just mentioned include not just tasks but various kinds of broadly defined activities (this is less the case for demands than for constraints or choices). Even so, they still can be differentiated from the components involved in the individual capability cluster of Figure 5.1. Indeed, Stewart (1982b) touches on the role of traditional leader behaviors in her demands, constraints, and choices model.

For our purposes, it appears that we could first assess the demands, constraints, and choices for leaders throughout the organization. Then, taking these into account, we should be able to use a time span of discretion measure to assess the overall task complexity, based on these demands, constraints, and choices, in much the same way as in the previous section. It also might be possible to develop an index based on such things as the number and homogeneity/heterogeneity of these elements. Still more perspective might be gained by combining the previously mentioned critical task perspective emphasizing strategies, organizational design, and so forth with some variation of Stewart's demands, constraints, and choices.

Scope and Scale

A third proposed approach is to use Bentz's (1987) scope and scale notions. Scope/scale is a multidimensional construct based on the interaction between organizational and leader individual characteristics as modified by socioeconomic conditions affecting an organization. It results primarily from organizational conditions, but is modified by leader, social, and economic factors inherent in these organizational conditions (Bentz, 1987).

Scope has horizontal implications and refers to the breadth of management (e.g., the number of functions embraced within a position). Scope reflects internal complexity and diversity of content, mission, or function within and across units led, within and across decisions made, and within and across varieties of personal relationships. As an example, scope might indicate the number of decisions made and the number of units and people influenced. In contrast, *scale* would accommodate issues internal to the decision process (ambiguity, complexity, and the like) as well as the quality of impact such decisions make in influencing the organization and the working lives of those within the organization. Figure 5.2 summarizes this description visually.

Bentz (1987) argues that scope and scale are both multidimensional but coexist and interact with the impact of a single construct. He shows one possibility for measuring the scope/scale construct to provide the hierarchical complexity levels shown in Figure 5.2 that are akin to the seven levels of Jaques.

At each level of the Bentz hierarchy of positions, degrees of uncertainty created by the job function are seen as varying—the higher the level, the greater the uncertainty. Responsibility within each level also is expected to vary, along the dimensions of size and complexity, along with diversity of functions (see Figure 5.2). Bentz contends that his preliminary work can be extended to devise measures appropriate to each dimension portrayed and to create a computer-based mathematical model of scope/scale useful for future research.

He doesn't specify exactly how the previous elements would be combined to determine various hierarchical levels. However, presumably this could be done using various job analysis or related techniques (see Spector et al., 1989). It also might be possible again to use time span of discretion to measure the complexity of the critical tasks arranged according to the scope/scale rationale. For instance, as the elements used in defining scope/scale increases in various jobs, the time span of discretion might well be expected to increase.

CRITICAL TASK IMPLICATIONS OF
THE ORGANIZATIONAL LIFE CYCLE

The previous discussion has emphasized leader critical tasks without considering changes in the content of these tasks over time. Let's expand our thinking by examining the organizational life cycle as shown in Figure 5.3. Baliga and Hunt (1988) and Hunt, Baliga, and Peterson (1988) propose such a cycle based on the work of Kimberly and Quinn (1984), Quinn and Cameron (1983), Quinn and Rohrbaugh (1983), and Tichy (1983), among others.

The figure shows growth, maturity, and revitalization/death stages as a function of an organization's development over time in response to external and internal forces. And, although not explicitly indicated,

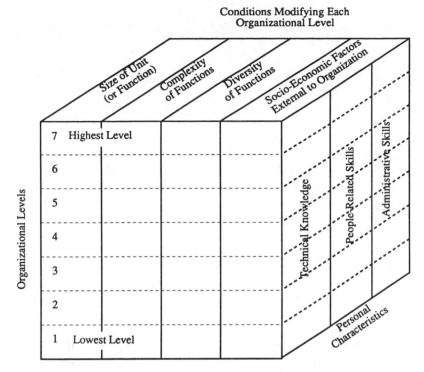

Figure 5.2. Components Involved in Bentz's Scope and Scale Construct
Source: Bentz (1987). Reprinted with permission. All rights reserved.

each stage is considered part of a phase that also includes a transition from one stage to the next (e.g., phase III consists of the maturity stage and the growth-to-maturity transition). Each transition and stage is seen as calling for:

• differing demands, constraints and choices in Stewart's (1982a, 1982b) terms;
• different kinds of leadership emphases, at various organizational levels, both vertically and horizontally;
• differing specific criteria or measures of organizational effectiveness; and
• changes in goal/mission/strategy, and organization/subunit and subsystems design, to fit the appropriate phase.

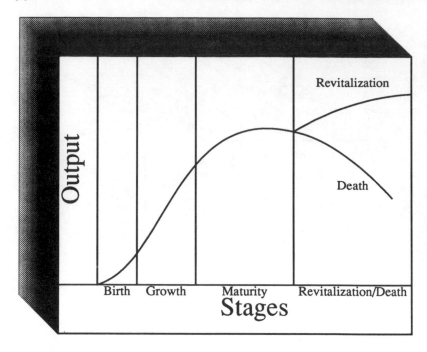

Figure 5.3. Organizational Life Cycle
Adapted from Baliga & Hunt (1988), p. 131. Used with permission.

In terms of the last point above, authors such as Greiner (1972) have proposed a linkage between the kinds of stages just mentioned and organizational design responses.

Essentially, I am making the argument that the temporal aspects emphasized in the extended multilevel model do not simply call for statically carrying out the critical tasks. Rather, leaders must recognize the importance of where the organization currently is and is expected to be in terms of the phases of its life cycle. Unfortunately, there are no definitive studies that provide an indication of the average span of the various transitions and stages of these life cycles. The above points must be taken into account when considering the critical tasks and the time spans of the various domains and levels. Particularly interesting is the revitalization/death stage. This stage makes explicit the point that there must be dramatic change in the content of the critical tasks as compared to the earlier maturity stage.

Carried out one way, the tasks can lead to revitalization; carried out another, they can lead to the demise of the organization. Western Union is an example of an organization that attempted substantial changes in response to deregulation of the telecommunications industry. Although attempts were designed to revitalize the hundred-plus-year-old organization, environmental events have overtaken it and Western Union appears instead to be in the death stage (see "Sad Saga," 1987). I might note in closing this section that Baliga and Hunt (1988) and Hunt, Baliga, and Peterson (1988) cover various life cycle and leadership aspects in more detail, and I refer to these as they apply later in the book.

EFFECTIVENESS

Figure 5.1 shows effectiveness as an "output" cluster in the extended model. Even so, we can properly consider it as an additional aspect of leader critical tasks. Mission/strategy development and organization/subsystems design, interpretation, and operation are closely related to development and operation of accompanying effectiveness criteria.

Current Treatments of Effectiveness

Current treatments of effectiveness look at it from four perspectives: goal attainment, strategic systems, strategic constituencies, and competing values. Table 5.1 summarizes the first three of these perspectives, and I consider below the more complex competing-values approach. The table outlines key aspects of each of these perspectives, including a short description, example criteria, assumptions, problems, and contributions. It also indicates that although the discussion is oriented toward the organization as a whole, many of the arguments also would hold at lower levels in the organization. For example, the use of traits or behavioral activities in lieu of end results at the individual employee level is consistent with the systems approach as discussed in the table.

Table 5.1 shows clearly the complexities and trade-offs involved when one looks at the various effectiveness perspectives. The competing-values perspective is a recent one developed to recognize these kinds of issues. It assumes that there is no best criterion, that it is

Table 5.1
Summary of Three Effectiveness Perspectives

Perspective	What it is and some example criteria	Assumptions	Problems	Contributions
Goal Attainment	Effectiveness measured by ends rather than means. Profit maximization, number of games won.	Organizations rational and goal-seeking. Must be ultimate goals generally agreed upon and defined so as to be understood. Must be few enough goals to be manageable and they must be measurable.	Who determines goals? Reconciliation of officially stated goals and goals actually pursued. Reconciliation of short and long-term goals and of multiple conflicting goals. Goals may be stated retrospectively in terms of actions previously completed.	Organizations exist to achieve goals. If deal well with problems, their ends can be useful effectiveness criteria and have an obvious connection with goal/mission/strategy package.
Systems	Based on ability to acquire resources, maintain itself internally as a social system and interact successfully with external environment. Emphasis on systems-oriented criteria believed to increase organization's long-term survival potential. Outputs/Inputs (Return on Investment); Transformations/Inputs (Inventory Turnover); Transformations/Outputs (Sales Volume); and changes in Inputs/Inputs (changes in Working Capital).	Organizations composed of interrelated subparts, where poor performance of one affects others. Must interact with environmental constituents. Must provide steady replenishment of resources consumed.	Measuring process variables may be more difficult than end result variables (e.g., goals) and constantly open to question. Emphasis on means to achieve effectiveness not as useful as effectiveness itself.	Tends to encourage long-run results and awareness of interdependency of activities. Useful where end result goals vague or defy measurement.

Strategic Constituencies	Satisfies demands of strategic constituencies from whom support is required for continuing existence (those who can threaten an organization's survival). Determine critical constituencies, compare various expectations and determine common and incompatible ones, assign weights to constituencies and develop a preference weighting for the various goals. Consider owners (Return on Investment); employees (Compensation); customers (Quality, Service); government (Compliance with Laws); etc.	Organizations composed of political arenas where vested interests compete for resources control. Are several strategic constituencies, differing in power with differing expectations. Goals selected by organization are in response to constituent expectations.	Difficult to identify strategic constituencies in dynamic environment and to separate from "less strategic" ones. Hard to identify accurately strategic constituency expectations.	Enhance survival by identifying strategic constituencies whose expectations are critical.

Note: Although these focus on the "organization," in many cases, similar arguments appropriate for subunits apply at lower-level units of analysis.
Source: Summarized from material in Evan (1976); Osborn, Hunt, & Jauch, (1980); Perrow (1961); Pfeffer & Salancik (1978); Robbins (1990); and Weick (1969).

STRUCTURE

Flexibility

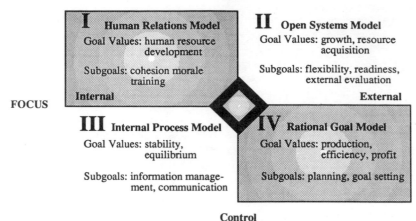

FOCUS

Control

Figure 5.4. Competing Values Effectiveness Criteria Based on Focus and Structure

Source: Adapted from Quinn & Rohrbaugh (1983) and Quinn & Cameron (1983), *Management Science.* Used with permission.

difficult to get agreement on goal priority, and that the goals chosen are a function of the person's individual values, preferences, and interests. Besides its contribution to dealing with effectiveness, this perspective is of special interest because it serves also as the basis for Quinn's (1988) competing-values approach to leadership, various aspects of which are examined in later chapters.

Figure 5.4 (for details see Daft, 1989; Quinn & Cameron, 1983; Quinn & Rohrbaugh, 1983; Robbins, 1990) summarizes essential aspects of the competing-values approach. The first aspect concerns *focus*: whether the primary emphasis is internal (employee well-being and efficiency) or external (organizational well-being with respect to the environment). The second major dimension is *structure*: whether stability (preference for top-down control) or flexibility (preference for structural adaptability and change) is the primary emphasis. The figure shows four kinds of organizational effectiveness criteria based on focus and structure:

- Human relations model (internal focus and flexible structure)—Development of human resources is the key, with an emphasis on such things as cohesion, morale, and training.
- Open-systems model (external focus and flexible structure)—The key is growth and resource acquisition, accompanied by the indicated subgoals relating to flexibility, readiness, and external evaluation.
- Internal process model (internal focus and structural control)—A primary outcome is a stable organizational setting that maintains itself in an orderly manner. Efficient information management and communication are stressed.
- Rational goal model (external focus and structural control)—Primary goals are productivity, efficiency, and profit, with subgoals emphasizing internal planning and goal setting.

This approach recognizes that there are contradictory models that must be considered when setting effectiveness priorities. Systems domain leaders must decide the relative emphasis on each of these, together with their goals and subgoals. Although there can be some overlap across the cells, some values *must* receive higher priority than others. The systems domain leaders could use their own preferences; however, they also could take into account the preferences of their strategic constituencies (these would include those constituencies identified earlier as defining the organization's specific environment). Of course this is easier said than done, but it is feasible and allows for differing effectiveness assessments as a function of key constituencies. The approach also allows for differing effectiveness criteria to be emphasized across the organizational life cycle as the strategic contingencies change (see Cameron & Whetten, 1981; Quinn & Cameron, 1983).

The competing-values approach includes both ends and means and thus combines aspects of the goal attainment, systems, and strategic constituencies approaches summarized in Table 5.1. Although it helps overcome some of the problems of the other approaches, it too is not without problems. For example, even though it includes strategic constituencies, it still leaves the kinds of problems with that approach that Table 5.1 summarizes. The approach also is better at evaluating constituency perceptions of how well an organization is doing on the eight criteria than at clarifying which criteria the constituencies are stressing (see Robbins, 1990). Rohrbaugh (1981) reports one example of operationalizing competing-values criteria.

Let's conclude by emphasizing a number of concerns implied or explicit in discussion of the previous perspectives. First, the perspectives involve multiple criteria (see, e.g., Korhonen, Santalainen, & Tainio, 1987). In some manner these criteria should cover aspects of human resource maintenance (the attraction and maintenance of a viable work force; see Osborn et al., 1980) in addition to whatever other criteria are used. This involves measures such as satisfaction, commitment, involvement, morale, turnover, and so forth and was explicitly recognized in the competing-values approach.

Second, the specific criteria may need to be different for domains and perhaps for levels (see Jacobs & Jaques, 1987). Even if different, they must be consistent with those at higher and lower domains/levels.

Third, the criteria should reflect adequately the focus on time emphasized in the other aspects of the model at the organizational level in question. In other words, if a key requirement is to deal with temporal aspects many years into the future, then the effectiveness measure should reflect this emphasis. Again, the competing-values approach seems to be sensitive to this, as was illustrated with the description of changes across organizational life cycles.

Finally, as with other aspects of the model and as mentioned above, the effectiveness levels of analysis should be conceptually and empirically consistent with each other and with the questions of interest. This question of level of analysis is so important that I consider it in the context of the entire model in Chapter 12. In terms of effectiveness, the argument is that micro level individual and group performance measures lower in the organization need to be consistent, at a unit of analysis level, with higher-order macro organizational effectiveness measures. For insights concerning macro and micro aspects of effectiveness see Lewin and Huber (1986), Cameron and Whetten (1983), and Campbell and Campbell (1988).

SELECTED RESEARCH AND CONCEPTUAL LINKAGES WITH THE EXTENDED MODEL

This is the first of the linkage discussions mentioned in Chapter 3 as a part of the treatment of the extended model's components. Let's start the section with external environment and societal culture aspects. We know from the extensive literature and the earlier discussion in this chapter that these components of the extended model are expected to be linked to various critical task aspects. We expect linkages with goal/mission development, strategy, and organizational/subsystem design. These linkages are expected to make their presence felt through aspects of the general environment. Such aspects as educational and socioeconomic levels, among others, would be expected to influence the nature of organizational employees.

Mission/strategy and organizational design elements also should reflect these environmental forces to a greater or lesser extent (e.g., there is some evidence that unions can influence organizational designs; that a labor force with a generally low educational level may encourage a more centralized structure and influence subsystem design). We particularly should expect societal culture to make itself felt through generally accepted national and community values (e.g., safety enforcement through OSHA, or a culture or subculture emphasizing egalitarianism). Similarly, those critical constituencies identified as a part of the specific environment might well be expected to have a bearing on mission/strategy aspects as well as organizational design.

Second, we should expect both direct and indirect vertical linkages as we consider integrating, interpolating, and translating these higher-level tasks and emphasizing lower-level standard operating procedures. These linkages can be expected to come about through the design and strategy parameters established in the systems and organizational leadership domains. As an example, a recent study links aspects of organizational design with personnel/human resources policies and procedures (Jackson, Schuler, & Rivero, 1989).

Third, if we take the temporal and organizational life cycle notions seriously, we could expect changes in the nature of various aspects of both the environment/culture and critical task clusters of the model and accompanying changes in relationships among these aspects. For example, the emphasis on various subunit/subsystem elements might be expected to differ in one life cycle stage compared with another.

Fourth, there is some evidence (e.g., Gupta, 1988; Osborn & Hunt, 1974b) suggesting that various facets of effectiveness are likely to be influenced by how well critical task aspects "fit" environmental/cultural components. Thus strategic contingencies are likely to be important (see Gupta, 1988).

Finally, although much more can be said about this in later chapters, after I have discussed each of the model's components in some detail, we still can identify some additional expected linkages. We would expect linkages between environment/culture and such aspects as individual value preferences and perhaps an emphasis on certain kinds of leadership skills (e.g., cultural forces might stress a more participative set of skills). Similarly, cognitive complexity and cognitive style as well as predisposition capability components might influence the specific environment in terms of what I describe later in the book as "enactment" (see Smircich & Stubbart, 1985; Weick, 1979). There a leader tends to enact parts of his or her own environment, depending on both perceptions and actualities. We also would expect linkages of both environmental and societal culture forces with organizational culture and vertical subcultures. Figure 5.1 summarizes these and the earlier mentioned linkages.

CONCLUDING COMMENTARY

This chapter began the detailed discussion of each of the extended model's components by considering the external environment and societal culture, along with leader critical tasks. There are many conceptions of critical tasks, and indeed a whole related literature has grown up covering managerial work, managerial jobs, and the like (see Stewart, 1982b). For our purposes, it's important to separate leader critical tasks, in the various domains and levels, from various leader individual capability aspects (especially leader behavior/skills). At the very least, we need to be sensitive to the differences between classes of tasks and capabilities in conceptualizing and testing the extended multiple-level model.

Given this sensitivity, there are still many possible conceptions of critical tasks. I have discussed some of these and have chosen to give special emphasis to a broad one that is consistent with the strategy and organizational literature and with works such as Jacobs and Jaques (1987) and Jaques (1989), while allowing for a great deal of flexibility in conceptualization and application. Thus I have conceptualized the critical tasks in terms of (a) an emphasis on strategy and organizational design; (b) the differences in the way these and their derivatives are developed and used vertically and horizontally in the organization; and (c) the extent to which the critical tasks lend themselves to measurement, with a primary emphasis on Jaques' time span of discretion notion.

While keeping these general ideas in mind in discussing various approaches, I have considered possible alternatives such as Bentz's (1987) scope and scale notion. Throughout, I've also recognized the key notions of those such as Simon (1977) and especially Katz and Kahn (1966, 1978) who conceive of ideas such as origination, interpolation, and use of existing structures to conceptualize hierarchical task differences.

At the same time, I've indicated that the critical task aspects discussed here, though based on the above points, were of necessity fairly general in their level of specification. In this, they correspond to the state of development of the literature. Even so, the tasks as conceived and specified here provide a useful starting point for detailed examination of the extended model. Having said this, I still would like to encourage the use of alternative conceptions and measures. I mentioned some here, but others are certainly needed.

Also, I have emphasized a couple of additional points. First is the importance of considering the critical tasks from an organizational life cycle perspective. Second is the importance of the conceptualization and use of various organizational and subunit effectiveness measures and their linkage with such things as the organizational life cycle.

In closing this chapter, I should note that its treatment of leadership is broader than most, encompassing as it does goal/mission, strategy, organizational design, and related aspects. Here it spills over into the way that many strategic management people think of leadership. However, it goes even further than most strategic management studies by tracing these components all the way down the organization using a systematic framework. Some would call this management rather than leadership, but given the extended multilevel model and broad treatment of leadership these fit naturally as leader critical tasks. And, as I have argued, they are considered both to influence and to be influenced by many aspects of the organization.

Not the least of these organizational aspects is the background and preference components of the individual capability cluster. It is to these components that I turn in Chapter 6.

THE FAR SIDE

By GARY LARSON

**And another thing . . . I want you to be more
assertive! I'm tired of everyone calling you
Alexander the Pretty-Good!**

6 Background Factors and Preference Aspects of Individual Capability

- **Individual Background Factors**
  Family and Childhood Experiences
  Educational Experiences
  Previous and Current Career Experience
  Age and Cohort History
- **Leader Predispositions/Preferences**
  Predisposition to be Influential and Self-Efficacy
  Value Preferences
  Cognitive Style Aspects
- **Selected Research and Conceptual Linkages with the Extended Model**
- **Concluding Commentary**

Skill is nil without will.
—Judah ibn Tibbon, Spanish translator
(quoted in Eigen & Siegel, 1989, p. 278)

Few Huns will sustain themselves as chieftains without strong personal desire—an inherent commitment to influencing people, processes and outcomes. Weak is the chief who does not want to be one.
—Wess Roberts (1987, p. 18),
Leadership Secrets of Attila the Hun

Proper training and experience develops in chieftains a personal feeling of assurance with which to meet the inherent challenges of leadership. Those who portray a lack of self-confidence in the abilities to carry out leadership assignments give signs [to others] that their duties are beyond their capabilities.
—Roberts (1987, p. 20)

Those who judge by their feelings do not understand reasoning, for they wish to get an insight into a matter at a glance, and are not accustomed to look for principles. Contrarily, others, who are accustomed to argue from principles, do not understand the things of the heart . . . and not being able to see at a glance.

—Blaise Pascal, French scientist and philosopher
(quoted in Eigen & Siegel, 1989, p. 111)

In this chapter, I do two general things. First, I examine the important individual background variables within the context of the extended model. Then I consider the leader predisposition and preference aspects of the leader individual capability cluster. That sets the stage for treatment of the other capability aspects in the remaining chapters in this part.

INDIVIDUAL BACKGROUND FACTORS

Let's start the discussion of individual background factors by looking at their role in the extended model as shown in Figure 6.1. Essentially, the argument is that while background factors can be expected to have the kinds of relationships shown in the figure, they will be particularly important in their impact on the individual capability cluster with its preferences and values, cognitive complexity, and leadership skills components. I argue that a key way through which these relations occur is by means of the kinds of long- and short-term leader developmental aspects discussed in Chapter 11.

My intent in the model is to use these background aspects, whenever possible, in conjunction with other variables. In contrast, they previously have been used by themselves in the organizational and strategic management literature to predict various organizational and strategic aspects (see Gupta, 1988). Gupta argues that, by themselves, they tend to predict various organizational actions and criteria less well than leader personality variables, which in turn are expected to predict less well than leader behaviors. This is because leader behaviors are "closer" to the actions and criteria. At the same time, background

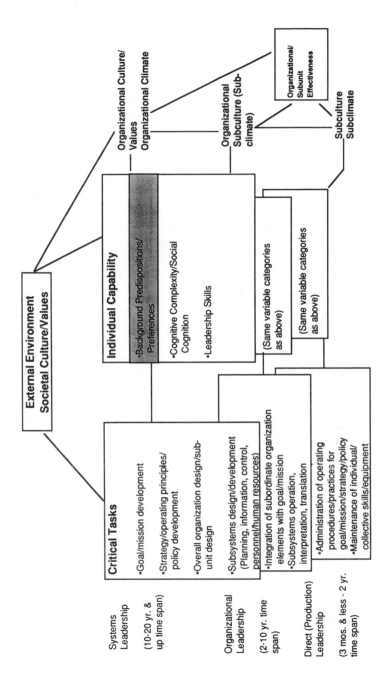

Figure 6.1. Extended Multiple-Organizational-Level Leadership Model
Note: For simplicity, some direct relationships, feedback, and arrowheads are not shown.

variables typically are easier to obtain than either of the other two kinds of leader variables. So there is a trade-off between predictability and ease of data collection. Of course, keeping the arguments in Chapter 4 in mind, the purpose of the data collection also makes a difference (e.g., top leaders interested in understanding how their behavior influences outcomes, versus security analysts desiring to predict future actions of many firms).

Finally, we need to recognize that sometimes background variables essentially are treated as proxies for more fundamental underlying variables (e.g., early leadership experiences for current leadership skills). Used in this way, the earlier genotypic/phenotypic differentiation becomes relevant because background variables are treated as phenotypic reflections of a genotypic variable.

Keeping these points in mind, let's now examine some specific kinds of background variables to be considered in the extended model. I list these below and then elaborate briefly on them.

Family and Childhood Experiences

Here we are interested in such aspects as parents' upward mobility, whether both original parents were at home while the leader was growing up, amount of education of parents, closeness of relationship with parents, father's occupation, and presence or absence of siblings (Kotter, 1982a). We also can consider such aspects as social class, race, and religious upbringing (Hambrick & Brandon, 1988). Based on findings reported in work such as that just mentioned, these kinds of variables are expected to influence especially the extended model's individual capability variables.

Educational Experiences

These include the kinds of schools attended (e.g., public versus private), general quality and nature of schools, whether the leader graduated or not, level of education, student leadership positions held, college major, and so forth (see Gupta, 1988; Jackofsky & Slocum, 1988; Kotter, 1982a). Again, these are expected to have their strongest linkage with various leader capability components.

Previous and Current Career Experience

Included here are such aspects as previous military service (if any) and branch, previous part-time and full-time jobs held while growing up, fit of jobs with interest and values, breadth and length of industry experience, breadth and length of firm functional experience, and rapidity of promotions (see Hambrick & Brandon, 1988; Hambrick & Mason, 1984; Kotter, 1982). These are expected to have a strong influence on occupational and professional socialization and, as were the earlier mentioned background variables, to be noticeably related to the individual capabilities cluster.

Age and Cohort History

Hambrick and Mason (1984) discuss research suggesting that age is especially likely to be related to organizational growth, volatility, risk-taking propensity, and other attributes. Typically, it also covaries with years of experience. Cohort history is indirectly indicated by age, but we need to be explicitly aware of it. Cohort history is concerned with the occurrence of major social events that have tended to shape a body of individuals in society. The "baby boomers" or 1960s antiestablishment cohorts are examples (see Hambrick & Brandon, 1988; Hunt, Boal, & Sorenson, 1990). Individual values, especially, are likely to reflect cohort history.

Summary

There is a wealth of literature arguing for the importance of background variables in organizational settings. I have touched on the major categories that can be used to classify these variables. In contrast to the wealth of empirical data linking background variables to important aspects of leadership, there is a dearth of theoretical rationale. One exception to this is their treatment in evolving theories of development to help explain why some leaders have developed differently than others, and this is discussed in Chapter 11. Although additional conceptual work is clearly needed to explain why specific background factors are important in specific situations , the fact that they frequently have been shown to be important is *not* at issue. Thus they are included explicitly in the extended model. Indeed, one place where they are expected to have an influence is on leader predispositions and preferences, to which I now turn.

LEADER PREDISPOSITIONS/PREFERENCES

Besides the abilities or skills represented by cognitive complexity and leader behavior skills, it's important that leaders have a predisposition to want to be leaders. In other words, one could have an extremely cognitively complex individual with many naturally occurring leadership skills, but that individual could only be a successful leader if he or she had the predisposition to be one. Indeed, this is simply a variation of the classic "performance is a function of motivation times ability" argument. More specifically, following the arguments of House (1988a, 1988b), Sashkin (1990), and McClelland (1985), among others, one key aspect of this predisposition is the need for socially oriented power.

However this is not enough. It needs to be accompanied by a feeling of competency or what sometimes is termed "self-efficacy" (see Wood & Bandura, 1989). The successful leader must both *want* to exert socially oriented power and *feel* competent in exerting this power and assuming a leadership role. Or, borrowing from the earlier quote and reinforced by Mintzberg (1983), the individual must both have the "will" and feel confident about the "skill." Finally, there must be an opportunity to lead (i.e., the person must be either in a formal leadership role or have the chance to become an emergent leader).

In addition to the predispositions just mentioned, a leader possesses a cognitive or intellectual predisposition or preference in terms of processing information. Thus two leaders may each be very intelligent or be very high on cognitive complexity and yet have different preferences for processing information as a part of this complexity. Finally, in addition to the preferences just discussed, leaders will possess a number of other preferences in the form of values. Thus if, say, collectivism were a value, the leader would tend to have a preference for valuing the wholeness of society and social systems and emphasize respect for all people (Hambrick & Brandon, 1988).

As we shall see, these predispositions or preferences can be tapped by a number of measures, commonly referred to as *traits*. After being widely used in early leadership studies, traits largely fell out of favor in the leadership field after a literature review by Stogdill (1948). Since that time they have been making a comeback, but in a more sophisticated form than in that earlier literature. House (1988a, 1988b; House & Baetz, 1979) essentially has argued that they can be grouped into three categories: (a) predisposition to be influential (covered in our approach here); (b) social aspects (e.g., cooperativeness); and (c) specific task objectives or organizational goals (e.g., initiative, emphasis on goal achievement). In terms of my previous arguments about linkage with other aspects of the extended model, I emphasize House's first category (along with self-efficacy) while making the point that an approach systematically developing all three categories appears potentially useful. The strategic management literature has been less reticent than the leadership literature in emphasizing traits (e.g., Gupta, 1988; Hambrick & Brandon, 1988; Hambrick & Mason, 1984).

Predisposition to Be Influential and Self-Efficacy

We can think of the predisposition to be influential in terms of dominance, and the need for socially directed power. The first of these can be measured by the Dominance scale of the California Personality Inventory (Gough, 1969). McClelland's (1985) power motive is a second individual characteristic indicative of power striving and acquisition. It is socially learned and typically is measured by a person's response to unstructured, ambiguous stimuli, such as writing an imaginative story about a picture. McClelland—as well as Howell (1988), Sashkin (1988), and others—argues that such power needs to be socially directed to empowering others, rather than selfishly directed, if it is to have a positive (rather than negative) impact. Hence the model's socially directed power factor. Again, House (1988b) cites many studies supporting the importance of this characteristic. And as I show in Chapter 10, emphasizing transformationally oriented leadership, this power preference is especially important in several charismatic approaches.

In addition to the predisposition to use power, I've argued for the importance of a leader's feeling of self-confidence, competency, or self-efficacy. Essentially, among other things, these provide a person with the feeling that he or she can be a leader and exert influence (although technically these are not preferences, I treat them as similar). Support for the use of these characteristics comes from House (1988b) and Sashkin (1988), among others, and is consistent with recent work by Wood and Bandura (1989) and the earlier work of White

(1959). Both socially directed power and self-efficacy are given special importance in the charismatic leadership literature, as is shown in Chapter 9.

Value Preferences

Besides the predisposition to lead and a feeling of efficacy concerning leading, values form another important part of the preference network of leaders. There is extensive literature both on values in general and on more specific values concerned with work and organizations (see Becker & Connor, 1986; Hambrick & Brandon, 1988). Like other areas in the behavioral sciences, the literature is quite diverse and not well integrated. It shows quite clearly, however, the importance and pervasiveness of values.

For our purposes, I'll use this literature selectively and emphasize primarily the role of individual value preferences on the part of leaders in our extended model. I should emphasize the term *individual* in the previous sentence for, consistent with the other aspects treated in this chapter, I am dealing with values as individual difference variables (as opposed to their treatment as part of societal and organizational cultures elsewhere in the book). Here they vary as a function of the individual, whereas elsewhere they vary as a function of societal and/or organizational cultures.

Following most of the literature, I treat values as preferences for courses of actions and outcomes (see Jacob, Flink, & Shuchman, 1962). And I differentiate them from ideologies or what are sometimes termed "beliefs" (see Beyer, 1981; Sproull, 1981), where ideologies refer to people's belief about the causal relations between courses of action and outcomes (Beyer, 1981). Values and ideologies are conceptually separate, even though they are hard to separate in practice and are not always separated in research (Beyer, 1981). I treat ideologies within the context of the discussion of cognitive or causal maps in Chapter 7. I also should note that though values are similar to attitudes, consistent with the literature I treat them as broader and relatively enduring. In contrast, attitudes are relatively transitory and focus on a specific object or situation (e.g., attitude toward a given job). Thus values shape attitudes (see Becker & Conner, 1986).

To make the long and complicated values literature short, we can deal with it in terms of four well-known value frameworks (see Hambrick & Brandon, 1988). These are: (a) Allport-Vernon-Lindzey; (b) Rokeach;

(c) England; and (d) Hofstede. In addition, I touch on a more recent framework (Meglino, Ravlin, & Adkin, 1990).

The Allport-Vernon-Lindzey (1970) "Study of Values" focuses on six value dimensions: theoretical, economic, aesthetic, social, political, and religious. Allport and associates measured the relative strength of these six dimensions using a forced choice instrument. The values are rather lofty in nature, and there has been limited usage in organizational settings.

The Rokeach (1973) framework divides values into 18 that are terminal (end-states; e.g., a sense of accomplishment) and 18 that are instrumental (modes of conduct; e.g., ambitious, logical). Again, application to managerial groups has been quite limited, although there has been some recent work using factor analysis to reduce the number of items (see Howard, Shudo, & Umeshima, 1983).

England's framework (e.g., England, 1967; England & Lee, 1974; England, Negandhi, & Wilpert, 1979; Whitely & England, 1980), is by far the most complex and was especially developed for managers. His "Personal Values Questionnaire" has 16 items each in five categories, from personal goals of individuals to ideas about general topics. England has focused especially on values of leaders across different countries. However, the instrument's complexity makes it relatively difficult to use and interpret.

Hofstede's (1980, 1983) framework was developed primarily for cross-national values comparisons and is discussed in more detail in the chapter dealing with societal culture. Essentially, he derived five dimensions that he used to classify societal culture differences across some 40 countries.

The frameworks just discussed are among the best-known in the values literature, are quite different from each other, and are seldom discussed in terms of the strengths and weaknesses of one framework relative to others. Hambrick and Brandon (1988, p. 14) did a conceptual analysis of these various frameworks and, based on overlaps and predicted relevance for organizations, derived five dimensions that they set forth as candidates for future values research with managers and leaders:

- Collectivism—to value the wholeness of humankind and of social systems; regard and respect for all people
- Duty—to value the integrity of reciprocal relationships; obligation and loyalty

- Rationality—to value fact-based, emotion-free decisions and actions
- Novelty—to value change, the new, the different
- Power—to value control of situations and people

The last dimension, of course, is similar to the power aspects discussed previously. Although these dimensions provide a conceptual base for leader values, for empirical use one would need to develop ways to measure them. The kind of empirical work needed is suggested in the discussion below, which deals with a different set of value preferences.

The Meglino et al. Framework

Whereas the Hambrick and Brandon (1988) framework currently does not have empirically developed measures of its dimensions, there is a recently developed values framework that does. That framework was specifically developed for organizational use by Meglino and his associates (e.g., Meglino, Ravlin & Adkin, 1989, 1990; Ravlin & Meglino, 1987). This values framework is based on four dimensions originally developed through the use of Flanagan's (1954) critical-incident approach:

- Achievement—getting things done and working hard to accomplish difficult goals in life
- Helping and concern for others—being concerned for other people and helping others
- Honesty—telling the truth and doing what one feels is right
- Fairness—being impartial and doing what is fair for all concerned

The format for this instrument uses an ipsative rank ordering approach that assumes a hierarchically organized value system, as opposed to an approach using Likert-type scales where each value is rated separately from the others. There is considerable justification for such ipsative treatment from the literature and from the work of Meglino and his associates. However, it does require different kinds of statistical analyses and assumptions than if the concepts were not treated ipsatively.

As pointed out earlier, values have been considered important in organizational research but, with the exception of England's work, have typically not been developed specifically for organizational use. The research just cited is an attempt to deal with this concern and is much simpler than England's work. Similar empirical work might be done with the suggested dimensions of Hambrick and Brandon (1988) to operationalize them. Together, the two sets of dimensions offer much potential for tapping organizationally relevant values.

Relations of Values to Other Variables

I've argued that value preferences are an important individual capability variable. Let's take a quick look at the values literature to see some ways in which they operate.

First, is an assumed direct effect—for example, a leader makes a particular decision based on his or her preferences. England (1967) uses the term "behavior channeling" to describe this direct effect of values on action (see Ravlin & Meglino, 1987). Second, and probably more common, are indirect effects, where values influence a leader's perceptions of stimuli and the perceptions influence action (see Ravlin & Meglino, 1987). This is sometimes called perceptual screening (see England, 1967), where a leader "sees what he wants to see" (Weick, 1979).

Third, Hambrick and Brandon (1988) propose a model where the amount of leader discretion (latitude of action) can moderate between values and perceptions and between perceptions and actions. Thus value-perception-action relations would be much stronger in situations where leaders had much discretion than where they had little.

Fourth, like attitudes, values may not only influence actions but be influenced by them (see Becker & Connor, 1986; Beyer, 1981). Fifth, congruence in values between leaders at the same and different levels and between leaders and subordinate employees may be operating (see Meglino et al., 1989, 1990) even where employees don't come in direct contact with upper-level leaders. This aspect shades into some of the organizational culture literature (see Chapter 10).

There is some literature to support each of the above relationships, although not very much within a leadership context. More specifically, there is evidence showing that values and value congruence influence various aspects of decision making and organizational design (Beyer, 1981). The organizational design implications are especially relevant for the critical leader tasks component of the extended model, discussed in the previous chapter. Hambrick and Brandon (1988) develop a table showing some possible organizational design linkages.

Khandwalla (1976-1977, 1977) some years ago reported related work that tends to mix together values and ideologies as I've defined them here. His results tied risk taking, technocracy, organicity, participation, and coercion into seven "styles" based on combinations of these and suggested that the neoscientific and entrepreneurial styles were most strongly related to organizational effectiveness. He stopped short of showing that his style measures actually led to specific organizational designs, but did make strong arguments that his ideology measures *should* influence organizational design.

An earlier review argued for the impact of administrative philosophies defined as traditionalistic (emphasizing organizational social function), moralistic (emphasizing employee morale, satisfaction, etc.) and individualistic (an emphasis on growth and power) as influences on organizational design (see Osborn, et al., 1980). These two works suggest still more possible dimensions to consider as candidates for organizationally-oriented value dimensions.

Still another preference aspect of the leader capabilities cluster in the extended model is concerned with what has variously been termed cognitive (or sometimes intellectual) style or preference variables. For the purposes of this model I look at these primarily in the context of information-processing preferences.

Cognitive Style Aspects

Cognitive style (sometimes labeled "decision-making style" or "problem-solving style") is one of the most frequently used individual difference concepts in organizational behavior. It is concerned essentially with preferences expressed by individuals for gathering information and evaluating information after it is gathered.[1] Although there are several cognitive style frameworks, the most commonly used is based on the work of Carl Jung (1921/1971) and typically is operationalized by means of the Myers-Briggs Type Indicator (MBTI; Myers & McCaulley, 1985). The MBTI taps the following emphases arranged along four continua where one emphasis in each pair is preferred to the other (see McCaulley, 1990):

- *Extraversion (E) or Introversion (I)*—Those with an E emphasis seek engagement with the environment and give weight to events in the world around them. Those with an I emphasis seek engagement with their inner world and give weight to concepts and ideas to understand events.
- *Sensing (S) or Intuitive (N) perception*—Individuals with an S perception are interested in what is real, immediate, practical, and observable by the senses. Those with an N perception are interested in future possibilities, implicit meanings, and theoretical or symbolic patterns.

- *Thinking (T) or Feeling (F)*—Those with a T emphasis rationally decide through a process of logical analysis of causes and effects. Those with an F emphasis rationally decide by weighing the relative importance or value of competing alternatives.
- *Judgment (J) or Perception (P)*—Individuals with a J emphasis enjoy organizing, planning, and moving quickly to a decision. Those with a P emphasis enjoy being curious and open to changes, preferring to keep options open in case something better turns up.

Sometimes these have been arranged into a 16-cell matrix (ISTJ, ISFJ, etc.) of types with accompanying percentages of various categories of MBTI respondents (see Barber, 1990; McCaulley, 1990). However, in terms of the earlier-mentioned information gathering/information evaluation aspects, a considerable amount of literature to be discussed shortly has tended to concentrate on the four combinations using the S, N, T, and F emphases from above (with information gathering first, evaluation second): ST (Sensing-Thinking), NT (Intuition-Thinking), SF (Sensing-Feeling), and NF (Intuition-Feeling). Hellriegel, Slocum, and Woodman (1989) provide detailed portraits of individuals occupying each of these four cells, but provide no documentation for the portraits. We can summarize the essence of each of these cells below (see Myers, 1976; Taggart & Robey, 1981):

(1) *ST (Sensing-Thinking)*—Focus on facts, stress impersonal analysis, emphasize practicality and matter-of-factness and technical skills with facts and objects. Harold Geneen, former CEO at ITT, fits this type.

(2) *NT (Intuition-Thinking)*—Focus on possibilities, stress personal analysis, logic, ingenuity, and theoretical and technical development. Soichiro Honda, president of Honda, fits this type.

(3) *SF (Sensing-Feeling)*—Focus on facts, stress personal warmth, sympathy, and friendliness, and emphasize practical help and service. Alfred Marrow, a people-oriented ex-CEO at Harwood Manufacturing, is characteristic of this type.

(4) *NF (Intuition-Feeling)*—Focus on possibilities, stress personal warmth, insight, and enthusiasm, and emphasize understanding and communication. This type is characterized by the late Edwin Land, founder and former CEO of Polaroid.

Together, these summaries show quite different preference portraits for leaders with orientations toward each of the four types. McKenney and Keen (1974; see also Whetten & Cameron, 1984) and Rowe and

Mason (1987) have developed two closely related frameworks that they compare to the Myers-Briggs type just covered.

Research literature has related the emphases above to such things as preferred decision-making strategies and career choices and organizational designs (see, e.g., R. Hunt, Krzystofiak, Meindl, & Yousry, 1989; Rowe & Mason, 1987). The organizational design aspect is especially relevant for us. For example, Mitroff and Kilmann (1976) showed relationships between differing cognitive styles and preferences for widely differing kinds of organizational designs. To illustrate, the ST's ideal organization focused on factual details, physical features of the work, impersonal organizational control, certainty, and specificity. The other types emphasized markedly different designs.

In terms of the emphasis on preferences and predispositions, following Jacobs and Jaques (1990, in press), it was mentioned earlier in the book that cognitive style might be important in quite another way—as an indicator of developmental inclination over time. Essentially, the argument is that NTs have a preference both for constructing an inner meaning structure and for analysis. Thus they may be more likely than the other types to make it through the lower-level analytical requirements while looking for ways to develop their cognitive maps and possessing the readiness for higher-level complexity. Nutt (1986) provides some support for this notion. Also, Barber (1990) and McCaulley (1990) show a tendency toward a higher proportion of NTs than NFs or SFs at higher levels. However, there also are data supporting STs at these levels. Clearly there is something about both NTs and Sts that tends to make them more prevalent at higher levels that NF or SF styles. However, support for the inclination suggestion is mixed and more systematic research needs to be done.

Also, in terms of the extended model, an especially relevant focus on cognitive styles is reflected in a recent strategic leadership framework that emphasizes the use of alignment of cognitive styles within top management teams in order to enhance creative strategic decision making over time (Hurst, Rush, & White, 1989). This is consistent with other research emphasizing homogeneous and heterogeneous MBTI team compositions (see McCaulley, 1990).

I have tried to convey the flavor of some of the cognitive-style work as it might relate to the extended model. McCaulley (1990) summarizes a considerable amount of additional MBTI work that does not restrict itself to the cognitive-styles emphasis above but sometimes looks at the earlier-mentioned aspects as well. That work touches on such areas as creativity, risk, stress and burnout, change, and organizational environments, among others. An area of special relevance for us considers MBTI differences in orientation to time. Extroverts tend to see time as continuous (Seiden, 1970). Sensing types tend to be short-term and present oriented (see Evans, 1976; Evered, 1973; Harrison & Lawrence, 1985; Yang, 1981). Thinking types tend to experience time on a past-present-future continuum, whereas feeling types emphasize the past (e.g., Yang, 1981). Finally, achieving management-by-objectives target dates tends to be easier for sensing, thinking, and judging preferences (Jaffee, 1980).

Mental Self-Government Framework

There are a number of other conceptualizations and measures of cognitive style. These are discussed by Robey and Taggart (1981), Sternberg (1990), and Streufert and Nogami (1989), among others. Let's conclude this section by touching on the recently developed, particularly intriguing *mental self-government* framework (Sternberg, 1990). This self-government framework emphasizes styles as analogous to governmental systems. They are differentiated by function, form, level, scope, and leaning.

In terms of *function*, there are legislative, executive, and judicial preferences of individuals.

- *Legislative*—prefer creating, formulating, and planning for problem solutions
- *Executive*—prefer implementation within the existing structure
- *Judicial*—prefer analyzing and evaluating existing things or ideas

In terms of *form*, there are monarchic, hierarchic, oligarchic, and anarchic preferences

- *Monarchic*—prefer single goal at a time; tend to be single-minded, decisive and driven; means justify ends
- *Hierarchic*—prefer hierarchy of goals with some more important than others; ends don't justify means
- *Oligarchic*—prefer multiple, often competing goals of perceived equal importance; ends don't justify means
- *Anarchic*—prefer potpourri of goals that are often difficult to sort out; virtually random in emphasis

In terms of *level*, there are globalists and localists.

- *Globalist*—prefer large and abstract issues
- *Localist*—prefer concrete, down-to-earth issues

In terms of *scope*, there are internalists and externalists.

- *Internalist*—tend to be introverted, task oriented, and aloof
- *Externalist*—tend to be extroverted, people oriented, and outgoing

Finally, in terms of *leaning* there are conservatives and progressives. Conservatives like to adhere to existing rules and procedures, and essentially minimize change. Progressives like to go beyond existing rules and procedures, and maximize change, and the like.

Sternberg (1990) argues that individuals will tend to have a preference for each of these aspects of mental self-government and that taken together the preferences will form a kind of archetype. Consistent with the emphasis here, he sees these as preferences or ways of using given cognitive complexity levels. He also indicates that there is current validation work on an inventory to measure these and speculates on developmental aspects of the styles.

Sternberg's work appears to be different than most of the other cognitive style measures and to have face validity in terms of relevance for the extended model—particularly in terms of the archetypes he mentions. This is especially the case if it is extended in terms of specific conceptualizations in organizational and leadership settings. Of course, its ultimate usefulness remains to be seen.

SELECTED RESEARCH AND CONCEPTUAL LINKAGES WITH THE EXTENDED MODEL

Starting with background variables, the previous discussion suggests relationships between them and values, influence predisposition, self-efficacy, cognitive complexity, and leadership skills (especially transformationally oriented ones) for individual leaders; primarily as a reflection of background developmental impact. Equally important, following the earlier arguments about leadership teams, is the increasing emphasis on upper-management team composition.

This composition emphasis is discussed conceptually by Hambrick and Brandon (1988) and Gupta (1988) and recent empirical work (e.g.,

Bantel & Jackson, 1989; A. Murray, 1989) considers the importance of heterogeneity and homogeneity of team composition using background factors of the type previously discussed. This work, as well as earlier work from the small-group literature, suggests more adaptive and innovative tendencies in heterogeneous teams and more long-term efficiency in homogeneous teams. However, the time period involved and the industry were shown to make a difference. These, as well as composition in terms of the kinds of preference variables treated in this chapter, appear to be relevant considerations within and between domains in the extended model. It seems likely that there can be too much or too little heterogeneity between and among the domains in terms of dealing with critical tasks.

Also, as with various aspects of the model discussed throughout the book, we might expect relationships between, for instance, values and cognitive style as predictors of various aspects of critical tasks. One critical task example is strategy, and another is organizational design archetypes (e.g., Hambrick & Brandon, 1988; Mitroff & Kilmann, 1976). Kets de Vries and Miller (1986) went so far as to argue that top leaders with neurotic personalities tended to design "neurotic" organizations.

Still another important area to investigate is the combining of such preference aspects as cognitive style with aspects of cognitive complexity discussed in the next chapter. Streufert and Nogami (1989) provide some useful insights here. Also, the direct and indirect relationships of values with organizational culture should be examined, as should the earlier-mentioned and related value-congruence notion of Meglino et al. (1990). Finally, it almost, but not quite, goes without saying that the kind of work above should be conducted and compared within and among the various levels and domains throughout the organization. Also, various direct and indirect effects should be considered, beyond those mentioned above.

CONCLUDING COMMENTARY

In this short chapter I first discussed the importance of background factors in terms of their role in the extended model and in leadership more generally. I then looked at the importance of various aspects of predispositions or preferences in the model. These covered the predisposition to exert influence, feelings of self-efficacy, a wide range of value preferences, and cognitive and intellectual preferences. Given the opportunity, these preferences are seen as working together with the other individual capability components of the model to encourage leadership. They are also seen as being related to various other aspects of the model, as illustrated in the preceding section.

From individual predispositions or preferences it is but a short move to individual cognitive aspects. It is to these that I turn in Chapter 7.

NOTE

1. Consistent with much of the literature, I have defined cognitive style as a type of preference. However, some literature defines it as a form of cognitive complexity (e.g., Driver, Brousseau, & Hunsaker, 1990; Rowe & Mason, 1987). Streufert and Nogami (1989) discuss this issue and treat cognitive style and cognitive complexity as two related but separate concepts and measures. I have done likewise, and have tended to follow Sternberg's (1990) approach to treating cognitive (intellectual) style as a preference for or way of using something as opposed to the level of something, such as cognitive complexity.

7 Individual Capabilities—Cognitive Complexity and Selected Social-Cognition Aspects

It is not enough to have a good mind. The main thing is to use it well.
—René Descartes, French philosopher

All things are ready, if our minds be so.
—William Shakespeare, *Henry V*
(quoted in Eigen & Siegel, 1989, p. 33).

A Hun's perception is reality for him.
—Wess Roberts (1987, p. 107),
Leadership Secrets of Attila the Hun

This chapter focuses on the cognitive complexity and selected social-cognition aspects of the extended model's individual capability cluster (see Figure 7.1).

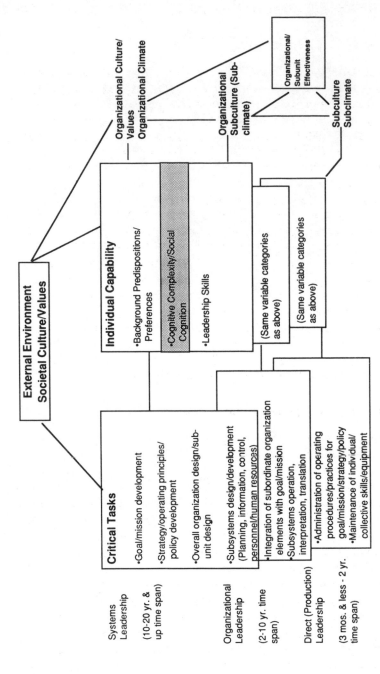

Figure 7.1. Extended Multiple-Organizational-Level Leadership Model
Note: For simplicity, some direct relationships, feedback, and arrowheads are not shown.

BACKGROUND

This chapter, even more than the previous one, involves "getting inside the heads" of leaders, or examining the leadership "black box" (Hunt, Boal, & Sorenson, 1990) to understand thought processes intervening between a stimulus and a response. Examining various aspects of this black box is one of the foundations of the extended model. This is consistent with the "cognitive revolution" (see Fiske & Taylor, 1984; Gardner, 1985; Markus & Zajonc, 1985), which has had a giant impact in several traditional disciplines and spawned new ones of its own. Essentially, it goes beyond the rigid behaviorism that was prevalent for so long in psychology, positing a stimulus $\rightarrow$ organism $\rightarrow$ response relationship and arguing that there must be a "level of representation" to bridge the gap between the brain and nervous system and behavior. Indeed, some (e.g., Markus & Zajonc, 1985) have gone even further and set forth an $O \rightarrow S \rightarrow O \rightarrow R$ relation, where the mental representations not only mediate between stimuli and responses but influence the stimuli attended to and ignored.

Be that as it may, this chapter's focus is on a variety of cognitive aspects that are considered as a crucial component of the capability cluster of the extended model. With this as a background, let's turn to a discussion of cognitive complexity and related aspects.

Cognitive Complexity and Related Aspects

Before moving into this more general discussion of cognitive complexity, recall the discussion of Jaques's notion of cognitive power or individual cognitive complexity in Chapter 2. Essentially, cognitive power was described as the raw mental power enabling a person to sustain increasingly complex decision processes. Maximum achieved time span was pointed out as a way of making the cognitive-power notion more specific and was defined as the maximum time span at which an individual is capable of working at a given time (the extent of a person's time horizon at a given point in his or her life). The longer the individual's maximum achieved time span, the greater the person's cognitive power or cognitive complexity. Jaques derived a series of eight maturation modes to link individual cognitive-power time horizon with required organizational complexity at each of seven organizational levels (Figure 2.1). For Jaques, individual cognitive power, as reflected in the maturation modes, was tapped by the Career Path Appreciation

(CPA) instrument, administered periodically to relevant individuals and briefly discussed in Chapter 2.

With this reiteration, we can examine the cognitive complexity notion less idiosyncratically. To do that, we can turn to an extensive body of cognitive complexity literature summarized in two book-length treatments (see Streufert & Streufert, 1978; Streufert & Swezey, 1986) and a recent review article (see Streufert & Nogami, 1989).

As used in this literature, cognitive complexity is based on the notions of differentiation and integration, mentioned in Chapter 3. Basically, differentiation is concerned with the separation of cognitions or structures of cognitions, and integration considers their combination. At the simplest level, a person responds differently to a stranger than to a familiar person. There is differentiation between the two categories of individuals. There is also integration, given that familiar people are seen as similar to each other because of the quality of familiarity, and strangers are seen as similar to each other because of their quality of strangeness. Any differentiation made between two sets of thoughts implies that an integration has been made within each set of thoughts (Wegner & Vallacher, 1977).

Streufert and Associates' Work

Streufert and his associates (e.g., Streufert & Swezey, 1986) argue that structural information processing is the central focus of what are called complexity theories (e.g., Bieri, 1955; Schroder, Driver, & Streufert, 1967; Scott, 1962). These theories consider the structural dimensions that underlie the flow, processing, and utilization of information. For Streufert and associates, complexity theory emphasizes our earlier-mentioned differentiation (defined as "the number of dimensions that are relevant to an information-processing effort"), and integration ("the relationships among these dimensions"; Streufert & Swezey, 1986, p. 2). The theory also looks at the impact of the organizational context on information flow and processing. Finally, the theory recognizes that the contextual impact may vary across differing cognitive or organizational domains (e.g., decision making versus interpersonal communication) that may have differing degrees of dimensionality (Scott, Osgood, & Peterson, 1979). Such differences in leader and organizational differentiation and integration are argued to have a potentially strong impact on how an organization functions and even whether it survives or not (Streufert & Swezey, 1986). As with the treatment of other cognitive aspects in this chapter, the emphasis is on *how* a person thinks or *how* an organization processes information, rather than on the specific nature of the information that is processed.

Table 7.1 provides a summary description, with some examples, of the key cognitive complexity notions of Streufert and associates. For accuracy, the table tends to use the specific language found in the material on which it is based.

Given the table as a foundation, we can now use an extended example of a cognitively complex versus a cognitively simple leader to extend the discussion of cognitive complexity in a leadership context. Thinking in terms of the leadership skills component of the model (to be treated in detail in later chapters), the cognitively complex leader emphasizes many leader behavior skills, rather than only one or two, and varies them according to the situation.

If the leader who emphasizes many such behaviors tends to see them as related in a deterministic way to each other and to, say, subordinate individual effectiveness, then he or she is emphasizing hierarchical complexity (Table 7.1). However, if he or she emphasizes insight about the use of the behaviors and possible relations to each other and to effectiveness, he or she is high on flexible complexity. If we assume that subordinate responses represent part of the information load on the leader from Streufert and Swezey's (1986) organizational context, then again we can think in terms of hierarchical complexity versus flexible complexity.

In the former case, our leader would tend to be more deterministic in the application of the leadership behaviors to each subordinate. Perhaps subordinates would be grouped into various classes to receive specified groupings of behaviors (e.g., short-service employees would almost automatically receive a number of behaviors oriented toward structuring, simplifying, and so forth). In the latter case, the leader would tend to vary leadership behaviors on a one-to-one basis in response to each individual subordinate's behavior, as in Graen's leader-member exchange theory (see Graen & Cashman, 1975).

Although both kinds of leadership are at a higher level of complexity than a narrower range of behaviors administered with virtually no regard for subordinate differences, the flexible-complexity individual is more complex. Flexible complexity is likely to be most compatible when there is novelty, change, and input that includes unexpected components. Fixed inputs with given meanings that can be quantified or set up in advance are most compatible with hierarchically

Table 7.1
Summary Descriptions and Examples of Key Cognitive Complexity Notions

---

Dimensions: A bipolar cognitive scale with two or more points of discrimination among stimuli. These have meaning in the space defined by the endpoints of the scale. For example, a person with a short-tall dimension (scale) in his/her cognitive space will find it relevant for "building" or "person" but not for the stimulus "weather." "Profit" and "effectiveness" cognitive dimensions are examples of those likely to be institutionalized in organizations.

Discrimination: Division of a cognitive bipolar dimension into subsystems for placement of stimuli relevant to the endpoints of the dimension. The minimum number of discriminations is two (the endpoints); the maximum number is limited only by the capacity of the individual or organization.

Differentiation: Division of cognitive or conceptual space into two or more orthogonal (independent) or oblique (related, but here nearly independent) bipolar dimensions, systems, or subsystems.

Integration: Relating a stimulus configuration of two or more orthogonal or oblique dimensions, systems, or subsystems in cognitive/conceptual space to produce an outcome determined by the joint demands of each dimension, system, or subsystem involved.

Hierarchical Integration: The fixed relationship among dimensions, systems, or subsystems with regard to stimulus configurations that produces a joint response to stimuli. Here, specific stimuli always affect the same dimensions in the same manner.

Flexible Integration: Varied, sometimes changing relationships among dimensions with regard to stimulus configurations, which produce diverse responses to stimuli. Flexible integration is responsive to anticipated environmental changes that require reconceptualizations of relationships between/among events; hierarchical integration is not.

Cognitive Complexity—Simplicity: Represents the degree to which a potentially multidimensional cognitive space is differentiated and integrated. A cognitively complex person functions multidimensionally. A cognitively simple person uses few or only one dimension and demonstrates little or no dimensional differentiation and integration.

Organizational Complexity—Simplicity: The organizational analogue to cognitive complexity. A conceptually complex organization would use a number of differentiated organizational goals, etc., and would generate outcomes based on the integrated weights of these conceptualizations. A conceptually simple organization would use one or a few conceptualizations (e.g., profit).

Domains of Complexity: The subdivision of cognitive or conceptual space into specific areas for which the degree of differentiation/complexity may differ widely. Managerially, the decision-making domain is different from the interpersonal communication domain and one might be high on one and low on the other, etc.

Source: Based on Streufert & Swezey (1986), pp. 15-18.

complex styles. Hierarchical complexity lends itself well to an artificial-intelligence-based computer system, flexible complexity does not (Streufert & Swezey, 1986).

Complexity within one domain does not necessarily ensure complexity across all domains, although complexity in one domain may help in developing complexity across other domains (Streufert & Swezey, 1986). Thus our leader with the highly complex leadership behavior may or may not be highly complex in his or her strategy-setting behavior. Let us take a final look at such a perspective. Integration without differentiation is impossible. Without the recognition of several dimensions, there is no way or need to relate those dimensions (Streufert & Swezey, 1986). Consistent with Streufert & Swezey, let's say that our leader considers one of his or her subordinates to be a nice person at work but a bad person at home. If our differentiating leader also is an integrator, he or she will look for some overriding principle to reconcile the work-home differences of the subordinate.

Moving from the previous example to a strategic decision-making one, we can state that a high-level integrator is more likely to consider a wide range of factors in a decision (concerning, for example, competitor information), then try to develop an overarching strategic reaction that emphasizes responsiveness to an overall view of the reasons (e.g., for the competitor's actions)—one that will be strategically best in terms of a number of possibilities. At the same time, our leader as a high-level integrator also may use available information and respond simultaneously to advance the future position of his or her organization (Streufert & Swezey, 1986).

The previous discussion should make it obvious that the need for being cognitively complex is a function of the situation (or the organizational setting) in which the person is operating. Streufert and Swezey argue for curvilinearity with an optimum level of complexity somewhere around the middle—there can be too much, as well as too little, individual complexity for complexity requirements of the organization. In other words, as with Jaques's conception, there needs to be a match or fit between organizational requirements and an individual's complexity.

Jaques's organizational requirements are expressed in terms of time span, whereas Streufert and Swezey think in terms of complexity of the organizational setting, with task information load as an example. In either case, an individual can be too complex for the requirements. Jaques (1989) discusses this in terms of the effects on an individual's level of satisfaction and the person's demonstrating behaviors more suitable to a higher-level position. Streufert and Swezey (1986) imply "overkill" on the part of a leader. For example, a problem may be "studied to death," or there may be too much emphasis on formalized planning.

Cognitive Complexity Research, Measures, and Theoretical Extensions

It's beyond my purpose to review and evaluate systematically the myriad of studies devoted to cognitive complexity. Rather, I will convey the nature of the research and provide a little history to show that the concept has been around for quite a while. Cognitive complexity has received a small amount of attention in mainstream leadership research (e.g., Streufert & Nogami, 1989; Wynne & Hunsaker, 1975), and is the basis for some current work related to leadership that I touch on below. Research most directly related to cognitive differentiation and integration goes back to the mid-1950s with the work of Kelly (1955), followed closely by Bieri (1961, 1966) and Zajonc (1960). Streufert and associates' work, emphasized here, starts in the early 1960s (see Streufert & Streufert, 1978).

Thus we have a concept that has been generating research for some 30 years, with a large number of studies. It has been found to relate to such things as differences in some aspects of personality structure, communication, attitudes, attraction, flexibility and creativity, and adaptation and adjustment to task demands. Complex persons tend to be more information oriented and have been found to use a more complex perceptual process than less complex individuals. Complexity also appears to be related to some aspects of individual and organizational performance and differences in decision making, as well as in planning and strategy, and analytic skills (Streufert & Nogami, 1989; Streufert & Swezey, 1986).

There also is some research focusing on complexity training. Some attempts have met with little success, whereas others have apparently been quite successful. Such training appears to work best when it is designed to deal with specific situations (see Streufert & Nogami,

1989). Cognitive training is related to the developmental discussion in Chapter 11.

Measurement

Like Jaques's CPA measure, the measurement of cognitive complexity can itself be complex. There are many measures in the literature, and even the programmatic work of Streufert and his colleagues has used a number of different ones. Their latest work embeds the measurement of complexity into quasi-experimental simulation technology assessing cognitive complexity evident in decision making (Streufert, Pogash, & Piasecki, 1988). Here, individuals or groups participate in an all-day computer-assisted task.

Essentially, this approach is a reflection of Streufert's conclusion that it's difficult to develop direct paper-and-pencil measures of complexity. According to this argument, individuals need to engage in a task that encourages the use of cognitive complexity. Thus relatively indirect, subjective sentence- or paragraph-completion or textual-analysis approaches are among those that have been used, along with the various kinds of decision-making analyses illustrated in the simulation (see Streufert & Swezey, 1986). Fortunately, although a wide range of measures of the kinds just mentioned have been used, research results appear to be quite consistent (Streufert & Nogami, 1989). In other words, different kinds of measures yield similar findings.

In contrast to the research just discussed is a very different kind of study reported very recently (Goodwin, Wofford, & Harrison, 1990). In this work the authors derived a complexity measure that they argued was suitable for the "organizational domain," based on the summation of four dimension scores. These dimensions were concrete activities and functions, the human side of the job, status structure at work, and interactive processes at work. The scale was derived from undergraduate and MBA students with some job experience; it consists of a series of Semantic Differential scales (Osgood, Suci, & Tannenbaum, 1957) to measure the dimensions. It does not appear to tap integration, and the only Streufert work cited is a 1968 study. It calls for task engagement in the broad sense that it asks subjects to respond to specific organizational stimuli, rather than to more general ones. However, the engagement is not nearly as direct as that recommended by Streufert. The scale is short and easy to administer. Its utility for the extended model and other leadership uses, however, currently is unknown.

Extensions

Two recent theoretical extensions of cognitive complexity are oriented toward leaders' cognitive complexity, along with a number of other variables, and recognize various situational contingencies operating in organizations. The first of these is by Schroder (cited in Streufert & Nogami, 1989), who focuses on a group of "competencies" (I discuss further the competency notion, in general, in the next chapter) that includes complexity aspects. One interesting finding, consistent with the emphasis here, is that high-performing leaders build teams that contain members with strengths that complement each other's and the leader's. Schroder also includes a set of what he terms individual values, which when integrated with the adaptive use of competencies requires leader capability to apply both differentiation and integration at a broad level.

The second approach is an extension of the earlier theoretical work of Streufert and his associates (e.g., Streufert & Swezey, 1986). Within the kinds of organizational settings included in the simulation mentioned earlier, this approach emphasizes not only differentiation and flexible integration but discrimination at both individual and organizational levels (see Table 7.1). It focuses on adaptability of individual leader cognitive complexity and other variables in meeting changing organizational task demands (see Streufert & Nogami, 1989). Thus we see complexity embedded within a dynamic setting. In another setting, such adaptability was discussed in much earlier cognitive complexity work, which suggested that the political survival of revolutionaries (e.g., George Washington, Che Guevara) depended on their demonstrating a much greater degree of complexity to maintain their position once a successful revolution was ended (see Suedfeld & Rank, 1976).

Integration of Diversity

In Chapter 5 I touched on Bentz's (1987) scope and scale notions as yet another way of broadening our perspective in looking at different organizational-level requirements and organizational complexity. Here I look at a companion individual capability measure by Bentz, called "integration of diversity." This measure, though developed differently, appears quite similar to the work discussed earlier in this chapter.

Instrument development started with in-depth, semistructured interviews of upper-level executives, who were asked to describe capabilities important for senior-level leader effectiveness. A content analysis of these provided a 51-item questionnaire consisting of short, narrative paragraphs representing complex managerial concepts. The questionnaires were administered to top executives and factor analyzed. Among the factors obtained was the "integration of diversity" scale representing top-management scope and scale aspects.

High-loading items covered such things as shaping events through a synthesis of related managerial functions, handling complex situations and coordinating diverse elements into a single overall managerial framework, ability to cope with new systems and integrate them into an overall system, and ability to shape events through strategy. Bentz (1987) then used multiple regression to relate scores on the nine factors obtained with a series of personality variables whose scores were obtained some *21 years* before. Although the results for integration of diversity alone are not reported, the multiple correlation was 0.46 for these data. These results suggest that the integration of diversity measure is worth developing further, in combination with the organizational scope and scale aspects of Bentz's work reported in Chapter 5.

To summarize, we've looked at a number of different notions and measures that propose to tap various aspects of cognitive complexity. Work is needed to compare and contrast these conceptions and measures, as well as others that might be relevant.

KEY SOCIAL-COGNITION NOTIONS

In this section I move from the cognitive complexity and related facets of the extended model to summary consideration of social cognition and some of its key aspects. I then look at some important implications of these social-cognition implications for the extended model; those readers familiar with cognitive concepts may want to go directly to this latter description. For those interested in a more extended discussion than provided here, check detailed treatments in Lockett and Legge (1989) and in Sims and Gioia (1986), and by Markus and Zajonc (1985), Peterson and Sorenson (in press), Fiske and Taylor (1984), and Lord and his associates, especially Lord and Maher (1989a, in press). These two sources not only provide state-of-the-art reviews but include extensive references to additional work by Lord and his associates and many others.

Let's start by describing social cognition as how individuals make sense of other people and themselves—how individuals think about people and how they *think* they think about people. There are at least four elements in the social-cognition process. First, we have *cognitions*, which help determine what a person will do or what direction behavior will take (Fiske & Taylor, 1984). A second element is *motivation*, a particularly important part of the discussion in Chapter 6 and of such mainstream leadership theories as path-goal (see House & Baetz, 1979). The strength of motivation determines whether behavior will occur at all and, if it does, how much it will occur (Fiske & Taylor, 1984). A third element is *causal attributions*—people's ideas about what causes things to occur and why things happen as they do (see Fiske & Taylor, 1984). Causal attributions are important to people's feelings of prediction and control. The fourth and final social cognition element is concerned with *affective response* (e.g., values, attitudes and emotions).

Although the process of social cognition emphasizes all of these elements in interaction with each other, in this chapter I am interested primarily in *cognitive schemas*, or what are sometimes called "cold" as opposed to "hot" (e.g., emotional) aspects of cognition (see Watson, 1982). I also touch on causal attributions in their relations to schemas; values, attitudes, and some motivational aspects were emphasized in the previous chapter. This discussion will not deal with emotions—for those interested in the role of emotions in social cognition in organizations, see Par, Sims, and Motowidlo (1986). Finally, we need to be aware that social cognition and its elements can be dealt with in a leadership context from both leader and subordinate perspectives. This book deals with it from both, but the primary emphasis is on leaders.

Schemas and Cognitive Processes

Let's define a *schema* as a cognitive structure that represents organized knowledge about a given concept or type of stimulus. It contains not only the attributes of the concept but the relationship among the attributes (Fiske & Linville, 1980; Hastie, 1981; Rumelhart & Ortony, 1977; Taylor & Crocker, 1981). Information is stored in abstract form, not merely as a collection of original encounters with examples of the general case. Schemas reflect the active construction of reality, as in

Chapter 4, where individuals create meaning and add onto it the raw data of the objective world. Organized prior knowledge shapes what is perceived and remembered (see Fiske & Taylor, 1984). Schemas are triggered primarily as a way of dealing with information overload and often are automatically called forth to make sense out of new situations. Previously, I've emphasized the importance of cognitive complexity in dealing with information. Now I am saying that even cognitively complex individuals will use schemas to reduce their information overload.

Let's take a quick look at how schemas are involved in the three key social-cognition process aspects of attention, memory, and inference. In terms of attention, schemas tend to filter information to be consistent with the schema(s) evoked. As an example we'll take the case of Don Burr, founder of the People Express airline, which was initially very successful and then ran into difficulties as it overexpanded and competition increased (e.g., Barrett, 1987; People Express, 1983; "Up and Away," 1985).

It can be argued that Burr had a "people-driven schema" with such key elements as the self-determining kind of people hired, a strong emphasis on employee self-actualization and superior customer service, and a deemphasis on bureaucratic elements. Thus we might expect these elements to filter Burr's interpretation of information that he received and to guide the kind of information to which he responded.

In terms of memory, people tend to remember information that is consistent with their schemas and to ignore or downplay information that is not—there is an emphasis on information-processing efficiency, rather than accuracy. In Burr's case, there is evidence suggesting that he tended to discount information arguing for more bureaucratization as his firm grew. His schema led him to remember the people-oriented aspects at the expense of information indicating a need for more structuring as things became more complex.

In terms of inferences, people tend to use preexisting schemas to draw inferences about data rather than examining the data carefully. Shortcuts or judgmental heuristics are often included as part of the schema. Two common heuristics are *representativeness* and *availability* (see Tversky & Kahneman, 1974). The representativeness heuristic means that a person judges the likelihood of an event on the basis of information about the generating process or inappropriately generalizes cause-and-effect models from one domain to another. Thus a leader may expect a Congress controlled by Democrats to enact legislation unfavorable to business without attempting to assess whether such inferences are supported by objective data. Or a CEO from the United States may have no hesitation in trying to implement Japanese management practices because he or she accepts the heuristic that Japanese companies are highly effective because they utilize the Japanese management style.

The availability heuristic results in a person interpreting new events in light of memories of very recent (and hence available) past events. Probably one reason Burr underestimated the later difficulties facing his firm was because of the widely available, favorable publicity about it in the media.

To summarize, schemas make themselves felt in social cognition through their impact on attention, memory, and inferences. They tend to be used to deal with information overload. The resulting socially constructed reality tends to be oriented toward efficient, although not necessarily accurate, processing of available information.

Types of Schemas

Essentially there are four types of schemas that are representative of those in the literature: self-schemas, person schemas, script (event) schemas, and person-in-situation schemas. Lord and Foti (1986) and Fiske and Taylor (1984) are among those discussing schema typologies of this kind.

Self-schemas (Fong & Markus, 1982; Markus, 1977) contain information about an individual's own appearance, behavior, and personality. For example, if a person has a "decisiveness" script he or she will tend to filter information and judge himself or herself in terms of that aspect in many circumstances, especially those calling for leadership. *Person schemas* relate to the way people sort others into categories, such as types or groups, in terms of similar perceived features. The term *prototype* often is used to represent these categories; a prototype is an abstract set of features commonly associated with members of that category.[1]

Once a prototype is formed, it is stored in long-term memory and the later categorization of an individual is based on the extent to which the person matches the prototype features. For example, if we have a leader prototype in mind that involves decisiveness and sociability, then that prototype may be triggered in categorizing a new manager as to whether or not he or she is a "real leader." This categorization would then be expected to make a difference in terms of responses to the leader and to later perceptions of his or her behavior.

Three levels of prototype categories have been identified in terms of specificity. The *superordinate level* is the most general and might involve characteristics separating, for example, good leaders from poor leaders. Then the more specific *basic level* prototype is triggered and might differentiate political from industrial leaders or those in one industry from those in another. Finally, a *subordinate level* prototype might be triggered. Here, specific organizational factors might make a difference (for a discussion, see Hunt, Boal & Sorenson, 1990; Lord, Foti & Phillips, 1982). As we shall see shortly, person schemas and prototypes play an especially important role in leadership.

Script schemas are the third major type of schema and are defined as knowledge structures that describe the appropriate sequence of events in a given situation (Abelson, 1981; Schrank & Abelson, 1977). They are especially useful for comprehending and understanding a given situation and providing behavior guides (e.g., steps in conducting a meeting; see Gioia & Manz, 1985). They may be thought of in terms of level of specificity in much the same way as prototypes (see Hunt, Baliga & Peterson, 1988) and are "strong" or "weak" depending on how closely they specify an exact sequence of events (Abelson, 1981).

Lastly, *person-in-situation schemas* combine an emphasis on schemas built around persons (self and person) and those emphasizing events (script schemas). These obviously are the richest kinds of schemas, and evidence indicates that they tend to be relatively accessible in memory (Cantor, Mischel, & Schwartz, 1982).

Although we don't know a lot about exactly what determines the choice of schema type, there is some information on this. The purpose of the perceiver is one such factor. For instance, a focus on goal achievement will tend to trigger a script schema or person-in-situation schema. Frequency and intensity of previous exposure to a schema are also important. Finally, salience or prominence of the person or situation encountered can have an impact on the type of schema emphasized (see Fisk & Taylor, 1984).

A final key aspect to consider in this quick treatment of social cognition and schemas concerns automatic versus controlled processing. This processing is relevant for any of the kinds of schemas just discussed. *Automatic processing* tends to demand little attention, can be applied to a number of activities simultaneously, is relatively unaffected by cognitive load, and is relatively difficult to change once it is learned. For example, if a leader's natural leadership schema is autocratic in nature, it will be difficult to change it to be participative. However, if the leader is satisfied with an automatic schema, he or she is "freed up" to concentrate on other aspects of the situation.

In contrast, *controlled processing* involves deliberate thinking and development of elaborate plans. Controlled processing places heavy emphasis on the limited information-processing capacities of even cognitively complex individuals. It tends to focus on one activity at a time, to be affected strongly by cognitive load, and to be easier to change than an automatic schema (for a discussion, see Langer, 1978; Lord & Foti, 1986).

Organizationally Oriented Social-Cognition Research

With the above brief discussion as background, let's now take a brief look at organizationally oriented cognitive process research that has implications for the extended model. Consistent with the emphasis in this book, there has been an increasing trend toward cognitively based work, with more than three times as many studies conducted recently as were conducted in the late 1970s (Lord & Maher, 1989a).

Organizationally oriented cognitive process research has been especially prevalent in the areas of performance appraisal, leadership perception, social processes (including superior-subordinate attributions and task perceptions), problem solving, and decision making. Current research in all of these areas has been carefully reviewed by Lord and Maher (1989a), and I invite those interested to read that review. The underlying theme tying all of the above areas together is the impact that social cognition has on the way information is processed in each of them. The basic message is that schemas, attribution, judgmental heuristics, and the like impact these areas to help explain such things as biases in performance evaluation, the fact that decision making does not follow the traditionally taught rationalistic mode, that leadership "behaviors" cannot really be taken at face value but are mediated by cognitive biases, and so forth.

For present purposes I'll concentrate most heavily on the leadership aspects of social cognition and will bring in other areas as they help in explicating the extended model. I'll start with the notion of implicit theories—which, as we shall see, are related to both attribution and prototypes. Both research in personality theory (Shweder, 1975, 1982) and a book on implicit psychology (Wegner & Vallacher, 1977) argue that individuals develop implicit theories (*implicit* because they are not spelled out) to give meaning to events, to attribute causes to phenomena, and to see patterns and regularity in the world around them. These theories are used to help explain a wide range of organizational phenomena, such as personalities best suited for high performance and appropriate leadership. And there are even implicit organization theories (what a successful organization design looks like, see Downey & Brief, 1986).

In terms of leadership there have been several studies, commencing in 1975, that have shown essentially that individuals' descriptions of leader behavior were biased by the subjects' beliefs about the performance of the leader's group. In other words, where people believed that performance was high, they attributed good things to the leader and their descriptions of the leader's behavior were more favorable than where they believed performance to be low. A related line of research showed that the factor structures of leadership questionnaires completed by subjects who were provided only general information about the work setting were very similar to those obtained from actual descriptions of leaders (Eden & Leviatan, 1975; Rush, Thomas, & Lord, 1977). In other words, the subjects don't literally have to have had experience with the leaders to describe them.

Taken together, this line of research suggests that implicit leadership theories were operating that influenced raters' attributions concerning leadership and their descriptions of leader behavior (e.g., leaders of groups that perform well must be "good"). Later research links attribution research with leadership prototypes to explain more completely the mechanisms underlying implicit leadership theory. Based on this, Lord (1985) argues that leadership can both be inferred from events or outcomes dependent on causal analysis, and be recognized through direct exposure to a leader's behaviors or traits (where, as mentioned earlier, they are compared against a "good" leader prototype that the subject brings into the setting). Lord and Maher (1989b; in press) have developed a model examining how both these processes are involved. This work is consistent with the arguments of those such as Fiske and Taylor (1984), Smith and Peterson (1988), and Baliga, Peterson, and Hunt (1990) that attributions may be influenced by schemas in affecting perceptions and descriptions of behavior.

I will discuss this implicit theory area in more detail in two chapters focusing on leadership skills, but for now it's important to recognize that implicit theories can have an impact on a leader's acceptance by subordinates. One recent model argues that the fit of leader behaviors and follower prototypes can influence such things as organizational effectiveness and individual performance and satisfaction, as well as the person chosen for a leadership position (Hunt, Boal, & Sorenson, 1990). Other related work focuses on the implications of schemas held by top-level leaders in terms of different phases of the organization's life cycle, and so forth (Hunt, Baliga, & Peterson, 1988). Consistent with the earlier discussion of schemas, the argument is that these developed schemas are likely to be very difficult to change as the organization changes. Finally, as pointed out previously, implicit organizing theories involving schemas and attributions about "good" organizations are likely to have a substantial impact on organization design as well as other components of our model.

The research and conceptual work just cited is highly suggestive in terms of the extended model and leadership in general. The actual research done has almost all been conducted in laboratory settings, although some of the conceptualization extends to upper-level leaders in organizations (e.g., Baliga et al., 1990; Hunt et al., 1990; Lord & Maher, in press; Peterson & Sorenson, in press). The laboratory research is particularly strong in emphasizing the dynamic processual aspects of leadership, and some recent review pieces discuss this in some detail (see Srull, 1984; Taylor & Fiske, 1981). This processual emphasis is consistent with that of the discussion of dynamic implications of the extended model in the final chapter. However, even with this and laboratory research's other strong points (e.g., Locke, 1986), I can only echo Lord and Maher (1989a) in calling for additional cognitive work outside the lab, particularly for the extended model. I'll return to some of these research and conceptual issues within the context of the model after examining cognitive maps in the next section.

COGNITIVE MAPS

Cognitive maps, originally developed by Tolman (1948) to deal with spatial maps of rats running a maze, are a kind of schema and might well have been treated immediately above. However, much of their literature base is different from that just discussed and, as suggested in Chapter 3, they are an especially useful additional way of tapping cognitive complexity. Bougan (1983) does a nice job both of linking schemas to cognitive maps and showing their representational qualities in bridging the gap between the brain and nervous system and behavior. He first sets the stage as follows:

> How does this flow of energy across the skin become knowledge about ourselves and our physical surroundings? The process transforming raw materials into knowledge relies on cortical schemas and particularly on the interplay between raw experience, schemas, patterns, perceptions and knowledge. . . . Schemas, perception and knowledge are intimately related and one cannot be isolated from the other. . . . Schemas have the property of handling the energy flow across the skin *as a whole*. Therefore, schemas empower us with such feats as recognizing patterns at a glance. For example, when you meet a person, you are often able to recognize that person at a glance by the *whole* pattern of face, look, demeanor, intonation, scent, mannerism, and so on. (p. 174, emphasis in original)

Bougan goes on to use an example of identifying the pattern in a mosaic and argues that we can't construct the whole from the parts. However, looking at the whole, we may see the pattern intended by the artists (Bougan, 1983, p. 175). Here we are reminded of the earlier-discussed cybernetic perspective.

In this view, schemas encompass processes that begin with an individual's raw experience, move through processing the neural signals, and culminate in perceiving, conceptualizing, learning, remembering, and behaving on the basis of wholes (Bougan, 1983, p. 175). Every schema is associated with concepts that also are the notions behind words. A schema can reconstruct the pattern of concepts that it records; this is called a "concept-structure." A person's concept-structure is the territory to be explored, and the recording of that exploration is a cognitive map (Bougan, 1983). Cognitive maps tap all kinds of relations occurring in patterns of concepts (e.g., contiguity, proximity, continuity, resemblance, and causality).

A simplified version of a cognitive map that is less abstract and easier to think about and use has been termed a *cause map*. Recall from Chapter 3 that a cause map displays a person's ends, means, conflicts, and contexts for sense making (Bougan, 1983, p. 181). It shows the means/ends beliefs necessary to the development of plans and the initiation of behaviors directed to desired end states (Axelrod, 1976). In terms of the mapping process, one can think of concepts (expressed in the respondent's own phrasing) linked by arrows representing a causal linkage between the concepts of the form "concept 1 has consequences for or can be explained by concept 2" (Eden, Jones, Sims, & Smithin, 1981, p. 40).

The concepts are variables (either continuous or discrete) and can be curvilinear and reflect such notions as "some amount of a variable is good, but too much of the same variable is bad" (or vice versa; Weick & Bougan, 1986). Of special importance is that elements of a cause map also can be interpreted in terms of the cognitive complexity notions of differentiation and integration (Weick & Bougan, 1986).

The previous discussion seems to imply that a cause map might be seen as a script and, indeed, Weick and Bougan (1986) argue that a script can be viewed as a "strip map" (a frozen deduction from a cause map). They contend that causal attribution work could allow for a sharper distinction between causes if it used a cause map. They also show that cause maps can be used to trace strategic implications across time (see Hall, 1984), as well as motivational structures.

There are a number of recent discussions of the use of causal maps and related concepts (sometimes termed "frames of reference," "belief structures," "influence diagrams," etc.) by those interested in organization theory and strategic management (e.g., Diffenbach, 1982; Ford & Hegarty, 1984; Jacobs & Jaques, in press; Khazanchi, 1990; Laukkanen, 1989; McCaskey, 1982; Shrivastava & Mitroff, 1984; Smithin, 1980; Voyer & Faulkner, 1986; Walsh & Fahey, 1986 and Walsh, Henderson & Deighton, 1988). This emphasis on cognitive maps joins the work of those such as Axelrod (1976) and Eden et al. (1981) in showing their efficacy for tapping complex thinking over time.

Of special interest here are examples of studies with a focus on cognitive maps at the top of the organization. The first of these looks at the contrasting role of cognitive maps in the strategic adaptation patterns over 15 years of a television receiver manufacturer that survived, versus one that failed. Data were obtained from trade journals and annual reports. Basically, it was found that the map of the survivor was more differentiated, complex, consistent, faster acting, and represented more aggressive goals than that of the failure (see Fahey & Narayanan, 1986).

Another study of interest examined cognitive maps to help explain how certain policies came to be adopted in an organization over a 20-year period and how, together with critical events, these policies caused the organization to evolve in specific directions (R. Hall, 1984). The study focused on cause maps at several different organizational levels, including top management. Of primary interest here is the demonstration that, although reasonable on the surface, these cause maps were what the researcher termed "maladaptive mutations" and ultimately led to the organization's demise.

A third study used a combined management-development program sample of middle managers and top managers seeking to improve their managerial skills (Walsh, 1988). The researcher was interested in how complex and functionally biased his sample's belief structures (i.e., cognitive maps) were. He concluded that these manager's belief structures were actually complex enough so that the managers tended not to be functionally biased and their information processing appeared to be relatively unrestrained, in contrast to arguments in some of the literature cited by him.

Finally, a Finnish study is of interest not only for its results, but for its detailed description of the methodology used. Essentially the study found that

(1) maps appeared to be formed by individual models of logical relationships inherent in each leader's mind, social influences (e.g., the accumulated knowledge base of various professional areas), and setting/environmental forces; and

(2) the three forces formed a reciprocal system influencing each other to form the map.

Among the study's conclusions was that the maps probably reflected a mixture of both memory and the capacity to generate causal notions when necessary. The study used a variation of Bougan's (1983) self-Q technique—where the subjects, as opposed to the researcher, provide the concepts to obtain the data. Both Bougan's original technique and the technique used here are time-consuming (about 10 to 12 hours per subject; see Laukkanen, 1989, for a description of the study).

Some recent work has used a simplified variation of the Bougan procedure and considerably shortened the time required per subject, at the expense of having the researcher provide more initial structuring (see, e.g., Walsh, 1988; Walsh et al., 1988). In these studies, concept cards were originally developed and the subjects were asked to sort them in various ways to get at different aspects of what the researchers termed "belief structures," which then were derived using multidimensional scaling. A careful reading of many of the previously cited references provides the essence not only of what cognitive maps are about but how to go about trying to tap them and analyze the resulting data.

Group Uses of Cognitive Maps

As with a number of other aspects throughout this book, Walsh et al. (1988) look at team aspects of cognitive maps (belief structures). An especially interesting part of their study in this context is "realized coverage" and "realized consensus." Coverage concerns the extent to which each aspect or dimension of the map appears at least once when the data are aggregated across group members. Consensus concerns the degree to which a member's map shares representations of each aspect of the information domain.

Even though high coverage and high consensus may exist, that is not enough. It's important to consider each group member's participation to determine if his or her coverage and consensus are ever utilized. Perhaps one person in a four-person group completely dominates the decision-making process. If so, the maps of the other individuals might as well not exist. Realized coverage and consensus takes this into account by weighting coverage and consensus by participation for a given decision. If there is no participation, even if the individual is present, dimensions in that map are not represented. Walsh and his associates, in a business simulation, found that realized map coverage and consensus were systematically related to team performance in the simulation.

For very indepth treatment of maps and related notions check very recent works by Huff (1990) and Walsh (1990). Let's turn now to a quick look at some research and conceptual linkages suggested by the work discussed throughout this chapter.

SELECTED RESEARCH AND CONCEPTUAL LINKAGES WITH THE EXTENDED MODEL

A couple of areas to start with concern schema antecedents and a focus on the attention, memory, and inference aspects of schemas. In terms of antecedents, Hunt et al. (1990) hypothesize some of these from the literature as they might apply to the prototype aspects of personal schemas. These essentially are similar to the background, environmental, and societal culture aspects of the extended model (see Figure 7.1), discussed in earlier chapters. Systems-level critical tasks also may have an impact on systems-level cognitive structures and particularly on lower-level ones, as I argue below. Fiske and Taylor (1984) also deal with such antecedents as demonstrated in a laboratory context and Laukkanen, as mentioned, does it with cognitive maps. Both conceptual and empirical work are needed to extend these treatments and to get at the related notion concerning when automatic versus controlled schemas are likely to be triggered (see Baliga et al., 1990; Peterson & Sorenson, in press).

Considering the role played by schemas in terms of attention, memory, and inference aspects, again Fiske and Taylor present some evidence within a social psychology context and with a laboratory emphasis. Lord and Maher (1989a; in press) serve as a good source summarizing some of Lord and associates' conceptual and empirical work (the latter being lab based) focusing on this concern. There is very little work emphasizing these cognitive process aspects in real-world organizations in general and the extended model in particular. Among other things, such findings could provide a better understanding of how schemas operate dynamically to influence strategies, organizational design, and many other relevant aspects of the extended model.

Equally as important as the points just mentioned is the relation of cognitive schemas to the other capability aspects, as well as to organizational culture and organizational and direct leadership domain aspects. Representative of the first point, we need work considering relationships among the values, cognitive style, and leadership preferences or predispositions in Chapter 6, and both cognitive complexity and cognitive structures in the present chapter. As developed in more detail in the next couple of chapters, we also need information within the context of the model linking cognitive complexity and cognitive structures to various aspects of leader behavior skills. These range from prototypes on the part of subordinates to the leader behavior-choice processes.

In terms of organizational culture, cognitive structures of the leader and others serve as the base for the leader's "management of meaning" involved in organizational culture (see Smircich & Morgan, 1982) and lower-level subcultures. Here, leaders treat actions and organizations as symbols whose meanings need to be shared with others in the organization. Implicit organization theories may help guide organization design and, if shared and agreed upon, help shape schemas and promote common understandings of those below (see Peterson & Sorenson, in press). Work is needed on these and related areas. Also, as I discuss with regard to other aspects of the model, ultimately we need work that cuts across time. Closely related to such work is that which focuses on how to change schemas. Again Fiske and Taylor (1984) touch on this, but the surface has only been scratched.

Finally, as with many other components of the model, there may be modest direct relationships with organizational outcomes. However, as before, the most interesting and important relationships are expected to be indirect, through linkages with other variables (both horizontally and vertically).

CONCLUDING COMMENTARY

The importance of cognitive complexity has been emphasized throughout the book, and I contended early on that it was a crucial component of the extended model. Arguments for the importance of the social-cognition aspects are essentially extensions of the complexity argument, and, indeed, in the case of cognitive maps, there is direct overlap in the concepts. However, beyond the complexity arguments, consistent with work in the previous chapters I've tried to continue to emphasize the importance of "getting inside the head" of leaders. I've also stressed some implications of this in terms of various aspects of the model—for example, strategy and organizational design schemas, as well as leader behavior choices and the perceptions of these as influenced by the cognitive structures of others.

One of the striking things in considering both the complexity concepts and other cognitive aspects discussed in this chapter is the difficulty of using "quick and dirty" measures to get at them. As an example, simple direct, paper-and-pencil questionnaires have not been used to measure Jaques's cognitive-power conception; neither are they the measure of choice to tap the kinds of cognitive complexity aspects dealt with by Streufert and associates. Finally, they typically have not been the primary data source in studies of schemas, cognitive maps, and the like (see Taylor & Fiske, 1981; Weick & Bougan, 1986).

Where used, questionnaires frequently are considered in combination with processual changes in simulations or laboratory studies. Or, relatedly, respondents have been asked to engage in activities such as paragraph completion that presumably call forth aspects of cognitive complexity involved. Clearly here, as much as any other area of leadership, the knowledge-content and knowledge-orientation aspects of paradigm pluralism are critical. The conceptualization and measurement of cognitive complexity, cognitive schemas and maps, and related concepts calls for very imaginative and ecumenical approaches if we are to be able to tap their full potential in the leadership area.

In summary, cognitive concepts and their measurement are an extremely important component of the leader capability cluster. Also important are a wide range of leader behavior/skills, which I turn to in Chapters 8 and 9.

NOTE

1. Although similar to stereotypes, some people restrict the term *stereotype* to racial, sexual, ethnic, and occupational categories, whereas the term *prototype* is use more generally (see Ilgen & Feldman, 1983).

THE FAR SIDE

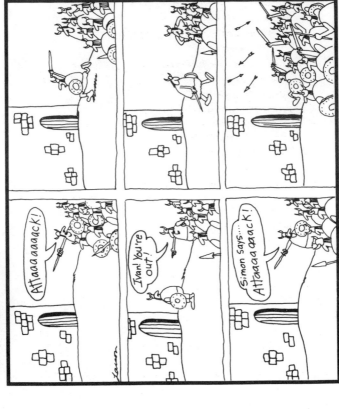

The Far Side © 1985 Universal Press Syndicate. Reprinted with permission. All rights reserved.

8 Individual Capabilities— Transactionally Oriented Leadership Skills

Lead, follow, or get out of the way!

—Anonymous
(quoted in Eigen & Siegel, 1989, p. 231)

Clear-water rivers with gravel bottoms change their channels very grad- ually, and therefore one needs to learn them but once; but piloting becomes another matter when you apply it to vast streams like the Mississippi . . . whose obstructions must be confronted in all nights and all weathers without the aid of a single lighthouse or buoy.

—Mark Twain
(quoted in Eigen & Siegel, 1989, pp. 229-230)

convince [people] that they should do
ing, articulating—trying to build con-

—Unidentified four-star general
ed in U.S. Army War College, 1988, p. 11)

cognitive aspects of the individual capability
clu   multi-level model. In this chapter, I continue the
treatmen   f the individual capability cluster by treating
leadership be   skills (see Figure 8.1). I further explore this topic
in Chapter 9 by focusing on transformationally oriented[1] components
of leadership. They are so important and have seen such an explosion
of literature recently that they justify their own chapter.

BACKGROUND

Historically, leadership research and research into managerial work,
jobs, and behavior have been carried out independently so that there has
been little cross-fertilization of ideas (Stewart, 1982b). The two areas
have traditionally attracted people from different backgrounds and
research interests. Many involved with leadership studies have tended
to have psychology backgrounds and emphasize structured questionnaires and surveys or laboratory studies for data gathering. There also
has usually been an interest in the relation of leadership to outcomes
such as performance, satisfaction, and the like.

In contrast, the much smaller number of individuals who have systematically examined managerial work or behavior frequently have
been outside the United States, with varied backgrounds and with a
primary interest in identifying the nature of managerial work by studying what managers do (Stewart, 1982b). Typically, the studies use
observations or diaries to obtain data. Almost never has there been an
accompanying interest in the linkage of this stream of work with
performance. Perhaps the best-known illustration of the leadership
research is the early Ohio State work and its derivatives (see Yukl, 1989,
for a review). Among the best-known illustrations of the managerial

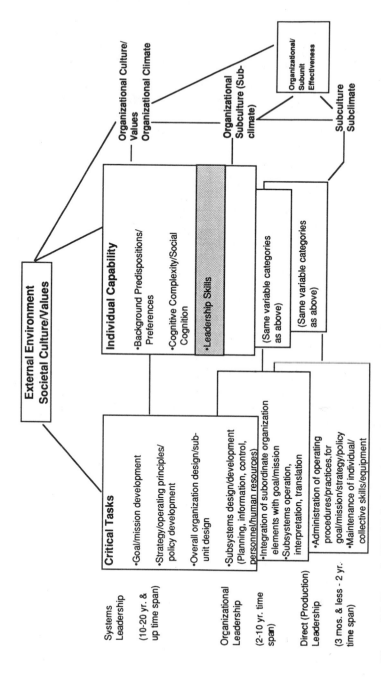

Figure 8.1. Extended Multiple-Organizational-Level Leadership Model

Note: For simplicity, some direct relationships, feedback, and arrowheads are not shown.

work/behavior stream is the research of Mintzberg (1973/1980) and Stewart (e.g., 1982a, 1982b).

There also is a stream of research that has aspects of both of those just mentioned. It focuses on the classical management functions or their analogues (e.g., planning, organizing, staffing, directing, and controlling), using a variety of methods and sometimes relating them to outcomes (see Carroll & Gillen, 1987). These classical management functions tended, in the eyes of many, to become almost passé when Mintzberg (1973/1980) argued that managerial settings and the manager's work were so dynamic and fragmented that managers really had neither the time nor inclination to engage in these highly systematic and abstract functions. This view was reinforced by the work of those such as Kotter (1982a) and Lombardo and McCall (1982), who showed the dynamic, apparently unplanned nature of much managerial work.

However, Carroll and Gillen (1987) have made the point that this conclusion misses the mark. Their careful review of the literature (much of it different than that covered by Mintzberg) showed that the functions were carried out, although not in as systematic a way as the management texts suggested. Planning tended to take place in short bursts in elevators, when people dropped by the office, and so on, as did the other functions. Carroll and Gillen then developed a model that linked the management functions with other aspects of managerial jobs.

These three largely separate research streams are clear examples of differing purposes and stakeholders (as discussed in Chapter 4)—relating leadership to outcomes versus finding out what a manager's job is like or what a manager does, versus examining the viability of the traditional management functions as set forth by authors such as Fayol (1949). And, of course, accompanying these different streams, purposes, and stakeholders has been sniping back forth concerning the usefulness of each (e.g., Carroll & Gillen, 1987; Mintzberg, 1973/1980, 1983; Snyder & Wheelen, 1981).

Recently, there have been attempts to reconcile various aspects of these differing approaches in order to develop a more comprehensive picture of managers and leaders (or management and leadership). Two recent examples by individuals outside North America are reviews and future research suggestions by Hales (1986, 1988) and Stewart (1989). These works are useful in terms of providing a feel for the literature and gaining insight into the perspectives of these non-North American scholars. They also are useful for emphasizing what for us is the special importance of being sensitive to differences between the critical task emphasis in Chapter 5 and the focus on leader behaviors and skills in this chapter.

LEADERSHIP BEHAVIOR TYPOLOGIES

Setting aside for the moment the definitional questions involved in how we are using the term *leadership* and what the difference is between "behavior" and "skill," let's start this discussion of leader behavior typologies with the nature of the issue examined and the importance of level of abstraction in typologies. These are influenced by a number of considerations (see Yukl, 1989). First, the categories used are abstractions, rather than tangible real-world attributes. This means, consistent with Chapter 4, that the purpose of the typology is important. A typology developed to focus on managerial effectiveness historically has emphasized different aspects than one used to describe observations of managerial activities. And especially for us, a typology to catalog leader critical tasks would differ from the previous two.

Second, even where the purpose is the same, the aspects can be more or less general. Some typologies contain a small number of broadly defined categories, whereas others contain a larger number of more specific ones. For instance, in an early version of the Ohio State work (Fleishman, 1953), initiating structure is broadly defined, whereas clarifying work roles would be a middle-range category and goal setting would be a narrowly focused category. Goal setting is a component of clarifying, which in turn is a part of initiating structure (Yukl, 1989). These differences have sometimes been lost sight of and we find mixed aspects and levels of abstraction in some typologies.

A typology most useful for the purpose of concentrating on situational aspects of effectiveness would need to focus most on the middle level of abstraction to reflect situational contingencies across a wide range of leaders. The argument is that if the categories are too few and/or too broad, they probably won't pick up the situational nuances. If they are too narrow, there are so many of them that it's hard to develop theories. For appraising performance or training purposes, we might well want narrower categories to help in more precise evaluation or specific skill development. For example, Alban-Metcalfe (1984) shows how very specific "micro-skills" are particularly useful for describing a leader's performance appraisal behaviors, and Wright and Taylor

(1984) develop such micro skills for a variety of management training exercises.

Third, the method used to develop the typologies can influence their nature and level of abstraction. For instance, factor analysis, rater judgments, and theoretical deductions all can be used to develop categories. Each of these can have a differential impact on the nature of the categories and their level of abstraction.

For us, these arguments are most important in two ways. First, they help us keep in mind differences between the leader behavior and skill typologies in this chapter and the critical tasks in Chapter 5. Second, they guide our thinking in terms of how broad or narrow the level of abstraction should be at the various organizational levels.

Mintzberg's Typology

Henry Mintzberg's (1973/1980) typology is now so well-known that it almost needs no description. However, I briefly summarize it below primarily to show the linkage between higher and lower levels of abstraction and to serve as a base to compare against other typologies. Mintzberg developed three higher-order categories to classify 10 roles used to code the content of activities he observed over a two-week period from watching five CEOs. These categories and roles are summarized as follows:

Interpersonal Category

- *Figurehead*—attend ceremonies and represent the organization/work unit to external constituencies
- *Leader*—motivate subordinates and integrate the needs of subordinates and the needs of the organization/work unit
- *Liaison*—develop and maintain contacts with outsiders to gain benefits for the organization/work unit

Informational Category

- *Monitor*—seek and receive information of relevance to the organization/ work unit
- *Disseminator*—transmit to insiders information relevant to the organization/work unit
- *Spokesperson*—transmit to outsiders information relevant to the organization/work unit

Decisional Category

- *Entrepreneur*—seek problems and opportunities and take action with respect to them
- *Disturbance handler*—resolve conflicts among persons within the organization/work unit or between insiders and external parties
- *Resource allocator*—make choices allocating resources to various uses within the organization/work unit
- *Negotiator*—conduct formal negotiations with third parties such as union officials or government regulators

I touched on Mintzberg's work in Chapter 2 and pointed out that a few studies had used a questionnaire to measure his roles. The specific items in those questionnaires, of course, tap an even greater level of specificity than each of his 10 roles, which in turn are more specific than his three interpersonal, information, and decisional categories. Of course, the specific questionnaire items were summed by role to enhance reliability and validity. Mintzberg's three higher-level-of-abstraction categories are useful in interpreting and grouping the more specific midlevel roles as a whole.

Luthans and Associates' Typology

A more recent typology that builds on Mintzberg, among others, is that by Luthans and his colleagues (e.g., Luthans, Hodgetts, & Rosenkrantz, 1988; Luthans & Larsen, 1986; Luthans & Lockwood, 1984; Luthans, Rosenkrantz, & Hennessey, 1985). Consistent with arguments in Luthans (1982), this typology is based on social learning theory. The emphasis is on behavioral observation, in combination with several other approaches. Besides the work of Mintzberg, these other approaches include a literature review recognizing especially the work of Kotter (1982a); obtaining of critical incidents; comparison with traditional leadership instruments, such as the LBDQ-Form XII (Stogdill, 1974); and comparison with an early version of the Management Behavior Survey (MBS) developed by Yukl and his colleagues (see Yukl & Nemeroff, 1979).

The offshoot of this multimethod work was the development of the Leader Observation System (LOS) with four higher-level-of-abstraction "activities"—routine communication, traditional management, networking, and human resource management—each with two

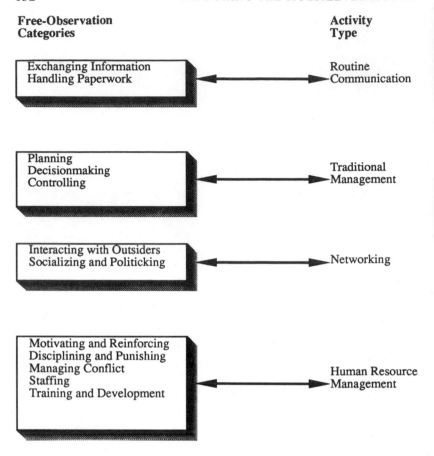

Figure 8.2. Leader Descriptive Categories and General Activities Developed by Luthans and His Colleagues

Source: Based on Luthans, Hodgetts, & Rosenkrantz (1988).

to five "descriptive categories," corresponding to our midlevel of abstraction (see Figure 8.2). And of course, each of these descriptive categories contained a number of specific behavioral descriptors. This observational instrument was designed to be used to supplement questionnaire measures.

A part of the work also included relating the activities and categories to aspects of leader performance and to an examination of top-, middle-, *what do successful managerials do?*

and lower-level managers (Luthans, Rosenkrantz, & Hennessey, 1985). For top-level leaders as compared to others, Luthans and his associates found more managing conflict, decision making, and planning. They found less socializing/politicking, controlling, and staffing. These findings appear to contain no surprises, although I don't want to make too much of them because they lack an organizational-level conceptual framework and we are not yet sure how Luthans and associates' levels compare with those of others.

Yukl's Typology

The Yukl (1987a, 1987b, 1989) typology is state-of-the-art in terms of recency and comprehensiveness. It has been designed to deal with the kinds of points described earlier and its basic purpose is to be used across different organizational situational contingencies to predict various outcomes. Thus that purpose is consistent with the one pursued here, as an aspect of individual leader capability in the extended multi-level model. The Yukl typology uses the earlier-mentioned Yukl work as well as that of several other major typologies as a base, as summarized in Table 8.1.[2]

Figure 8.3 shows the latest version of the typology with its 4 general (higher level of abstraction) categories and 11 mid-range categories (each containing eight or nine specific items). Table 8.2 lists the 11 behaviors, together with brief definitions that are reflected in the specific items. Each of these mid-range behaviors also contains both an internal and external organizational focus. In this, they are consistent with work arguing for the importance of both vertical and lateral internal and external leadership (e.g., Hunt, Baliga & Peterson, 1988; Hunt et al., 1981; Osborn et al., 1980). Note that Yukl has reconfigured some of his 13 behaviors (e.g., harmonizing, developing, interfacing) in Table 8.1 in his later 11 behaviors shown in Table 8.2 and Figure 8.3. This is typical of his ongoing revision of the instrument as he obtains new information and data.

I have devoted so much space to Yukl's work because of its state-of-the-art nature. Questionnaire measures of concepts have taken a real beating lately from a wide range of behavioral scientists. Yukl is aware of the arguments raised and has tried to deal with them, based on his background as a methodologically oriented objectivist psychologist. I return to this point later in the chapter, after discussing some leadership skills (or competencies) typologies.

Table 8.1
Comparison of Yukl Typology with Earlier-Developed Ones

Integrating Taxonomy	Yukl	Morse & Wagner	Stogdill	Bowers & Seashore	House & Mitchell	Luthans & Lockwood	Mintzberg	Mahoney et al.	Page
Supporting	Consideration	****	Consideration	Leader Support	Supportive Leadership	Socializing		****	****
Consulting & Delegating	Decision Participation; Delegation	****	Tolerance of Freedom	****	Participative Leadership			****	****
Recognizing & Rewarding	Praise; Structuring Rewards	****	****	****	****	Motivating & Reinforcing		(Evaluating)	
Motivating	Performance Emphasis; Inspiration	Motivating & Conflict Handling	Production Emphasis	Goal Emphasis	Achievement oriented Leadership		Leader Role	Supervising	Supervising
Harmonizing	Conflict Mgt.; Inter. Facil.		Integration	Interaction Facilitation	****	Managing Conflict		(Staffing)	
Developing	Training; Counseling	Providing Development	****	Work Facilitation	****	Training & Developing			
Clarifying	Clarifying; Goal Setting	****	Initiating Structure		Directive Leadership				
Planning & Organizing	Planning; Innovating	Organizing & Coordinating				Planning & Cooordinating	Resource Allocator; Entrepreneur	Planning	Planning & Organizing; Strategic Planning

154

Problem Solving	Problem Solving	Strategic Problem Solving	Role Assumption: Demand Rec.	****	Problem Solving & Deciding	Disturbance Handler	Supervising, Evaluating	Decision Making
Informing	Information Dissemination	Information Handling	****	****	Exchanging Information	Disseminator	****	****
Monitoring	Monitoring Operations	****	****	****	Monitoring/Controlling	Monitor	Investigating	Monitoring Indicators; Controlling
Representing	Representing	****	Representing; Influencing Superiors	****	Interacting with Outsiders	Spokesman, Negotiator	Representing, Negotiating	Representing
Interfacing	External Monitoring	Managing Environment & Resources	****	****		Liaison	Coordinating	Coordinating

Source: Yukl (1987a), p. 38. Reprinted by permission.
Note: **** Indicates behavior not included in the earlier typology

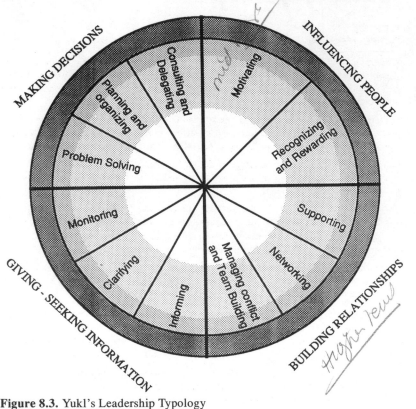

Figure 8.3. Yukl's Leadership Typology

Source: Adapted from Gary A. Yukl (1989), *Leadership in Organizations* (2nd ed., pp. 129). Englewood Cliffs, NJ: Prentice-Hall. Reprinted by permission.

LEADERSHIP SKILLS/ COMPETENCIES TYPOLOGIES

We can think of skills and competencies as similar concepts. Let's define them generally as the ability to translate knowledge into action that results in desired performance (for a detailed discussion of competencies, see Klemp, 1979). Let's also keep in mind the level-of-abstraction notion in organizing this section. Like the leader behavior typologies, the skill typologies vary in their level of abstraction from quite general to very specific. As we shall see, in some cases skills and leader behaviors are linked together by conceptualizing the skills as specific ways of carrying out higher-order behaviors. A good place to

Table 8.2

Definition of Behavior Categories in Yukl's (1989) Typology

Networking: Socializing informally, developing contacts with people who are a source of information and support and maintaining relationships through periodic interaction, including visits, telephone calls, and correspondence, and attendance at meetings and social events.

Supporting: Acting friendly and considerate, showing sympathy and support when someone is upset, listening to complaints and problems, looking out for someone's interests, providing helpful career advice, doing things to aid someone's career advancement.

Managing conflict and team building: Encouraging and facilitating constructive resolution of conflict, fostering teamwork and cooperation, and building identification with the organizational unit or team.

Motivating: Using influence techniques that appeal to emotions, values, or logic to generate enthusiasm for the work and commitment to task objectives, or to induce someone to carry out a request for support, cooperation, assistance, resources, or authorization; also, setting an example of proper behavior by one's own actions.

Recognizing and rewarding: Providing praise, recognition, and tangible rewards for effective performance, significant achievements, and special contributions; expressing respect and appreciation for someone's accomplishments.

Planning and Organizing: Determining long-range objectives and strategies for adapting to environmental change, identifying necessary action steps to carry out a project or activity, allocating resources among activities according to priorities, and determining how to improve efficiency, productivity, and coordination with other parts of the organization.

Problem solving: Identifying work-related problems, analyzing problems in a systematic but timely manner to determine causes and find solutions, and acting decisively to implement solutions and deal with crises.

Consulting and delegating: Checking with people before making changes that affect them, encouraging suggestions for improvement, inviting participation in decision making, incorporating the ideas and suggestions of others in decisions, and allowing others to have substantial discretion in carrying out work activities and handling problems.

Monitoring operations and environment: Gathering information about the progress and quality of work activities, the success or failure of activities or projects, and the performance of individual contributors, also, determining the needs of clients or users, and scanning the environment to detect threats and opportunities.

Informing: Disseminating relevant information about decisions, plans, and activities to people who need it to do their work, providing written materials and documents, answering requests for technical information, and telling people about the organizational unit to promote its reputation.

Clarifying roles and objectives: Assigning tasks, providing direction in how to do the work, and communicating a clear understanding of job responsibilities, task objectives, deadlines, and performance expectations.

Source: Gary A. Yukl (1989), *Leadership in Organizations* (2nd ed., pp. 129-130). Englewood Cliffs, NJ: Prentice-Hall. Reprinted by permission.

start this discussion is with the classic, broadly conceptualized trium-virate of skills set forth by R. L. Katz (1955, 1970) and Mann (1965) and first mentioned in Chapter 2.

Technical, Human Relations, and Conceptual Skills

I call these classic because virtually any discussion of leader or manager skills treats them and they are now covered in virtually any elementary management or organizational behavior (OB) text. Let's define them as follows:

(1) *Technical skills*—knowledge about methods, processes, procedures, and techniques for conducting a specialized activity, and the ability to use tools and operate equipment related to the activity

(2) *Human relations (interpersonal) skills*—knowledge about human be-havior and interpersonal processes; ability to understand the feelings, attitudes, and motives of others from what they say and do (social sensitivity, empathy); ability to communicate clearly and effectively (speech fluency, persuasiveness); and ability to establish cooperative and effective relationships (tact, diplomacy, etc.)

(3) *Conceptual skills*—general analytical ability; logical thinking; concept formation proficiency; conceptualization of complex and ambiguous relationships; creativity in problem solving and idea generation; ability to analyze events and perceive trends, anticipate changes, and recognize potential problems and opportunities (deductive and inductive reasoning)

Conceptually, Katz and others have argued that technical skills are most needed at the bottom leadership levels, conceptual skills at the top, and human relations skills are about equally needed at all three levels. Interestingly, given these categories' ubiquity it's surprising that there hasn't been very much empirical work on them. Mann (1965) did some, as did Pavett and Lau (1983). Results showed partial support for the hypothesized relationships, with increasing conceptual skills by level perhaps the most consistent finding (this finding should apply to the extended model, even recognizing that there is not exact correspond-ence between the levels used). I might note in passing that the Pavett and Lau (1983) study also included "political skills" as a fourth general category and found them to be equally important at all of their organi-zational levels.

This skill classification is at a relatively high order of abstraction and lends itself to sets of less abstract, lower-order skills. Its wide usage and underlying face validity makes it a useful conceptual anchor point in discussing different leader skill mixes. Let's now move to more specific sets of skills.

More Specific Skills

Mintzberg (1973/1980) talks about a skill typology in his widely cited book. However, although his 10 roles are frequently discussed in the literature, his skills are not. Essentially, he argues that the skills are needed to implement his roles. However, there is not a one-to-one correspondence between the skills and roles. Indeed, a comparison of the skills listed presently with the roles mentioned earlier in the chapter shows that skills such as *peer* and *introspection* appear useful for several roles.

The eight skills, with quick synopses, are:

* *Peer*—ability to enter in and maintain peer relations, networking, and so on
* *Leadership*—ability to deal with subordinates
* *Conflict resolution*—ability to mediate between conflicting individuals and to handle disturbances
* *Information processing*—ability to establish informational networks, find information sources, and so on
* *Decision making under ambiguity*—ability to find problems/opportunities, diagnose unstructured problems, jiggle parallel decisions, and so on
* *Resource allocation*—ability to choose among competing demands
* *Entrepreneurial*—ability to search for problems/opportunities and implement organizational change
* *Introspection*—ability to understand job and be sensitive to impact on organization

Pavett and Lau (1982) operationalized Mintzberg's skills in questionnaire form and found that only decision making was significantly related to leader job performance for middle- and lower-level managers. For present purposes, this finding is not as important as their use of this particular skill typology.

The preceding discussion sets us up for treatment of three additional typologies. These link skills at different levels of abstraction with each other or link leader behavior (or its equivalent) with leader skills where each is at a different level of abstraction.

Clement and Ayers's Typology

Consistent with the earlier discussion, Clement and Ayers (1976) were concerned that such dimensions as "consideration" and "planning" were at too high a level of abstraction but that neither would more narrowly defined dimensions be sufficient by themselves. Thus they used a systematic literature review to derive skill "dimensions," "elements," and "items." They developed nine dimensions each with two to three elements that, in turn, used several items. For example, there was an ethics dimension with individual behavior/values, professionalism, and organizational responsibility as elements. Then for each of five organizational levels they specified specific skill items that would tie back to the elements in the dimension. Particularly interesting was the fact that their items varied for each organizational level (although the dimensions and elements did not). Clement and Ayers estimated the relative importance of each of the dimensions at each level by counting the number of elements and items. Based on this reasoning, they concluded the following:

Increase in importance by level	*Decrease, or increase and then decrease*
• communication	• human relations
• decision-making	• counseling
• planning	• supervision
• ethics	• technical
	• management science

It's unfortunate that Clement and Ayers's work appeared only in technical report form and thus has not received wide coverage. It is also unfortunate that there does not seem to have been empirical followup. Although their "skill dimensions" are similar in many ways to various leader behavior dimensions, they are particularly notable for their inclusion of technical skill and ethics. The former was included in early work by Comrey, Pfiffner, and High (1954) and then did not receive much attention until considered more recently by Fiedler and Garcia (1987) and Podsakoff, Todor, and Schuler (1983), among others. Ethics has received even less attention as a leadership dimension. Finally, we can fit Clement and Ayers's nine skills into the earlier higher-order technical, human relations, and conceptual categories as follows:

Technical	*Human relations*	*Conceptual*
• technical	• communication	• decision making
• management science	• human relations	• planning
	• counseling	• ethics
	• supervision	

In summary, Clement and Ayers (1976) used nine "skills" varying in terms of dimensions, elements, and items, and levels of abstraction with different items used within elements across each of five organizational levels.

Boyatzis's Managerial Competencies Typology

A second skill typology is reported in a book by Boyatzis (1982). It has been widely cited and focuses on different types of managerial "competencies." Essentially, competencies are conceptualized in terms of types and levels. *Types* are associated with various aspects of behavior and an individual's capability to demonstrate such behavior. For example, planning competency is associated with such factors as setting goals, assessing risks, and developing a sequence of goal-related actions (Boyatzis, 1982). Competency *levels* (of abstraction) are conceptualized in terms of (a) the motive and trait level, (b) the self-image and social role level, and (c) the skill level. For planning at the motive/trait level, a person might desire to achieve goals as a reflection of improving performance; at the self-image/social role level the person would have a self-image of being deliberate and thinking ahead, and that image would tend to be projected in the social role; at the skill level (the ability to demonstrate a system and sequence of behavior that is functionally related to obtaining a performance goal), the person would tend to develop a plan of action, assess risks in achieving the plan, and so forth (Boyatzis, 1982).

Boyatzis used this competency type and level notion to derive empirically a number of competency clusters (such as human resource management, leadership, and goal and action) at the motive/trait, self-image/social role, and skill levels. For example, his leadership skill cluster consisted of self-confidence, use of oral presentations, conceptualization, and logical thought. Among other things, Boyatzis then examined the competency clusters related to entry-, middle-, and executive-level managerial samples.

Because there is not an organizational-level conceptual base, and because the competencies are unique to the Boyatzis framework, the specific findings are less important than his general conclusions and his use of differing levels of abstraction. First, different competencies are relevant at different organizational levels and the ways in which these emerge in specific behavior and action appear to differ. Second, the focus and orientation at each level are different enough that new competencies are needed and those useful at the previous level may actually impede performance. Essentially, these conclusions are consistent with the general orientation of the extended model and this book.

Some (e.g., Sashkin, 1990), are critical of aspects of the Boyatzis study, such as not entirely clear differentiation between traits and behaviors. Even so, this study is cited almost invariably when managerial or leader competencies or skills are discussed, and thus it needs to be mentioned. Conceptually it tends to reinforce the notion of level of abstraction and does suggest some *possible* ties among traits and behaviors, as well as emphasizing possible organizational-level differences. Basically, though, it is so different from the other work discussed here that its results are hard to compare very specifically.

Quinn's Competing-Values Typology

The third typology that I cover in this section is Quinn's competing-values leadership framework. It and the competing-values effectiveness approach in Chapter 5 are brothers under the skin, although this book emphasizes somewhat different aspects in each. The leadership framework uses a combination of values (orientations), leadership roles, and leadership competencies (see Quinn, 1988; Quinn, Faerman, Thompson, & McGrath, 1990). On the surface, Quinn's eight leadership roles appear much like Mintzberg's roles or the behaviors emphasized by Luthans and associates or Yukl. However, in addition to the inclusion of separate value and competency components, Quinn's conceptual base is very different and has substantial implications for the way in which the various dimensions are used. Figure 8.4 summarizes the various components. It shows four quadrants, each containing one of the models of organization mentioned in Chapter 5: human relations, open systems, internal process, and rational goal. The eight driving values or orientations for these are shown on the outer part of the diagram and are consistent with the organizational models.

The eight leadership dimensions—facilitator, mentor, and so forth—are shown inside the square. Immediately outside the square are numbered elements (3 to a leadership dimension, for a total of 24) termed *competencies* ("the knowledge or skill necessary to perform a certain task or role"). Again, we have more general and more specific levels of

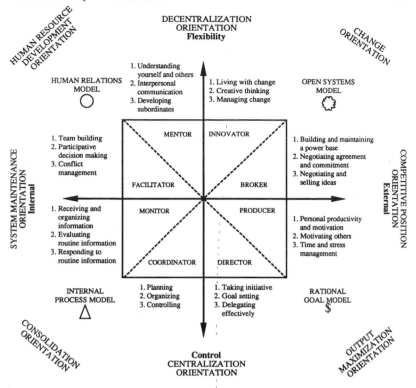

Figure 8.4. Quinn and Associates' Competing-Values Leadership Approach

Source: Adapted from Schermerhorn, Hunt, & Osborn, 1991, p. 477. Copyright © 1991 by John Wiley & Sons. Reprinted by permission.

abstraction—this time in terms of quadrants, roles, and competencies (as shown in the figure), with the roles and competencies each including separate items.

The part of this framework that most differentiates it is the "competing values" aspect. This perspective assumes that each value both complements the two values next to it and contrasts with the one directly opposite to it. Similarly, the roles both complement the ones next to and contrast with those opposite to them. The values overlap the roles and quadrants and help tie similar roles together.

The four models of organization are clearly different from each other and encompass the differing ("competing") values shown in the figure. For example, we want our organizations to be adaptable and flexible, but we want them also to be stable and controlled. These are assumed to be opposites in a leader's mind, and typically the assumption is that these opposites can't exist at the same time.

Quinn and associates assume that many leaders blindly pursue values in one of the models (i.e., carry out the accompanying roles) without considering the values and roles in the others. They argue that leaders need to be able to break out of this restricted line of thinking and to embrace other values and roles, particularly those opposite, at the same time or at least sequentially.

Such behavior calls for a whole new way of thinking and operating called "Janusian" (after the two-faced Roman god, Janus). As I show in Chapter 11, such thinking and behavior are both difficult and time-consuming to develop. Those that are successful at balancing the eight roles are called "master managers" (Quinn, 1988; Quinn et al., 1990).

Quinn and his associates have developed instruments to test various aspects of the model (see Quinn, 1988). Like Yukl's work, these are undergoing "running revisions." The individual items making up the eight dimensions are similar to the competencies listed in Figure 8.4. In the later Quinn et al. (1990) skill-building text, the authors emphasize development of the 24 individual competencies shown in the figure, and questionnaires are available. In terms of consistency with the earlier typologies, it appears reasonable to use the work reported in Quinn (1988). For individual developmental purposes (which I focus on in Chapter 11), Quinn et al. (1990) and accompanying material appear appropriate.

Quinn (1988) reports some interesting results that apply to multiple organizational levels. Based on his framework, descriptions of nearly 300 managers constituting five organizational levels were obtained (Quinn, 1988). Among other things, these managers were described in terms of how frequently they engaged in each of the role behaviors and how effective they were perceived to be. The researchers then separated individuals who scored very high or very low on perceived overall effectiveness and used cluster analysis to group together the individuals who had similar patterns of emphasis on the eight roles in the competing-values framework. The researchers then computed a profile for each of these groups, checked demographic variables and qualitative statements prepared by respondents, and finally prepared archetypes of effective and ineffective managers.

The results, in terms of organization level, are shown in Figure 8.5 for "effectives." Here we see the second managerial level characterized

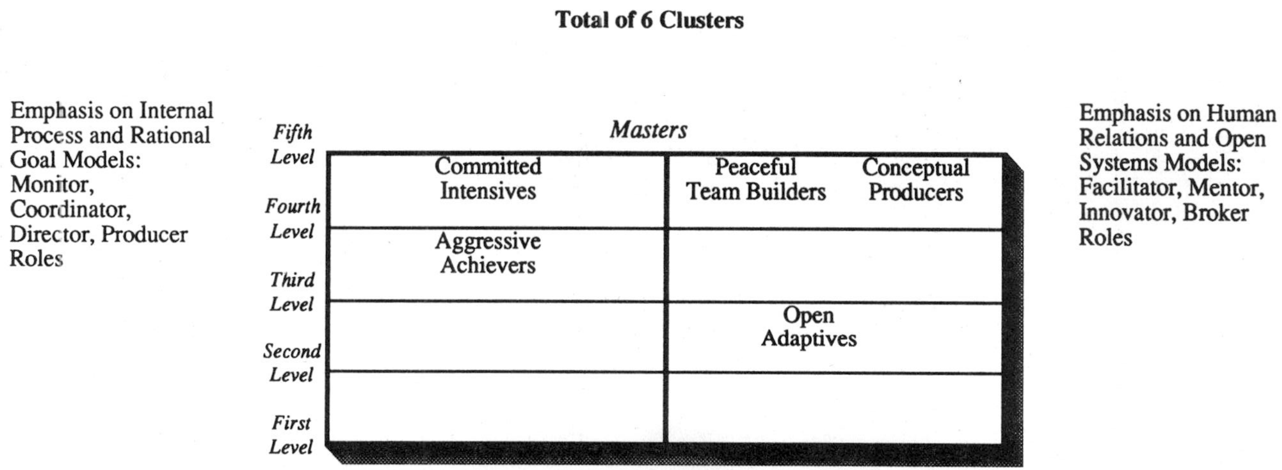

Total of 6 Clusters

Masters

Emphasis on Internal Process and Rational Goal Models: Monitor, Coordinator, Director, Producer Roles

Emphasis on Human Relations and Open Systems Models: Facilitator, Mentor, Innovator, Broker Roles

	Committed Intensives		Peaceful Team Builders	Conceptual Producers
Fifth Level				
Fourth Level	Aggressive Achievers			
Third Level				
Second Level		Open Adaptives		
First Level				

Figure 8.5. Organizational Levels of Effective Archetypes

Source: Based on Quinn (1988), p. 108.

by *open adaptives* (high scores on innovator, broker, facilitator, and mentor roles, emphasizing open-systems and human relations models; and near the mean on the other four roles, emphasizing internal process and rational goal models). The third level has *aggressive achievers* (high on the coordinator, monitor, producer, and director roles, with some strength in the innovator role).

The fourth level finds archetypes emphasizing each of the competing orientations and role groups. The *committed intensives* tend to be high on innovator, producer, monitor, and facilitator roles, and near the mean on mentor, director, and coordinator roles. In contrast, the peaceful team builders are above the mean on all the roles, except those for broker and producer, where they are near the mean. The *conceptual producers* also are high on six of the roles but are below the mean on the monitor role and are only at the mean on the coordinator role. The *master managers* at the top-management level show a balanced high score across all the roles.

The figure does not show results for ineffectives, for which there were a total of seven archetypes. Basically, however, they tend to be more extreme on their role groupings than effectives. Four of the seven archetypes were at the lower two organizational levels, and none was at the top.

Quinn's data basically argue that, rather than looking at each dimension separately, it is fruitful to consider them in paired opposites and look for trade-offs across the dimensions. The objective is to strive for balance. Because the data are time collapsed, one cannot tell empirically if the balance must be obtained simultaneously or across time. However, those at the top of the organization hierarchy tend to display it and are examples of Quinn's master managers.

There are several implications of Quinn and associates' work for the multi-level model. First, the work is conceptualized and operationalized in terms of varying levels of abstraction, systematically related. Second, it presents effective and ineffective leader archetypes by level based on the competing roles reflecting competing organizational models. As I argue later in this chapter and in Chapter 12, I believe such archetypes to be a particularly important way of combining leadership aspects at different levels of abstraction—the general archetype encompasses the more specific nuances. Third, Quinn's results suggest a high level of complexity at his top level if we assume that a leader who is able to balance competing leader roles as a master manager has to be more complex than those who can't or don't.

Finally, the study is one of the few recent ones to examine several levels of management systematically and empirically. This examination shows clear differences, and future work is needed to check such differences in various organizations and to tie them more tightly to the extended model.

BEHAVIORS AND SKILLS REVISITED

As I've shown, the treatment of leadership skills ranges from typologies linking them with roles or behaviors to typologies using skill dimensions that look very much like roles or behaviors in other typologies. This suggests that we would not be off the mark to consider altering a comprehensive leader behavior typology such as Yukl's to reflect skills. Indeed, Carroll and Gillen (1984) did something similar when they translated the management functions, such as planning, into skills.

Essentially, one could modify the response stem on items in Yukl's (1989) 11 mid-range leadership dimensions. Like most such instruments, these now use a frequency or magnitude response variation for each item; usually, to a great extent; sometimes, to a moderate extent; seldom, to a small extent; never, not at all; not applicable; and don't know. Note that these do *not* reflect how *well* a given behavioral item is performed. Simply performing something frequently or displaying a given magnitude of response is not the same as doing it skillfully or proficiently. Although there are somewhat different definitions of skills or competencies, it is difficult to conceive of one that does not reflect how *well* something is performed.

Thus I am arguing that we can tap the skill or competency aspect of what a leader does by using a response stem that reflects proficiency and not simply frequency/magnitude. One might be tempted to use both frequency and proficiency, and this is worth exploring.[3] Also, in tapping proficiency or how well a given behavior was done, one would need to be careful not to use a stem with "effectiveness" in it such as "describe how effective the leader was doing X." If one did this, it would be tautological with leader performance or effectiveness measures.

As previously mentioned, Yukl's typology is consistent with the range of literatures covering various aspects of leadership and managerial behavior as well as the management functions. Thus we can feel confident that it could serve as a useful base for tapping skills. This is so even though Yukl himself does not do this but emphasizes the earlier-mentioned technical, human, and conceptual skills in the skills treatment in his book. The higher-level-of-abstraction conceptual and human skills are clearly represented in his dimensions. Technical skills is less obvious, although a close look at the individual items suggests that it appears to be covered.

In closing this section, I refer readers to the developmental aspects of Chapter 11 for further discussion of leadership skills. I also refer you to Porter and McKibbin (1988), the AACSB (1987) Outcome Measurement Project, and Whetten and Cameron (1984) for additional treatments of leadership skills.

LEADERSHIP TYPOLOGIES, IMPLICIT LEADERSHIP, AND LEVELS OF ABSTRACTION

Regardless of whether one uses Yukl's or any other leadership behavior or skill typology, one must recognize the importance of implicit leadership theories or leadership prototypes as discussed in the previous chapter. Simply put, the concern is that good and bad leader prototypes (implicit leadership theories), once stored in long-term memory, will influence future leadership perceptions. Indeed, descriptions of leadership sometimes may be based as much on responders' implicit theories of "appropriate leader characteristics" as on the leader's "actual" behaviors (see Phillips, 1984; Phillips & Lord, 1982). In other words, implicit leadership theories will influence leadership descriptions to an unknown extent, whenever they are obtained.

Could one eliminate questionnaires and substitute observer observations to deal with this concern? The answer is no, because one simply would be substituting the observer's implicit theory for those of the questionnaire respondents. Even if this were not the case, given their relatively low cost, ease of administration, and extensive treatment in the literature, questionnaires would still be with us. And although one sometimes hears pleas for a moratorium on the use of questionnaires pending their improvements, this is simply unrealistic. Their use will continue unabated. Given this, let's look at a couple of broad ways of dealing with the issue. The first involves an objectivist orientation, whereas the second has a much more subjectivist (symbolic interaction) thrust. And though the discussion emphasizes questionnaires, much of it also is relevant to observational measures.

Objectivist Emphasis

Although discussion of various kinds of validity and reliability is the sine qua non of objectivist approaches, I would like to focus instead on the notion of accuracy. Here, consistent with current debates in the literature, the question is: What is the accuracy of leadership questionnaires? The literature suggests at least three approaches to answering this question. The first equates accuracy with reliability (stable and replicable factor structures can be used to develop highly reliable leadership scales). However, any systematic source of bias (such as implicit theories) can produce high internal-consistency reliability. The second approach considers accuracy in terms of consistent factor structures. However, these structures are possible to generate by implicit theories (Phillips & Lord, 1986).

Finally, experimental studies sometimes have been used to approach the accuracy question. Here leadership behavior is varied systematically across different leadership conditions and compared with the degree to which questionnaire descriptions reflect these effects (see Lord, Binning, Rush, & Thomas, 1978; Rush, Phillips, & Lord, 1981). Alternatively, observers have been asked sometimes to distinguish between the presence and absence of specific, conceptually equivalent behaviors in videotaped stimulus materials. Here subjects were found able to report accurately that a behavior was present or absent on the tape if the behavior was equally characteristic of effective and ineffective leaders. They could *not* make such a distinction for behaviors more characteristic of effective than ineffective leaders. There, accuracy and reliability were inversely related, as questionnaire items tapping behavior characteristics of effective leaders had a higher internal reliability than did those measuring behaviors equally characteristic of effective and ineffective leaders (see Phillips & Lord, 1986).

Distinctions among these three aspects of accuracy allow us to speak of *classification accuracy* and *behavioral accuracy*. Classification accuracy allows us to categorize or classify a person as a leader; whereas behavioral accuracy allows us to detect the presence of specific *types* of leader behavior (Phillips & Lord, 1986). Findings suggest that both "actual" behavior (as manipulated in laboratory treatments) and information concerning previous performance (performance feedback) tend to influence classification accuracy (see Calder, 1977). Once an individual is so classified, based on behavior and performance feedback, then a rater's implicit leadership theory is used to generate plausible behavioral ratings (Phillips & Lord, 1986). Thus a high degree of behavioral-level accuracy may be difficult to obtain.

Which kind of accuracy is required depends on the purpose of the leadership research, or the leadership theory or topic in question (once again, the emphasis on purpose in Chapter 4 is reinforced). As an example, classification-level accuracy typically would be appropriate for attributional approaches and leadership emergence. In contrast, all of the mainstream theories previously indicated and the extended multi-level approach call for behavioral-level accuracy to distinguish separate leadership dimensions. Often, behavioral-level accuracy will be required where leadership is an independent variable, and classification-level accuracy required where leadership is a dependent variable (Phillips & Lord, 1986).

The previous discussion suggests the importance of assessing whether classification- or behavioral-level accuracy is likely to be needed for a given purpose. At the same time, the discussion and points raised by Phillips and Lord suggest the importance of being sensitive to the possible confounding effects of such things as respondent knowledge of performance or tendencies toward rating leniency. Where there is an indication of this kind of confounding, results should be treated with appropriate caution.

Also:

- In some cases, it may be possible to develop elaborate respondent training concerning information encoding and the like to facilitate more accurate leader descriptions (of course, this typically is not very feasible).
- More feasible is the statistical correction for respondent tendencies to integrate leadership description information into a unified whole. Here, in addition to the responses involved in describing specific leadership dimensions, some overall measures should be obtained. One of these is a measure of respondent leniency (see Ganster, Hennessey, & Luthans, 1983; Schriesheim, Kinicki, & Schriesheim, 1979). Another is a global leadership rating (e.g., how well the leader in question fits a respondent's image of a leader; see Cronshaw & Lord, 1987). Once measures such as these are obtained, their scores are partialled from the more specific descriptions on the assumption that the global ratings reflect classification-level accuracy and that the residual represents behavioral-level accuracy. Of course this

technique needs to be used with caution, because the partialling removes more than just classification-level variance.

Other work suggests that more behaviorally specific measures may move us closer to behavioral-level accuracy. Gioia and Sims (1985) found that the measure of initiating structure (using the well-known LBDQ-Form XII instrument) was significantly susceptible to implicit leadership theory. However, more behaviorally specific measures did not have this susceptibility and indeed appeared to be relatively good reflections of the study's measure of "objective reality." Of course, one must not forget the earlier level-of-abstraction point that one must balance specificity and generality with the specific purpose. One may use a larger number of more specific measures to ameliorate implicit theories but move away from parsimony in the process.

I might note in passing that Gioia and Sims's measurement of consideration was not influenced by implicit leadership theory even though an inspection of its items suggests that they are not very behaviorally specific. However, the implicit theory manipulation was based on performance, which is probably less relevant for consideration. It may be that situational aspects inferred by the subjects from the laboratory setting of the study had more relevance for the description of initiating structure than for consideration here.

MORE SUBJECTIVIST EMPHASIS

The previous discussion has basically assumed that there is a leadership "reality" to be tapped and that implicit leadership theories keep us from that reality; somehow, we should be able to refine the measuring instrument or the respondents' perceptions to reflect such a reality. An important approach that uses questionnaires but has a more subjectivist focus is Misumi's PM theory (see Misumi & Peterson, 1985, 1987, in press). Misumi is a well-known Japanese leadership researcher with a long-term program emphasizing PM leadership. P (performance oriented) behavior prompts and motivates goal achievement. M (maintenance oriented) leadership behavior is directed toward prompting and reinforcing the tendency toward self-preservation (Misumi & Peterson, 1985).

On the surface, this sounds much like the initiating structure and consideration dimensions mentioned above and emphasized heavily in traditional United States leadership research. Indeed, this initial reaction has caused many U.S. researchers to treat PM theory, like initiating structure and consideration, as virtually passé. However, this is a gross misinterpretation.

For present purposes, we can think of the PM theory in terms of the genotypic notion I've emphasized. The P and M dimensions are interpreted by Misumi as the genotypic (general) or underlying aspects of leadership. These are inherent in the leadership process and will be present in all settings. However, the phenotypic (specific) aspects concern the manner in which a given dimension is interpreted within a given setting.

In other words, there is an emphasis on the differences between leader behaviors and the functions that they fulfill when experienced by subordinates. They are seen as helping to clarify some of the symbolic cues in the leadership interaction process that are most distinctive in various settings. Thus the emphasis is on a set of leadership functions experienced by subordinates in various settings, as opposed to a set of behaviors seen as objective stimuli. The settings vary within and between various societal cultures and within and between various organizational cultures (see Misumi & Peterson, in press; Smith & Tayeb, 1988).

As an example, initiating structure is typically measured and interpreted the same regardless of where it is used. In contrast, P, although the underlying goal-achievement function, is measured by different specific items depending on the specific setting in which it is operating. Indeed, Misumi and Peterson show a large number of different forms of the PM instrument as a function of particular settings. Recall here that Clement and Ayers's (1976) work was similar in that it used different items for each organizational level. This general point has also been mentioned by Hales (1986) in reviewing the managerial work literature.

Peterson (1985), although not using PM theory per se, conducted a study along related lines. Essentially, he found that some of the items in his questionnaire measures were seen by subordinates as situationally contingent to a given leadership situation in question (e.g., do the subordinates consider participation consequential in their particular setting?) and other items as more general and noncontingent.

Consistent with the discussion above, and like Sashkin (1984), Peterson argues that the *meaning* of a behavior is not the same as an abstract description of an action. For example, "giving work-related guidance to subordinates" might define adequately an important category of observable behavior. However, a simple frequency count of such behavior or a description at a higher level of abstraction will not. In summary, the previous discussion suggests that the higher the level of abstraction (the more general the leadership aspects), the more impact implicit theories are likely to have. This supports the use of relatively specific items for different settings where the items are embedded within umbrella concepts at a higher level of abstraction.

Of course, we don't want to forget the fact that questionnaire development calls for a high level of skill (as many can attest, it is not nearly as simple as it looks). Thus there is much to be said for using a well-developed and comprehensive instrument such as Yukl's (and as indicated previously my preference would be to use a skill-oriented stem, reflecting how well an action is performed). However, regardless of what instrument is used, one needs to be sensitive to the kinds of issues and possible solutions just discussed. Of crucial concern is the recognition of cognitive aspects, namely, implicit theories in interpreting results. We must not forget that we are not really getting at measures of leader behavior or skills. Instead we are getting perceptions of these reflecting respondents' cognitive structures (i.e., attributions and prototypes). As I have argued throughout, these are important in their own right and arc what respondents act on.

GESTALTS AND PROFILE DEVIATIONS

Given that one has been sensitive to the points above and obtained data concerning several different leadership behavior/skill aspects, then how should one deal with these data? I subscribe strongly to the arguments of those such as Quinn (1988) that examining leadership predictors one at a time, or even in a traditional multiple regression approach, probably does not capture reality very well. Rather, what we need are approaches that look at the effects of such predictors in terms of configurations, gestalts, or profiles. In Miller's (1981) terms: "Instead of looking at a few variables or at linear associations among such variables we should be trying to find frequently recurring clusters of attributes or gestalts" (p. 5). Miller and Friesen (1977) argue that these gestalts or archetypes represent relationships in a temporary state of balance and that they form holistic, ordered equifinalic patterns or configurations. Miller (1981) and Miller and Friesen (1984) provide a comprehensive discussion of such gestalts and include a treatment of alternative statistical approaches useful for gestalt development.

Among the more common of these approaches are various types of cluster analyses. Quinn's competing-values archetypes at different organization levels, discussed earlier, provide an illustration of such cluster analysis. Typically, a sample will be subdivided on the basis of a criterion such as effectiveness. Then, some form of cluster analysis will be used to identify the differing clusters or gestalts for each of the subdivided criteria (e.g., low versus high effectiveness gestalts).

A somewhat different alternative that focuses on a holistic perspective is profile deviation. As discussed by Venkatraman (1989), this approach is more precise than is the gestaltic one. Profile deviation calls for "degree of adherence to an externally specified profile" (Venkatraman, 1989, p. 433). As an example, if a leader's ideal leadership profile (e.g., the level of behavior along a set of leadership dimensions) is specified for a particular situation, then the leader's degree of adherence to such a profile will be positively related to effectiveness if there is a high degree of situation-leadership coalignment. Deviation from such an ideal profile implies a shortcoming in situation-leadership coalignment, leading to a negative impact on effectiveness. Because this approach calls for specifying an "ideal profile," it is less exploratory and calls for a higher degree of knowledge than does a gestalt approach, which interprets empirically derived clusters after the fact. Drazin and Van de Ven (1985) and Venkatraman and Prescott (in press) discuss the profile deviation perspective.

In terms of level of abstraction we can see this overall profile or gestalt as being at the most general level comprising a pattern of specific lower-level-of-abstraction individual components. As discussed here, although taking a holistic orientation, these approaches have neglected the temporal concerns so important in the extended model. I discuss these within a temporal context in Chapter 12.

SELECTED RESEARCH AND CONCEPTUAL LINKAGES WITH THE EXTENDED MODEL

A Good starting point in this section on linkages is to examine the relationships between the leadership dimensions here and the other individual capability components of the model. Referring to Figure 8.1, and Chapter 6, we can first examine linkages with various background variables and the kinds of leadership dimensions treated in the present chapter. Consistent with much of the literature we might expect generally modest relations with these background variables.

In terms of the predispositions, self-efficacy, and individual values aspects of our individual capability cluster, we might generally expect some relationships between these and the relative emphasis on various leadership dimensions. For example, we might speculate that need for socially oriented power would influence the relative emphasis on some dimensions. Relatedly, self-efficacy might influence the intensity or level with which some dimensions are pursued. Individual value preferences also might be expected to play a role in the dimensions emphasized (e.g., a preference for consulting and delegating; consideration of some of the value aspects in the Quinn et al., 1990, framework). Following the arguments in the chapter and elsewhere in the book, we might think of these relations in terms of gestalts or constellations of emphasis for both the other individual capability aspects and those for leadership. Also, we would want to be sensitive to the level-of-abstraction discussion in the chapter. An important question would be the relationship between these empirically devised gestalts and the conceptually derived higher-level-of-abstraction "umbrella."

Also, following arguments in the chapter, we might expect linkages between various leadership aspects and cognitive complexity. In Chapter 7, I used an example of differentiation, and both hierarchical and flexible complexity and expected emphasis on various aspects of leadership. Essentially, one would expect more differentiation and an emphasis on flexible integration for more cognitively complex leaders.

Of course, one would be interested not only in examining the previously mentioned kinds of linkages horizontally but in investigating direct and indirect linkages up and down the extended model's levels and domains. Here, some of the studies conducted earlier on leadership heterogeneity and homogeneity across organizational levels might be suggestive (e.g., Hunt, 1971; Nealey & Fiedler, 1968; Storm, 1977), especially within the context of the gestalts mentioned earlier.

As I develop further in Chapter 9, not only are the leadership aspects treated in this chapter important, but so also are the transformationally oriented ones discussed there. Certainly, as discussed in more detail in that chapter, the linkage between the more transactionally oriented leader behaviors in this chapter and the transformationally oriented ones in Chapter 9 is important, as is the use of both together to determine the relative impact of each.

As part of all this, following the speculations of Baliga et al. (1990), one might expect a tendency for the more routine or transformational leadership here to be used to influence lower-level behaviors within the present schemas of these individuals. In contrast, the more transformational leadership discussed in the next chapter would tend to be used to try to alter the lower-level schemas themselves.

Besides the linkages just discussed, the linkage of external environment and societal culture with leadership would be relevant. Osborn et al. (1980) and Hunt et al. (1981) provide suggestive arguments here.

In addition, the linkages between the extended model's critical task components and leadership are particularly important. As I've pointed out, essentially we can view the critical tasks as the "what" aspects of the leaders' positions, and the leadership behaviors/skills as ways in which the leaders carry out the critical tasks (the "how" aspects). Here again, the level of abstraction of the leader behavior/skills is important, this time in terms of its linkage with the critical tasks. We might speculate that this level of abstraction would differ by organizational level, with behaviors or skills becoming more broadly defined at higher organizational levels. If we consider this in terms of gestalts or archetypes, we might expect higher-level gestalts to be more complex, consisting either of different dimensions than those at lower levels or of a largely different mix of dimensions.

Along with the previous points, one could argue that organization design can influence lower-level discretion or opportunity to exert leadership, discussed at various points throughout the book. One also could expect that implicit organizing theories and organizational configurations almost certainly will be linked to leader behaviors/skills both horizontally and up and down domains and levels as leaders attempt to carry out these organizational configurations.

At the same time, we cannot forget the potential linkage of leadership and organizational culture. Although, as we shall see in Chapter 9, most of the literature concentrates on transformationally oriented kinds of leadership as influencing organizational culture, the role of the more traditional leadership aspects discussed in this chapter is important to explore. Consistent with their usage for lower-level cognitive schemas, these transactionally oriented aspects may be useful primarily as ways of maintaining the currently established organizational culture (or subcultures) as opposed to attempting to change the culture.

An additional important area is consideration of the possible linkage of leadership to effectiveness. Traditional leadership theories suggest such relationships, although they are more likely to be stronger if contingencies or indirect effects (via other variables) are considered. There also is evidence that the linkages are likely to be reciprocal, with both leadership and effectiveness influencing each other. Finally, I conclude this section with three more considerations. First, as always, I am concerned with examining across time the kinds of linkages I have discussed. Second, we are concerned with leadership team implications of various leadership aspects. Third, we are concerned with examining the role of implicit leadership theories and prototypes in various aspects of the model. Hunt et al. (1990) provide some suggestions in terms of prototype fit, and so forth.

CONCLUDING COMMENTARY

As a part of the coverage of leadership skill capabilities I've focused on a number of transactionally oriented behavior/skill typologies in this chapter. Although these generally are quite comprehensive, they place relatively little emphasis on charismatic and related notions. Thus I devote Chapter 9 to that transformationally oriented aspect of leadership.

The approaches in the present chapter use two or more levels of abstraction so that more specific dimensions are covered under the umbrella of higher levels of abstraction. In this way it's possible to get both breadth and depth in the treatment of behaviors and skills. Though sometimes skills or competencies are treated as more specific aspects of higher-level-of-abstraction behaviors or roles, they also quite often are used by themselves. In the latter case, they are especially likely to reflect similar dimensions to those of behaviors or roles. Indeed, such similarity led to my suggestion that it should be feasible to alter the stems on a comprehensive typology, such as Yukl's, to reflect how well something is done and not just indicate frequency or magnitude.

Along with the emphasis on level of abstraction, there are other points that are important. One of these separates job duties, or leader critical tasks, from the leader behaviors or skills related to them. Another point focuses on leader prototypes and implicit theories. Here there is evidence that specific behaviors/skills tailored to specific settings but embedded within a more genotypic framework are useful. They not only help minimize implicit leadership effects, but specifically recognize the pervasiveness of such effects within a symbolic interaction perspective.

Still another point is the question of the level of abstraction by organizational level and the linkage with gestalts or prototypes. Level of abstraction can theoretically serve as a useful umbrella concept for grouping large numbers of more specific aspects by organizational level. An important part of this is how consistent this might be with empirical groupings of dimensions in terms of gestalts or configurations. In other words, how similar or different are these likely to be with regard to the a priori conceptual umbrellas? Also, to what extent might such archetypes at higher levels encompass different, as compared with simply more, dimensions? The level-of-abstraction notion sensitizes us to these kinds of questions, along with the earlier ones.

Most of the work in this chapter has emphasized questionnaire measures. In contrast, a behavioral observation approach such as that used in Luthans and associates' typology might serve as a useful supplement in the extended model (although it is much more expensive and time-consuming). It's an example of a technique normally used in ethnomethodological/symbolic interaction-type work that has been used by Luthans et al. as a supplement to an objectivist questionnaire approach.

The dimensions identified in the work emphasized in the chapter are state-of-the-art and reflect good coverage of what is known. Thus they are useful as starting points, if not more, in objectively oriented leadership studies. Certainly it makes no sense to develop "homegrown" instruments in the absence of the information contained in this work. Even if specific items are used for specific settings, they should start with the kind of work illustrated here. Having said all this, I also must point out that authors such as Martinko and Gardner (1985) make the point that reliance on what is currently used restricts innovative ways of thinking that might lead to important new findings. Again, the purpose and nature of the knowledge needed are important considerations.

It's difficult to relate comprehensive treatments of leadership dimensions such as those in this chapter with the previous findings concerning differences or similarities by organizational level. I have argued earlier that findings from these studies are so inconsistent that they provide little specific basis for future work, except for the general theoretical underpinnings that have been developed as part of the extended multi-level model. Previous studies have typically had little or no conceptual emphasis and the leadership concepts have tended to differ substantially from study to study. In this they are much like the managerial work studies reviewed by Hales (1986). We can hope that the extended model conceptualization, together with the kind of state-of- the-art frameworks just discussed, can help with this problem. It is exacerbated still more as we go to more complex analytical techniques, such as cluster or profile analysis, to provide a more accurate reflection of our findings.

The leadership typologies covered in this chapter often include such a broad range of behaviors/skills that some would call them management typologies. Even so, as I have said, they underemphasize transformationally oriented aspects (which some consider to be synonymous with leadership). I turn to these in Chapter 9.

NOTES

1. Transactional leadership traditionally denotes a much narrower set of stable, day-to-day activities than the typologies included here. However, these typologies tend to put relatively less emphasis on the more change-oriented kinds of leadership typically covered in transformational, charismatic, or visionary frameworks. Thus, to reflect these points, I've termed the typologies in this chapter "transactionally-oriented." Similarly, in the next chapter, I've lumped together as similar transformational, charismatic, and visionary leadership typologies that have varying degrees of relation to each other, depending on their particular underlying conceptualizations.

2. Also, although Yukl does not consider Hale's (1986) piece, based largely on different literature, the two derive similar dimensions.

THE FAR SIDE

By GARY LARSON

Chronicle Features, 1982 Larson 11-2

"Wait! Wait! Listen to me! . . . We don't HAVE to be just sheep!"

9 Individual Capabilities— Transformationally Oriented Leadership Skills

Be absolutely accessible but always remote.

—James L. Fisher (1984, p. 54)

Charisma is that wonderful quality of being taken more seriously than you deserve.

—Kenneth Shaw
(quoted in Fisher, 1984)

Who can say that government is not about charismatic leadership after watching Ronald Reagan. It's important to build a consensus but leadership must first be bold and have a direction.

—Jesse Jackson (1990, p. 50)

You cannot manage men into battle. You manage things; you lead people.

—Grace Hopper, retired admiral
(quoted in Eigen & Siegel, 1989, p. 221)

In Chapter 8, as a part of the individual capability cluster, I looked at the various transformationally oriented leadership behavior/skill typologies based on work in leadership and managerial work and behavior. I continue that emphasis in this chapter by focusing on transformationally oriented aspects of leadership as another part of the individual capability cluster (see Figure 9.1).[1] Though recently developed, this area has become so important that it needs its own chapter.

BACKGROUND

Although laypersons can immediately conjure up an image of transformationally oriented leaders and, indeed, frequently think of all leadership in this way, serious study of the topic in organizations really only started to take hold in the 1980s. This is in spite of the work of the well-known sociologist Max Weber, who dealt with the topic many years ago. This general lack of attention is probably because of the perceived difficulty of operationalizing and measuring a concept often treated as mystical or metaphysical.

Charisma also is an easy concept to get caught up in nonproductive ideological arguments, which may have impeded its careful study. For example, it is not infrequently compared with participative or consensual leadership, which generates both strong positive and negative feelings (see, e.g., Little, 1988; Locke, Schweiger, & Latham, 1986; Sashkin, 1984, 1986; Zalesnik & Kets de Vries, 1975).

Weber's Contribution

As just implied, Max Weber's (1924/1947) charismatic work is seminal and it helps lay the groundwork for later efforts and for our own

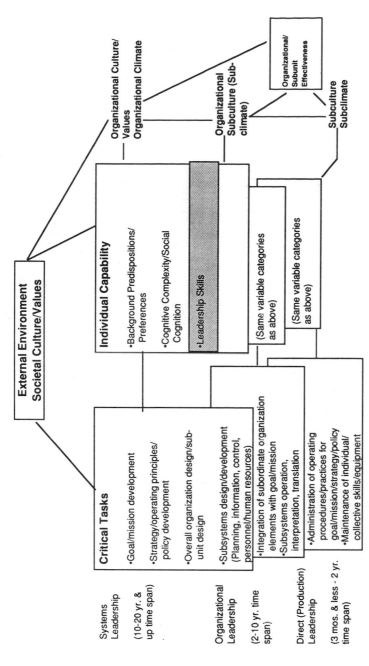

Figure 9.1. Extended Multiple-Organizational-Level Leadership Model
Note: For simplicity, some direct relationships, feedback, and arrowheads are not shown.

understanding (see Table 9.1). The table shows many assumed differences between charismatic and traditional and rational-legal forms of leadership (e.g., charismatic leaders are chosen by followers, or are extraordinarily gifted). Based on Weber's work, political scientists and sociologists struggled for some time with three key charismatic issues whose answers have influenced current work (Conger & Kanungo, 1988):

- What is the locus of charisma? It resides in the leader and his/her relational and attributional relations with followers.
- Does charisma only reside outside bureaucracies? It resides either outside or within.
- Does charisma apply outside religious institutions? It applies to both religious and secular institutions.

TRANSITIONS AND CURRENT MAJOR DIRECTIONS

In spite of the just-mentioned work by sociologists and political scientists, it wasn't until recently that organizational scholars and traditional leadership researchers became seriously interested in transformationally oriented research. This research has taken off in two related but separate directions—an examination of transformationally oriented versus transactional leadership, and a comparison of "leaders" to "managers" (or leadership to management).

The work of the well-known political scientist James McGregor Burns (1978) was important in developing current transformationally oriented leadership thinking, as was the theoretical model developed by Robert House (1977). The leader-versus-manager focus was emphasized by Zaleznik (1977) more than a decade ago, and has led to considerable later work. I briefly discuss these influential works for each direction and then look at follow-up work particularly appropriate for the extended model.

Transformational/Transactional Leadership

Burns notion of transformational leadership is related to, but not identical with, charismatic leadership, or what he called "heroic" leadership (because he felt that the usage of *charisma* had lost its

Table 9.1
Summary of Weber's (1924/1947) Charismatic Authority Conceptualization

	Theoretical Systems of Authority		
Key Distinguishing Features	*Charismatic*	*Traditional*	*Rational-Legal*
	Based on faith in leader's exemplary character. Set apart from the ordinary and treated as having superhuman or at least exceptional qualities of divine origin.	Based on established belief in sanctity of immemorial traditions.	Based on belief that obedience owed to legally established impersonal order.
	Emphasis on extraordinary and mystical	——————— Emphasis on logic ———————	
Rank vs. Personal Authority	Found in personal qualities of individual leader	——————— Invested in rank or office ———————	
	Chosen by followers because believe extraordinarily gifted	——— Appointed/elected under existing traditions and rules ———	
	Possesses personal power base (must perform miracles or heroic deeds)	——— Power bases: traditions, positions, expertise, rewards, coercion, rules ———	
Rational vs. Heroic	Origins in revolution (against "divine right of kings" or abstract legal statutes)	Origins from some divinity	Origins in revolution (against tyranny of tradition)
	Exclusive glorification of prophet and hero		

(continued)

Table 9.1
Continued

Key Distinguishing Features	Theoretical Systems of Authority		
	Charismatic	*Traditional*	*Rational-Legal*
	Seeks to overturn existing social order stagnant or in crisis		
	Must come from margins of society		
	Appears instantaneously		Gradual process of disenchantment
Stable vs. Transitory	Unstable and transitory	———————— May exist for centuries ———— Stable	
	Does not exceed founder's lifetime		
	Bridges transition from one to another existing order		
	Creates and institutionalizes new orders then fades or is institutionalized.		
	Must have success to sustain charisma		
	If institutionalized, assumes the form of traditional or rational-legal authority.		
Formal vs. Informal Organization	Organized informally through human relationships	——— Organized around permanent and formal structures ———	
	Commitment is to a powerful bond to leader	——— Commitment to set of rules or hierarchical bodies of authority ———	

Source: Summarized from Conger & Kanungo (1988); Eisenstadt (1968); Etzioni (1961); Schein (1980); and Willner (1984).

meaning). For Burns (1978), transformational leadership is a process where "leaders and followers raise one another to higher levels of morality and motivation" (p. 20). Transformational leaders go beyond basic emotions such as fear, jealousy, or greed to appeal to such ideals and moral values as justice and liberty. The leader seeks to satisfy the followers' higher needs and to engage the full person of the followers—resulting in a mutually stimulating and elevating relationship that converts followers to leaders and may convert leaders into moral agents (Burns, 1978, p. 4).

Burns asserts that not all leadership is transformational; some is transactional. Transactional leadership motivates followers by appealing to their self-interest. Pay, status, and similar kinds of rewards are exchanged for work effort and the values emphasized are those related to the exchange process. For details on these and other aspects of Burns's approach see Burns (1978), Conger and Kanungo (1988), Yukl (1989), and Bass (1990).

House (1977) proposed a model of charismatic leadership that differentiates the behavioral and personality characteristics of charismatic leaders and those of noncharismatics. Charismatic leaders are differentiated by dominance, self-confidence, need to influence, and strong conviction in the moral rightness of their beliefs. They also tend to articulate appealing ideological goals and to engage in behaviors that create a sense of success and competence in followers and that arouse motives relevant to mission accomplishment. House emphasized that, whereas traditional (transactional) leadership approaches emphasize instrumental aspects such as expectancies and cognition, charismatic leaders have their greatest effects on follower emotions.

For House, the charismatic leader's emotionally appealing goals and behaviors arouse followers' needs for achievement, affiliation, or power, and motivate task accomplishment. At the same time, these leaders also communicate high performance expectations and confidence that their followers can meet these. Thus there are increased follower expectations that their efforts will lead to performance accomplishments (Conger & Kanungo, 1988; House, 1977).

Bass and Associates

Bass (1985) considered earlier charismatic literature (especially that of Burns) in developing a transformational/transactional leadership theory for use by organizational leadership researchers. Although based heavily on Burns's approach, Bass's theory has at least three important differences.

First, Bass emphasizes expansion of the followers' portfolio of needs and wants. Second, unlike Burns, Bass allows for positive and negative transformation (e.g., Hitler was negatively transformational). Third, whereas Burns saw transformational and transactional leadership at opposite ends of a continuum, Bass does not. Instead, he sees transformational leadership ("leadership that broadens and elevates goals and instills subordinates' confidence to go beyond ordinary goals") as higher-order leadership. Such higher-order leadership is needed *in addition* to transactional leadership (leadership that gets things done through leader-subordinate exchange relationships) to go beyond accomplishment of ordinary, day-to-day activities.

Bass argues that transformational leadership consists of three dimensions: (a) *charisma* (the leader instills pride, faith, and respect, and has both a gift for seeing what is really important and a sense of vision that is effectively articulated; (b) *individualized consideration* (the leader delegates projects to stimulate and create learning experience, pays attention to followers' needs—especially of those who seem neglected—and treats each follower as an individual); and (c) *intellectual stimulation* (the leader provides ideas that result in a rethinking of old ways, that is, the leader enables followers to look at problems from many angles and to resolve those at a standstill). For Bass, then, charisma is a necessary (and extremely important) but not sufficient component of transformational leadership.

In terms of the transactional base, Bass defines two dimensions: (a) *contingent reward* (the leader is seen as frequently telling followers what to do to achieve a desired reward for their efforts); and (b) *management by exception* (the leader avoids giving directions if the old ways are working and intervenes only if standards or specifications are not met). Bass considers transactional leadership to be a necessary but not sufficient leadership condition.

Bass and his associates have been quite active in instrument development work and partial tests of his theory. Later work is moving beyond this in various ways, particularly with regard to leader developmental aspects (e.g., Avolio & Bass, 1988; Avolio & Gibbons, 1988). Essentially, Bass and his colleagues have found transformational leadership to predict incrementally beyond transactional leadership and to be related to such things as higher performance ratings, higher-performing work groups, higher potential for advancement, and more transformational and satisfied subordinates (e.g., Avolio & Bass, 1988; Avolio, Waldman, & Einstein, 1988; Bass, 1985; Hater & Bass, 1988; Perevia, 1987).

Although Bass's approach is encouraging, there are a number of criticisms (see Sashkin & Burke, 1990; Smith & Peterson, 1988: Yukl, 1989). First, Bass is using questionnaires prematurely, before we have sufficient knowledge of transformational leadership. More emphasis should be placed on descriptive interview and observational research. Second, leadership outcomes (e.g., follower enthusiasm) are indiscriminately mixed with leader behavior. What's needed is a clear and consistent conception of whether transformationally oriented leadership is a leader behavior or subordinate response to a behavior, and then consistent usage in the measuring instruments. Also: (a) the most "behavioral" of Bass's scales (individualized consideration) has items much like those of scales going back 40 years or more; and (2) some of the transactional items are written so as to imply an ineffective leader.

Third, Bass gives insufficient attention to the two-way aspects of leader-follower relations that are very important in Burns's approach. As we shall see, other recent approaches have attempted to deal with some of these criticisms.

Recent Work by House and Associates

House and his associates recently have conducted studies of the United States presidency based on aspects of House's (1977) theory, discussed earlier (see House, Spangler, & Woycke, 1990; House, Woycke, & Fodor, 1988) In addition to illuminating charisma in the presidency, the studies are useful in illustrating research not reliant on the kind of questionnaire measures just discussed and in highlighting different conceptions of charisma.

Earlier I mentioned that transformationally oriented leadership could be operationalized in terms of behavior of the leader or in terms of follower reactions to leader behavior. To these, House and his associates add observer assessments of leaders and their effects. And, consistent with the implicit leadership discussion in several places throughout this book, they argue that charismatic assessments may be biased by reputational factors and perceptions of performance. They define charisma as "influence exerted on followers' normative orientations, emotional involvement with the leader, and follower performance, that is due to the actual behavior of the leader" (House et al., 1990, p. 216).

House and associates examined a number of different aspects of presidential charisma (including its relation to need for power, achievement, and affiliation) using a variety of conceptualizations and measures. For example, charisma was measured both from content analysis of cabinet members' biographies and from classifications by well-reputed historians. An attempt was made to control for implicit leadership biases. Performance measures were obtained from historians' ratings and from several research coders using presidential biographies as a base. The power, achievement, and affiliation needs were obtained from content analysis of presidential first-term inaugural addresses, and additional sources were used to get at what I earlier termed the "socially directed" aspect of power. The range of approaches and measures used really is quite impressive and sensitizes us to ways of moving beyond questionnaire measures of transformationally oriented leadership.

Some of the more interesting findings were (a) considerable support for various aspects of House's (1977) theory; (b) a number of differences between effective charismatic and noncharismatic presidents; (c) no relationship between the various needs and charisma; and (d) that needs and charisma together accounted for 37% of the variance in presidential overall performance and up to 45% of the variance in selected aspects of overall performance. The latter findings are relevant for arguments at various places in this book concerning the extent to which leadership is consequential.

Leaders and Managers

So much for transformationally oriented leadership. Let's now look at the second direction mentioned earlier—leaders versus managers. Leader-manager definitional differences can be traced back to the military, where they have been institutionalized (see Segal, 1981). As noted earlier, Zalesnik (1977) emphasized such differences more generally in an article. He then followed this up with a book (Zalesnik, 1989) using case histories and psychoanalysis to expand his original theme—essentially, that managers try to avoid appealing to subordinates' emotions and are interested in maintaining an orderly, smooth-running status quo. Leaders, on the other hand, are interested in instituting change.

Others sharing a similar view are Bennis and Nanus (1985) and Kotter (1988, 1990), and I elaborate on Kotter's work later in the chapter. The leader/manager difference is very similar to the transformational/transactional leadership difference. However, its proponents typically don't emphasize charisma, and their backgrounds and literature bases often are different from those with a charismatic focus.

Kouzes and Posner

Kouzes and Posner (1987) illustrate the leader/manager theme well in their recent book. They feel that *charisma* is so overused as to not be useful, although they tend to be less negative about transformational leadership. They develop five leadership "practices," ranging from "challenging the process" and "inspiring a shared vision" to "encouraging the heart."

The authors derived these dimensions by asking a series of open-ended questions focusing on a leader's personal best—an experience in which the leader got something extraordinary accomplished in the organization. This may make these measures subject to the kinds of criticism leveled at Hertzberg's critical-incident methodology in the job satisfaction/motivation literature (see Pinder, 1984). The measures were supplemented with in-depth interviews. The contents of the data from these sources were content analyzed by two outside raters, and from this Kouzes and Posner developed their 30-item Leadership Practices Inventory (LPI).

Wrap-Up

I have conveyed the essence of earlier and current transformationally oriented and leader versus manager research. This provides the base for the more specialized treatments to follow. For those readers wanting additional very recent transformationally oriented reviews, I suggest several of the individual chapters in Conger and Kanungo (1988), as well as Avolio and Bass (1988), Conger and Kanungo (1987), or Conger (1989).

Turning now to the first of the more specialized treatments, I look at current developments in strategic leadership transformation, charisma, vision, and related notions.

STRATEGIC TRANSFORMATIONALLY ORIENTED LEADERSHIP

Let's start this section with consideration of the TPC (technical design, political allocation, cultural value problems) framework developed by Tichy and his associates (Tichy, 1983; Tichy & Devanna, 1986; Tichy & Ulrich, 1984a, 1984b).

TPC Framework

In contrast to much of the work in this chapter, which has a psychological or organizational behavior background, the TPC framework is based on the strategic management literature. Consistent with this background, Tichy and Devanna's (1986) application of the framework has a primary emphasis on *organizational* transformation and a secondary emphasis on *individual* transformation. Thus it can be linked to the more general organizational change or transformation literature (see Levy & Merry, 1986), as well as the transformationally oriented leadership literature in this chapter. It also fits nicely with a recent visionary piece by Robbins and Duncan (1988), which derives a model with a number of similarities to the TPC one.

More specifically, Tichy and Devanna (1986) are interested in how strategic leaders transform or revitalize organizations so that they can deal with the often dramatic and turbulent changes that they are facing, or that their leaders anticipate them facing in the future. Examples include increased competition (especially foreign), rapid technological change, and changes in societal culture.

The basic framework, emphasizing organizational dynamics has five phases:

(1) *a trigger event*—a crisis or realization by the transformational leader that events call for movement beyond the status quo

(2) *a felt need for change*—the trigger must lead to a felt need for change by key actors

(3) *creation of a vision*—the transformational leader must convey the vision of a desired future state

(4) *mobilization of commitment*—a critical mass of people must make the vision happen

(5) *institutionalization of change*—consistent with Weber (Table 9.1), a new organizational culture must be developed to reinforce the vision (I have more to say on this later in this chapter and in Chapter 10)

Accompanying the phrases above, if the transformational process is to be successful, are three individual phases (see Bridges, 1980):

(1) *endings*—individuals must recognize that traditional assumptions/behaviors are no longer appropriate
(2) *neutral zone*—reorientation by completing endings and beginning new patterns
(3) *new beginnings*—if there is successful movement through the neutral zone, then the transformation can be carried out

Tichy and associates suggest that in playing out their role across the phases of the organizational transformation model, strategic leaders need to (a)have a thorough understanding of the technical, political, and cultural aspects of the TPC framework; (b) articulate new values and norms and use multiple action levers (e.g., role modeling, symbolic acts) to support transformational changes; and (c) as Kenny Rogers would say, "know when to hold and when to fold" or when to push and when to back off and, when pushing, to make quick decisions (see Tichy & Ulrich, 1984a).

Also, based on case studies, Tichy and Devanna (1986) derived seven characteristics differentiating transformational and transactional strategic leaders. Essentially, the transformational leaders tend to identify themselves as change agents and emphasize visions embodying change, to take risks and empower others, and to be cognitively complex.

Conger and Kanungo's Framework

If we compare Conger's (1989) recently developed four-stage charismatic model, summarized in Figure 9.2, based on related work by Conger and Kanungo (1987, 1988), we see many similarities across the whole cycle with the framework just discussed. However, individual phases/stages differ somewhat. Conger's (1989) work is based on extended case studies of charismatic and noncharismatic strategic leaders.

Conger sees each stage as requiring differing leadership behaviors or skills. Also, for him the extent to which the leader is seen as charismatic

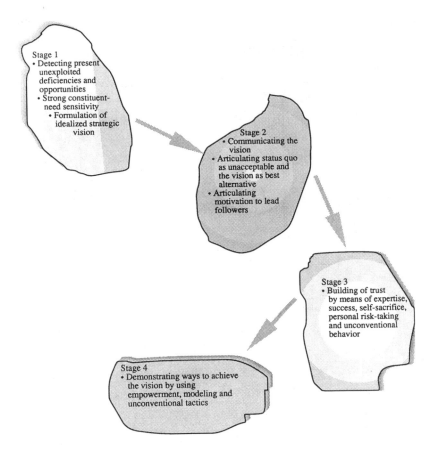

Figure 9.2. Conger's Four-Stage Charismatic Leadership Model
Source: Based on Conger (1989), p. 27.

depends on how many of the behaviors are exhibited, their intensity, and their relevance to followers. For example, just demonstrating a vision, in the absence of other behaviors, would not be enough to ensure charisma. Indeed, Conger shows some examples of charismatic versus noncharismatic visions.

Most recently Conger and Kanungo (1990), have developed preliminary questionnaire measures based on a broader, three-stage articulation of their model in terms of environmental assessment, vision formulation, and implementation. The two researchers derived six dimensions reflecting subordinates' attributions of charisma to their leaders. The following dimension labels convey the essence of the dimensions and suggest also a high level of consistency with Tichy and Devanna's work:

- vision and articulation
- environmental sensitivity
- unconventional behavior
- personal risk
- sensitivity to member needs
- not maintaining status quo

I should mention also that the overall measure had a wide range of relationships from low to high with more traditional people, task, and participative leadership and was correlated 0.66 with the charisma dimension of Bass's work.

Sashkin: Visionary Leadership

Besides the work just cited, Sashkin and his associates have actively been involved with what they call a "visionary" strategic leadership framework (see Sashkin, 1988; Sashkin & Burke, 1990; Sashkin & Fulmer, 1988; Sashkin & Sashkin, 1990). This visionary leadership framework uses questionnaires to measure leadership and other dimensions, and both descriptions of the framework and the questionnaires have been refined over time to reflect new empirical data and evolutions in thinking.

Essentially, in the visionary leadership framework, strategic leaders believe they can have a major impact on the organization by empowering organization members to realize the leader's long-range organizational vision. The leaders do this by developing or modifying organizational cultures (they are long-term culture builders). The visions and cultures created by visionary leaders strengthen and support four critical organizational functions identified by Parsons (1960). The vision- and culture-creating process is carried out by means of five leader behaviors or skills derived from Bennis and Nanus (1985). Thus the approach emphasizes leader personal characteristics, organizational settings within which visionary leaders act, and specific actions that they take to build vision and culture.

The personal characteristics are similar to those discussed at other places in this book—socially oriented power, efficacy, and a questionnaire measure of Jaques's time span of discretion notion. These are involved in the leader's impact belief, and the empowerment of followers to carry out the long-term vision.

The organizational setting variables are questionnaire measures involving the functions of adapting, goal attainment, coordinating, and cultural maintenance. The visionary leadership behaviors consist of focusing attention on the vision; communicating the vision personally; demonstrating trustworthiness; displaying respect; and taking risks. Although the framework is more comprehensive than the previous ones in terms of its three categories of variables, we can see similarities in terms of such aspects as emphasizing vision, taking risks, communicating trust, and the like (I could draw more explicit comparisons had the visionary leadership dimensions been included in the earlier-mentioned Conger and Kanungo instrument development work). The visionary framework's personal characteristics also are similar to some of those in the previously mentioned work of House.

The visionary framework is quite explicit in terms of organizational culture building. For example, recent work (see Sashkin & Sashkin, 1990) examines this framework to predict a questionnaire measure of various aspects of organizational culture in schools (I have more to say about organizational culture in Chapter 10).

Agenda Setting and Network Building

If this chapter has done nothing else, it has emphasized vision—this, in one way or another, cuts across the chapter's content. Accompanying the vision have been ways of communicating it, operationalizing it, and so on. Essentially, these discussions look remarkably like Kotter's (1982a, 1982b) early treatment of general managers in his widely cited work. However, instead of speaking of vision and charisma, he talks about agenda setting and network building—activities that appear more down-to-earth and doable than vision setting and transforming organizations. He describes similarities and differences in agenda-setting and network-building activities for a sample of 15 "successful" general managers. They had profit center responsibilities for revenues from about one million to about one billion dollars. In terms of hierarchical position, they appeared to be located at SST level IV and higher.

Kotter's agendas tend to be unwritten, less detailed concerning nances, more detailed concerning strategies, to cover a broader time horizon (both short and long), and to be less rigorous and logical than traditional formal strategic plans. And unlike the formal plans, typically generated hierarchically from below as a part of "strategic planning" (see Hunsicker, 1980), these agendas were developed and implemented through informal networks.

In terms of network building, Kotter's general managers used as wide a set of people as possible. Thus they tended to develop relationships (of varying duration and intensity) with such parties as financial experts; bosses (and/or board of director members); peers (and their bosses and subordinates); immediate subordinates; their subordinates' subordinates; government; press; public; and customers, suppliers, and competitors. Once the agendas and networks were established the leaders used the networks to help implement the agendas. This process called for using interpersonal skills, budgetary resources, and information to influence people (any and all in the network) and events—directly and indirectly. In using the network, the leaders were attempting to get some action on agenda items that would not be accomplished without intervention on the leader's part. The people approached could provide help, often uniquely so. These leaders worked on shaping the "setting" of the network to encourage teamwork and so forth, using such formal tools as planning processes and organization structure, as well as more informal means.

I must admit that this description struck me as remarkably similar to the previous treatment of transformationally oriented leadership—but with less mystique. And, indeed, others such as Luthans and his associates (e.g., Luthans & Lockwood, 1984) and Yukl (1989) incorporated the networking aspects of it into their leadership typologies (see Chapter 8) but made no claim that these tapped "charisma."

Indeed, the closest Yukl's current framework appears to come to charisma is a few items in his motivating dimension. The Luthans et al. and Yukl typologies appear to concentrate on transactional leadership and are consistent with Yukl's (1989) argument that, "It is difficult to base behavior constructs on questionnaire research when our knowledge of transformational behavior is still so primitive" (p. 224).

Based on all this, the question arises as to what relation, if any, the agenda-setting networking material has with the previously discussed material. It is here that Kotter's (1988, 1990) later books, contrasting leaders and managers, are particularly relevant.

...agers Revisited

...seriously the notion of leader and manager differences. ...ok, he discusses some of these differences and argues that ...iortage of leadership in U.S. firms today. In his 1990 book, K.. ...ntrasts leaders with managers, or leadership with management, ..nd asks and answers in some detail how the two differ.

He starts by making the point that leadership and management are both very important processes and that the current widely held belief that leadership is "good" and management is "bad" is wrong. For Kotter, the two processes can work together well, and some people can be both effective managers and effective leaders. Also, he contends that many organizations currently lack sufficient leadership, but that this is often correctable.

For Kotter, like a number of others, the essential function of leadership is to produce adaptive or useful change, whereas management is used essentially to make the current organization operate smoothly. Planning is a managerial process quite different from what he calls the "direction-setting" aspect of leadership, a process that produces not plans but vision and strategies (akin to his earlier "agenda setting"). He speaks of the key leadership aspect of *alignment*—getting individuals to understand, accept, and line up in the direction chosen—and differentiates it from the managerial function of *organizing*.

Kotter also emphasizes motivation and inspiration as central components of leadership and argues that leadership roles and relationships in complex organizations are so complex that they require more than one person. Finally, he discusses the inadequacy of traditional managerial structural arrangements (e.g., hierarchy, plans, job descriptions) and argues that they need to be supplemented by "thick networks of relationships". Figure 9.3 conveys the essence of his arguments.

It's apparent that Kotter's treatment of leadership is very similar to the earlier treatments of transformationally oriented leadership. Also, his treatment of managers is similar in some ways to Conger's treatment of the vision of noncharismatic leaders.

Much of the previously cited literature on visionary strategic leadership (and the related transformational and charismatic notions), with the exception of Kotter's leader versus manager visions, has tended to emphasize process rather than content. That is, it has looked at what led to visions, how they were transmitted, and so forth rather than the nature

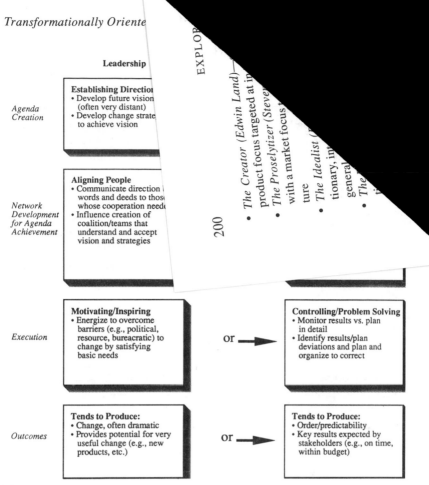

Figure 9.3. Kotter's General Comparison of Leadership and Management
Source: Based on Kotter (1990), p. 6.

of visions. Here I extend this previous literature by considering both content and process aspects of strategic vision.

Content and Process Aspects of Strategic Vision

One set of strategic vision studies derived five different styles of strategic leadership vision, based on inferences drawn from biographical and related literature on five well-known strategic leaders (see Westley & Mintzberg, 1988, 1989). Their essence is as follows:

sudden, holistic introspective vision with a
dependent consumers and scientific community
Jobs)—incremental, interaction-dependent vision
argeted at a collective market and computer infrastruc-

Rene Levesque, ex-premier of Quebec)—incremental-evolu-
rospective vision, with an idealistic focus targeted at the Quebec
population
Bricoleur (forms new ideas from collecting junk; Lee Iacocca)—induc-
ive, incremental, interactional-built vision, with both a product and organization focus, targeted at the government, union, and customers
- *The Diviner (Jan Carlzon)*—incremental-development/sudden crystall-
ization, interaction-stimulated vision, with a service focus, targeted at
employees

The styles just summarized vary substantially in terms of their focus
and source and the group(s) toward which they are targeted, as well as
in other respects not summarized here (see Westley & Mintzberg, 1988,
1989). They have clear implications in terms of their linkage with
strategy, planning, organizational design and other leader critical tasks,
their temporal implications, and so on. For example, there appears to
be a relation to the configuration and stage of the organization. The
styles also appear to call for different salient leader capabilities and
perhaps even different levels of cognitive complexity.

A set of exploratory studies from the Organizational Vision Project
Team (1990), consisting of Larwood, Kriger, Falbe and Miesing, derived three vision clusters from business school deans and CEOs.

- *Reactive leaders*—relatively low in risk, flexibility, and bottom-line orientation
- *Lone imagers*—keep visions close to self; little formal expression, communication, or acceptance by others; difficult to describe visions
- *Strategic actors*—action-oriented; inspirational; integrated with others'
visions; long-term; strategic; responsive to competition

A number of other aspects of vision were examined, including a
questionnaire measure asking how far into the future the vision extended. Data suggested substantial variations but a sizable number of
the sampled executives reported visions of 10 years or longer, with a
few visions extending beyond 20 years. These data join some reported by Jacobs and Jaques (1990) covering three- and four-star Army

generals. They found that 15% of the three-star generals and 50% of the small sample of four-star generals reported visions of 20 years or more. Taken together, these studies provide some support for the kind of long-time horizons discussed in the extended model. Furthermore, the Jacobs and Jaques (1990) piece suggests increasing individual complexity from the three- to four-star level.

The visionary material discussed up to now, and cases from consulting or the popular media (e.g., Delbec, 1990; *Fortune*, 1990), suggest quite strongly that establishing a strategic vision is not the same as traditional strategic planning, and the way these visions are established varies considerably. Some, such as Sashkin, argue that visionary leaders understand implicitly or explicitly the nature of organizations and leadership and structure the process and content of their visions accordingly—that is, they are relatively systematic.

We can think of these visionary styles in terms of James Quinn's (1981a) logical incrementalism, a widely acknowledged perspective in the strategic management literature. I discuss this in more detail in Chapter 12, but essentially logical incrementalism involves the flowing together of internal and external decisions from a broad range of parties to promote consensus. As I use the term in Chapter 12, logical incrementalism appears to be most applicable to those emphasizing interactions and consensus in their visions. Thus Jobs, Iacocca, and Carlzon all appear to emphasize variations of logical incrementalism in their strategic visions. And although, at first glance, Kotter's managers might appear more likely than his leaders to follow logical incrementalism, this might not be true. The managers appear to be less consensually oriented than his leaders.

CRISIS AND CHARISMA

In addition to the earlier emphases on transformationally oriented strategic leadership and differences between leaders and managers, there is the important question of the role of crisis in considering transformationally oriented leadership. Much of the charismatic literature explicitly or implicitly argues that there must be a crisis situation for charismatic leadership to be established. We can see this kind of thinking, for example, in the previously discussed work of Tichy and Devanna (1986) on organizational transformation.

Some, such as Conger and Kanungo (1988), go so far as to argue that if there isn't a crisis, the leader may need to create one or something very close to one if he or she is to be able to exert charismatic leadership. Bass (1988) cites literature supporting crises or at least distressful situations and situations in transition as opportunities for transformationally oriented leaders. Post-World War I Germany and the ascendence of Hitler or the rise of Martin Luther King in the United States are cases in point.

Although the arguments above tend to support the importance of crisis in providing charismatic opportunities, there is not complete agreement on this point (Conger & Kanungo, 1988). To provide additional insight concerning this issue, let's look at some recent works that take contrasting views about the relationship between crisis and charismatic leadership.

Crisis Is Necessary

The first of these pieces was a case study examining a leader's charismatic leadership, first when she was a direct superintendent of education and then when she was promoted to head of the education system of an entire state (see Roberts & Bradley, 1988). Using a charismatic framework developed by Bradley (1987), the researchers present evidence suggesting that, at the district superintendent level, the leader was found to be very charismatic. However, after her promotion to the state level she was not seen as charismatic at all, even though she was able to get much accomplished.

The authors argue that there was a crisis at the district level but not at the state level—and that the leader's charisma could not be transferred. Indeed, they take the very strong position that charisma lies beyond the realm of purposeful, rational action and needs a crisis to set it off—it can't be manufactured by a leader or organization. Of course, this position is strongly at variance with that of most others in this chapter that transformationally oriented leadership can be developed. There are a number of other interesting aspects of the study, and for these I refer you to Roberts and Bradley (1988).

Visionary and Crisis-Induced Charismatics

Boal and Bryson (1988) proposed an interesting approach that clearly differs considerably from the one just discussed and provides additional insight on this crisis question. They propose that there are two different kinds of charismatics—visionary and crisis induced. The visionary charismatic begins with ideology or vision and then moves on to action. A leader such as Iraqi President Saddam Hussein would illustrate this, if we assume that he is indeed charismatic. In contrast, the crisis-induced charismatic begins with solutions to a crisis and then develops ideological or visionary justification for those solutions (i.e., a leader "makes" circumstances). President George Bush would illustrate this, again with the assumption that he does, indeed, demonstrate charisma in his response to the Iraqi invasion of Kuwait. Both kinds of charisma produce the kinds of effects discussed earlier by means of creating a new and different "phenomenologically valid" world—one that is "real" to followers (see Brickman, 1978).

Leaders do this by creating or heightening internal and external correspondence for followers. A person's behavior must correspond with his or her feelings for *internal correspondence* to exist (e.g., in a game where an actor shoots someone, the actor only pretends anger, whereas where internal correspondence exists the actor's anger would be real). *External correspondence* involves a correspondence between a person's behavior and its consequences (e.g., in a game where an actor shoots someone, that person only pretends to be hurt, whereas in reality he or she would be dead). The visionary charismatic is argued to promote reality by helping to heighten internal correspondence, whereas crisis-induced charismatics tend to heighten external correspondence (Boal & Bryson, 1988).

Boal and Bryson develop a conceptual framework involving these two different kinds of charismatics but present no data. If they are right, we should not be looking for just one kind of charismatic leader under all circumstances, but rather should be looking for one of two different kinds depending on whether there is a crisis or not. This is a particularly important area for future research.

CHARISMATIC LEADERSHIP FROM A DISTANCE

Another important specialized area—and a tantalizing one, indeed—is the at-a-distance impact of transformationally oriented leadership (see Madsen & Snow, 1983; Oberg, 1972). This point is illustrated in Fisher's chapter-opening quote. How is it that a charismatic person can have an impact on a mass audience or collectivity when there is only an image and a name with which to identify? How can upper-level leaders ever hope to have a transformationally oriented impact on people deep within their organizations when, if there is any contact, it will be at most cursory, superficial, and probably highly mediated?

Katz and Kahn (1978), Hollander (1978), and Etzioni (1975) are among those who have argued not only that it is possible to have charismatic impact at a distance but that because of "feet of clay" and human fallibility, close day-to-day contact destroys illusion. However, the top-level leader is far enough removed to make charisma possible. Katz and Kahn go on to argue that there must be a fit on readily perceptible dimensions (such as basic values and traits) to ensure bonding. A recent, previously mentioned study of value congruence between employees and video presentations of charismatic leaders provides some support for this notion (Meglino et al., 1990).

There are a couple of very new charismatic approaches, each very different from the other, that address this issue. The first develops a model to explain subordinate motivation allowing both for these at-a-distance circumstances where the leader contacts subordinates as a collectivity and for closer, more individualized contact. The second proposes a "leadership contagion theory." Let's look at these in turn.

At-a-Distance Motivation

The approach that I have labeled "at-a-distance-motivation" emphasizes both follower motivation effects (termed "transformational effects of charismatic leadership") and leader charismatic behaviors (see Shamir, House, & Arthur, 1990). It is a charismatic analogue to House's transactional, path-goal leadership theory (see Yukl, 1989, for a review). Essentially, the transformational effects in the present approach are seen as being achieved through influencing the self-concepts of followers. The leader's values and goals are internalized by linkage to valued aspects of the followers' self-concepts through harnessing follower self-expressions, consistency between self-concepts and behaviors, self-competency, and feelings of virtue and moral worth. The leader also changes the salience hierarchy of the followers' values and identities within their self-concept so that these values and identities will be reflected in follower behavior.

In a nutshell, followers are moved to a feeling of both self- and collective efficacy and to internalize a strong moral commitment or commitment to the "spirit of the organization" (see Hodgkinson, 1983)—they develop a strong moral commitment to the organization as a collectivity.

The leader is seen as influencing these things either directly or at a distance through a primary emphasis on learning (symbolism, and so forth; see Bandura, 1986), and through such things as teaching and focusing on leader-follower schema congruence. (See also institutionalization of charisma later in this chapter, schema changes in Chapter 7, and organizational culture changes in Chapter 10 for related aspects.)

Social Contagion Approach

This approach, by Meindl (1990), is a follower-centered one, as opposed to the previously discussed approaches that were leader centered. Thus, rather than depending on a leader who exhibits a set of charismatic behaviors, charismatic symptoms are caught like a disease from fellow group members (hence the term "social contagion"), and charisma is then attributed to the leader (see Figure 9.4).

Essentially, the contagion works as follows. First, some outside person or event serves to activate one or more group members' needs or motives. The outside stimulus might be, for example, a visibly salient leader delivering a speech before a large gathering of people at a political convention. We can expect there to be a high level of excitement and energy based on the saliency and the large number of people gathered. These serve as sources of arousal, particularly among high-status opinion leaders, for example. These people might themselves be formal or informal "leaders" and indeed, have sometimes been called "secondary leaders" in the social movement literature (e.g., Madsen & Snow, 1983). They are probably in a better position than most, because of what Hollander (1985) terms "idiosyncratic credits," to act out unusual or deviant behavioral manifestations that may be involved in their articulation of the "charismatic syndrome" to be discussed below.

Second, the arousal provides the context for the contagion process (see Figure 9.4). This process has two forms: behavioral contagion and hysterical contagion. In behavioral contagion, the release of inhibitions wins out over the two forces of fear of uncontrolled expression and of acting out in public—there is open expression of the kinds of charismatic-syndrome symptoms shown in the figure and based on House's (1977) charismatic theory. They are labeled as a syndrome because they

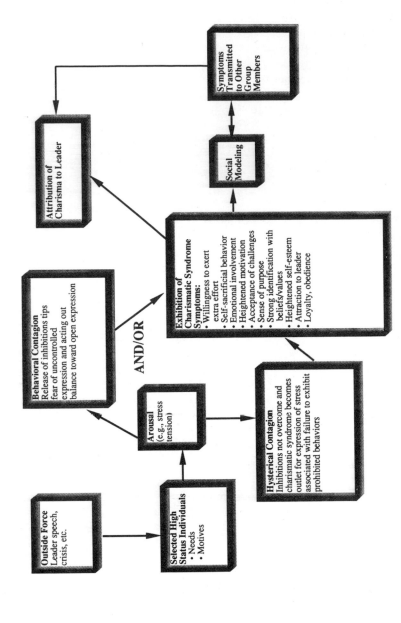

Figure 9.4. Illustration of Follower-Centered Social Contagion Charismatic Process

Source: Based on Meindl (1990).

represent a set of "symptoms" or experiences likely to occur together (Meindl, 1990).

Hysterical contagion may arise from the failure to engage in other, more direct displays of frustration, anxiety, and/or fear. Such emotional displays may be inhibited enough to preclude their normal occurrence. The charismatic syndrome then becomes a symptomatic expression of stresses associated with the failure to display other expressive, but strongly prohibited behaviors. With the assistance of social models, the prohibited desires may be rechanneled and redefined in terms of charisma. And there will be symptomatic displays of the charismatic syndrome consistent with that redefinition (Meindl, 1990).

Third, the charismatic symptoms demonstrated by the opinion leader as a result of either or both behavioral or hysterical social contagion serve as a model for the other group members, and the symptoms are transmitted to them. Accompanying this are attributions of charisma to the leader. These attributions may be influenced at least partially by implicit leadership theories and prototypes, as discussed in earlier chapters, and by group members' prototypes of how people in the members' situation should behave. For example, at a rally a prototype might be triggered of a group member displaying various aspects of the charismatic syndrome.

Note that the leader's actual behavior is almost irrelevant in this follower-centered approach. The members are influenced by one or more opinion leaders and then influence each other. The opinion leaders do not themselves possess charisma, they simply transmit it (note also that the self-concept so important in the approach discussed just before this one may also be important here, but in a quite different way). Here, there may be latent "heroic motives" tied to one's self-concept and activated by external threats. Such heroic motives may be reflected in the charismatic syndrome symptoms (see Meindl, 1990).

The Meindl approach assumes that there are four process phases: latency, social isolates, social network, and normative. In the latency phase, there is general onset of arousal but visible manifestations of the charismatic syndrome have not yet occurred. In the social isolates phase, when arousal reaches threshold levels, marginal group members tend to be the first to be influenced. This is because they are believed to have less well-developed social reference points compared to better integrated members, and to have less inhibition against "wierd"behaviors. The social network phase occurs when the contagion moves from the fringes to the social network, where those most central are argued to be most susceptible and modeling becomes very important. Finally, the normative phase occurs when the contagion leaves sociometric channels. It is now diffused very rapidly, and network position contagion probabilities are random. Soon, the syndrome becomes normative and takes on symbolic status representing solidarity and group identity. Snake-handling religious groups are an example.

Summary

I consider at-a-distance conceptions of charisma to be extremely important—particularly for the extended model. Both of the emphases just mentioned are so new that they are difficult to evaluate. However, if they do nothing else, they serve as starting points toward systematic examination of this important issue. Both perspectives emphasize the follower. However, the first one does so within parameters set by the leader; thus it is still a kind of leader-centered emphasis. The self-concept notion serves as a potential point of integration between these two very different approaches, although it serves a different role in each.

IMPLICIT THEORIES AND TRANSFORMATIONALLY ORIENTED LEADERSHIP

The follower-centered perspective, previously discussed, touched on follower prototypes or implicit leadership theories. Here I extend that treatment, keeping in mind the discussion in Chapter 8 that argued that leadership descriptions were to a greater or lesser extent influenced by such theories.

One might expect implicit theories to have an even greater impact on charismatic leadership perceptions than on other aspects. Recently, Bass and Avolio (1987) showed that this was, indeed, the case. They found a correlation of 0.83 between subordinates' descriptions of their leaders' charismatic behavior (using Bass's scale, discussed earlier) and subordinates' ratings of the prototypical leader using Lord, Foti, and Phillips's (1982) measure of prototypicality. The correlations with Bass's other dimensions were also substantial but lower (e.g., 0.61 with contingent reward and 0.38 with management by exception). House et al. (1990) were concerned about this possibility and attempted to control for it in their earlier-mentioned study.

Meindl (1988) also reports some related results using his Romance of Leadership Scale (RLS), based on the romance of leadership notion mentioned in Chapter 4. He found that for business school students there were a number of significant correlations between their RLS scores and their descriptions using Bass's leadership instrument of Reagan and Iacocca (two assumed high-charisma leaders). For the overall transformational leadership score, the correlations between the two measures were in the thirties for both Reagan and Iacocca, and for the charisma dimension they were 0.44 for Reagan and 0.53 for Iacocca. They were lower and sometimes nonsignificant for the individualized consideration and intellectual stimulation transformational aspects and were generally nonsignificant for transactional leadership and its components.

Finally, a related study by Meindl, Tsai, and Lee (1988) looked at the degrees of responsibility subordinates would feel under "leaders" versus "managers" in different scenarios where difficulties occurred. As in our earlier discussion, leaders essentially were described as "taking charge," whereas managers "kept things running smoothly."

One scenario described a situation where a worker was primarily responsible for inadequate task performance but a coworker also contributed to the negative event in a small way. In essence it was found that the worker tended to diffuse the blame more to the coworker when the boss was a manager than when the boss was a leader. The "normal" management backdrop apparently let the main perpetrator off the hook to some extent.

In another scenario, the worker's superior, rather than a coworker, contributed in a small way to the negative event. This time, however, the results were not the same as before. Here, where the boss was a leader, there tended to be more diffusion of blame away from the worker than where the superior was a manager. In other words, more responsibility tended to be attributed to "take charge" superiors who were "real leaders" than to "mere managers" who were responsible for the status quo.

All these results reinforce the attribution aspects of transformationally oriented leadership and the strong linkage to implicit theories. They provide additional insight into the process, and some of them again caution us even more than in the previous chapter that questionnaire measures are indications of the describer's cognitive structure and not measures of "actual" leader behavior.

ROUTINIZATION OF CHARISMA

Thinking again in terms of a leader-centered emphasis, an area of particular importance in the extended model is that of routinizing or institutionalizing transformational/charismatic/visionary leadership. As Table 9.1 shows, such institutionalization was an important aspect of Weber's perspective, and there was an emphasis on institutionalization in some of the work cited earlier. Routinization of charisma appears similar to that involved in trying to institutionalize a new organizational culture and many of the same "action levers" seem relevant. Even so, the concepts are conceptually distinct enough to be treated in separate chapters, though one may recognize underlying similarities. For starters, one commonality is that there is little systematic empirical evidence examining either charismatic or organizational culture routinization.

In terms of charisma, there are less than a dozen such studies (Clark, 1970, 1972; Constas, 1961; Day, 1980; Drachkovitch, 1964; Kanter, 1968, 1972; Madsen & Snow, 1983; F. C. Miller, 1966; Van de Ven, Ludwig, Oppenheim, & Davis, 1983), with Trice and Beyer (1986) having conducted the most recent and systematic one. Based on the Trice and Beyer study and the work of Weber, five charismatic routinization criteria can be listed:

(1) development of an administrative apparatus, separate from the charismatic, to deal with the ongoing operating needs generated by putting the charismatic's program into action;

(2) transformation and transference of charisma to other organizational members by means of rites, ceremonies, and symbols;

(3) incorporation of the charismatic's message and mission into the organization's written and oral traditions;

(4) selection of a successor who resembles the charismatic closely enough to be like a "reincarnation"; and

(5) the degree to which the organization (or collectivity) continues to express, work toward, and cohere around the charismatic's message or vision.

Trice and Beyer investigated charismatic routinization in terms of these criteria by using case histories of the founders of Alcoholics Anonymous and the National Council on Alcoholism—both founded as part of the social movement to redefine alcoholism as an illness rather than as a moral weakness. Both leaders were, indeed, found to be charismatic in terms of such things as possessing extraordinary personal characteristics and advancing a radical message and mission widely perceived as relevant.

However, based on the five criteria above, the founder of Alcoholics Anonymous was judged to be far more successful in routinizing his charisma. The structure was simpler, allowing for less involvement in mundane administration; there were many rites and ceremonies; and a saga or tale about the founder was developed and elaborated upon during his lifetime. Although his successor was not, strictly speaking, a "reincarnation," the previously mentioned activities were so deeply embedded that the charisma continued. Finally, the structure and mission remained about the same. All this was in marked contrast to events in the National Council on Alcoholism, where the founder's charisma was not institutionalized.

These descriptions and the criteria provide insights into the kinds of activities needed to sustain a vision once it gets accepted and implemented. They also reinforce the earlier point about the obvious dearth of studies in this important area. Let's now broaden the discussion by examining some general research and conceptual linkages of transformationally oriented leadership with various aspects of the extended model.

SELECTED RESEARCH AND CONCEPTUAL LINKAGES WITH THE EXTENDED MODEL

The discussion in this section is built around the assumption that we need to consider transformationally oriented aspects of leadership from both process and content perspectives as used earlier in the chapter. There, I argued that most of the transformationally oriented leadership work tended to emphasize charismatic leader characteristics or behaviors, what might trigger charismatic/visionary behaviors, the process that a visionary leader would use to instill a vision, and similar subjects. Accompanying this focus was another stream of literature that tended to stress more the content of the vision, its relation to strategy setting, and so forth.

The assumption above is consistent with the notion that all leaders, and not just transformationally oriented ones, have some sort of vision. However, among other things, the nature of that vision and its implementation and institutionalization are a function of the strength of the transformationally oriented behaviors that the followers attribute to the leader (recall the leader-versus-manager visions or charismatic/noncharismatic visions treated earlier in the chapter).

Given this basic assumption, then, let's start by emphasizing the linkage of transformationally oriented leadership both to other elements in the individual capability cluster and to the external environment and societal culture component. For openers, one would expect relations between various background variables and both the process and content of visionary leadership. Relations of societal and individual values to both perspectives of vision also should be examined, as should efficacy and predisposition to lead, which House and Sashkin have posited are likely to be especially important for transformationally oriented leaders. Cognitive complexity is likely to be especially important in terms of visionary content and complexity, as well as how far into the future the vision is extended. At the same time, cognitive style might influence the nature of the vision.

The relation of the transformationally oriented leadership variables to the more transactionally oriented leadership variables discussed in the previous chapter also is important. Given the arguments in that chapter, one would need to be concerned about using analyses that would maintain the nuances of the separate transformational/transactional clusters to the greatest extent possible. In that way one would be less likely to oversimplify complex relations into a two-variable transformational/transactional world.

As a part of the linkages to the individual difference cluster I would be interested in comparing and contrasting, up and down the model's levels and domains, the kinds of relations just suggested. Some, such as Bass and his colleagues (e.g., Bass, Waldman, Avolio & Bebb, 1987), have presented evidence suggesting that organizations with highly transformational upper-level leaders also tend to have more transformational leaders at lower levels. This would be a particularly important aspect to examine in comparing and contrasting. Also, I would be interested in the group or collegial aspects of these, especially at the top of the organization.

A second important area to examine is the relationship of transformationally oriented leadership to various aspects of the extended model's critical tasks. Here, one would expect to find substantial linkages, particularly with vision content. Goal/mission development, strategies, and organizational/subsystems design have obvious ties to the nature of a vision and may be linked in more subtle ways to the more processual transformationally oriented aspects. Once again, these kinds of relations should be examined for leader collegiums and up and down the organization.

A third set of linkages to examine is concerned with organizational culture and its lower-level analogues. Much of the discussion in this chapter argues for strong organizational culture relations with various aspects of transformationally oriented leadership. Indeed, those such as Sashkin contend that organizational culture is the primary action lever for the visionary leader. Thus it's extremely important to examine these kinds of linkages, both vertically and horizontally, in the extended model. Indirect upper-level leadership relationships with organizational culture are likely to be especially important at lower levels.

A fourth area to examine concerns possible direct relationships between transformationally oriented leadership and various individual and organizational outcomes. The work of Bass and House and their associates is among the research that has found such relations.

A fifth area concerns the question of implicit leadership theories and prototypes and their impact on the perceptions of and responses to questionnaire measures of transformational/charismatic/visionary leadership. The model proposed by Hunt et al. (1990) has some implications in terms of fit and misfit of leader-subordinate prototypes.

A sixth area concerns the direct versus at-a-distance aspects of transformationally oriented leadership. This question is at the heart of the study of such leadership, and recent work cited in the chapter has begun to focus on it. In the extended model context, we are interested primarily with to what extent and how upper-level transformationally oriented leadership is translated indirectly to those deep within the organization. This was implicit in some of the earlier discussion but is a key issue in its own right.

Finally, as with other components of the extended model, temporal considerations cut across all these relations and have implications for the institutionalization of vision, how far into the future the vision is projected, and so on.

CONCLUDING COMMENTARY

Let's look at several thoughts in concluding this chapter. First is the issue of whether we consider transformationally oriented notions to be a leader behavior (regardless of the attributional source) or a follower response. Work cited in the chapter has looked at it either way, and sometimes (as in the case of Bass, for example) the two are mixed together. Either alternative is appropriate, given our purpose, but we must be clear about the perspective we choose. We also must be careful to avoid a tautology where, in effect, we define a charismatic leader simply as "one who has charisma." It's interesting to note that we usually don't define traditional leadership dimensions in terms of responses or outcomes. This occurs with charisma because the perspective is so heavily oriented toward extraordinary follower responses.

Related to the previous concern is the use of questionnaires in transformationally oriented studies. The phenomenon clearly lends itself to more subjectivist-oriented approaches, and some of this is evident in the studies reviewed. Nevertheless, what is arguably the most frequently cited work by Bass and his colleagues uses questionnaires and has relied heavily on objectivist approaches (probably largely because of Bass's objectivist background). The questionnaires used in this research have come under fire for several reasons, with some arguing that they need substantial revisions.

Sashkin and associates offer one alternative, which is revised on a running basis as they obtain new data. However, much of this work is reported in more practitioner-oriented outlets, and it has not received the attention among scholars that Bass's work has. Conger and Kanungo (1990) offer another alternative questionnaire but one still so new that we know little about it. A related questionnaire that has some developmental history is that of Kouzes and Posner, and it focuses on the leader-versus-manager question. Perhaps, as we pointed out earlier, the original critical incident base is subject to the same kinds of criticisms as Hertzberg's work. This issue needs clarification. Regardless of whatever questionnaire is used, there is evidence that implicit theories and prototypes loom large in responses to it. Indeed, they loom larger than for transactional leadership dimensions. Once again, we are reminded that it is wise not to treat questionnaires as if they reflect objective reality.

A particularly important point is the one raised by Yukl (1989)—that we are in danger of a two-factor theory of leadership. It is as if years and years of leadership findings have been swept away in embracing transformationally oriented leadership. As I've stressed more than once, a wiser choice would be to look for the kinds of nuances suggested in the previous chapter, including examination of gestalts and profiles to provide a more complete picture. Kotter has the right idea in arguing for balance between leadership and management. There have to be situational contingencies operating that have an impact. In pursuing this we need to be aware of definitional and operational treatment of the dimensions in both the transformational and transactional approaches. We also need to examine the ideas put forth by Boal and Bryson. To what extent are there two kinds of charismatics? If there are, what are the conditions surrounding them? At the very least, Boal and Bryson's model should make those pause who argue that we must have crises for there to be charisma.

In addition, it's important to understand better the linkage between individual models and those emphasizing organizational transformation. Certainly one can't transform an organization without some individual transformation, but what is the linkage? By and large, the people studying each are different as are the literature bases.

This book has covered some additional important issues (e.g., at-a-distance leadership) in the preceding section. For those who would like to gain still more perspective, I invite you to consider especially Conger and Kanungo (1988), Bass (1990), and a comprehensive paper that I received during the late stages of this book's production (see House, Howell, Shamir, Smith, & Spangler, 1990).

Finally, with the previous chapter as a background, it's appropriate to consider the much-mentioned organizational culture component of our model. I turn to this in Chapter 10.

NOTE

1. I use *transformationally oriented* to refer to transformational, charismatic, or visionary leadership unless the context calls for one of the more specific labels.

10 Organizational Culture

Right off, he told me to forget about the meaning of poetry."A poem doesn't mean," the poet said. "A poem is."
　　　　　　　　　　　　　　　—Joe Murray (1989, p. A8), columnist

Chieftains and leaders in every subordinate office are responsible for establishing the atmosphere in which they lead. This atmosphere may have periods of change even as the seasons change. Nonetheless, unlike our lack of influence over the weather, our leaders can and must influence and control the spirit of our tribes.
　　　　　　　　　　　　　　　—Wess Roberts (1987, p. 61),
　　　　　　　　　　　　　Leadership Secrets of Attila the Hun

Nothing reveals more of what [an organization] really cares about than its stories and legends . . . Listening to [an organization's] stories is the surest route to determining its real priorities and who symbolizes them.
　　　　　　　　　　　　　　　—Tom Peters and Nancy Austin
　　　　　　　　　　　　　(quoted in Eigen & Siegel, 1989, p. 91)

BACKGROUND AND TYPOLOGIES

Organizational culture is the organizational analogue to societal culture. As such, we might start with the definition we used for societal culture—"collective mental programs of the people in the environment"—and substitute the term *organization* for *environment*. As we shall see, this mental programming covers a wide range of values, beliefs, assumptions, behaviors, norms, and so on. And, just as with societal culture, the emphasis here is on *collective* (reflected in the organization or organizational subpart as a whole) mental programming as opposed to the individual values, beliefs, and the like emphasized in Chapter 6. And again, though we expect individuals to reflect shared cultural aspects, we also expect each individual to possess values separate from those shared. Of course, it is not always easy to maintain a sharp collective-individual separation, as demonstrated in studies examining value congruence between or among various individuals or organizational groups (e.g., Meglino et al., 1990).

Be that as it may, I consider organizational culture to be a particularly important linkage among critical tasks, subcultures, and various facets of effectiveness up and down the organization (see Figure 10.1).

Within the last decade or so, organizational culture has become one of the most active research areas within organizational studies (Allaire & Firsirotu, 1984). It also has been emphasized heavily in recent popular, practitioner-oriented management books (e.g., Deal & Kennedy, 1982; Peters & Waterman, 1982). One impetus for the study of organizational culture came from a realization by a number of people in the 1970s that traditional organizational approaches were not as useful as they might be in leading to an understanding of observed disparities between organizational goals and outcomes or between strategy and implementation (Ouchi & Wilkins, 1985). Reinforced by comparisons of U.S. firms with foreign ones, this general line of reasoning began to suggest that organizational models were incomplete without inclusion of cultural aspects.

The general rationale, not often explicitly stated for this position, goes something like this: Shared values or assumptions form the basis for consensus and integration, which encourages motivation and commitment of meaningful membership. The same shared values that define

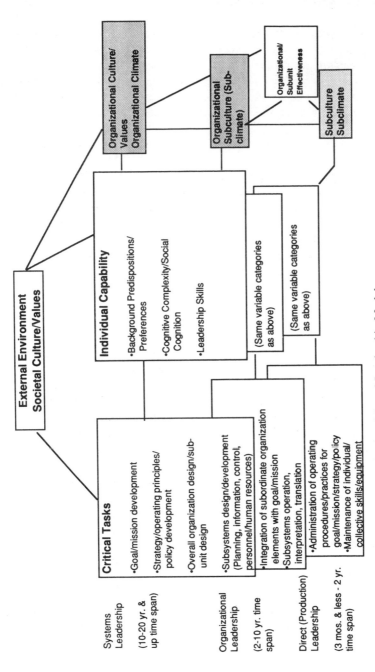

Figure 10.1. Extended Multiple-Organizational-Level Leadership Model
Note: For simplicity, some direct relationships, feedback, and arrowheads are not shown.

organizational purpose also provide meaning and direction. From these come organizations with high levels of built-in coordination and the capacity to adapt by projecting existing values and assumptions on ambiguous situations. Thus, consistent with its usage in the extended model, there should be a linkage between culture and various organizational variables—especially effectiveness or performance (see Denison & Mishra, 1989).

This general kind of thinking led to a spate of book-length publications in the early and middle 1980s emphasizing organizational culture (e.g., Frost, Moore, Louis, Lundberg, & Martin, 1985; Jelinek, Smircich, & Hirsch, 1983; Kilmann, Saxton, & Serpa, 1985; Schein, 1985). However, in spite of the arguments linking organizational culture to effectiveness, with the exception of a practitioner-oriented book by Peters and Waterman (1982), there was not much attempt to examine this proposed linkage explicitly. To see why, let's examine this earlier thrust in more detail.

Most of the earlier work was by subjectivists who essentially staked out the field and argued that organizational culture could not appropriately be tapped by traditional objectivist methods (typically questionnaires). Their argument, like that of the poet in the chapter-opening quote, is that culture "is." More specifically, they contend that culture is something an organization "is"(a root metaphor), rather than something an organization "has" (a variable).

Under the subjectivists' root metaphor notion, there is an emphasis on within-unit interpretations of organizational culture, avoiding reports of its distribution, pattern, and generalizability across organizations. It is viewed as particular and idiosyncratic rather than as replicable and well-defined. In contrast, those toward the objectivist end of the objectivist-subjectivist continuum (Chapter 4) would tend to emphasize the "has" aspects of culture and treat it as a variable. That is, they would treat culture much like structural or other variables dealt with by organizational researchers, and a natural off-shoot would be to examine the variable's relationship with effectiveness and the like.

Ott (1989) illustrates the subjectivist, root metaphor notion by using a color analogy. It's easy to agree that something is green once there is agreement on what *green* means. In this view, each person uses a different deciphering process and will find a different culture in the same organization. Hence, they can't agree on what constitutes green.

As Rousseau (in press) indicates, the concept's concurrent appearance with that of subjectivist orientations toward OB have almost inextricably linked it with such subjectivist approaches as ethnography and such arguments as:

- culture's fundamental content is unconscious and highly subjective;
- interactive probing must be done to tap otherwise inaccessible and unconscious cultural material; and
- every culture is idiosyncratic and unique, and thus standardized assessments with researcher-constructed categories cannot be used. Such a priori categorization misrepresents experiences of respondents and thus is invalid.

Schein (1984, 1986) goes even further by arguing that categories derived by researchers distort the respondent's perspective (i.e., are not his or her own) and thus presume unwarranted generalizability and therefore are unethical.

Organizational Culture Typologies

If taken literally, these arguments would preclude anything but subjectivist assumptions and approaches in dealing with organizational culture. Recently, however, some typologies have been developed whose usage allows for a broader treatment of culture. These start with Edgar Schein's (1985) three-level typology, summarized in his well-known book. Ott (1989) developed this typology further and extended it to three-and-one-half levels. Rousseau (in press) proposed a layered analogue that I like to think of in terms of layers in an onion. I summarize this "peeled onion" in Figure 10.2, which synthesizes points from the Schein, Ott, and Rousseau typologies.

Let's now examine each of the layers in the figure.

Artifacts and Patterns of Behavior

Included here are behavioral patterns and visible or audible results of behaviors, such as logos or badges. Examples are written and spoken language and jargon, office layouts, organizational structure, dress codes, technology, and behavioral norms (members' beliefs regarding acceptable and unacceptable behavior). Habits, rites, and rituals also are found here. The content of this layer is generally easily seen but hard to interpret without direct information from members and without

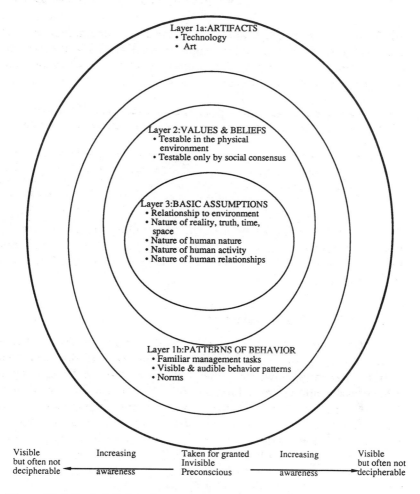

Figure 10.2. Peeled-Onion Conception of Organizational Culture
Source: Based on Schein (1985), Ott (1989), and Rousseau (in press).

some consideration of the deeper levels (Rousseau, in press; Sathe, 1985).

Values and Beliefs

Consistent with usage of the term in Chapter 6, values are considered "what ought to be, as distinct from what is" (Schein, 1985). Beliefs are an indication of "what is." This layer shows ways in which individuals communicate, explain, and rationalize or justify what is said and done as a community. In other words, it shows how they make sense of the first layer of culture (Ott, 1989). This layer also includes ethos, philosophies, ideologies, attitudes, and ethical/moral codes. At first glance, this layer appears to provide accurate information about a *true* organization culture, thus making the basic assumptions layer unnecessary. However, the difference here is analogous to Argyris and Schön's (1978) espoused values (what people say; second layer) and values-in-use (what people will do; basic assumptions level), mentioned in Chapter 4 and further discussed in Chapter 12. Espoused values often serve important symbolic functions and may remain in an organization for a long time even though they are inconsistent with values-in-use (Ott, 1989). As indicated in Figure 10.2, values/beliefs are closer to the third layer (basic underlying assumptions) than are the artifacts and patterns of behavior in the outer layer.

Basic Underlying Assumptions

These are fundamental, unconscious assumptions and perceptions, not directly knowable even to members. They have become so taken for granted that there is little variation within a given culture. As theories-in-use they tell organizational members how to perceive and think and feel about things, and tend to be unconfrontable and nondebatable (Schein, 1985). These are reflections of what I call "automatic" schemas in Chapter 7. We can get an idea of just how fundamental these are from Table 10.1, which is similar to Parson's (1960) action framework.

This peeled-onion configuration is useful for several reasons. First, it helps tie together a wide range of different definitions, concepts, and literature from those dealing with and writing about organizational culture. Second, it's useful in understanding how cultures form, are maintained, and can be changed. The outer layers are easier to change than the deeper ones. Third, configuring culture as layers of processes (interpretive/behavioral, conscious/unconscious) varying in depth, accessibility, and changeability allows the concept to reflect multiple knowledge assumptions and purposes, as argued for in Chapter 4. Finally, where all of the layers of the onion are used, in totality, and they are thought of as linked together with the transmission of one facet through the use of others, the model is consistent with the organization "is," rather than "has," concept of culture. The use of the outer layers as variables would emphasize the "has" notion.

Table 10.1

One Conception of Basic Underlying Assumptions

1. *Organization's Relationship to Environment.* Extent to which key organizational members see this relationship as one of dominance, submission, harmonizing, finding an appropriate niche, and the like.

2. *Nature of Reality, Truth, Time, Space.* The linguistic and behavioral rules that define what is real, and what is not, what is "fact," how truth ultimately is to be determined, and whether truth is "revealed" or "discovered"; basic concepts of time as linear or cyclical, monochronic (one kind only) or polychronic (several different kinds); basic concepts such as space as limited or indefinite and property as communal or individual; etc.

3. *Nature of Human Nature.* What does it mean to be "human," and what attributes are assumed to be intrinsic or ultimate? Is human nature evil, good or neutral? Are human beings perfectible? Is theory X or Y more appropriate?

4. *Nature of Human Activity.* What is the "right" thing for humans to do, on the basis of the above assumptions; should they be active, passive, self-developmental, fatalistic, or what? What is work and what is play?

5. *Nature of Human Relationships.* What is assumed to be the "right" way for individuals to relate to each other, to distribute power and love? Is life cooperative or competitive; individualistic, group, collaborative, or communal; based on traditional lineal authority, law, or what?

Source: Based on Schein (1983), p. 16.

Let's elaborate a bit more on this last point. The peeled onion analogy assumes that the many elements of culture are layered along a range of subjectivity and accessibility. The more objective elements become vehicles for transmission of more subjective, less tangible subjective aspects of culture. The outer layers (artifacts, behaviors, and norms reflected in such activities as decision making and communicating) are major considerations when organizational processes directly related to these (e.g., use of formal structures) are of interest. Or if we are interested in the deeper layers (e.g., studies of socialization, assimilation, and the like) the more tangible elements, such as the way people respond to mistakes, can be interpreted as transmitters of the highly internalized and often unconscious aspects of culture (Rousseau, in press). In other words, more visible aspects can sometimes be used as proxies for deeper aspects. Adolf Hitler and his chief architect, Alfred Speer, serve as an example here. They demonstrated an intuitive feel for these linkages in the carefully planned use of space, architecture, and other artifacts both to reflect underlying assumptions and values and to shape these and reinforce Hitler's leadership. The consistent theme throughout was the "Thousand Year Reich" (see Speer, 1970).

Schein (1985, 1990) essentially argues for a holistic approach, such as the one just discussed, in data gathering where a consultant has been called in to decipher aspects of organizational culture to help deal with organizational problems. Schein uses a 10-step clinical approach where there is close and continuous interplay between the outsider consultant and various motivated insiders who live in the organization and embody its culture. The outsider continues to probe or peel away layers of the onion until both insider(s) and outsider are satisfied that they have surfaced the underlying assumptions. In so doing, the deeper layers provide interpretive information for the outer ones.

We also should note that although Schein (1985, 1990) argues that the real meaning of culture is picked up in the core underlying assumptions, most definitions and treatments by those interested in culture deal with it at the values or behavior/artifacts layers (Rousseau, in press).

Finally, there are two other aspects I'd like to emphasize, although I don't have the space to develop them in greater detail. The first of these concerns the historical development and support of the perspectives represented at each layer. Ott (1989) discusses this historical background in some detail and links later work with some of the classical earlier work from a range of literature.

The second of these is a framework developed by Smircich (1983) and extended by Smircich and Calas (1987) and Deshpande and Webster (1989). This framework argues that the focus of culture can be viewed along five positions: (a) as an exogenous, independent variable (societal culture); (b) as an endogenous, independent variable (organizational culture); (c) as a metaphor for organizational-knowledge systems; (d) as a metaphor for shared symbols and meanings; and (e) as a metaphor for the unconscious mind.

These bear an obvious resemblance to the earlier typology presented here (although they express differences as well). The first position deals with societal culture and the second is its organizational culture analogue. Both treat culture as something an organization "has." The other three positions are consistent with the root metaphor ("is") treatment of culture. I invite readers to refer to the sources above for more details and for the literature base and references underlying these various positions.

Cultures and Subcultures

Much of the literature treats organizational cultures as monolithic—there is one culture for a given organization. Indeed, this notion is implied in discussions of "strong culture" by Deal and Kennedy (1982), among others. However, others such as K. L. Gregory (1983) and Ouchi and Wilkins (1985) argue that we should think in terms of subcultures (and, of course, the extended multi-level model does, indeed, recognize this as we move down the hierarchy).

Van Maanen and Barley (1985) illustrate the notion of subcultures in terms of Venn diagrams where small circles cluster and overlap as the collective understandings of one group approximate those of another. The extent to which smaller circles combine onto a larger, hypothetical circle determines the justification for talking about a single organizational culture. In extreme cases, where there is a large proportion of nonbasic assumptions and these are counter to each other, there may exist "organizational countercultures " (Martin & Siehl, 1983). The assumption of a single organizational culture is risky on two counts. First, assumptions of a single culture may cause one to overlook possible diversity in subcultures. Second, aspects detected in a subculture are not necessarily a determining force in the overall culture of the organization in question (Louis, 1985).

It's useful here to think in terms of "sites of culture." The previously emphasized top of the organization is one such site. Then there is a "vertical slice," such as a division. General Motor's Chevrolet division is quite likely to have a different culture in many ways than the Cadillac division, even though both will tend to share common elements of the overall GM culture.

A third focus is the "horizontal slice," such as a particular type of job or (an especial emphasis of this book) a hierarchical level. Here, design engineers at company X may have developed a unique shared set of understandings, just as there could be unique shared understandings across the organizational domain (see Cooke & Rousseau, 1988). Finally, a particular unit, such as a department, may reflect a characteristic culture (e.g., maybe the finance and marketing departments in a business school each have somewhat different subcultures; Louis, 1985).

It's also useful to think in terms of cultural intensity (sometimes called cultural strength) and integration. *Intensity* is the extent to which members of a unit agree as to various aspects of the cultural content associated with the unit. Organizations with strong norms (e.g., innovation) tend to have intensive cultures as contrasted with new organizations or those in transition (e.g., as a result of strategic reorientation), which tend to have less intense cultures. Intensity is demonstrated by high intraunit agreement among members concerning culture aspects. Greater consistency in member behavior is expected in intensive cultures (Rousseau, in press).

Integration reflects the degree to which organizational units share a common culture. Organizations with a pervasive dominant culture, such as at least some hierarchically controlled power-oriented military units (e.g., Rousseau & Cooke, 1988), tend to have cultures high in integration. Low cultural integration is associated with within-organization functional differentiation or differentiation in such aspects as goals, structure, and personnel practices (Rousseau, in press). Louis (1985) discusses similar notions.

A recent study showing the importance of organizational subcultures and illustrating mixed methodologies is worth describing briefly (see Jermier, Slocum, Fry, & Gaines, in press). Perhaps the most interesting aspect of the study is that it demonstrates the presence of a number of different subcultures in a police department (a paramilitary organization with a highly developed top-down hierarchy). The authors argued and provided support for the notion that the organization projected a rigid exterior appearance, symbolizing what key stakeholders expected, while masking a loosely coupled set of interior practices.

The official culture (crime-fighting command bureaucracy) was investigated as an arbitrary set of meaning structures and symbols arranged according to top-management preferences. Top management was unable to impose organizationwide conformance with the official culture, and there were five distinct clusters of subcultures. In all these subcultures but one, the officers substantially modified or rejected the projected organizational culture.

The authors defined culture as shared beliefs and typical patterns constituting how an organization produces goods and services. They used semistructured interviews and ethnography where officers were accompanied on patrol on "several occasions," and a questionnaire based on the interview and ethnographic information. Cluster analysis and associated statistical techniques to determine profile similarities were then used to test for subcultures. The questionnaires tapped traditional quantitative perceptual measures of such things as formalization and task interdependence, and the cluster analysis also was quantitative.

The cultural aspects essentially were derived from the combination of ethnographic and interview data and the subjectivist, symbolic conceptualization used in interpreting the quantitative material. This study gets its "cultural" claim from the latter.

Quantitative Approaches to Measuring Culture

I've indicated that the peeled-onion typology clearly calls for multiple methods. I've touched on the general nature of some of these previously and the Jermier et al. (in press) study, just summarized, illustrates how differing approaches can be combined. Smircich and Calas (1987) and Louis (1981), as well as pieces in Frost et al. (1985) and Morey and Luthans (1985), provide additional insights on subjectivist (and sometimes combined) approaches. What I discuss here is the use of objectivist approaches (primarily questionnaires) in dealing with appropriate layers of culture.

The approaches in general consist of techniques that can have content specified in advance, are replicable, and use standardized techniques for obtaining and scoring the relevant cultural aspects. Besides questionnaires, these may include such techniques as cards in a Q-sort and interviewing. The essence is *a priori* structuring of the stimuli to which people will be exposed during collection of data. Although this common content facilitates uniform categorization and scoring systems, and thus encourages statistical analysis (as mentioned in the public/private approach in Chapter 4), it does not *require* such analysis. There also are other concerns, such as who provides the data, and these as well as the above material are discussed in detail by Rousseau (in press).

Questionnaires

Let's hope the previous discussion has brought us to the point where I can discuss seriously questionnaires in culture research without the discussion being anathema to readers. Carefully developed questionnaires are appropriate for the outer two layers, particularly when used and/or developed in combination with other methods. Rousseau (in press) summarizes seven of these that are not simply relabeled questionnaires used previously to measure such concepts as organizational climate (discussed further below), or practitioner-oriented inventories that lack research concerning their psychometric integrity.

The content of the specified dimensions included varies, but three general underlying dimensions, expressed as either values or behaviors, cut across several of the instruments. First are task-related aspects such as quality and risk-taking. Second are interpersonal aspects such as supporting and communicating. Finally, are individual aspects emphasizing organizational member personal enhancement, such as freedom and self-expression. Together these dimensions illustrate the etic (outsider's analytic categories) perspective mentioned in Chapter 4 (see Rousseau, in press).

In closing this section, it's worth noting that although societal and organizational cultures are analogous, they have tended to use different dimensions. For example, Hofstede's (1980) societal culture measures differ from those used in organizational culture research. Furthermore, the values literature, treated in Chapter 6, also uses different dimensions. An important future research direction is to try to reconcile the differences across these related areas.

ORGANIZATIONAL CULTURE AND ORGANIZATIONAL CLIMATE

Those readers with an objectivist orientation, and who have been around a while, may remember the emphasis on organizational climate in the 1960s and 1970s. They may also wonder how it is similar to and different from organizational culture. I address this issue in this section. I would argue that organizational culture research is to the 1980s and 1990s what organizational climate research was to the 1960s and 1970s.

Both concepts have numerous definitions and have been operationalized a number of different ways. Each is seen as a kind of bridge between the individual and the organization. However, epistemological and methodological differences have tended to keep their proponents in separate camps (e.g., climate has tended to use objectivist assumptions and methods and, as I have shown, there has been a heavy subjectivist emphasis in the culture area). In the 1980s, as climate waned in interest, interest in culture seemed to increase. Perhaps the apogee for the early climate studies was reached in the 1970s with extensive reviews (e.g., Hellriegel & Slocum, 1974; James & Jones, 1974; Joyce & Slocum, 1979; Olmstead, 1973; Payne & Pugh, 1976; Schneider, 1975).

Now, however, climate seems to be experiencing a resurgence. In one form (misguided or opportunistic, in my opinion) it is treated as synonymous with culture (e.g., Gordon, 1985; Lippitt, Langseth, &

Mossop, 1985). In a more enlightened form, climate is treated in combination with culture (e.g., Ashforth, 1985; Rentsch, 1989; Schneider, 1985, 1987; Schneider & Gunnarson, in press; Schneider & Rentsch, 1988). For our purposes, the combination of both culture and climate seems particularly useful. Although there still is not complete agreement on what either of these concepts means, and probably never will be, Schneider and his associates have gone a long way in using the two concepts to complement each other.

Schneider and Rentsch (1988) consider climate to be the message that organizational members receive from organizational routines (policies, practices, procedures, etc.) and the reward system (supports, expectations, and various kinds of rewards). They define culture as the values and norms underlying such organizational routines and rewards, in addition to the shared assumptions about organizational life reflected in these norms and values. We can see, then, that their definition of culture is reasonably consistent with this book's treatment.

Schneider and Rentsch see culture as communicated through interpretations of routines and rewards. Such interpretations are passed on and help explain the norms and values underlying the routines and rewards. For these authors, climate and culture overlap in terms of meaning. For climate this is reflected in the interpretations that members make about the organization when confronted with particular patterns of routines and rewards. For culture, this is reflected in terms of what routines and rewards connote for underlying norms, values, and assumptions.

Climate researchers typically have asked for nonevaluate descriptions of the presence or absence of some organizational event. These events or routines can be see as manifestations of culture—they are what is being interpreted and given meaning. In other words, the organizational routines (the "what") measured in climate research are interpreted and given meaning (the "why") by organization members, as assessed in culture research.

As an example, think of an organization that operates under the shared assumption that people are basically lazy and dislike working (McGregor's Theory X). As a result, there might be a tightly controlled climate where organization members punch time clocks, and so forth. Culture would be communicated through members sharing their interpretations of why they think things happen the way they do ("they are bringing in computers to monitor our work more closely") or through storytelling ("one day an employee came in late for work and his work materials were left in a pile outside of his office"; see Schneider & Gunnarson, in press).

This treatment appears to be consistent with, but more highly elaborated than, Ashforth's (1985). Essentially, like Schneider and Rentsch, Ashforth sees culture as shared assumptions and climate as shared perceptions. Rousseau (in press) also interprets the two concepts in a similar manner.

For our purposes, then, this treatment reinforces the use of both concepts, a critical pluralist perspective and the use of multiple methods in assessing the importance of culture/climate in the extended model.

Specific Aspects of Culture/Climate

Although early treatments of climate, much like those of culture, tended to treat it as monolithic, later treatments recognize more specific aspects. Following the above definition of climate that emphasizes perceptions of organizational routines and rewards, some (e.g., Schneider & Gunnarson, in press; Zohar, 1980) have tended to focus on specific aspects related to particular routines and rewards. Thus there has been emphasis on "safety climates," "innovation climates," or "service climates." Some recent work has also extended the subculture/ subclimate notion by examining specific interaction groups (e.g., specific account auditors) that share perceptions and meanings *within* functionally defined units that typically serve as subcultures or subclimates (see Rentsch, 1989).

Unit of Analysis Considerations

The previous discussion has particularly strong unit of analysis implications. Climate is often considered to be an individual measure (sometimes termed "psychological climate") that can be aggregated to various levels to provide for organizational climate or subclimate (e.g., Joyce & Slocum, 1984). Consistent with this, it is then possible to check on consistency of shared perceptions and so forth through selected statistical procedures (e.g., Joyce & Slocum, 1984). However, recently this approach has led to controversy. Glick (1985) has argued that aggregation from psychological to organizational climate is not appropriate on conceptual grounds and contends that the unit of analysis for climate should be the organization or subunit, not the individual. This has led to a lively response by James, Joyce, and Slocum (1988) and to a rejoinder by Glick (1988). I will not attempt to reconcile this issue here. However, I do want to call readers' attention to the unit of analysis as an especially important aspect not only of climate and culture but of the extended multi-level model and, indeed, the organizational field in general. The unit of analysis issue is so pervasive and so important, in fact, that I discuss its implications for the extended model in general in Chapter 12.

ORGANIZATIONAL CULTURE AND EFFECTIVENESS

As I pointed out previously, because of the subjectivist emphasis and treatment of culture as something an organization is, earlier work does not usually try to link culture and effectiveness. This seems to be changing, and the peeled-onion approach allows for investigation of this kind of linkage quite easily.

A recent review located some half-dozen studies in the literature that did concentrate on such a linkage (see Denison & Mishra, 1989). In addition, some recent conceptual pieces develop models that examine this question (e.g., Arogyaswamy & Byles, 1987; Saffold, 1988). The first of these discusses organizational culture in terms of tight or loose internal fit (agreement concerning dominant organizational values and ideologies and values/ideologies compatibility) and external linkage to environment and strategy. Saffold (1988) not only develops a sophisticated model but discusses methodological and other implications. He also makes the point that it is possible to investigate the effects of culture on performance using either objectivist or subjectivist approaches. Saffold's argument thus is consistent with a critical pluralist perspective. I recommend both of these pieces for additional detail.

Finally, Denison and Mishra (1989) not only review much previous work but also use that review to develop a culture-effectiveness model consistent with competing-values aspects as discussed in several places in this book. The model shows the importance of emphasizing the cultural dimensions of involvement, consistency, adaptability, and mission in terms of a range of different aspects of effectiveness. The study also illustrates using a two-phase approach where case studies provide input for developing questionnaire measures of culture and drawing on subjective and objective performance measures.

Essentially, then, we can conclude from all this that a critical pluralist perspective appears useful in examining various models linking culture to effectiveness. This, linked with earlier treatment of the peeled-onion approach and the linkage of culture with climate, suggests some ways in which organizational culture can prove useful in our extended model.

CREATING AND MANAGING CULTURE

Given the divergence in the basic notions of organizational culture, what can be said about creating and managing it? The answer is that one can offer a synthesis of arguments from various sources with varying degrees of empirical support. Like other aspects of organizational culture, this one is ripe for systematic development with research conducted across time. I also should note that *managing culture* here ranges from sustaining and transmitting the current culture to taking an active role in trying to change it. Schneider and Rentsch (1988) call this "grappling effectively" (p. 181).

In terms of culture creation, first, we can think of the role of the external environment and societal culture (see Ott, 1989). I described the nature of these in Chapter 5; here I simply argue that they are expected to play a potentially important role in the creation of organizational culture. We expect the general and specific external environment segments to have an impact on the basic nature of the kinds of employees hired and the organizations with which a given organization must deal. These, in combination with the values ideologies and assumptions brought in from the outside, are expected to have a direct impact on organizational members, including management and employees. This point is well illustrated in terms of the new plant locations in Riverton and Coal Town described in Chapter 5. Recall that the two towns were located in parallel valleys separated by a mountain range, and that Riverton was a farming retail center, whereas Coaltown was a mining town with strong United Mine Worker ties. Clearly, the dramatic cultural and environmental differences in these two towns would be expected to have a strong impact on the organizational cultures of the plants locating in each.

Second, we can think of the impact of the founder, or of the founder functioning as a dominant elite in combination with other influential leaders (e.g., Dyer, 1986; Schein, 1983, 1985). The founder's values, beliefs, and basic assumptions about how to succeed are expected to be particularly important, along with the founder's cognitive complexity and other attributes. All these come together in a vision or archetype of what the organization should be. Founder impact is likely to be especially important for entrepreneurs. This vision is influenced by the previously discussed external environment and societal culture in which the founder was raised and is located, and by a whole host of the kind of individual background factors (education, family history, previous work experience, etc.) discussed in Chapter 6. In turn, the founder will tend to hire people with compatible values, basic assumptions, and so on, and these peoples' learning experiences inside the organization will have an influence on the organizational culture (Schein, 1983).

As a part of creating and managing culture, these "right type" people are moved into managerial positions and bring in later generations of right-type people. Thus environmental and societal culture forces are reinforced by the founder's basic assumptions, selection and socialization emphases, and the continuing action of top management (see Wiener, 1988).

Let's look at the socialization and top management aspects in more detail. Socialization starts with an emphasis on hiring right-type members initially because they will require less formal socialization. At best, however, training and acculturation will be required (see Feldman, 1988; Ritti & Funkhouser, 1987; Van Maanen, 1977). There are a number of different dimensions along which socialization can vary and that can have an impact on the socialization process and organizational culture (e.g., group versus individual, or self-destructive/reconstructive versus self-enhancing). For example, a self-destructive/reconstructive focus emphasizes tearing down previous aspects of the self and replacing them as in boot camp. A self-enhancing focus is represented in professional development programs (Van Maanen, 1978).

As a part of the socialization process and reinforcement of the strong impact that many argue top-level leaders have on organizational culture (e.g., Franklin, 1975) there is leader role modeling, so that organizational members can identify with the leaders and internalize their values and assumptions (Schein, 1990). Schein (1983, 1985, 1990) argues that there are a number of "embedding mechanisms" that can be used to reinforce leaders' underlying assumptions. Primary ones include such things as what leaders pay attention to, measure, and control, how they react to critical events, how the reward system is set up, and so forth. Secondary ones, which work only if consistent with primary ones, are oriented around organizational design characteristics and a wide range of artifacts as summarized in layer 1 of the peeled-onion framework. These include stories, language, rituals, legends, physical facilities, symbols, and so forth (see Pettigrew, 1979).

The forces just indicated are important in establishing and sustaining an organizational culture. Over time we can expect there to be a natural evolution in culture (Schein, 1990). Changes in these forces tend to produce group stresses and strains leading to new learning and adaptation. Also, new people coming in will bring in new assumptions (in spite of selection efforts). These forces are in contention with those to maintain the status quo, but over time one can expect a natural evolution in the culture. Age and size tend to lead to more differentiation; hence subcultures are likely to emerge and there will be some variation in their relative impact versus that of the overall organizational culture (Schein, 1990).

Managing Change

A key question for leaders is whether to allow culture to change slowly through natural evolution or to try to induce "forced-draft" change. There is debate among management scholars about the extent to which leaders really can induce substantial change (see Kilmann et al., 1985; Meyerson & Martin, 1987; Schein, 1985). However, for practitioners there is little debate—they take it almost as a matter of faith that culture can be changed. As has been said earlier in the chapter, the layer of culture makes a difference. The outer layers are more amenable to change in general and quick change in particular than arc the core assumptions (sce Ott, 1989).

What all of this suggests is that the most reasonable stance is to ask under what conditions and how organizational culture can be changed (Robbins, 1990). Let's look at these as suggested in the literature.

Dramatic crisis. There is virtually universal agreement that a crisis that is perceived as one by the organization's members is a triggering mechanism for cultural change (see Dyer, 1984; Tichy & Devanna, 1986). This argument also is a relevant one in considering the occurrence of charismatic or transformational leadership, as shown in Chapter 9. A key point in both cases is that the members must perceive the crisis; although it is sometimes obvious to everyone, often it falls upon the leader to make it "obvious".

Leadership turnover. Turnover in top management and other levels allows for the opportunity for new values/assumptions to be introduced (see Pettigrew, 1979). Of course, the new leadership must have a clearly articulated alternative vision and know how to implement it (Dyer, 1985). Again, transformationally oriented leadership is relevant (see Chapter 9).

Stage of organizational life cycle. I touched on the organizational life cycle in Chapter 5. Here, the argument is that cultural change should be easier when the organization is moving from birth to the growth stage and from maturity to the decline or revitalization stage (Robbins, 1990). It is at these transition points that the need for change is likely to be most apparent and organizational members most responsive (see Baliga & Hunt, 1988). Receptivity during these transitions is likely to be enhanced if organizational members are less than satisfied about previous developments (see Siehl, 1985).

Other factors. Organizational age and size, and intensity and integration of the current culture, are other factors likely to be important (Robbins, 1990). In terms of age, the argument simply is that the older the culture, the more deeply entrenched it is likely to be. In small organizations there are less likely to be strong subcultures, and it is expected that top leaders can more easily both communicate with and serve as a role model for organizational members. Cultural intensity (within organization/unit agreement) and integration (subunit sharing of common cultures) have an obvious impact on how easy or hard a given current culture/subculture is to change. Change should be easier when there is less agreement and where subcultures are not highly developed.

How. Robbins (1990) and Schein (1990) are among those who present methods that can be used to bring about the changes just mentioned. I won't discuss these here other than to indicate that they are similar to the kinds of steps discussed in terms of visionary leadership in Chapter 9, are related to schema changes as touched on in Chapter 7, and are consistent with change efforts in general (see Robbins and Schein for further discussion).

Postscript

As a part of the direct and indirect sources involved in the previous discussion, I invite readers to consider especially pieces by Meyerson and Martin (1987) and by Schneider and Rentsch (1988). The first of these contrasts some implications of managing organizational culture under three different cultural views. The second develops an organizational culture management framework oriented around six issues (e.g., membership and authority issues). Also, there is a piece by Gagliardi (1986) that develops a framework for organizational culture creation and change. Finally, a very recent book describes in considerable detail the difficulties involved in attempting to merge the two very different and intensive cultures of General Motors and Electronic Data Systems (EDS; see Levin, 1989). Even a quick reading of this interesting book shows the importance of the factors discussed in this section and what can happen where they are disregarded.

These pieces, in combination, can reinforce this chapter's insights on managing organizational culture.

SELECTED RESEARCH AND CONCEPTUAL LINKAGES WITH THE EXTENDED MODEL

It seems appropriate to start this linkage section with the consideration of organizational culture as something the organization has, versus something the organization is. Clearly the variables and linkages in Figure 10.1 support the "has" approach, built around variables and relationships (and I will return to this point shortly). Nevertheless, a holistic approach based on culture as something an organization "is" is inviting.

Such an approach might well attempt to link leadership up and down the organization in a "management of meaning" context (see Smircich & Morgan, 1982) with organizational culture and perhaps other aspects as well. It would make subjectivist-oriented assumptions and use research approaches consistent with these (e.g., some type of ethnographical approach). In many respects it might well resemble the ethnographical liberal-arts college study touched on in Chapter 4 (Tierney, 1988). One important aspect of this would be an emphasis on the organization's history and its impact on current findings. Among other things, such a study should help illustrate the kinds of organizational configurations or archetypes that I've mentioned so many times. All told, this could prove to be a very enlightening study and have something important to say about limited aspects of the extended model.

Of course, as stated earlier, more typical in terms of other aspects of the model would be studies treating organizational culture as a series of variables and relationships—something an organization has. Given this, following the chapter's peeled-onion analogy, we still must determine how deep we need to go for our questions of interest. For example, systems domain leader background aspects and those of the external environment and societal culture could be linked to organizational culture using the outer layers of the peeled onion. In contrast, one might attempt to look at these relationships at the deeper, unstated assumptions layer of organizational culture. The literature suggests relationships among these variables, though it does not address them in terms of the peeled onion's layers. Similarly, the literature suggests that organizational design and other leader critical tasks are likely to both influence and be influenced by organizational culture. And, once again, the peeled-onion approach is apt, as it is for the later areas that I discuss in this section.

Another important area to consider is the relationships among organizational culture and the various subcultures up and down and horizontally throughout the organization. What is the relationship of these to the cultural intensity and cultural integration concepts discussed in the chapter? In turn, how are such aspects related to the various leader and subordinate capability components, particularly individual values, at different levels in the organization? To what extent are organizational culture and subcultures related to various kinds of cognitive schemas? To what extent do organizational culture and subcultures serve as a bridge between leader critical tasks and effectiveness aspects at different organizational levels and over time? A related question is what happens to the above kinds of linkages when organizational climate and subclimates (where they are differentiated as in the chapter) are considered in conjunction with the earlier organizational culture aspects.

Returning to leadership, an important set of linkages to examine is that between organizational culture and various aspects of transformational and charismatic (as well as other) aspects of leadership as we move up and down the domains. Also, what is the linkage with vision as articulated in some of the different ways discussed in the book? Some recent work by Sheridan, Hogstel, and Fairchild (1990), showing the effects of different kinds of leadership under different kinds of what they define as climates, appears consistent with this general thrust.

Still another important area is concerned with managing culture and subcultures up and down the organization. Consistent with the chapter discussion, the question is how some of the conditions (turnover, crisis, life cycle stages, etc.) influence the culture-sustaining and change process.

Also, the role of the various kinds of leadership teams in the diverse organizational culture relationships is important, as it has been for other facets throughout the book. Finally, the impact of organizational culture across time is important. In an "is" mode it could be examined using a dynamic case study approach like that in Chapter 12. It also could be examined across time using variables.

CONCLUDING COMMENTARY

This chapter illustrates quite clearly the virtue of a critical pluralist approach. The study of organizational culture has now evolved to the point where it is clear that entire reliance on either subjectivist or objectivist orientations is not the most appropriate way to use organizational culture in the extended model. The peeled-onion framework allows us to emphasize those aspects of culture most germane to whatever particular focus we are emphasizing at a given time. Furthermore, it makes us aware of easier-to-obtain proxy measures that sometimes can be used in place of those that are more difficult to obtain.

The question of whether one is interested in culture as something an organizational has, as opposed to something an organization is, is also useful in guiding thinking. Interestingly, both this and the peeled-onion label represent the use of metaphors so prized by subjectivists. The conception of culture vis-à-vis climate, discussed in this chapter, also should prove helpful in using the two concepts to reinforce each other while recognizing their separateness.

Finally, the role of subcultures and subclimates and the notions of intensity and integration should help in extending our thinking about the appropriate role of organizational culture and its relation to other organizational aspects. Such usage is particularly important as one moves down to lower organizational levels.

It's useful to return to Figure 10.1 to help reinforce understanding of the pervasive role of organizational culture in the extended model. This, and the other linkages in the model, illustrate the kind of complex series of relationships with which leaders in the model must deal. These have a great number of important implications for leader development and for the extended model in general. These are discussed in Chapter 11, which concludes Part II of the book.

11 Developmental Implications and Enriching Schema Variety

Those of you who are overly ambitious may attempt to acquire [leadership] qualities over a short period. As I, Attila have found in my own life, these qualities . . . simply take time, learning and experience to develop. There are few who will find shortcuts. There are simply rare opportunities to accelerate competence, and without paying the price, no matter how great or small, none will become prepared to lead others.

—Wess Roberts (1987, p. 22),
Leadership Secrets of Attila the Hun

A man has no ears for that which experience has given him no access.

—Friedrich Neitzsche,
German philosopher

And then for the next ninety minutes the Other Voice takes over, and He or It, the Comedy Deity, lets you leave the world while He talks, and then after it's all over, He sets your weak, trembling and insecure body down.

—Joe Bob Briggs (1990, p. 77),
stand-up comic

The opening quotes capture the nature of the developmental aspects that are important to leaders in the extended model. Generally, these leaders must be concerned about developmental shortcuts, about the role of experience in their development, and about being so competent at their role that an internal "Leadership Deity" helps them in complex leadership situations. More especially, they must be concerned with developing the capabilities recapitulated in the section below.

RECAP OF NEEDED TOP-LEVEL LEADERSHIP CAPABILITIES

For openers, top-level leaders in the model need to be cognitively complex—in simplest terms, to be very high on differentiation and integration both in the short run and across long periods of time. I've argued earlier that these aspects should be reflected, among other ways, in cognitive maps—special kinds of schema that summarize the strategic interrelationships seen by leaders across time. The more cognitively complex the leader, the more sophisticated the map and the longer the time period over which the leader is able to map these complex interrelationships. At the very highest level, I've argued that these maps, at least in broadest outline form, probably should extend 20 years or more into the future.

A part of this complexity must surely involve being able to combine both rational and intuitive knowledge and skills over time. It also probably involves what I later in the chapter call "street smarts," practical intelligence or tacit knowledge in some as yet unknown amount.

Another part that I see as important concerns the stylistic cognitive or intellectual preferences that tap inclinations or preferred ways of using cognitive aspects. The previously mentioned Myers-Briggs and Sternberg Intellectual Style instruments illustrate this. As one example, following Jacobs and Jaques, I speculated earlier that lower-level Myers-Briggs intuitive thinkers might be particularly likely to work at building the kind of sophisticated cognitive maps that could provide possible future payoff at higher organizational levels.

I've also contended that inclination is important in terms of the motivation to exert the kinds of efforts involved in being a successful top-level leader. Here I especially emphasize self-efficacy and need for socially oriented power as indicators of a leader's feeling of competency and inclination to lead and empower others. At the same time, I recognize the potential importance of other personality variables (e.g., those relating to social skills, or to task objectives), although the major emphasis here has been on the inclination or predisposition aspects. I've further reinforced this orientation with a focus on value preferences and ideologies, which along with other variables help shape such critical tasks as goal and strategy setting and organizational design.

Finally, I have argued that the cognitive and personality/value aspects just mentioned will be complemented by complex sets of leadership behaviors/skills. These behaviors/skills can be grouped roughly into transactionally oriented and transformationally oriented aspects, with more specific sets of skills delineating these general categories.

I've summarized the important capabilities that I am concerned with developing in the extended model. Let's now turn to some basic learning concepts involved in developing these capabilities.

LEARNING CONCEPTS AND AN APPLICATION

The basic learning concepts of importance are summarized in Figure 11.1 and are then considered in light of how they might apply to expert versus novice leaders. After that, I use the concepts as appropriate throughout the rest of the chapter. The figure contrasts an emphasis on cognitive learning with an emphasis on skill learning, and learning of a logical/rational nature versus that of an intuitive/judgmental nature. Cells I and II reflect a detached and informational approach to logical/rational and intuitive/judgmental learning, respectively (e.g., reading a book or listening to a lecture *about* leadership or *about* how to develop intuition). Cells III and IV, in contrast, represent an emphasis on skills—learning *to do* something logical/rational (such as solving mathematical problems) or something more intuitive in nature (such as leadership).

Many continue to argue that our education system, at all levels, tends to underemphasize cell II and IV learning. In terms of collegiate business school education (BBA and MBA programs) the underemphasis on these two cells, and particularly cell IV, recently has become a major issue (see Porter & McKibbin, 1988). Projects such as the American

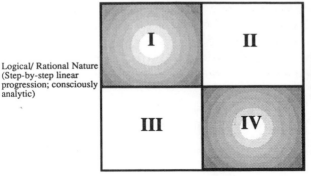

Cognitive Emphasis
(What and why; learning
about something)

Logical/ Rational Nature
(Step-by-step linear
progression; consciously
analytic)

Intuitive/Judgmental
Nature (Multiple cues;
not capable of being
expressed adequately in
words)

Skill Emphasis
(How to; learning *to*
do something)

Figure 11.1. Learning Emphasis and Nature of What Is Learned

Assembly of Collegiate Schools of Business (AACSB, 1987) Educational Outcome Project have been established to deal with it.

At the same time, Kotter (1982a) and Isenberg (1984), among many others, contend that the management literature has traditionally over-emphasized rationality. Lombardo and McCall (1982) capture this well by contending that rational analytical management models fail to capture the complexity involved in "thresholds and constantly changing relations among elements" (p. 67).

Some who share this view, such as Mintzberg (1976), have argued in terms of split, right brain/left brain thinking and action. Here, the left side of the brain is thought to be oriented toward logic, with the right side oriented toward intuitive aspects. However, Hines (1987) asserts that this "hemisphere mythology" is an oversimplification. Simon (1987) calls it a "red herring." The argument does not negate the importance of both kinds of learning; it simply puts in question the hemispheric argument.

Consideration of both rational and intuitive aspects together has been variously referred to as dualities, dialectics, linear versus nonlinear, competing, and red mode versus green mode, among other terms (see Isenberg, 1985; Kolb, 1983; Mitroff, 1978; Pondy, 1983; Quinn, 1988).

Indeed, Bogen (1969) has compiled from the literature more than 30 adjectives describing such dualities. For our purposes, an especially representative term for this complex combination of thinking and behaving is *Janusian* (from the two faces of the Roman god, Janus; see Quinn, 1988). Pondy (1983) goes so far as to assert that there is a union of these two modes in an interactive process where rational and intuitive are equal partners. Fry and Pasmore (1983) describe this kind of learning as "frame breaking" and argue that it tends to be underemphasized in management education and training programs.

Experts Versus Novices as an Application

An extremely important application illustrating the learning concepts just discussed is concerned with experts versus novices. One can argue that the whole intent of this chapter is to discuss some key ways of developing novice leaders into expert leaders, able to deal with progressively more complex critical organizational tasks.

For openers, we should be aware that there are different definitions of novices and experts, as discussed by E. Ropo (1989a) and others. Also, some of the definitions are more comprehensive than others. The conception of Janusian thinking and behaving presented here appears to be consistent with the more comprehensive perspectives.

The general notion is that the schemas of experts differ in numerous ways from those of novices (essentially, then, there is a concern with how novice schemas change as the novices move toward becoming experts). Empirical work is needed to examine systematically such novice-to-expert schema changes in the leadership area. One study does suggest different leadership prototypes between experts and novices (see Baumgardner & Forti, 1988). In contrast to the leadership area per se, there is considerable evidence (from both the United States and abroad) from other areas that appears relevant for leadership (e.g., Chi, Glaser, & Farr, 1987; Messick, 1984, 1988; E. Ropo, 1989a, 1989b; Ropo & Jahnukainen, 1990; Simon, 1987). I only touch on this literature here, and I encourage interested readers to turn to the original sources.

Experts tend to obtain a large amount of specific information concerning their expertise area. Such information is hierarchically or otherwise organized to be consistent with the underlying structure of the area or domain in question. However, although the novice too attempts to obtain specialized information, the expert and novice process their information very differently (Chi et al., 1987; Messick, 1984, 1988).

For instance, an expert in physics will concentrate initially on ways of representing a problem and tend to work forward from this representation to a desired outcome. In contrast, a novice tends to work backward, leading the novice more quickly to ostensibly feasible equations. Similarly, social problem-solving experts, as contrasted with novices, tend to devote much more effort toward analysis of their abstracted problem representations, as opposed to problem specifics (Chi et al., 1987; Messick, 1984). Essentially, experts internalize "knowing what" in their emphasis on "knowing how" (see Dreyfus & Dreyfus, 1986).

The summary above conveys some of the flavor of expert and novice differences. Dreyfus and Dreyfus (1986) have developed a five-stage model showing the movement from novice to expert:

- *Novice stage*—Learn facts and rules concerning a task. These are not to be violated.
- *Advanced beginner stage*—Experience becomes very important. Performance improves. Understanding begins to exceed facts and rules.
- *Competency stage*—The learner begins to appreciate the complexity of the task and to recognize a much larger set of cues. The most important cues are concentrated on. Reliance on rules begins to disappear.
- *Proficiency stage*—Calculation and rational analysis appear to vanish. Unconscious, fluid, and effortless performance begins to emerge. The learner unconsciously knows how to "read" the system.
- *Expert stage*—Here, the expert does what comes naturally or intuitively. The expert has programmed into his or her head multidimensional cognitive maps or schemas. He or she sees and knows things intuitively.

Using Intuition

The model just described suggests that, in addition to rational learning, experts have developed a high level of intuition. However, we should recognize that the term *intuition* has been used in a number of different ways (see Agor, 1984); Isenberg, 1984, discusses five of these. First, it can reflect "gut feel" that something should be done or is wrong. An example is a top-level leader who forecast a difficult year ahead for his organization and, sensing that something was wrong, analyzed one particular group (Isenberg, 1984).

Second, leaders rely on intuition or judgment so that they can rapidly perform skillfully learned behavior patterns. Once this schema is internalized it becomes automatic (and, as described in Chapter 7, the leader is unaware of the effort involved). Third, intuition can be used to synthesize isolated bits of data into an integrated picture (differentiation and integration). Frequently this is what is called an "aha" experience. Fourth, some leaders use intuition to check the results of more formal analyses. The data have to "feel right" to them before they are accepted. Finally, leaders sometimes use intuition to forgo in-depth analysis and move rapidly toward a plausible solution. Here, as with chess experts, intuition is a virtually instantaneous cognitive process where expert leaders recognize familiar patterns.

Basically, what all this suggests is that intuition is something more than a process of random guessing (for the expert, although it might not be for the novice). It typically involves extensive skill learning. In union with rational analysis, described earlier, we have the Janusian notion.

As applied specifically to leading, Isenberg (1985) embeds this Janusian notion within the context of what he calls "leading empirically." Expert leaders vary their behaviors on the basis of an incomplete understanding of a typical, fast-paced situation while monitoring the situation and adjusting behavior as the situation unfolds. Isenberg sees this as a skill developed through experience that encourages filling holes in incomplete data by organizing problems into a network of broadly related concerns. These concerns can be dealt with as one structure (schema) and used to guide problem management (see Hunt & Phillips, in press). Similarly, Weick (1983) argues that leader thinking occurs simultaneously with behavior. This notion was alluded to in Joe Bob Briggs's description of the "Comedy Deity."

Intuition and Street Smarts

There is a recently discussed concept called *street smarts* (Wagner & Sternberg, 1990) that appears related to intuition. As the name implies, it is concerned with the practical knowledge and judgment required for on-the-job success, (e.g., "learning the ropes," "learning what goes without saying around here"). Its hallmark is facile acquisition of tacit knowledge learned informally on the job (Wagner & Sternberg, 1990). Three specific tacit knowledge aspects concern managing oneself, managing others, and managing tasks. As I show later in the chapter, Wagner and Sternberg have developed a way to measure street smarts and have proposed a couple of training approaches.

Wrap-up

I've argued that Janusian thinking and behavior essentially involve all four cells shown in Figure 11.1 and that novices become more Janusian along the road to expertise. In other words, experts, as defined here, use a combination of both cognitive and skill emphases and rational and intuitive emphases. I've also contended that Janusian thinking and behaving may be related to cognitive complexity. Although I am unaware of any data on this, I would expect that those high on the differentiation (a kind of analysis) and integration (a kind of synthesis) concepts—particularly flexible integration—discussed in Chapter 7 would also tend to be high on Janusian learning involving those concepts. However, this would not necessarily be true for other, unrelated concepts.

What about cognitive styles? As has been shown, one of the Myers-Briggs dimensions calls for a breakdown between "intuition" and "sensing." In other words, a person expresses a preference for either *sensing* or *intuition*. If taken literally, this might suggest an either-or situation. However, if we include both gathering and evaluating information, then again the earlier-emphasized NT (intuitive thinking) style comes to mind. That style combines an intuitive information-gathering preference with rational information evaluation. Elsewhere I have discussed intuitive-thinking and other cognitive style relationships with differing aspects of individual and organizational functioning. Here I argue that there may be relationships between various MBTI preferences (or other intellectual style preferences, for that matter) and the extent to which one develops Janusian skills.[1]

The learning concepts and their application clearly show the importance of Janusian thinking and behaving in complex situations requiring development of leadership "experts." Let's look at the role of education, training, and experience in such leadership development.

EDUCATION, TRAINING, AND EXPERIENCE

The leadership development model in Figure 11.2 summarizes similarities and differences in education, training, and experience activities as they relate to the kind of expert leaders called for by the extended model. This leadership development model is similar to other recent approaches in the literature (see Keys & Wolfe, 1988; Wexley &

Baldwin, 1986). It serves as an organizing framework for much of the rest of the chapter.

Education

The education component in Figure 11.2 is broad in scope and has both immediate and long-term applications. Education typically involves exposure to contrasting perspectives and requires personal intellectual initiative that tends to be cumulative and geometric in building understanding about complex matters. Often, however, the effects are uncertain in terms of utility (Brascombe & Gilmore, 1975). For our purposes, education includes degree programs (BBA, MBA), nondegree short courses, and in-house seminars oriented to specific organizations (see Heisler & Benham, in press).

I've already touched on the BBA and MBA programs in the earlier section on learning concepts, particularly intuitively oriented skill learning. There I pointed out that one key criticism was the programs' lack of emphasis on skill learning. That point, in one form or another, has come up again and again over the years in the literature (see Cohen, 1988-89; Fromm, 1966; Hays & Abernathy, 1980; Kahn & Bruce-Briggs, 1973; Kilmann, 1984). Similar criticisms, as well as that of a lack of understanding of adult learning processes, have sometimes been leveled at university nondegree (management development) courses and executive MBA programs.

In spite of these and other criticisms, such university programs continue to be the primary source of education for middle- and upper-level leaders (Executive Knowledgeworks, 1986). Their most commonly expressed goals are the individual development of management skills and broadening individual perspectives (Executive Knowledgeworks, 1986; Saari, Johnson, McLaughlin, & Zimmerle, 1988).

A more complete feel for the nature of these programs is available from Heisler and Benham (in press), Porter and McKibbin (1988), and Keys and Wolfe (1988). The programs, in combination with training and experience, appear to be key means for development of cognitive complexity and the other leader capabilities in the extended model—provided that they emphasize Janusian learning.

As a part of this kind of emphasis and at least partly in response to the previously indicated criticisms, we are beginning to see Janusian-oriented courses that can be used either as a part of a degree program

Leadership Development
Activities

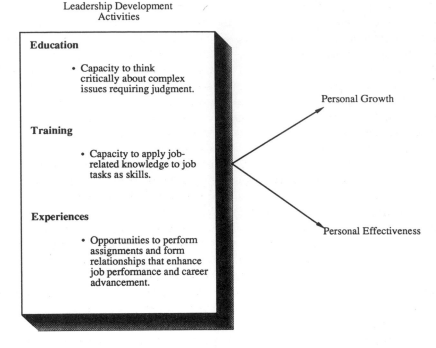

Figure 11.2. A Leadership Development Model
Source: Adapted from Heisler and Behham (in press). Used with permisssion.

or as a short course for managers. Quinn's (1988) competing-values work is at the vanguard of these.

Quinn—Competing Values

Recall the different hierarchical archetypes of leaders developed by Quinn in Chapter 8. At the top organizational level tend to be Quinn's "master managers," who were found capable of balancing the competing demands in his eight-dimension framework.

As shown in Chapter 8, Quinn and his associates have designed a series of courses or programs to develop the complex Janusian thinking/behaving required of his cognitively complex master managers. The intent is to facilitate the growth of these skills in leaders at any organizational level. As indicated earlier, this kind of growth is very difficult. It calls for emphasizing new schemas, frame breaking (see Fry & Pasmore, 1983), or changing one's cognitive maps. Quinn (1988) discusses such complex Janusian learning issues in some detail. For example, he deals with deliberate self-examination and change, a couple of surprising instances of "spontaneous transformation" caused by crises or extremely frustrating situations, and a detailed curriculum of systematic education and training. The latest version of this is reflected in the skills-development program covered in Quinn, Faerman, Thompson, and McGrath (1990; see Chapter 8). This program, in some ways, is patterned after Whetten and Cameron's (1984) *Developing Management Skills*, but is oriented to the competing-values framework. Both this and the Whetten and Cameron approach have been designed to try to integrate the cognitive learning and skills notions discussed earlier.

Essentially, they involve a variation of individual assessment, learning (via directed reading), analysis (typically cases), practice (role plays or similar activities), and application (trying out the new skill or competency). These and other recently appearing "management skills" books are consistent with the earlier mentioned recent push by AACSB (the accrediting agency for business/management schools) to go beyond cognitive learning and develop critical managerial skills as a part of the education process.

As such, the programs are logical extensions of the earlier experiential learning approaches used in management and organizational behavior courses in business schools (e.g., Kolb, Rubin, & McIntyre, 1984). How successful the skills movement will be remains to be seen—although it certainly is a step in the right direction, particularly in the context of the extended model.

So much for the educational component of Figure 11.2. Let's turn now to the training component.

Training

The training component tends to be relatively narrow in scope and to have immediate job-specific applications. It typically is more focused and more short-term in nature than either the education or experience components. Although it is employer sponsored, it can be delivered by either internal trainers or external vendor/consultants (Heisler & Benham, in press).

A recent interview of leadership training (Latham, 1988) tended to place a heavy emphasis on training concerned with the traditional leadership approaches mentioned in Chapter 4. For our purposes, we need to focus on training concerned with various aspects of cognitive complexity, transformationally oriented leadership and the other kinds of notions discussed in the earlier section on complex thinking and behaving. Let's start with transformationally oriented training.

Transformationally Oriented Training

As of this writing, some of this training has only been proposed, whereas some has been implemented. All of it, in one way or another, uses a combination of the cognitive learning function (the what) and the skill-learning aspect (the how-to) discussed earlier. The training also assumes that certain baseline dispositions such as goal commitment and work involvement (Conger & Kanungo, 1988), as well as the previously emphasized need for power and desire to use it in prosocial ways (Sashkin, 1988), are probably necessary and need to be assessed. Then, based on this information, the programs propose training individuals in terms of the specific skills involved in the particular transformationally oriented approach.

As an example, Conger and Kanungo (1988) propose development of (a) skills in critical evaluation of the context- and problem-finding, (b) visioning (goals) and planning (tactics) skills; (c) communication (articulation and interpersonal sensitivity) skills, (d) exemplary personal behavior and impression management skills, and (e) empowering skills. These are closely related to the Conger (1989) four-stage model discussed in Chapter 9.

Sashkin (1988) presents a similar list of skills to be developed that correspond to his model. The key point here is that the authors of each of these approaches discuss their potential implementation using a combination of currently available organizational development (action research) and training techniques for which they provide references and brief descriptions. That is, they propose building these transformationally oriented skills using a range of previously developed techniques. Unlike some (e.g., Roberts & Bradley, 1988), these authors believe that such leadership skills can be trained.

Bass (1987) has begun to use training programs built on his transformational/transactional approach, discussed in Chapter 9. The programs take various directions, depending on the desired managerial objectives. Let's convey the tenor of a typical program.

First, Bass's Multifactor Leadership Questionnaire (MLQ) is completed by leaders and subordinates. Then survey feedback is used to provide the leaders with information about their transformational/transactional leadership as described by subordinates. Second, individual counseling or group workshop sessions are used to deal with discrepancies between self-descriptions and those of subordinates. The counseling-workshop sessions involve examination of why the discrepancies might have occurred.

Then, depending on specific objectives, other facets used singly or in combination include: (a) participants' use of the MLQ to describe an effective leader they have known and discussion of these results in combination with the leaders' self-descriptions; (b) workshops where leaders consider new organizational design and organizational culture aspects to enhance transformational leadership; (c) workshops where leaders learn how to serve as mentors for each other in developing various aspects of transformational leadership; (d) creative exercises to develop the intellectual stimulation component of transformational leadership (e.g., Zuker, 1985); and (e) workshops where leaders develop action plans to help enhance various aspects of their leadership.

Some preliminary results using the Leadership Practices Inventory (LPI) of Kouzes and Posner (1987), discussed in Chapter 9, also have been reported. Posner and Kouzes (1990) claim an average 15% increase in LPI behaviors over a 10-month period from a one-week training program at AT&T. This program was a part of these authors' emphasis on examining and identifying key behaviors of leaders, how these behaviors manifest themselves, and how these practices can be nurtured and developed in people (Posner & Kouzes, 1990, p. 214).

None of these programs uses mysterious techniques; all borrow heavily from established organizational development and related approaches (survey feedback, workshops, and so on). Thus we can anticipate that they will be subject to the strengths and weaknesses of such programs in terms of the difficulty of changing behavior, sustaining the change, and so forth (see Yukl, 1981, for a review of several facets of leadership training and its effects). Although not directed toward transformationally oriented leadership, much of that discussion still is relevant.

I should note also that only Bass has shown explicit concern with transactional leadership—for the others it is almost as if it doesn't exist. Given the emphasis in Chapter 8 on the wide range of relevant transactionally oriented leader behaviors, we certainly don't want to fall into the trap of ignoring these other components. Yukl and Lepsinger (1989) deal with feedback intervention based on the Yukl typology discussed in Chapter 8. Thus the message, in terms of the extended model, is to combine a range of different kinds of leader skills/behaviors in addition to transformationally oriented ones.

Tacit Knowledge (Street Smarts) Training

In addition to the kind of training in leadership skills just described, it's useful to conclude this section with a look at training for the recently recognized street-smarts notion discussed earlier. The developers (Wagner & Sternberg, 1990) propose two kinds of training—direct and indirect. The direct program involves a pretest with the Tacit Knowledge Inventory (TKI) for managers, followed by instruction and application of rules of thumb, and finally by posttest TKI administration.

The indirect approach does not involve the training of tacit knowledge per se, but rather training in strategies people can use to facilitate acquisition of tacit knowledge. One approach to this involves working on aspects of schema change (encoding, etc.) that are believed to lead to various successful aspects of leadership or management (e.g., promotion, strategy setting). Wagner and Sternberg (1990) discuss this and an additional approach to indirect tacit learning.

Experience

Experience as used here, includes both experience in general (developed throughout life) and more specific job-related experience and the relationship of these to growth in cognitive complexity and the other leader capability aspects in the extended model.

General Experience

In terms of general experience, there is evidence that even unprogrammed experiences such as marriage and child rearing produce deep-seated changes in the way adults handle problems and risks and organize their thinking (Botwinick, 1967; Flavell, 1970). There are a number of life cycle and career stage of development models that have relevance for general aspects of experience across different life or career stages (see Dalton & Thompson, 1986; Hall, 1976; Kegan & Lahey, 1984; Levinson, Darrow, Klein, Levinson, & McKee, 1978). Systematic coverage of these goes beyond the scope of this book. Instead, I borrow some aspects of them for discussion as it relates to developmental contributions for the leader capabilities in the extended model.

Avolio and Gibbons (1988) combine many of the notions reflected in models such as those above, and particularly the one by Kegan and Lahey (1984), to derive an illustrative life span events model. The original Kegan and Lahey framework comprises stages reflecting increases in an individual's cognitive complexity level. Avolio and Gibbons do not restrict themselves to stages, and focus specifically on transformational leadership, but their treatment provides insights into the developmental process that appear relevant for a wide range of leader capabilities in the extended model.

Essentially, their approach starts with high parental expectations across many aspects of life. Their potential leader, as a child, is active in family responsibilities. Parents accompany these expectations and responsibilities with an appropriate balance of resources so the potential leader does not get overwhelmed and can feel successful. The potential leader learns how to handle emotions, conflict, and so on through the family and/or other ongoing experiences. The potential leader has engaged in many leadership opportunities and reflected upon these while growing up (e.g., being a team captain, class or club officer, etc.).

The potential leader also has a strong developmental inclination (e.g., recall the importance of cognitive style and need for socialized power as possible indicators). This inclination tends to become a way of life and uses the high standards developed earlier. Related to this, the potential leader seeks out broad, personal development workshops and structured developmental activities. Finally, the potential leader learns to treat *all* experiences as learning ones and is very self-reflective.

These convey the essence of the nonstage developmental model that Avolio and Gibbons articulate and for which they provide some suggestive empirical support (for a related four-stage transformational/ transactional developmental model, see Kuhnert & Lewis, 1987). There are similarities here with the longitudinal work conducted at the AT&T assessment center (see Bray & Howard, 1983; Howard & Bray, 1989). I also should note that Avolio and Gibbons reinforce the importance of family background and general experience shown by those such as Kotter (1982a, 1985, 1988, 1990), and illustrate the importance of the background component of the extended model discussed in Chapter 6.

Finally, we can relate the previous discussion to Elliott Jaques's (e.g., 1986) life span emphasis. As indicated throughout this book, he assumes that an individual's cognitive complexity increases through that person's life span. Earlier, he was quite emphatic that such development could take place only within an individual's maturational band and that a person's genetically determined potential interacts with that individual's potential life experiences (see Chapter 2).

Furthermore, Jaques saw these life experiences as overriding the effects of specific education and training. More recently he and his associates (e.g., Jacobs & Jaques, in press) have begun to consider these issues less deterministically and have proposed a systematic developmental effort involving education, training, and guided experience. I discuss this effort in more detail later in the chapter.

Experience Within the Job Setting

I've argued the importance of lifelong learning for successful leadership and the potential role of various developmental models in the growth and development of leaders. Now, it's important to look at the contribution of experience within the job setting on growth and development. In spite of the recognized importance of such on-the-job experiences as early job challenge (see Margerison & Kakabadse, 1984; Sonnenfeld & Kotter, 1982), there has been surprisingly little systematic emphasis on this in U.S. organizations (see Heisler & Benham, in press; Kotter, 1988; McCall, Lombardo, & Morrison, 1988).

Such experience has been a kind of seat-of-the-pants operation even among major corporations known for progressive human resource programs (Kotter, 1988; McCall et al., 1988). Although many of these major firms have succession planning functions and managerial job rotation programs, frequently the experience provided is not very different in its demands and what is learned from that in previous positions (Davies & Easterly-Smith, 1984). These organizations do not have systematic guidelines to relate the experience to orderly development for leaders. One indication of just how little is known in this area is that even the most sophisticated and expensive assessment technique—the assessment center—accounts for only 10% to 20% of the variance in management promotion rates (Klimoski & Brickner, 1987), where promotion rates are taken as one measure of leadership success.

Fortunately, recent work has begun to address this experience issue programmatically. One set of studies conducted with high-level managers (probably at SST level V or above) in six major corporations in Canada and the United States examined critical career events and developmental lessons learned from these events. These studies, in combination with work focusing on successful managers who got derailed (demoted, fired, or plateaued) just before reaching the top (McCall & Lombardo, 1983) led to development of instruments to shed light on on-the-job experience and its developmental lessons. Figure 11.3 shows an overall summary of this work. Based on several hundred key events described, the researchers used content analysis to condense these to 16 categories. These covered the following kinds of job assignments: the first supervisory job, task force assignments, line/staff switches, managing a larger scope, and business turnaround. Also categorized were: bosses as positive or negative role models, various kinds of hardships (personal trauma, career setback, etc.), purely personal events related to values playing out, and course work.

These led to 34 categories of lessons learned (e.g., how to direct and motivate subordinates, how to cope with situations beyond one's control, management values). Finally, 10 derailment problems, such as problems with interpersonal relations and overdependence, were included.

The combination of these events, lessons, and derailment problems led to the Benchmarks measure, currently containing 18 scales—each with multiple items. This measure has scales tapping the extent to which the respondent demonstrates resourcefulness, being a quick study, decisiveness, acting with flexibility, and difficulty in making transitions (a derailment factor) that appear to be related to cognitive complexity. It also seems to measure a number of other implicit or explicit aspects of the extended model, such as setting a developmental culture and so forth. All of these are considered to be capabilities that leaders are not born with and do not automatically bring to the job but that might realistically be developed.

The authors report early validation work that shows how Benchmark relates to other feedback instruments, how it relates to cognitive styles, and how it relates to promotability and performance assessments. All these suggest that it holds promise for helping to assess specific contributions of on-the-job experience more systematically.

Where Benchmark is an instrument for tapping capabilities that leaders need, the Job Challenge Profile (JCP) is an instrument that focuses on identifying and classifying the different types of developmental job elements—(i.e., assessing sources of on-the-job development; Ruderman, Ohlott, & McCauley, 1990). Twelve scales measuring such developmental aspects of jobs as supportive boss, conflict with

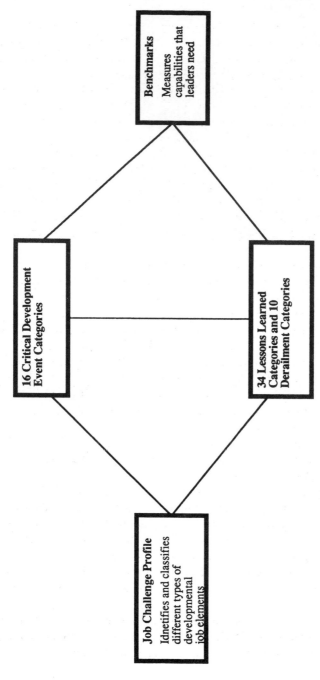

Figure 11.3. Summary of Programmatic Work Covering Critical On-the-Job Events, Lessons Learned, and Executive Derailment

Source: Based on McCauley & Lombardo (1990) and Ruderman, Ohlott, & McCauley (1990).

boss, intense pressure, downsizing/reorganization, problem subordinates, and inherited problems were based on 155 items describing the developmental aspects of jobs. These items were derived from the developmental descriptions discussed earlier (see Figure 11.3).

Once initially developed, the JCP was subjected to various measures of validity. It was found to be related to both general ratings of development of leaders' current jobs and to the 34 lessons of experience previously discussed for the Benchmark measure (see Figure 11.3). It also was found to detect the developmental potential of very different kinds of jobs (e.g., line versus staff). The JCP thus shows promise as a method for assessing the developmental potential of job assignments. Organizations can use it to help identify sources of development in different parts of the organization. It also has the potential to help leaders understand the learning potential of their own jobs (Ruderman et al., 1990).

The programmatic research just described illustrates well the interplay between a range of subjectivist- and objectivist-oriented approaches to obtain a better understanding of the role of on-the-job experiences in developing assessment instruments.

Key events identified from this programmatic research were used as an important aspect of a study to examine the importance of job experience on leader development in New York Telephone, a subsidiary evolving from the 1984 AT&T divestiture. AT&T longitudinal work over more than 20 years (see Bray & Howard, 1983; Howard & Bray, 1988), among other things, has shown the importance of job challenge in the development process for AT&T managers in the aggregate. With the divestiture, the study described here was conducted to answer questions within the context of a particular company that was once a part of AT&T (Valerio, 1990).

Results supported the importance of job challenge in the early years, as shown in the previously conducted AT&T studies. They also revealed that the three most frequently occurring key events reported by Lombardo et al. (1983) also were the most frequently reported in New York Telephone. These were increase in scope, special projects, and exposure to role models. Close behind were self-initiated activities and learning from a negative experience, mentioned not quite as often in the earlier work.

Other recent work focusing on the developmental impact of career experiences is touched on in Kotter (1982a) and treated in more detail in Kotter (1985, 1988, 1990). Although even Kotter's later work on this aspect of experience is not as detailed as that above, it is largely consistent with it. Taken together, the studies reinforce each other and provide much needed preliminary evidence on the growth and development role of experiences within the job setting.

The work just described is an important first step in helping pin down more precisely the role of experience in the overall leader developmental and growth process and making the process less seat-of-the-pants. Another part of an increasing understanding of the role of experience is *how* individuals learn from it. We know even less about this than about the aspects of experience discussed above, but it's an important issue.

Feldman (1986) includes a summary of much of the work relating to how and when individuals learn from experience and, consistent with the earlier discussion in this work, points out the different kinds of learning required in logical/rational and intuitive-type tasks. This book doesn't cover his complex discussion in detail other than to mention its heavy emphasis on various kinds of schemas and information-processing biases. However, it will take a quick look at his action suggestions, based on his earlier discussion.

Feldman argues strongly for increasing the amount and immediacy of feedback by attempting to provide experiences that can make even intuitive tasks more subject to analysis. Of course, this is not easy, but he makes some very general suggestions and sensitizes us to the issue. He also argues for using experiences that *require* learning—in other words, experiences that are not just "the same one repeated twenty times".

A third suggestion is that both substance (content) and process need to be emphasized. The leader not only learns about content (e.g., strategic management in the specific organization) but is sensitized to learning processes, schemas, and "learning how to learn." The final suggestion (much easier said than done) is to try to make the setting a less risk-aversive one to encourage learning from risk taking. Feldman suggests that, instead of penalties for being wrong, there be penalties only for refusing to learn.

Systematic Integration of Education, Training and Experience

As has been shown throughout this chapter, there are relatively few examples of systematic, long-term development combining education, training, and experience. This tends to be so even in our largest corporations. However, the U.S. uniformed services are a major exception. Thus in this section I first examine briefly the strengths and weaknesses of the systematic development programs for the officer corps. Then I look at a systematic development program proposed by Jacobs and Jaques (in press) that moves beyond Jaques's earlier arguments by focusing on orderly development efforts to enhance cognitive complexity. The Air Force, Army, Coast Guard, and Navy all have academies to direct the initial flow of talent. Although selection to these academies differs somewhat across the uniformed services, all strive for very bright, well-rounded entrants. In terms of development, the academies differ from colleges and universities in general because of the relative uniformity of their input and especially of their output.

Let's look at the Army program at West Point as an example. Its purpose is stated quite simply as "developing leaders." Its graduates are expected to be appointed to leadership positions upon commissioning and then to progress to positions of increasing responsibility throughout their careers (Prince, 1987). The culture is one of high expectations and each cadet is anticipated to develop into an effective leader by graduation. The new officer should be able to lead a platoon of 45 soldiers and should have acquired a foundation for continuing development toward higher leadership positions.

The development process starts with selection of the kind of well-balanced people believed to serve as appropriate raw development material. Besides such selection, West Point emphasizes education, skill training, practice opportunities, socialization, evaluation, feedback, and remediation. These are designed to be progressive and sequential so that there are prerequisites and each step offers something new (Prince, 1987).

There is a mix of in- and out-of-class emphases on leadership and organizational behavior. Cadets perform many leadership roles, accompanied by assessment and feedback. The faculty are primarily military officers, who serve as role models for the cadets in their in- and out-of-class activities. The leadership roles include an emphasis on self-development and take in athletic and other activities with leadership implications. A couple of recent empirical studies report on the role of transformational leadership in two programs similar to West Point (see Clover, 1990; Yammarino & Bass, 1990).

After academy graduation, there is then a series of developmental assignments and schools in each academy to which the officers are assigned throughout their careers. Once again we can summarize these, using the Army as an example (see Jacobs & Jaques, in press):

(1) *The Officer Basic Course*—This is formal schooling where the technical skills of the Army and the branch of service are emphasized.

(2) *Period of application of basic junior officer skills*—This application period is then followed by the Officer Advanced Course, formal schooling at a more advanced level.

(3) *Junior service in staff organizations or in command of more complex organizations, followed by schooling in staff procedures*—There are two schools: the Combined Arms Staff, Support School and the Command and General Staff College. Selection to the latter is based on merit and somewhat less than 50% of all officers are selected.

(4) *Extended service period in successively higher staffs, ending for some with battalion command and selection to attend the Army War College or one of several other equivalents*—Selection is based on merit and the percentage selected is small. Yet a smaller percentage is selected to command a brigade. With but few exceptions, only those who command at both battalion and brigade level have a serious opportunity to be promoted to general officer.

The typical form of progression is attendance at a school to prepare for subsequent responsibilities, a period of responsibility with a staff serving the command position for which the officer is being prepared, and then a period of performance in the command position (Jacobs & Jaques, in press). Jacobs and Jaques (1987) argue that the just-described developmental sequence is similar for the Air Force and Navy. Furthermore, the leadership focus at the various academies appears similar, although its exact form differs and there appears to be a varying emphasis on behavioral science findings as a base (compare the Naval Academy description by Katz, 1987; the Air Force description by Gregory, 1987; and the Army description by Prince, 1987). Finally, I might note that the various uniformed services also place a heavy emphasis upon graduate education at civilian universities.

There is no civilian counterpart to this elaborate system that controls inputs from college entrance to retirement. Until recently, the emphasis at the college level was almost entirely focused on cognitive, rational learning (see Figure 11.1). As pointed out, AACSB has become quite concerned about this and it appears that there will be a much heavier focus on Janusian learning. We are beginning to see this on an isolated basis with experiential learning courses (e.g., Kolb, Rubin, & McIntyre,

1984) and even more so with recent skill-development courses (e.g., Quinn et al., 1990; Whetten & Cameron, 1984). Even so, as shown, the developmental efforts once the individuals graduate tend to be far less systematic than those for the uniformed services. In one sense, then, we might put these uniformed services programs forward as models to strive for. However, Jacobs and Jaques (in press), among others, question their "survival value" or at least their adequacy. This issue has been raised for the Navy in terms of narrow conformity, and lack of vision and transformational leadership (see French, 1987; although, as indicated above, Yammarino & Bass, 1990, have begun to focus on this concern.) Of course, to the extent that these criticisms are true, we can only speculate as to some of the reasons. Perhaps the process is appropriate but the specific content is faulty. Perhaps there is too much structure and homogeneity to provide the necessary capabilities—especially cognitive complexity. Perhaps they do not focus enough on the kinds of novel situations likely to be encountered in time of war (see Hunt & Blair, 1985; Hunt & Phillips, in press). Regardless, the uniformed services' methods are not a panacea.

Jaques Revisited

As previously mentioned, Jaques's work with others (e.g., Jacobs & Jaques, in press) has moved beyond his earlier assumptions that a pro-active developmental stance is not necessary. Thus he and his associates have examined some systematic developmental considerations for increasing leader cognitive complexity (see U.S. Army War College, 1988; Jacobs & Jaques, 1987, in press). Briefly, Jaques and his colleagues see leader development as the process of acquiring successively more complex cognitive maps (i.e., capacity to comprehend increased complexity, understand indirect cause-effect relations, and combine logical with intuitive learning and other necessary "equipment" over time. As the tools that are required for successfully operating at increasingly higher levels are acquired, upper-level leaders are ready to make the transition to the next higher level.

For these authors, the key issue is to gain an understanding of how cognitive maps develop over time through the maturational process. They see cognitive map development to depend on the leader's (a) basic cognitive capacity, (b) inclination to develop, and (c) opportunity to develop through increasing interactive exposure to ongoing complexity.

Cognitive capacity. In Chapter 2 I showed Jaques's emphasis on maturational bands and his argument that the Career Path Appreciation

(CPA) measure shows substantial correlations between initial complexity assessment and predicted subsequent hierarchical position at time of follow-up. To this measure one would add other means of tapping complexity and maps (e.g., Bentz, 1987; Streufert & Nogami, 1989; Streufert & Swezey, 1986; Weick & Bougan, 1986) to avoid being method bound by Jaques' approach.

Developmental inclination. For Jaques and his associates a leader's time and effort can be spent in many ways, and only some people will be inclined toward activities leading to increasing cognitive complexity. As previously indicated, they speculate that the intuitive-thinking (NT) cognitive style may tap this inclination. NT leaders may be predisposed to construct internal meaning structures *and* to emphasize the necessary analytical skills at lower organizational levels to be promoted. As we saw earlier, support for upper-level NT styles is mixed. However, I argued for more systematic followup research.

Opportunity. Here, the authors suggest various assignments to provide appropriate education, training, and experience. The earlier discussion in the experience section clearly is relevant here. For Jaques and his colleagues, coaching, mentoring, and counseling should be used to help with this "guided discovery process." Coaching is current on-the-job training by the immediate superior. Mentoring (see Kram, 1985) is teaching longer-term skills by a superior-once-removed. Counseling uses a career specialist with quite varied duties but counseling responsibilities and ready access to the leader in question (Jacobs & Jaques, in press; Jaques, Clement, Rigby, & Jacobs, 1986). Finally, these authors suggest the use of sabbaticals, leaving the current position shortly before promotion, and frequent focused training courses.

ENRICHING SCHEMA VARIETY

A key aspect of the education, training, and experience developmental aspects previously discussed is the enrichment of the individual leader's schema or cognitive map variety. Such enrichment is related intimately to increases in cognitive complexity. Here, I want to touch briefly on some approaches that can facilitate variety in organizational schemas across a wide range of people that may be involved, and also to sensitize leaders and others to their own schemas, the relation of these schemas to those of others, and the value of enriching schema variety. I also invite the reader to think of the treatment here in terms of the earlier discussion of managing organizational culture. There is a very clear linkage.

Organizational Self-Reflection Approach

This approach presents an organization with a description of its current enacted strategy (its strategy-in-use; see Argyris, 1985) and thus is particularly useful at the systems leadership domain. To reveal underlying schemas, this enacted strategy is then compared with the organization's espoused strategy and with its proposed strategy. Displaying inconsistencies between the present strategy, the espoused strategy, and the proposed strategy surfaces the consensual meaning of embedded strategy at the present time. This process helps reveal various schemas and helps provide sensitivity to them and to what might be involved in their change (Finney & Mitroff, 1986). Although a key purpose of such intervention is to influence organizational strategy and structure, as I have said, it can also serve to enhance leadership development.

Finney and Mitroff (1986) discuss a five-stage process that is a variation of the dialectic assumptions involved in Mason and Mitroff's (1981) Strategic Assumption Surfacing and Testing (SAST) process. In dialectics, an idea generates its opposite, leading to a reconciliation of opposites (synthesis) through discourse. Thus it is much like the Janusian emphasis accentuated throughout this chapter. The Organizational Self-Reflection (OSR) process surfaces and examines the schemas associated with the current strategy-in-use.

The five stages essentially call for (a) clear statement of espoused strategy; (b) identification of critical stakeholder groups; (c) surfacing assumptions of the stakeholders (who could be a wide range of people from inside and even outside the organization); (d) comparison of the product of stage (a) for inconsistencies against the product of stage (c); and (e) the developing of an action plan with new cognitive schemas.

These steps involve a considerable amount of time and effort, but the authors' description of their use in a case study suggests their potential usefulness in leadership development (among other things). The OSR process also has been used to contrast schemas between an organization's board of directors and its executive staff (Finney & Mitroff, 1986). Other similar uses come to mind.

Relatedly, Khazanchi (1990) proposes an interactive management information system designed to allow leaders to model their cognitive maps via what is termed a "cognitive lens" perspective. These maps can be compared to and combined with those of others to provide potentially useful insights. Khazanchi (1990) also provides a useful review of literature related to his proposed system.

Additional Approaches

Hunt, Baliga, and Peterson (1988) argue that other approaches that can be used for enriching schema variety involve such things as creating an office of the CEO (where different kinds of people operate as a team in performing the CEO function), participation in activities outside the industry (to introduce different schemas), and even structural mechanisms to separate new, innovative units from their traditional schema counterparts.

IMPLICATIONS FOR LEADERSHIP RESEARCHERS

I made the point in Chapter 4 that even though one might sensitize a person to the different objectivist-subjectivist knowledge assumptions, this sensitization might not be enough to change that individual's knowledge-orientation perspective. This is particularly the case for leadership researchers. These individuals, like the leaders in this chapter, bring with them the baggage of past education, training, and experience that may have provided them with limited schemas/scripts concerning appropriate ways of knowing.

Such schemas may inhibit these individuals' ability to utilize approaches beyond those built into the schema. Here, the espoused schema would differ from the schema-in-use, to paraphrase Argyris. If that is the case, and these researchers are serious about broadening their schemas-in-use, then some of the change approaches might be called for as discussed earlier. Alternatively, the techniques discussed by Argyris, Putnam, and Smith (1987) might be used. In any case, I am reiterating the point that changes in schemas and development of more complex thinking and behavior are not just restricted to practicing leaders, but are applicable to those studying leadership as well.

CONCLUDING COMMENTARY

My conclusion concerning cognitive and skill learning is similar to that of Keys and Wolfe (1988). They conclude that there seems to be a convergence between the skill preferences of practitioners and the theory or knowledge preferences of academics. They argue that recent movements in the management development area are addressing the issue of combining knowledge and conceptualization, development of skills, and assessment processes, and that these movements are attempts by the field to provide itself with a much-needed reappraisal. Clearly, the material in this chapter is consistent with that conclusion.

The chapter material also is heavily life span oriented and reinforces one of the book's key emphases on the importance of considering long time periods. Along with this, the material tends to blur distinctions among education, training, and experience in preparing leaders. Although each of these was treated in a separate section, the whole development process tends to entail a mix of these and to involve Janusian learning.

In addition, the emphasis on combined rational/intuitive learning is striking and is in line with the related focus on increasing cognitive complexity, along with the other leader capabilities in the extended model. Accompanying these emphases is the stress on schemas as underlying learning concepts. The work demonstrates, for me, a convergence in thinking across these different areas as well as a link with the cognitive learning/skill learning thrusts. If we are to develop more capable leaders, we must be concerned with combining rational and intuitive modes, altering schemas, and utilizing both cognitive and skill learning.

Given the differential inputs in most organizations, the process for doing these kinds of things appears relatively nonsystematic. However, more homogeneous inputs allowing for more predictable approaches (as demonstrated by the uniformed services) may not necessarily be better. Indeed, they can suffer from too much tradition, too similar a set of inputs, and too similar a set of developmental assignments. As always, it's useful to think in terms of requisite variety—where "messy" environments call for "messy" developmental approaches or at least approaches that allow for a great deal of diversity.

Finally, I've argued here and elsewhere in this book that those studying leadership, and particularly leadership researchers, may be thought of as similar to leaders in terms of development. They too tend to have fixed schemas, though of a different nature than those of leaders. Thus the content of this chapter is as relevant for changing the schemas related to leadership knowledge orientation as it is for the schemas of the leaders who are studied.

This chapter is the last in Part II of the book. We now have the task of looking back over the book's content, tracing out some additional implications and reinforcing previously discussed ones. It is to this task that I turn in Chapter 12, the concluding chapter in the book.

NOTE

1. Of course, I haven't considered possible differences here between the MBTI intuition conception and my comprehensive one involving Janusian learning.

12   Last Things Last

I have seen the future and it is vague.

—Alex Heard

Time . . . is nothing absolute; its duration depends on the rate of thought and feeling.

—John W. Draper, English scientist
(quoted in Eigen & Siegel, 1989, p. 477)

We are living in the first period of human history for which the assumption that the time-span of major cultural change is greater than the life-span of an individual is false. Today this time-span is considerably shorter.

—Alfred North Whitehead, English philosopher
(quoted in Eigen & Siegel, 1989, p. 34)

WHERE WE'VE BEEN

The book's leadership synthesis emphasis started with the argument that traditional leadership approaches are too narrow and restrictive.

267

The book has attempted to deal with this in two ways. First, it expands the content of leadership knowledge by considering leadership at multiple organizational levels. Second, it stresses pragmatism in orientation toward leadership knowledge. The extended multiorganizational-level leadership model has been developed to deal with knowledge content. A knowledge-orientation framework, emphasizing underlying leadership assumptions, purposes, definitions, and stakeholders, has been developed to deal with knowledge-orientation aspects. In terms of this orientation toward knowledge, I argued for critical pluralism.

Critical pluralists are flexible in their underlying objectivist-subjectivist reality assumptions. They also are sensitive to the differing purposes, definitions, and stakeholders involved in gaining, using, and assessing leadership knowledge.

The extended model, so important in this leadership synthesis, has as its base the stratified-systems theory (SST) core notions of (a) increasing organizational complexity as leaders move up in the organization, and (b) a concurrently increasing required amount of leader cognitive complexity at higher organizational levels. Organizational complexity in the extended model has been expressed in the form of leader critical tasks. Earlier description of these has been in terms of hierarchical organizational levels, within domains, based on the time span of feedback of the longest-feedback task for which leaders at each level are responsible. Along with this, the extended model has considered the corresponding required leader cognitive complexity—the leader's ability to differentiate and integrate cognitive elements faced by him or her as a function of the critical tasks that are encountered. The greater the degree of integration and the greater the ability to integrate diverse cognitive elements, the greater the leader's cognitive complexity.

Using the previously mentioned notions and a strong temporal emphasis as a base, the extended model includes:

- key mission, strategy, and organizational design elements as the basis for critical task levels in each domain;
- various leader background factors, preferences, capabilities, and skills (including a mix of transactionally and transformationally oriented leadership skills) in addition to cognitive complexity at each level;
- aspects such as external environment and societal culture and organizational culture and climate at various levels; and
- differing aspects of organizational effectiveness at various levels.

Additional conceptions and measures of both organizational complexity and individual leader complexity have been proposed as possible supplements or alternatives to the initial measures. Even so, the classification of levels and domains based on time span feedback has been maintained. Shortly, however, I specifically address this matter and also extend our discussion of temporal considerations.

In the process of discussing the extended model and each of its components, I've focused on many issues. Let's briefly reiterate some of the more important of these. First is the relation of this model to mainstream leadership models and to recently developed models oriented toward strategic leadership. The major differences between the extended model and traditional models are three: its hierarchical as opposed to bottom-level, face-to-face focus; its emphasis on longer-term temporal aspects; and its stress on a critical pluralist approach to gaining, using, and assessing leadership knowledge. In terms of the various strategic leadership approaches, I've tried to relate the model to them wherever there seemed to be obvious connections. The extended model generally differs from these because of its specific focus on multiple levels, whereas their major or exclusive emphasis is on the strategic level.

Second, the model has an emphasis throughout on direct effects among sets of variables, and on indirect effects that take place at various organizational levels based on what happened at the same or higher levels. A same-level example is where leader charisma has an indirect effect on an aspect of organizational effectiveness via its direct effect on organizational culture. Third, a wide range of organizational variables, as well as external environment and societal culture, is emphasized. The organizational variables are not taken strictly as givens. They are placed within the context of leader critical tasks, over which the leaders have varying degrees of discretion. The amount of discretion depends very importantly on their hierarchical location within the organization.

Fourth, there is a focus on various individual background aspects (e.g., education, experience, family history) as well as leader predispositions and preferences. The latter include predispositions to lead, feelings of leadership competency, value preferences, and cognitive (intellectual) style preferences. These preferences represent the "will" or motivational part of the leader capability cluster. They join cognitive complexity and a range of leader behaviors/skills as the "skill" or ability part of the cluster. Joining both the will and skill aspects of this cluster are the opportunity aspects, partly reflected in what I called leader discretion (latitude of action). A person can't exert leadership if there is no discretion.

Fifth, and closely related to the point above, is a heavy emphasis on social cognition. This is reflected in the various ways of looking at cognitive complexity. It's also reflected in a focus on different kinds of scripts and schemas and the processes involved in their activation and development. Particularly important as well are implicit theories, especially those related to leadership and organizations. These theories are seen to have substantial influence on such things as leadership skill perceptions and responses and various aspects of organizational design. I develop these arguments at more length later in this chapter. The basic theme is that we must "get inside the head" of the leader and subordinates to understand leadership fully.

Sixth, and still in a similar vein, is the model's focus on vision as a part of what I termed "transformational orientation." Such vision, with its many manifestations, is a key way of demonstrating the importance of temporal aspects in the model. How are leader strategies and visions demonstrated across time spans of up to 20 years and even more?

Seventh, the model's emphasis on increasing organizational complexity leads to a stress on a wide range of leader development considerations. Such development is seen as starting early in life and being influenced by a whole host of background experiences as well as experience gained on the job. Experience is seen, in combination with education and training, as necessary to develop the will and skill components of leadership. An especially important aspect of the all-important cognitive complexity in this model is the development of what I've called Janusian thinking and behaving. This is the ability to bring together the appropriate mix of rational and intuitive cognitive and skill learning. Among other things, the cognitively complex leader must be skilled at this Janusian thinking and behaving.

Eighth, the underlying organizational and individual leader complexity notions in the model encourage a genotypic as opposed to phenotypic perspective. Leadership studies examining organizational levels have tended to treat these levels phenotypically. That is, they are treated as a surface manifestation of some underlying (genotypic) characteristic. Here, that genotypic characteristic is conceptualized in terms of organizational and leader complexity. This way of thinking is seen as allowing for genotypic comparisons across organizations. Genotypic comparison is very difficult to do in traditional phenotypically oriented studies (e.g., how comparable is the fourth organizational level in IBM with that in American Motors or United Airlines?).

Ninth, the model stresses at all levels the importance of leadership teams. Even though I typically speak in terms of "the leader," the intent throughout is to focus on the mix of characteristics of the designated leader and his or her key players as a team in performing leader critical tasks. This emphasis suggests the relevance of the plentiful small-group literature and consideration of the small-group concepts developed in that literature.

Tenth, along with the kinds of leadership knowledge-content aspects discussed above, I've interwoven—sometimes explicitly and sometimes implicitly—a knowledge-orientation focus. Thus I've been concerned with differing assumptions, purposes, definitions, and stakeholders in exploring the extended model. I'll explore this area still further later in the chapter.

Finally, I've discussed selected research and conceptual linkages for various aspects of the model. It's important to emphasize that there is very little empirical research concerning most of these linkages. Indeed, consistent with my critical pluralist philosophy, I strongly encourage as many people as possible to help fill this void, using the extended model as a starting point, within the context of their own work. Standing out even among this general dearth of empirical work is the lack of work attempting to relate the model and its various components to effectiveness. Clearly, such studies are not easy to do. This is so especially if we recognize the model's temporal emphasis and the complexities involved in appropriate criteria (emphasized especially in Chapter 5). However, empirical work is particularly critical here.

So much for where we've been. Let's now focus on a number of directions reflecting where we might go from here. I start by revisiting the model in terms of alternative organizational designs.

ALTERNATIVE ORGANIZATIONAL DESIGNS

In developing the extended model, I pointed out early on that various aspects of it were more flexible and less deterministic than those in Jaques's original stratified-systems theory (SST). However, I still maintained the basic SST characteristics of domains, levels, and time span of feedback (while suggesting some other possible measures, such as scope and scale, to get at organizational complexity). Essentially, the extended model has been implicitly oriented toward traditional large-scale bureaucracies, even though I touched on the possibility of alternative designs along the way. These hierarchical, bureaucratic organizations, by and large, have served society well since the advent of large-scale corporations.

And indeed, in spite of predictions of the demise of this kind of organization, Robbins (1990) makes the point that it still is far and away the predominant type of organizational design. He argues that there are two contradictory organizational trends—toward extreme flexibility or adhocracy, and toward high certainty. Those such as Peters (1988) essentially argue that flexible organizational designs are needed to deal with the increasingly more frequent, rapidly changing environments. However, Drucker (1988) makes the case for designs recognizing technologies dealing with the certainty requirements of the "information age."

Regardless of exactly what the future holds, we need to look at the extended model explicitly in terms of alternative organizational designs. These include not only small entrepreneurship designs but participative-type, new-wave organizations. Mintzberg's (1979) simple structure and adhocracy configuration (touched on in Chapter 5) are examples. So are the participative-type designs advocated by those such as Lawler (e.g. 1984) and Kanter (1989) and by sociotechnical theorists (see Pasmore, 1988).

Some Basic Issues

In examining the extended model in the context of these alternative designs, let's consider two basic issues:

- boundary conditions (conditions specifying the limits of the model's applicability); and
- linkage of critical tasks and organizational complexity.

If one argues that the model is a midrange one (i.e., it attempts to explain only certain segments of the total universe; see Pinder, 1984), rather than a grand one, then boundary conditions become particularly important to consider. Consistent with the previous discussion, one might start by arguing that the model represents a traditional bureaucratic one. It would be suitable primarily to large organizations operating in relatively stable environments. If defined that way, it would be useful for a large number of organizations. However, there would be questions about its applicability to the other kinds of organizations mentioned above—especially those in extremely turbulent environments. The argument would be either that the model only applies to these large, bureaucratic organizations or that its general notions could be applied to other kinds of organizations but that its specifics would have to be modified to do so.

One modification would be to consider equifinality or functional equivalency. For example, a 20-year time span in a relatively stable environment (e.g., as once experienced by utilities) might be equivalent in complexity to a 10- or even a 5-year time span in the increasingly more dynamic and turbulent environments faced in many industries. This equifinality notion suggests that it may be possible to reconcile and equate shorter-term flexibility versus the uncertainties encountered in long time periods in more stable environments.

To the extent that this possibility is true, it would be consistent not only with the issue here but with related expressed concerns (see Streufert & Swezey, 1986; Streufert & Nogami, 1989). Some argue that effective top-level leaders are those who are flexible in responding to problems as they arise, and not just problems with long planning and feedback horizons. Rivera (1990) uses an example of a crisis. A crisis may call for very high levels of complexity and last an indefinite period but less than 15 or 20 years, and be equivalent in complexity to longer but stable time periods.

To deal with this boundary-condition issue, then, we are talking about including the notion of equifinality—which allows us to extend the boundary conditions for the model.

The second issue, the linkage of critical tasks and organizational complexity, is related to the one just discussed. However, it's trickier. Following SST and other work by those such as Katz and Kahn (1966, 1978), the extended model has argued that goal and mission development, strategy and policy development, and organizational design are responsibilities of the systems leadership domain. The tasks involved in these areas are argued to have high levels of organizational complexity, one indication of which is the time span of feedback. Then, in the organizational leadership domain, the main tasks are to operate, interpret, translate, and integrate the elements designed above; and there is correspondingly less complexity. Finally, more detailed aspects of these tasks are handled at the direct leadership level, again with correspondingly less complexity.

As before, these arguments appear relatively straight forward for a traditional bureaucracy operating within the kind of boundary conditions mentioned earlier. However, how might these apply in a small entrepreneurship or in a new-wave organization where there frequently is downward delegation or sharing of traditional upper-level tasks? The general tasks still have to be carried out, regardless of the nature of the organization. However, the amount of organizational complexity (e.g., time span of feedback) probably is quite different. In other words, both an entrepreneur and the CEO of a large corporation are responsible for the previously mentioned mission/strategy and organizational design tasks. However, the tasks' relative complexity is almost certainly not the same.

Likewise, if some of these critical tasks are delegated downward in a new-wave organization, what are the implications for upper-level organizational complexity? Does it decrease, or does it stay the same or even increase even though critical tasks have been delegated downward? It could well remain the same or increase because the accountability is still retained at high levels and coordination requirements and the like increase with the change in tasks.

Essentially, these questions again raise the issue of comparability across different kinds of organizations. Do we consider an entrepreneurial CEO as comparable to a large-corporation CEO because they both have the critical tasks of mission development and organizational design, even though the organizational complexity (time span of feedback) may be different?

In line with the genotypic emphasis, I argue that organizational complexity should be the governing factor in comparing one organization with another. In other words, one would use organizational complexity, rather than the specific function of the critical tasks. Thus the CEO level of an entrepreneurship might, indeed, be more comparable to a lower level in a larger organization. Or a lower level in a new-wave organization could well be equivalent in terms of comparability to a higher level in a more traditional bureaucracy.

In summary, I've argued that we can broaden the boundary conditions of the extended model in two ways. First, by considering equifinality, and second, by emphasizing organizational complexity as the key factor in comparing different kinds of organizations. These arguments obviously have implications for domain and level treatment under these circumstances. Work is clearly needed to explore and extend them, both empirically and conceptually.

SELECTION, TAKING CHARGE, AND SUCCESSION

Although I explicitly devoted Chapter 10 to developmental aspects of leadership, the topics in this section have only been implicitly considered in the treatment of the extended model. Their importance belies their lack of earlier discussion. As but one example, we can think about trying to institutionalize long-term strategy and vision. Here I ask, to what extent do top-level leaders selected to succeed former ones deviate from or reinforce the former leader's long-term strategic visions and develop and implement their own? In some cases this would involve ensuring continuity with the previous strategic vision; in others, it would involve a frame-breaking departure. The successor selected would make a big difference here, as could his or her actions upon "taking charge." Let's look at some suggestive research directions based on the topics in this section.

In terms of selection, it almost goes without saying that there is much to be learned from the application of the various industrial/organizational psychology approaches in an attempt to match leaders with critical task requirements. This should continually be done. However, for present purposes, I want to start by emphasizing an approach that compares selection and development as strategy alignment alternatives. The argument is that selection is used basically to fit leaders with critical task demands; however, development can be used dynamically to align leaders and strategy (Kerr & Jackofsky, 1989).

In other words, selection involves a more mechanistic orientation toward organizations. Leader characteristics are viewed essentially as fixed, and the leaders are reassigned or leave when their capabilities don't fit strategic demands. In contrast, the developmental emphasis is consistent with a fluid, dynamic organizational view. Here both capabilities and strategic aspects are seen as evolving over time. Of course, the end goal is the same—to contribute to organizational capacity to adapt to strategic and environmental change (Kerr & Jackofsky, 1989).

In terms of suggested research, this contrast of selection versus developmental fit suggests investigation of a series of propositions with different environment, strategy, structure, and organizational culture aspects as suggested by Kerr & Jackofsky (1989). Results from these propositions, among other things, provide useful information on the role of development and selection in the dynamic functioning of the extended model.

Once the selection decision has been made, if we think about it, it's obvious that the way in which a new top-level leader "takes charge" can set the tone in terms of the long-term strategic vision emphasized in the extended model. That is, it has particular relevance for linking the new mission/strategy package with or separating it from the one that went before. Yet there has been practically no research on this important topic until Gabarro's (1988) recent work.

Garbarro developed a process model of leadership succession that, among other variable categories, includes one emphasizing a number of individual leader characteristics of the kind in the extended model. It also focuses on cognitive aspects, particularly cognitive maps. I invite readers to investigate Gabarro's process framework further in terms of (a) its potentially useful insights for the succession aspects of the extended model, and (b) its emphasis on the importance of process (a topic that I discuss shortly).

We've considered selection and taking charge—both focusing on the inside of the organization looking out. Now let's look at succession—emphasizing a view of the organization from the outside looking in. The literature from this view is quite different from most of that emphasized throughout the book. However, it's directly related to the question of whether leadership matters or not, which was raised in one of the opening quotes in Chapter 1.

There is now extensive literature on leadership succession (see Day & Lord, 1988; Romanelli & Tushman, 1988). Typically, it has focused on such questions as how much impact an incumbent CEO has on organizational outcomes relative to environmental and organizational factors or how outcomes compare before and after succession. There has been considerable controversy in this literature on the relative impact of leadership relative to other factors. Some have concluded that top-level leadership is inconsequential—that is, that leadership doesn't matter. Others have argued that if methodological shortcomings in the literature are dealt with, leadership does indeed matter (e.g., Day & Lord, 1988).

For us, following those such as Romanelli and Tushman (1988), the more important question is not whether top leadership matters, but under what conditions does it make a difference, and how much and what kinds of difference? Indeed, this question is implicit in the extended multi-level model. Thus for this book the appropriate emphasis in the succession literature is extended to include such concerns as the kinds of things a CEO does in succession (e.g., kinds of decisions, strategies, and "taking charge" behaviors) and how well (see Pfeffer & Davis-Blake, 1986); the length of pre- and postsuccession time periods considered; and the nature of the postsuccession change (e.g., insider versus outsider or, of special relevance to the preceding discussion, previous strategy continuation or change; see Helmich & Brown, 1972). In other words, the kinds of variables looked at in the extended model become relevant to the extent that they can be included in studies of the above types. The ability to track organizational and broad top-management characteristics over relatively long time periods is a strength of this kind of work. Of course, the chief trade-off is that the studies don't (and usually can't) provide a detailed inside look, and typically depend on what can be obtained from archival data. However, they can provide a nice complement to the studies with an inside perspective, which I've emphasized so heavily in the extended model.

TEMPORAL CONSIDERATIONS

I've argued throughout the book that a part of our extended view of leadership must include an emphasis on temporal aspects. And I've touched on the importance of these via such things as critical task time span of feedback; and emphasis on time and historical background in Tierney's (1988) college-president ethnographical study; the organizational life cycle discussion in Chapter 5; and the emphasis on time in the linkage section of various chapters. Here, and in much of the remainder of the chapter, I expand the treatment of the extended model by discussing temporal issues much more systematically and in much more depth than before. In keeping with the spirit of the book, I discuss temporal aspects both in terms of variables emphasized in more objectivist-oriented approaches and in terms of emphases that have a very different orientation.

Fortunately, even though temporal aspects traditionally have been underemphasized in United States organizational and leadership literatures (as argued in Chapter 1), that underemphasis is now being dealt with. Recent articles by those such as Bluedorn and Denhardt (1988), and books by Kelly and McGrath (1988) and McGrath and Kelly (1986), join works of earlier European scholars such as Heller (1984) and Clark (1984) to shed light on temporal concerns in the organizational and psychology literature. I emphasize especially the two books by Kelly and McGrath in the discussion to follow.

Philosophical Assumptions

Although many people do not think much about this, underlying philosophical assumptions concerning time are as important as they are for the knowledge-orientation aspects emphasized in Chapter 4. Essentially, conceptions of time are influenced heavily by culture. In North America and Western culture, in general, time has a strongly Newtonian flavor, as illustrated in classical physics. A number of assumptions follow from this conception—time is divisible and homogeneous, it flows uniformly, it is considered as existing independently from objects and events (an objectivist orientation), it is regarded as independent of space and motion, and it is assumed to be singular (only one "correct" time) as opposed to multiple (more than one "correct" time). Though the "new physics" does not subscribe to these Newtonian assumptions, its assumptions have not generally become a part of our culture (see Capra, 1975).

To a large extent, these Newtonian assumptions are reflected in "organizational time" and in most work in organizational behavior and leadership (see McGrath & Kelly, 1986). Even so, other alternative conceptions are not uncommon. A particularly relevant one for our purposes is "biologic" time, which emphasizes epochs, phases, and oscillations, among a number of other things that differentiate it from Newtonian time (McGrath & Kelly, 1986).

One illustration is the notion of entrainment, where one cyclic process becomes "captured by" and set to oscillate in rhythm with a higher-order process and the two systems sometimes get "out of sync" (e.g., individual jet lag). In terms of the extended model, we can think of entrainment of the organization with the environment, or of lower-level or lower-domain leadership entrained by that at upper levels.

Causality and Time Lags

If Newtonian assumptions influence our conceptions about time, the English philosopher David Hume's (1748/1955) arguments influence traditional assumptions about causality. Essentially these arguments are: (a) cause must precede effect; (b) all causal processes take some finite and specific amount of time; and (c) there can be no action at a temporal distance (the time between X and Y must be filled by the causal process). Also, the closer X and Y are in time and space, the more likely it is that X causes Y. The longer the lag, the more likely that other variables can confound the results. If the period is too short, other variables may not have had a chance to have an impact. In terms of the epochs or cycles of biologic time, the time intervals must be appropriate to capture the various phases of the cycle or erroneous conclusions are drawn (see Kelly & McGrath, 1988).

I want to make two comments about the preceding discussion. First, although many of the points may seem almost self-evident, that is only because of the pervasiveness of the Newtonian and Humean assumptions in our culture. Second, the fit of the X-Y time intervals to the cycles reinforces the importance of what Lawrence (1984) has termed the "historical perspective." One illustration of this was provided in the college-president study in Chapter 4. Essentially, this perspective focuses on understanding a subject in light of its earliest phases and later evolution. Thus we would use historical information about an organization's founding years to help explain the evolution of current leadership. Lawrence argues for consideration of age effects (from chronological age) and cohort and period effects (from similarities among those born during a certain time period, and events occurring in the period during which the observations were conducted). Failure to disentangle these effects over an extended time period (e.g., an organizational life cycle) leads to erroneous conclusions concerning such findings as leadership stability. Subjectivist approaches, in general, tend to recognize the importance of the historical perspective.

So much for underlying temporal assumptions. Let's now consider three different kinds of analyses that illustrate differences and similarities in underlying temporal conceptions.

Static, Comparative Statics, and Dynamic Analysis

Let's start this discussion by thinking in terms of snapshots and movies. *Static analysis*—for example, between leadership and effectiveness—is analogous to a snapshot taken at a moment in time. The basic Newtonian assumptions are implicit and time is considered as only a medium, rather than as a "real" variable (Kelly & McGrath, 1988). Typically, time is not even mentioned, much less measured. As I show shortly, static analysis has been the dominant mode of study of leadership and organizational phenomena.

If a static analysis is a snapshot, then a *comparative statics analysis* is a series of snapshots with the time periods between them clearly identified. Again, many of the previous assumptions are implicit. However, we could capture the effects of cyclical patterns if the time periods were selected with that in mind. A common comparative statics example is a comparison of leadership effects at a given time 1 and a given time 2. Motion pictures best reflect *dynamic analysis*. Here, the temporal *process* involved in the variable relationships across time is the central focus, just as it is in the motion pictures. Although what happens at two or more time periods is not lost sight of, it is the process involved in moving from one time period to another that is of primary interest (see Mohr, 1982, for a related book-length discussion). Here, many of the Newtonian assumptions about time have been replaced by assumptions better reflected in a biological temporal conception.

I've summarized more detailed characteristics of these three modes of analysis in Table 12.1. In terms of earlier chapters, especially Chapter 4, the table suggests that dynamic analysis is consistent with the cybernetic, holistic position, emphasizing variables. As previously indicated, I'll also discuss later a holistic orientation that is not based on variables per se.

Summaries of Current Longitudinal Empirical Work

With the previous discussion as background, let's look at the extent and kind of work in the organizational and leadership literature focusing on longitudinal analysis with an emphasis on causal, temporal aspects. A recent review of these studies at the micro level (considering individual and/or group units of analysis) traces them back to the work of Lawler (1968). That review (see Williams & Podsakoff, 1989) and another recent one (Aldag & Stearns, 1988), together found less than 40 longitudinal studies through 1986. Of these, less than 10 focused on leadership (of which all were face-to-face, lower-level leadership studies). These reviews generally do not cover related work outside North America (see Heller, 1984; Heller, Drenth, Koopman, & Rus, 1988).

Neither do they do much with such North American temporally oriented work as that by Graen and his colleagues (see for example, Graen & Cashman, 1975; Graen & Scandura, 1987). Nevertheless, the dearth of temporal studies in general and leadership studies in particular is apparent.

In addition to the micro-oriented works above, there is literature on macro-oriented temporal studies that focus on organizational as opposed to micro-level individual and group analyses. These do not

Table 12.1
Summary Characteristics of Three Kinds of Temporal Analyses

Static

* Unidirectional relationships (a change in some independent variables results in a change in one or more dependent variables)
* Stable relationships
* Deterministic rather than probabilistic (stochastic) relationships
* Assumes equilibrium exists

Comparative Statics

* Similar to statics except the stability of the relationship over time becomes the central purpose of the study. Tries to explain what caused changes in functional relationships at each time period
* Assumes equilibrium exists or there is movement toward equilibrium

Dynamic

* Eliminates assumption of unidirectionality
* Instead of assuming *a* causes *b*, assumes all variables exert a direct or indirect effect on each other (feedback)
* Assumes time lags long enough for feedback to occur
* Focuses on tracing the processes of change and not just the relationships
* Focuses on whether equilibrium occurs and what level is achieved if it does occur

Source: Summarized from the work of Emmett & Melcher (1978), Melcher (1979), and Melcher & Melcher (1980).

emphasize leadership per se, but their discussion is relevant for the organizational aspects of the extended model. Miller and Friesen (1982) review these studies and classify them into five different types ranging from nonquantitative case studies to quantitative, multivariate, multi-organizational kinds of work. To these reviews we can add the laboratory experimental process literature examining cognitive aspects that was touched on in Chapter 7 (e.g., Taylor & Fiske, 1981), and the temporally oriented quality of work life literature (e.g., Macy, Izumi, & Smith, in press). Essentially, this latter literature in combination (a) conveys well the flavor of work emphasizing variables, and (b) reinforces the earlier arguments concerning the general lack of temporal emphasis.

Temporal Methodologies Emphasizing Variables

The above literature not only shows the small number of studies with a temporal emphasis but contributes to our understanding of temporal methodologies using variables. A particularly important methodology, touched on in Chapter 4 and elsewhere in the book, that is useful for static, comparative statics, and dynamic analysis is "structural equation modeling" or "latent variable causal modeling" (e.g., the computer program LISREL; Joreskog & Sorbom, 1985). Williams and Podsakoff (1989) discuss its use in longitudinal studies, whereas Taylor and Fiske (1981) discuss its usefulness for assessing process in experimental social cognition studies. Williams and Podsakoff argue that the analyses used in the small number of longitudinal organizational behavior and leadership studies were inappropriately done by today's standards. They show how structural equation modeling deals with the concerns they raise and demonstrate the approach by reanalyzing data from two of these earlier studies.

The structural equation modeling approach is one way (using variables) of illustrating the holistic, cybernetic (or brain) perspective discussed earlier. The approach involves a combination of path analysis and factor analysis, and Kenny (1979), Williams and Podsakoff (1989), Harris and Schaubroeck (1990), Hughes, Price, and Marrs (1986), and James and James (1989) are useful references. What follows are some important points concerning the modeling (Taylor & Fiske, 1981; Williams & Podsakoff, 1989).

First, these models allow for an explicit linkage of measures and abstract theoretical (latent) constructs as well as linkage between various theoretical constructs. Second, they allow for multiple ways of measuring differing constructs. Third, they provide a way to estimate structural parameters while dealing with both random and systematic errors of measurement. Finally, and especially relevant for us, they allow simultaneous testing of reciprocal relationships among several variables and the recognition of appropriate time lags.

These points suggest the particular appropriateness of the structural equation approach for the extended leadership model. Structural modeling is suitable for capturing the hypothesized complex direct and indirect effects and temporal aspects of the extended model. Even so, this approach is not magical. To utilize it calls for clear specification and measurement of models and variables. These models can become very complex very quickly, and conceptual fuzziness and sloppy measurement gets compounded. In other words, garbage in, garbage out, as the saying goes. Also, the very complexity of the technique calls for relatively large sample sizes. Given these caveats, these structural equation models have the potential to add much to our arsenal of approaches to study leadership and especially to consider its temporal aspects.

Structural equation modeling is useful for some aspects of temporal and other kinds of analysis. Additional approaches are suggested by Williams and Podsakoff (1989). Also, if we are interested in searching for cyclic patterns, then spectral analysis and Fourier transform analysis are the methods of choice. These are mathematical and statistical procedures designed to show recurrent regularities within a series of observations that is time ordered. They also can show the frequency of each cycle. Kelly and McGrath (1988) discuss these in greater detail and provide several references dealing with the methodologies.

Still another methodology useful for some kinds of temporal analysis is called *event-history analysis*, and Aldag and Stearns (1988) discuss it with accompanying references. An event-history structure contains the times of occurrence of events and corresponding values of independent variables at the times in question. It appears to be particularly useful for using archival data over time periods extending for 100 years or even longer (see Aldag and Stearns, 1988). It also allows for the previously discussed "historical perspective." In terms of the extended model, it appears most useful for the selection and succession emphases discussed earlier in this chapter.

Laboratory Settings and Simulations

Even though the methodologies mentioned earlier can facilitate temporal studies, we should not lose sight of the difficulty of conducting these, particularly over the long time periods envisioned in the systems leadership domain. Thus it is important, even necessary, to supplement leadership studies in real organizations with laboratory studies and simulations.[1] As I've shown, laboratory studies are a popular mode for examining dynamic process aspects of social cognition (see Taylor & Fiske, 1981). A recent example is the investigation of individual decision-making processes through concurrent verbal protocols (think-aloud descriptions by the decision maker; Todd & Benbasat, 1987).

One key problem with the use of laboratory experiments in the examination of process is that tight experimental processes can easily backfire. Laboratory researchers may force behavioral processes into "experimental time" by artificially creating order, duration of events, and the time intervals between them (e.g., 15-minute production periods). These times often are based on quite atheoretical, arbitrary grounds such as the "experimental hour" (Kelly & McGrath, 1988). Thus we lose fruitful opportunities to treat "experimental time" in "real time" terms.

A very promising approach, within a laboratory study format, is that of the "generational study" (see Kurke, 1988). Some very interesting research has been done using this general approach (Insko et al., 1982; Insko et al., 1980; Jacobs & Campbell, 1961; Weick & Gilfillan, 1971; Zucker, 1977). Essentially, the experiment is conducted over several time periods. Then specific individuals, such as the leaders, periodically are withdrawn and replaced.

These kinds of studies have been used to examine such issues as the effects of institutionalization and the formation, maintenance, and decline of various small-group ("organizational") cultures. They offer a potentially powerful means of tracking many of the concepts that I have emphasized so heavily throughout this book. Leadership and organizational culture are a case in point. Procedures for this approach are indicated in the studies just mentioned. These works have tended to focus on comparative statics but could readily accommodate an emphasis on dynamic analysis.

Manned Simulations

Manned simulations are similar to laboratory experiments because they provide an artificial context within which those participating can operate. Typically, however, they provide more realistic settings than do most laboratory experiments. As an example, consider the recent, carefully developed manned simulation called Looking Glass (e.g., Lombardo & McCall, 1982; McCall & Lombardo, 1982). Here, for six hours (or more or less time), 20 participants playing various managerial roles run Looking Glass, Inc., a moderate-sized manufacturing corporation with different divisions facing different environments. During this simulation, the participants deal with concerns such as supply shortages, pollution problems, and the like. Decision making, power, information processing, politics, and, of course, various aspects of leadership in action can be observed.

Looking Glass is but one example of a free simulation, where events are shaped in part by the behavior of the participants (see Fromkin & Streufert, 1976). In these simulations, those participating are allowed to choose their own course of action within the simulation's rules and resource limitations (Swezey, Davis, Baudhuin, Streufert, & Evans, 1980). Researchers may introduce independent variables by selecting starting points or by varying constraints from one run to another (Fromkin & Streufert, 1976). These simulations are in contrast to experimental simulations where members are led to believe that they can affect their fate somewhat, although they really cannot because all independent variables are controlled by the experimenter. The participants can behave and cope with their surroundings with some freedom, but all events over time are predetermined (for a discussion see McGrath, 1964). Either of these kinds of simulations allows for dynamic analysis. However, the free simulation, because it does not place process restrictions on the participants, can operate in a time frame closer to real time than does an experimental simulation (see McGrath & Kelly, 1986). Either of these simulations also can, but does not have to, involve computers to a greater or lesser extent (see Barton, 1970).

In contrast, an all-computer simulation is not dependent on human participants. Here, the computer's key simulation role is as a logic machine and symbol manipulator (Barton, 1970). Thus, in this situation, the computer is a natural for dynamic modeling, provided certain kinds of very specific information are available. Computer models used for this purpose emphasize a way of systems thinking and expression that is more specific and formalized than models expressed in everyday language. However, it is less formalized and restrictive than mathematical statements of dynamic models (even though it involves some mathematical statements). Indeed, Hanneman (1988) argues that behavioral scientists should learn to restate their theories in computer-based language. He also discusses dynamic computer modeling in considerable detail.

As in the earlier discussion, the use of computer models to focus on dynamic aspects of leadership and related concepts is not new. An early example, and one of the few published in a mainstream organizational journal, was a study reported in the late 1960s (see Kaczka & Kirk, 1967). This study developed a computer simulation model of an organization. The model included, among other things, work groups and top-, middle-, and lower-level leaders linked by information systems designed to simulate real systems and procedures. An early example, in a military context, is discussed by Olmstead (1974) and Olmstead, Christensen, and Lackey (1973).

A careful look at these studies provides a feel for the types of information necessary in the kind of computer models I am emphasizing. The provision of appropriate data for these models is quite complex; probably that complexity helps explain why we have not seen wider usage of such models in the leadership and organizational literature. We seem to be in a catch-22 situation here. To develop this kind of model we need realistic and relatively complex data. However, if we could easily obtain such data, we might not need the computer simulation. Is there a way out? A recent paper by Hurd and Hunt (1991) contends that there is. In that paper the authors argue that we can combine use of a manned simulation such as Looking Glass with a computer simulation to investigate dynamics of behavioral models in general and the extended model in particular.

As a starting point, they suggest videotaping the behaviors displayed by the participants in Looking Glass or a similar simulation and then developing a procedure to analyze the videotapes to provide data for input into the desired computer model. Although this is not easy, it is feasible, and it gets at a wide range of aspects relevant to leadership, effectiveness, and many other concerns. The videotaped information also should be supplemented with background information and whatever questionnaire information seems relevant. All this is discussed in enough detail in Hurd and Hunt (1991) that people should be able to implement the authors' recommendations, provide the implementation is carried out by a team involving both a knowledgeable leadership (or organizational behavior) scholar and a person familiar with computer-based modeling. Typically, either alone would not be sufficient. The piece thus builds on other "how-to" oriented computer behavioral modeling works (e.g., Emmett & Melcher, 1978; Hanneman, 1988) to encourage the reader to use this neglected tool.

Once the model is developed, following the general outline above and based on appropriate aspects of the extended model (or whatever model is of interest), the parameters can be changed as needed to answer what-if questions over various time periods. Then the results from the computer simulation can be used in role plays involving the original manned simulation, and relevant data gathered and analyzed. Thus it's possible to see how some of the computer-generated findings replicate when people are involved. Finally, a field experiment could be conducted to examine pertinent findings in an ongoing organization. Of course, the researcher would then have to face the usual real-time problems in the organization. However, the previous steps would provide a starting base. In closing this section, I refer leaders to two additional pieces of relevant literature. The first is a very recent comprehensive review of management games and simulations by Keys and Wolfe (1990). The second is a study by Streufert, Pogash, and Piasecki (1988) briefly describing the latest version of a simulation developed by Streufert and his colleagues and summarizing results concerning a number of aspects of cognitive complexity.

A Dynamic, Generative, Holistic Perspective

Until now I've emphasized temporal aspects, even holistic ones, in terms of variables or sets of variables. Here I want to focus on the very different *generative perspective* that is both dynamic and holistic. Tsoukas (1989) sets the stage for us by differentiating among *real, actual,* and *empirical* ontological assumption domains. The real domain is seen as the one where *generative mechanisms* (core explanations) reside. These mechanisms are structural in the sense that they exist independently of what an observer sees but are capable of producing what is seen. The actual domain is the one where *observed events* or patterns of events occur. The empirical domain is that of *experienced events.* These experiences assume the occurrence of events in the actual domain, independent of whether the observer sees them or not. At the same time, events assume the existence of mechanisms in the real domain (Tsoukas, 1989).

Thus the explanatory structure resides as a generative mechanism in the object of study. If we can reveal a generative mechanism we are able to redescribe our research in a theoretically meaningful way. These explanatory mechanisms operate as causal powers to generate tendencies (rather than deterministic causal laws, as assumed in the more objectivist positions).

The realization of these tendencies is contingent upon specific contextual circumstances that may or may not favor certain patterns of events (Tsoukas, 1989). Here, we would be interested in revealing and conceptualizing the causal *experiences* probabilistically associated with leadership.

The generalizability of the findings from such work relies on its capability to (a) conceptualize generative mechanisms of research projects, and (b) shed light on contingent conditions under which these generative mechanisms combine and operate. The redescription of the research object can take several forms, including a type of conceptual framework, a process model, or a middle-range theory (see Eisenhardt, 1989).

Let's look more explicitly at how temporal aspects might be reflected in this generative and holistic perspective. Here, the notion of tracks is useful. *Tracks* refer to the temporal association of an organization with one or more design archetypes (Greenwood & Hinings, 1988). These archetypes (Miles & Snow, 1978), gestalts, or configurations (Miller & Friesen, 1980) are illustrated in the five Mintzberg typologies discussed in Chapter 6. They involve a configurative conceptualization of interacting components when an organization seeks a fit or congruence to function appropriately (Miller & Friesen, 1980). These interacting elements may be environmental, structural, and behavioral, and an understanding of the components can be gained only by looking at the pattern of overall design.

Overall, leaders are concerned either with maintaining the current archetype or with moving toward an alternative one (e.g., top-level leader strategic vision). This movement is reflected in tracks that essentially are maps of the extent to which organizations move from the constraining assumptions of a given archetype and assume the characteristics of an alternative archetype. The specific track, followed by an organizational archetype, is a function of the compatibility between structures and environmental/contextual contingencies (Chapter 5), commitment to prevailing and alternative values/schemas and implicit organization theories (Chapter 7), and the impact of various stakeholders (Greenwood & Hinings, 1988). Tracks, like organizational archetypes, can take many different forms. Four of these are: (a) status quo-oriented; (b) aborted excursions, where a change is attempted but is unsuccessful and there is movement back to the original archetype; (c) reorientation, where the change is successful; and (d) unresolved excursions, where the change is unsuccessful and the organization remains in a kind of never-never land (see Greenwood & Hinings, 1988).

Dynamic Case Study Illustration

Dynamic case studies are one appropriate way of providing access to the discovery of generative phenomena and illustrating holistic, dynamic archetype/track notions. They are particularly useful in specifying the contingent circumstances where supportive or constraining mechanisms favor or hinder the operation of causal powers (see A. Ropo, 1989; A. Ropo & Hunt, 1990a, 1990b). Let's look at a recent illustration of such a case study.

This study focused on the leadership behavior changes of five high-ranking Finnish bank leaders in an organizational change setting. The setting included mergers and service structure changes as a result of strong banking industry deregulation and other industry-level structural changes. The purpose of the study was to provide empirical descriptions of bank manager's leadership behavior tracks in changing organizational settings and to discover underlying generative mechanisms for these tracks. The key interest was the dynamic interplay of individual and organizational configurations across several years.

The study developed the argument that the bank managers' leader behavior (transactional and transformational activities and representation activities—network development beyond superior/subordinate contact) is in dynamic interaction with organizational change processes (mergers and changes from functional to profit-center organizational structure). The structural change was seen as calling for certain kinds of leader behaviors that, in turn, might support or direct or be inconsistent with the change. The basic link between leadership and organizational change was argued to be changes in managerial work (described in terms of task, goal, and time perspectives and analogous to critical tasks in the extended model).

Three different leadership behavior tracks, varying by the timing, intensity, and extent of adapting change-oriented behavior, were traced: *proactive* (highly progressive and anticipatory), *reactive* (involving big, sudden shifts in response to an organizational change), and *contractive* (an occasional peak of change-oriented behaviors followed by contraction and withdrawal of activities).

Generally, the role of leadership in organizational change processes was seen as a configurative function of individual and organizational (i.e., cumulative know-how and experience built into the strategies, structures, and so forth) capabilities developed over time. Where these were high, a positive proactive track was able to develop, and where they were mixed, the other tracks developed. The underlying causal power seen as having the generative capability to produce the tracks was a drive toward renewal. It was triggered by the frame-breaking environmental and organizational changes in the banking industry.

Dynamism, Life Cycles, and Punctuated Equilibrium

Discussions of dynamics are clearly related to the treatment of organizational life cycles in Chapter 5. Recall that the life-cycle model in that chapter had four or five phases from birth through growth, through maturity, and finally through revitalization or death, each with a corresponding transitional stage (Baliga & Hunt, 1988; Hunt, Baliga, & Peterson, 1988). The emphasis in Chapter 5 was on the implications of these in terms of mission/strategy and organizational design, and the argument was that the phases/stages would influence these. And, although it was hinted at in Chapter 5, I want to reiterate the point that we would expect the relative mix of transformationally and transactionally oriented leadership as well as leadership schemas to vary by phase/stage for leaders at various levels (see Baliga & Hunt, 1988; Hunt, Baliga, & Peterson, 1988).

Such a life-cycle model and its implications are similar to the metamorphosis model tracking organizational evolution (Miller & Friesen, 1984; Tushman & Romanelli, 1985), except that the life cycle model's evolution across time is more regular. The metamorphosis model considers simultaneously the dynamics of inertia *and* processes of change that influence the course of an organization's development over time. Essentially this is a "punctuated equilibrium" framework with some notions borrowed from biology (see Eldredge & Gould, 1972). It has periods of equilibrium where a relative emphasis on symbolic compared to substantive aspects of leadership is hypothesized to be called for. These equilibrium periods are punctuated periodically by reorientation periods (caused by sustained low effectiveness or environmental forces) where there is a push for change of a "radical and discontinuous nature, i.e., metamorphosis" (Romanelli & Tushman, 1988, p. 139). For these reorientation periods it is hypothesized that an emphasis on both substantive and symbolic leadership is needed (Romanelli & Tushman, 1988).

Relation of Punctuated Equilibrium to Other Concepts

Tushman, Newman, and Romanelli (1986) see punctuated equilibrium as involving painful, discontinuous, systemwide change following from long periods of incremental change. The incremental periods or periods of convergence are seen as fine-tuning, whereas the reorientations are necessary evils. Levy and Merry (1986) call the former "first-order change" and the latter "second-order change." They suggest "catastrophe theory" from mathematics as a pragmatic approach to capture the kinds of dynamics involved. This has been applied on a limited basis to help explain differing phenomena in the social sciences (e.g., Bigelow, 1982; Olivia, Day, & MacMillan, 1988), and has recently been used in the leadership approach proposed by Lord and Maher (in press). It requires a high level of both mathematical and behavioral science research skills to be used effectively (Duran, 1990).

Catastrophe theory also has reemerged as the "science of chaos" (Duran, 1990) that is discussed by Gleick (1987) and Briggs and Peat (1989), among others. Essentially, it is a way of seeing order and pattern out of random, erratic, unpredictable events (Gleick, 1987). Punctuated equilibrium may be one aspect of chaos, which could prove useful in explaining organizational transitions. James Quinn's (1978, 1981) notion of logical incrementalism, discussed briefly in Chapter 9, may be part of the punctuated equilibrium process and consistent with some of the implications of catastrophe theory or chaos (Duran, 1990).

Most people probably would associate logical incrementalism with the convergence periods in punctuated equilibrium (see, e.g., Dunphy & Stace, 1988, and their discussion of takeovers, mergers and other examples of turbulence). However, Duran (1990) spins out the following description to make the case that logical incrementalism better covers the reorientation periods. Logical incrementalism essentially involves the flowing together of internal decisions and external events, thus creating a widely shared consensus for action. There is a combination of strategies from lower levels, blended incrementally and opportunistically into a coherent pattern (Quinn, 1978). The precipitating events are dealt with incrementally. Early commitments are kept free and tentative, subject to later review and change because the timing, nature, and severity of precipitating events is not known (see Hollings, 1976, for a related view).

Accompanying all this are trial balloons involving interactive testing, during which top leaders may substantially modify their original positions (see Hosking & Morley, 1988). Thus even major reorientation decisions can allow for flexibility testing and feedback. This is in contrast to Tushman et al. (1986), with their assumptions that reorientation is painful and should be carried out quickly. Instead, logical incrementalism's assumption is that effective reorganizations and reorientations unfold with time and room for flexibility (Duran, 1990).

Work is needed concerning these alternative views, and I expect that the different strategic vision orientations discussed in Chapter 9 would have a bearing on this issue. Duran (1990) helps sensitize us to the increasingly important role of approaches such as catastrophe and chaos theory (e.g., Summey & Bovinet, 1989) from the physical and biological sciences in helping us to understand dynamic organizational aspects.

It seems reasonable to expect the dynamism issues discussed throughout this chapter would add yet another view to leader cognitive complexity requirements of the extended model. Here, I argue that the tracks would tend to call for differing degrees of complexity across time. A 20-year vision with an inertia track is quite a different story than a more complex one reflecting several reorientations or configurational changes across the 20 years.

I've emphasized work relevant to organizational change and transition and with implications for the extended model. Additional source books are Kimberly and Quinn (1984), Quinn and Cameron (1988), and Pettigrew (1987).

UNIT OF ANALYSIS AND FIT

Previous sections have shown the importance of temporal aspects for the extended model and, indeed, for a broadened view of leadership in general. Now let's look at unit of analysis and fit among leadership components as another important set of knowledge-orientation considerations. As with the temporal aspects, I discuss these first in terms of variables, then look at them from the kind of dynamic configurational perspective discussed earlier. It has been known for some 40 years that various biases in results can occur if the unit of analysis is inappropriately handled (e.g., see Robinson, 1950). However, with few exceptions (e.g., Hofstede, 1980; Korukonda, 1989), there has been inadequate attention devoted to this issue in the organizational and leadership literatures. Rousseau (1985) makes the point that many of the phenomena in these literatures are "mixed level."

Here, for example, a dependent variable may be tapped at the individual level of analysis (e.g., individual effectiveness). However, the independent variable may be at the organizational level of analysis (e.g., technology). It's erroneous simply to correlate technology measured at the organizational level with aggregated individual performance. This is because the organizational level of analysis is inherently different than the individual level and data aggregation does not make that argument go away (although many people act as if it does). Thus organizational or leadership analyses should start with identifying the relevant level of analysis, and the level should not be changed without a specific statement that this has been done (Miller, 1978). The unit of analysis just mentioned (individual, group, department, etc.) may be called the *focal unit*. There is also a *level of measurement* and a *level of analysis*. The level of measurement is the unit to which the data are directly attached (e.g., self-report questionnaires at the individual level). The level of analysis is the unit to which the data are assigned for hypothesis testing and statistical analysis. The problem is that in practice, the focal unit frequently is not the same as either of the other two levels. Thus, for example, information on an individual's measured sense of autonomy and the number of formal job rules erroneously may be used to conclude that an organization's technology affects its structure (e.g., Bell, 1967).

Rousseau (1985) discusses some biases and fallacies that can occur when there is confusion among the focal unit, level of measurement, and level of analysis. This discussion should be studied carefully. Perhaps even more important is Rousseau's level-of-analysis typology. This typology covers three kinds of what she terms "mixed-level models" (together with variations within) encountered in organizational and leadership research. She also specifies their nature, provides examples, and shows when to use each of them.

Of special interest for us is her cross-level model, which focuses on relations among independent and dependent variables at different levels in the organization. Typically, the dependent variable is at the individual analysis level and independent variables are global ones operating higher in the organization. In this situation, she argues that all individuals in the *same* unit should be assigned the same global score for any global variable and correlations should be computed at the individual level. I interpret this to mean that the appropriate sample size for analysis purposes in a combined organization sample of say, 600 first-level employees and 10 top-level leaders would be 600, rather than 10. Thus the use of large-sample analytical techniques, such as the earlier discussed structural equation modeling, would be facilitated—a very important consideration, indeed, for a top-level leadership analysis.[2]

Although Rousseau emphasizes the conceptual aspects of unit of analysis considerations, a recent statistically oriented approach (but with a conceptual focus as well) has been developed by Dansereau, Alutto, and Yammarino (1984) and reviewed by House (1987). It is called *Varient*, because it emphasizes both variables and entities. It's quite complex and sophisticated and is presented in a book with accompanying software. Essentially, Varient allows for specifying and testing theories involving all of the kinds of level-of-analysis models just covered. The approach includes procedures to test hypotheses asserting competing predictions about the level of analysis where relationships between variables occur.

In summary, Varient is useful in generating hypotheses that include explicit consideration of single and multiple levels of analyses. These include corresponding grouping of entities (persons, dyads, groups, and collectivities) and multiple variables with multiple relationships among those variables. Varient also includes tests to allow for hypothesis falsification.

To illustrate, think of two hypotheses about three variables and two levels of analysis. Hypothesis I asserts that various aspects of leader behavior are related to satisfaction, independent of a person's political ideology and applicable to groups but not collectivities. An alternative hypothesis might be that leadership aspects, satisfaction, and ideology are all related but they are applicable only to collectivities. The first (group) hypothesis implies that multiple interpersonal processes underlie the variables and their relationships. The second (collectivity) hypothesis implies that collectivized or large-scale social movements, rather than lower-level group processes, may underlie variables and relationships. Varient allows for testing each of these competing hypotheses. Single- and multiple-level analyses may be used to examine assertions about entities. Multiple-variable and multiple-relationship analyses may be used to examine assertions about variables (Dansereau et al., 1984).

Dansereau et al. argue also that Varient can be used to reflect temporal aspects. They claim that the approach can be extended to permit the simultaneous consideration of variables, entities and time. Thus Varient appears to encompass some of the kinds of comparative statics and dynamics issues highlighted earlier.

Fit

Along with unit of analysis consideration, issues of fit also are important. I have explicitly or implicitly dealt with various aspects of fit or "match" throughout the book. Indeed, the fit notion is at the heart of mainstream contingency leadership approaches, which I touched on in Chapter 4. It also is at the core of contingency organization theory (see Daft, 1989; Robbins, 1990), and the strategic contingencies approach in the strategic management literature, touched on in Chapter 5 (see Gupta, 1988).

In the contingency leadership literature, outcomes such as effectiveness are seen as being a function of the fit between, for example, a micro situational variable (such as task dimensions) and leadership behavior or style. In the organization theory literature, organizational effectiveness is argued to be a function of a fit among, for example, environment, context (size and technology), and organization structure. A strategic contingencies approach treats organizational outcomes as a function of the fit among various organizational aspects, including leader characteristics, and various aspects of strategy. An example of fit in the extended model includes the frequently mentioned heterogeneity or homogeneity of fit among various leader capability variables among strategic apex members, or between the strategic apex and lower-level leaders.

Although the fit notion is pervasive and important, it's not as simple as it first seems. Indeed, there are as many as six different commonly used conceptions of fit that consider variables (see Venkatraman, 1989), and these do not include the issue of dynamics or comparative statics fits, which I will look at shortly. Also, there are likely to be varying mixtures of universalistic (important regardless of fit) and contingency fits that are operating in many cases. Let's look at these points in more detail.

The six different kinds of fit range from moderation to profile deviation and covariation (see Venkatraman, 1989). *Moderation* involves the classical statistical interaction where two variables, other than the criterion, are involved in the specification of fit. For example, one might examine the interactive effects of type of strategy and leadership skill on organizational effectiveness.

Recall that I discussed *profile deviation* briefly in Chapter 8. It was described in terms of adherence to a specified profile involving multiple variables. As an example, the closer the fit with a specified leadership profile, the better we expect organizational effectiveness to be (see Drazin & Van de Ven, 1985; Venkatraman, 1989; Venkatraman & Prescott, in press).

Finally, fit as *covariation* conceives of internal consistency among a set of underlying theoretically related variables. For instance, when appropriate leadership is best represented as a pattern across two transformational and two transactional dimensions, any one dimension is insufficient for effective leadership. Effective leadership requires constant attention to all four dimensions as reflected in a specified pattern of covariation among the four variables.

The preceding discussion has covered only three of Venkatraman's six kinds of fit. Nevertheless, it should be obvious that although all these approaches represent "fit" in its loosest sense, they are really quite different both conceptually and analytically. Thus a key implication is that we should devote increasing attention to the nature of the fit in various leadership approaches. Hunt et al. (1990) provide an example of this when comparing the fit of leadership prototypes (discussed especially in Chapters 8 and 9) and leader behaviors.

Now let's look at the universalistic and contingency notions of fit mentioned above (see Gupta, 1988). The basic argument is that every leadership characteristic can be thought of in terms of one of the following contingency types:

- Those that have little or no impact on other variables or criteria, regardless of the strategic or environmental setting—they are irrelevant, regardless of the values of the environment or strategy.
- Those that have a significant effect on other variables or criteria attributable solely to strategic and/or environmental contingencies, for example. These are called *strictly contingent.*
- Those that have a significant effect on other variables or criteria, but the effect is universalistic and not contingent on either the strategic or environmental setting. These are called *strictly universalistic;* reward and punishment behavior might fit this category (see Podsakoff, Todor, Grover, & Huber, 1984).
- Those that have a universal impact on other variables or criteria, but the strength of the universal impact is contingent on environmental and/or strategic factors. These are simultaneously universalistic and contingent relations.

Once again, it's useful for us to go beyond a simple all-or-nothing contingent or universalistic notion of fit. We need to recognize some of the nuances involved and to think in terms of these when dealing with profiles and various other aspects of fit in the extended model.

Unit of Analysis and Fit Dynamic, Holistic Implications

The previous unit of analysis and fit discussion assumes the use of variables. Furthermore, the fit perspectives are based on static relations, and their relevance for comparative statics or dynamic analysis is unclear at this time (Venkatraman, 1989). One perspective that is relevant, however, for both unit of analysis and fit considerations is the previously emphasized dynamic, holistic one, illustrated by the Finnish bank study.

A dynamic case study, such as the one mentioned earlier, focuses on the interplay and configurative nature of the individual, organizational, and environmental levels across time. It illustrates an embedded and stratified design, wherein a phenomenon can be explained only within a wider organizational, environmental, and societal context. Multiple levels of analysis are an integral part of the configurational nature of the study. The tracks involved in attempting to move from one configuration to another provide shifting fits (due to the supporting and countervailing generative explanatory forces) across a dynamic context. We see these notions illustrated in the differing leadership tracks of the Finnish bank managers as they attempted to deal with rapidly changing environmental and organizational forces.

In summary, in this dynamic, holistic perspective, unit of analysis considerations are an integral part of the configurations. And fit is a function of the shifting configurations across time as they are influenced by underlying generative supportive and countervailing notions. Altogether, these paint a very different unit of analysis and fit picture than do the variable-oriented approaches discussed previously.

CONCLUDING COMMENTARY

In this final chapter I've revisited the development of a new synthesis in leadership. I have done this by emphasizing high points of the book's content and by moving into new areas or expanding the discussions of previously covered areas. This has gotten us into treatment of selection/succession, alternative organizational designs, a wide range of temporal considerations, and unit of analysis and fit aspects applied to the extended multilevel model. Parts of this discussion have considered both leadership knowledge-content and knowledge-orientation aspects of leadership synthesis.

Now I would like to encourage readers to internalize their approach to leadership in terms of the "Texas dozen" thoughts summarized in Table 12.2. They embody the book's content and critical pluralist notions. As my final comment, I want especially to emphasize point 15

Table 12.2
A "Texas Dozen" Final Thoughts for Readers

1. Think extended multilevel model with all its broad-ranging implications.

2. Think critical pluralist in terms of leadership knowledge-orientation; don't be either an extreme objectivist or extreme subjectivist.

3. Think genotypically in terms of both organizational and leader individual complexity.

4. Think leadership predispositions and efficacy and cognitive and value preferences.

5. Think cognitive with its various manifestations—complexity, schemas, maps, implicit theories, Janusian thinking/behaving, and the like.

6. Think environment, culture, values, and organizational culture and climate and their role and impact.

7. Think mission/goal/strategy and organizational design and their role and impact.

8. Think transactionally oriented and transformationally oriented leadership skills and their role and impact.

9. Think leadership team rather than single leader.

10. Think temporally and generatively, recognizing especially dynamics, archetypes, and tracks.

11. Think level of analysis and component "fit" and their conceptual and empirical implications.

12. Think organizational effectiveness and its multidimensional, multilevel, and dynamic aspects.

13. Think indirect (deep within the organization) as well as direct leadership effects.

14. Think long- and short-term developmental implications when considering leadership education, training, and experience.

15. Think mutual contribution of your leadership interests and the extended multilevel leadership model.

in the table, which reiterates a key purpose for the proposed synthesis. I hope readers will think about how their interests and the extended model might reinforce each other.

There are many forms that this reinforcement can take. For example, the book's discussion can lead to various aspects of the model of interest to the reader; readers can use the model to help extend their own theoretical work; readers can refine and extend the many general points discussed in the book; or, finally, readers can use the book as a source book for enhancing their overall leadership knowledge and/or research. There are many more directions that these can help suggest. Indeed, a project with which I have been involved (see Phillips & Hunt, 1989) focuses on a number of such directions. As I've said more than once, the basic point is to encourage the model's use to broaden leadership knowledge, and not (as happens with so many models) to see this model as restricting creativity.

NOTES

1. Some may question this recommendation in terms of external validity. Locke (1986) and Korukonda and Hunt (1989) provide discussions of this issue for laboratory studies in general. In terms of cognitive complexity, Stamp's (1988) work can be interpreted as providing some support for the use of students, even though their complexity has not yet been fully developed.

2. An early study, based on similar assumptions, related upper-level leader treatment philosophies toward mental health to lower-level leadership and outcome measures (see Hunt, Osborn, & Larson, 1975).

References

Abelson, R. P. (1981). Psychological status of the script concept. *American Psychologist, 36,* 715-725.

Adler, N. (1984). Understanding the ways of understanding: Cross-cultural management methodology reviewed. In R. Framer (Ed.), *Advances in international comparative management* (pp. 31-67). Greenwich, CT: JAI Press.

Adler, N. (1986). *International dimensions of organizational behavior.* Boston, MA: Kent.

Agar, M. (1986). *Speaking of ethnography.* Newbury Park, CA: Sage.

Agor, W. H. (1984). *Intuitive management.* Englewood Cliffs, NJ: Prentice-Hall.

Alban-Metcalfe, B. (1984). Microskills of leadership. A detailed analysis of the behaviors of managers in the appraisal interview. In J. G. Hunt, D. M. Hosking, C. A. Schriesheim, & R. Stewart (Eds.) *Leaders and managers: International perspectives on managerial behavior and leadership* (pp. 179-199). New York: Pergamon.

Aldag, R. J., & Stearns, T. M. (1988). Issues in research methodology. *Yearly Review of Management of the Journal of Management, 14,* 253-276.

Aldrich, H. (1979). *Organizations and environments.* Englewood Cliff, NJ: Prentice-Hall.

Alexander, L. D. (1979). The effect level and functional area have on the extent Mintzberg's roles are required by managerial roles. *Academy of Management Proceedings,* pp. 186-189.

Algera, J. A. (1987). Job and task analysis. In B. M. Bass, P. J. Drenth, & P. Weissenberg (Eds.), *Advances in organizational psychology* (pp. 137-149). Newbury Park, CA: Sage.

Allaire, Y., & Firsirotu, M. C. (1984). Theories of organizational culture. *Organizational Studies, 5,* 193-226.

Allport, G. W., Vernon, P. E., & Lindzey, G. (1970). *Study of values.* Boston: Houghton Mifflin.

American Assembly of Collegiate Schools of Business. (1987). *Outcome measurement project: Phase III report.* St. Louis: Author.

Argyris, C. (1976). Problems and the directions for industrial psychology. In M. D. Dunnette (Ed.), *Handbook of industrial and organizational psychology* (pp. 151-184). Chicago: Rand McNally.

Argyris, C. (1979). How normal science methodology makes leadership research less additive and less applicable. In J. G. Hunt & L. L. Larson (Eds.), *Crosscurrents in leadership* (pp. 47-63). Carbondale: Southern Illinois University Press.

Argyris, C. (1982). *Reasoning, learning, and action.* San Francisco: Jossey-Bass.

Argyris, C. (1984). Double loop learning in organizations. In D. A. Kolb, I. M. Rubin, & J. M. McIntyre (Eds.), *Organizational psychology* (4th ed., pp. 45-59). Englewood Cliffs, NJ: Prentice-Hall.

Argyris, C. (1985). *Strategy, change and defensive routines.* Boston: Pitman.

Argyris, C., Putnam, R., & Smith, D. M. (1987). *Action science.* San Francisco: Jossey-Bass.

Argyris, C., & Schön, D. A. (1978). *Organizational learning: A theory of action perspective.* Reading, MA: Addison-Wesley.

Arogyaswamy, B., & Byles, C. (1987). Organizational culture: Internal and external fits. *Journal of Management, 13*(4), 647-659.

Ashby, W. (1952). *Design for a brain.* New York: Wiley.

Ashforth, B. E. (1985). Climate formation: Issues and extensions. *Academy of Management Review, 10,* 837-847.

Avolio, B. J., & Bass, B. M. (1988). Transformation leadership, charisma, and beyond. In J. G. Hunt, B. R. Baliga, H. P. Dachler, & C. A. Schriesheim (Eds.), *Emerging leadership vistas* (pp. 29-50). Lexington, MA: Lexington.

Avolio, B. J., & Gibbons, T. C. (1988). Developing transformational leaders; A life span approach. In J. A. Conger & R. N. Kanungo (Eds.), *Charismatic leadership* (pp. 276-308). San Francisco: Jossey-Bass.

Avolio, B. J., Waldman, D. A., & Einstein, W. O. (1988). Transformational leadership in a management game simulation. *Group & Organizational Studies, 13,* 59-80.

Axelrod, R. (Ed.). (1976). *Structure of decisions: The cognitive maps of political elites.* Princeton, NJ: Princeton University Press.

Baliga, B. R., & Hunt, J. G. (1988). An organizational life cycle approach to leadership. In J. G. Hunt, B. R. Baliga, H. P. Dachler & C. A. Schriesheim (Eds.), *Emerging leadership vistas* (pp. 129-149). Lexington, MA: Lexington Books.

Baliga, B. R., Peterson, M. F., & Hunt, J. G. (1990). *Senior level transformational and transactional leadership from a cognitive sciences perspective.* Unpublished manuscript, College of Business Administration, Texas Tech University, Lubbock.

Bandura, A. (1986). *Social foundations of thought and action: A social-cognitive view.* Englewood Cliffs, NJ: Prentice-Hall.

Bantel, K. A., & Jackson, S. E. (1989). Top management and innovations in banking: Does the composition of the top team make a difference? *Strategic Management Journal, 10,* 107-124.

Barber, H. F. (1990). Some personality characteristics of senior military officers. In K. E. Clark & M. B. Clark (Eds.), *Measures of leadership* (pp. 441-448). West Orange, NJ: Leadership Library of America.

Barley, S. B. (1983). Semiotics and the study of occupational and organizational cultures. *Administrative Science Quarterly, 28,* 393-413.

Barnard, C. I. (1938). *The functions of the executive.* Cambridge, MA: Harvard University Press.

Barrett, W. P. (1987, March). Top gun. *Texas Monthly,* pp. 98-103, 185-190.

Barton, R. F. (1970). *A primer on simulation and gaming.* Englewood Cliffs, NJ: Prentice-Hall.

Bass, B. M. (1981). *Stodgill's handbook of leadership.* New York: Free Press.

Bass, B. M. (1985). *Leadership and performance beyond expectations.* New York: Free Press.

Bass, B. M. (1987). Policy implications of a new paradigm of leadership. In L. Atwater & R. Penn (Eds.), *Military leadership: Traditions and future trends* (pp. 155-164). Annapolis, MD: U.S. Naval Academy.

Bass, B. M. (1988). Evolving perspectives on charismatic leadership. In J. A. Conger & R. N. Kanungo (Eds.), *Charismatic leadership* (pp. 40-77). San Francisco: Jossey-Bass.

Bass, B. M. (1990). *Bass & Stodgill's handbook of leadership* (3rd ed.). New York: Free Press.

Bass, B. M., & Avolio, B. J. (1987). *Biases in transformational leadership ratings.* Working Paper No. 87-124, School of Management, State University of New York, Binghampton.

Bass, B. M., Waldman, D. A., Avolio, B. J., & Bebb, M. (1987). Transformational leadership and the falling dominoes effect. *Group & Organization Studies, 12,* 73-87.

Baumgardner, E. L., & Forti, J. C. (1988). *The implications of experience for leadership categorization theory: A field study.* Unpublished manuscript, University of Akron.

Becker, B. W., & Connor, P. E. (1986). On the status and promise of values research. *Management Bibliographies & Reviews, 12*(2), 3-17.

Bell, G. D. (1967). Determinants of span of control. *American Journal of Sociology, 73,* 100-109.

Bennis, W., & Nanus, B. (1985). *Leaders.* New York: Harper & Row.

Bentz, V. J. (1987). *Explorations of scope and scale: The critical determinant of high-level effectiveness* (Technical Report 31). Greensboro, NC: Center for Creative Leadership.

Beyer, J. M. (1981). Ideologies, values, and decision making in organizations. In P. C. Nystrom & W. H. Starbuck, (Eds.), *Handbook of organizational design (pp. 166-202).* Oxford, UK: Oxford University Press.

Bhagat, R. S., & McQuaid, S. J. (1982). Role of subjective culture in organizations: A review and directions for future research. *Journal of Applied Psychology Monograph, 67,* 653-685.

Bieri, J. (1955). Cognitive complexity-simplicity and predictive behavior. *Journal of Abnormal and Social Psychology, 51,* 263-268.

Bieri, J. (1961). Complexity-simplicity as a personality variable in cognitive and preferential behavior. In D. W. Fiske & S. R. Maddi (Eds.), *Functions of varied experience.* Homewood, IL: Irwin-Dorsey.

Bieri, J. (1966). Cognitive complexity and personality development. In O. J. Harvey (Ed.), *Experience, structure and adaptability.* New York: Springer.

Bigelow, J. (1982). A catastrophe model of organizational change. *Behavioral Science, 27,* 27-42.

Blair, J. D., & Hunt, J. G. (1986). Getting inside the head of the management researcher one more time: Context free and context specific orientations in research. *1986 Yearly Review of Management of the Journal of Management, 12,* 147-166.

Bluedorn, A. C., & Denhardt, R. B. (1988). Time and organizations. *Yearly Review of Management of the Journal of Management, 14,* 299-320.

Boal, K. B., & Bryson, J. M. (1988). Charismatic leadership: A phenomenological and structural approach. In J. G. Hunt, B. R. Baliga, H. P. Dachler, & C. A. Schriesheim (Eds.), *Emerging leadership vistas* (pp. 11-28). Lexington, MA: Lexington Books.

Bogen, J. E. (1969). The other side of the brain: An oppositional mind. *Bulletin of the Los Angeles Neurological Societies, 34*(3), 135-162.

Botwinick, J. (1967). *Cognitive processes in maturity and old age.* New York: Springer.

Bougan, M. (1983). Uncovering cognitive maps: The self-Q technique. In G. Morgan (Ed.), *Beyond method)* (pp. 173-188). Beverly Hills, CA: Sage.

Boyatzis, R. E. (1982). *The competent manager.* New York: Wiley-Interscience.

Bradley, R. T. (1987). *Charisma and social structure: A study of love and power, wholeness and transformation.* New York: Paragon House.

Brascomb, L. M., & Gilmore, P. C. (1975). Education in private industry. *Daedalus, 104*(1), 222-233.

Bray, D. W., & Howard, A. (1983). The AT&T longitudinal studies of managers. In K. W. Schaie (Ed.), *Longitudinal studies of adult psychological development.* New York: Guilford.

Brickman, P. (1978). Is it real? In J. G. Harvey, W. Ickes, & R. F. Kidd (Eds.), *New directions in attribution research* (Vol. 2, pp. 5-34). Hillsdale, NJ: Lawrence Erlbaum.

Bridges, W. (1980). *Making sense of life's transitions.* Reading, MA: Addison-Wesley.

Briggs, J., & Peat, F. D. (1989). *Turbulent mirror.* New York: Harper & Row.

Briggs, J. B. (1990, July). My life as Joe Bob Briggs. *Texas Monthly,* p. 77.

Brisset, D., & Edgley, C. (1975). *Life as theater: A dramaturgical sourcebook.* Chicago: Aldine.

Bruner, J. (1966). *Toward a theory of instruction.* New York: Norton.

Burns, J. M. (1978). *Leadership.* New York: Harper & Row.

Burns, T., & Stalker, G. M. (1961). *The management of innovation.* London: Tavistock.

Burrell, G., & Morgan, G. (1979). *Sociological paradigms and organizational analysis.* London: Heinemann.

Calas, M. B., & Smircich, L. (1988). Reading leadership as a form of cultural analysis. In J. G. Hunt, B. R. Baliga, H. P. Dachler, & C. A. Schriesheim (Eds.), *Emerging leadership vistas* (pp. 201-226). Lexington, MA: Lexington Books.

Calder, B. J. (1977). An attribution theory of leadership. In B. M. Staw & G. R. Salancik (Eds.), *New directions in organizational behavior* (pp. 179-204). Chicago: St. Clair.

Cameron, K. S., & Whetten, D. A. (1981). Perceptions of organizational effectiveness over organizational life cycles. *Administrative Science Quarterly, 26,* 525-44.

Cameron, K. S., & Whetten, D. A. (1983). *Organizational effectiveness: A comparison of multiple models.* Orlando, FL: Academic Press.

Campbell, J. P. (1977). The cutting edge of leadership: An overview. In J. G. Hunt & L. L. Larson (Eds.), *Leadership: The cutting edge* (pp. 221-235). Carbondale: Southern Illinois University Press.

Campbell, J. P., & Campbell, R. J. (Eds.) (1988). *Productivity in organizations.* San Francisco: Jossey-Bass.

Cantor, N., Mischel, W., & Schwartz, J. (1982). Social knowledge: Structure, content, use and abuse. In A. Hastorf & A. Isen (Eds.), *Cognitive social psychology.* Hillsdale, NJ: Lawrence Erlbaum.

Capra, F. (1975). *The Tao of physics.* Berkeley, CA: Shambhala.

Carroll, S. J., & Gillen, D. J. (1984). The classical management functions: Are they really outdated? *Academy of Management Proceedings,* pp. 132-136.

Carroll, S. J. & Gillen, D. J. (1987). Are the classical management functions useful in describing managerial work? *Academy of Management Review, 12,* 38-51.

Casti, J. (1979). *Connectivity, complexity, and catastrophe in large scale systems.* London: International Institute for Applied Systems Analysis.

Certo, S. C., & Peter, J. P. (1988). *Strategic management.* New York: Random House.

Chandler, A. D. (1962). *Strategy and structure: Chapters in the history of American industrial enterprise.* Cambridge: MIT Press.

Chi, M., Glaser, R., & Farr, R. M. (Eds.). (1987). *The nature of expertise.* Hillsdale, NJ: Lawrence Erlbaum.

Clark, B. R. (1970). *The distinctive college: Antioch, Reed and Swarthmore.* Chicago: Aldine.

Clark, B. R. (1972). The organizational saga in higher education. *Administrative Science Quarterly, 17,* 178-184.

Clark, B. R. (1970). *The distinctive college: Antioch, Reed and Swarthmore.* Chicago: Aldine.

Clark, B. R. (1972). The organizational saga in higher education. *Administrative Science Quarterly, 17,* 178-184.

Clark, K. E., & Clark, M. B. (Eds.). (1990). *Measures of leadership.* West Orange, NJ: Leadership Library of America.

Clark, P. A. (1984). Part 5 integrative comments: Leadership theory—the search for a reformulation. In J. G. Hunt, D. M. Hosking, C. A. Schriesheim, & R. Stewart (Eds.), *Leaders and managers* (pp. 375-381). Elmsford, NY: Pergamon.

Clement, S. D., & Ayers, D. (1976). *A matrix of organizational leadership dimensions (United States Army Leadership Monograph Series, monograph 8). Ft. Benjamin Harrison, IN: U.S. Army Administrative Center.*

Clover, W. H. (1990). Transformational leaders: Team performance leadership ratings, and firsthand impressions. In K. E. Clark & M. B. Clark (Eds.), *Measures of leadership* (pp. 171-184). West Orange, NJ: Leadership Library of America.

Cohen, A. R. (1988-1989). Some uncomfortable comments on "The MBA program: Views from a student and a professor." *Organizational Behavior Teaching Review; 13*(3), 72-74.

Comrey, A. L., Pfeffner, J. M., & High, W. S. (1954). *Factors influencing organizational success: A final report.* Final Technical Report, Los Angeles, University of Southern California.

Conger, J. A. (1989). *The charismatic leader: Behind the mystique of exceptional leadership.* San Francisco: Jossey-Bass.

Conger, J. A., & Kanungo, R. N. (1987). Towards a behavioral theory of charismatic leadership in organizational settings. *Academy of Management Review, 12,* 637-647.

Conger, J. A., & Kanungo, R. N. (1988). *Charismatic leadership.* San Francisco: Jossey-Bass.

Conger, J. A., & Kanungo, R. N. (1990, August). *A behavioral measure of charismatic leadership in organizations.* Paper presented at 50th annual meeting of the Academy of Management, San Francisco.

Constas, H. (1961). The USSR—from charismatic sect to bureaucratic society, *Administrative Science Quarterly, 6,* 282-298.

Cooke, R. A., & Rousseau, D. M. (1988). Behavioral norms and expectations: A quantitative approach to the assessment of organizational culture. *Group and Organizational Studies, 13,* 245-273.

Cronshaw, S. F., & Lord, R. F. (1987). Effects of categorization, attribution, and encoding processes on leadership perceptions. *Journal of Applied Psychology, 72,* 97-106.

Dachler, H. P. (1988). Constraints on the emergence of new vistas in leadership and management science: An epistemological overview. In J. G. Hunt, B. R. Baliga, H. P. Dachler, & C. A. Schriesheim (Eds.), *Emerging leadership vistas* (pp. 261-285). Lexington, MA: Lexington Books.

Daft, R. L. (1989). *Organization theory and design.* St. Paul, MN: West.

Dalton, G. W., & Thompson, P. H. (1986). *Novations: Strategies of career management.* Glenview, IL: Scott, Foresman.

Dansereau, F., Alutto, J. A., & Yammarino, F. J. (1984). *Theory testing in organizational behavior: The Varient approach.* Englewood Cliffs, NJ: Prentice-Hall.

Davies, J., & Easterly-Smith, M. (1984). Learning and developing from managerial work experiences. *Journal of Management Studies, 21,* 164-183.

Day, D. V., & Lord, R. G. (1988). Executive leadership and organizational performance: Suggestions for a new theory and methodology. *Journal of Management, 14,* 453-464.

Day, P. J. (1980). Charismatic leadership in the small organization. *Human Organization, 19,* 50-58.

Deal, T. E., & Kennedy, A. A. (1982). *Corporate cultures: The rites and rituals of corporate life.* Reading, MA: Addison-Wesley.

Delbec, A. (1990, August). *Vision as a change strategy in health care crises.* Paper presented at 50th annual meeting of the Academy of Management, San Francisco.

Denison, D. R., & Mishra, A. K. (1989). Organizational cultures and organizational effectiveness: A theory and some preliminary empirical evidence. *Academy of Management Proceedings.*

Deshpande, R., & Webster, F. E., Jr. (1989). Organizational culture and marketing: defining the research agenda. *Journal of Marketing, 53,* 3-15.

Diffenbach, J. (1982). Influence diagrams for complex strategic issues. *Strategic Management Journal, 3,* 133-146.

Downey, H. K., & Brief, A. P. (1986). How cognitive structures affect organizational design. In H. P. Sims, Jr., & D. A. Gioia (Eds.), *The thinking organization* (pp. 165-190). San Francisco: Jossey-Bass.

Drachkovitch, M. M. (1964). Succession and the charismatic leader in Yugoslavia. *Journal of International Affairs, 18,* 54-66.

Drazin, R., & Van de Ven, A. H. (1985). An examination of alternative forms of fit in contingency theory. *Administrative Science Quarterly, 30,* 514-539.

Dreyfus, H. I., & Dreyfus, S. E. (1986). *Mind over machine: The power of human intuition and expertise in the era of the computer.* New York: Free Press.

Driver, M. J., Brousseau, K. R., & Hunaker, P. L. (1990). *The dynamic decisionmaker.* New York: Harper & Row.

Drucker, P. F. (1988, January-February). The coming of the new organization. *Harvard Business Review,* pp. 45-53.

Dunphy, D. C., & Stace, D. A. (1988). Transformational and coercive strategies for planned organizational change: Beyond the OD model. *Organizational Studies, 9,* 317-334.

Duran, C. A. (1990). *Punctuated equilibrium: Logical, revolutionary, or chaotic?* Unpublished manuscript, College of Business Administration, Texas Tech University, Lubbock.

Dyer, W. G., Jr. (1984). Organizational culture: Analysis and change. In W. G. Dyer, Jr. (Ed.), *Strategies for managing change,* Reading, MA: Addison-Wesley.

Dyer, W. G., Jr. (1985). The cycle of cultural evolution in organizations. In R. H. Kilman, M. J. Saxton, R. Serpa et al. (Eds.), *Gaining control of the corporate culture.* San Francisco: Jossey-Bass.

Dyer, W. G., Jr. (1986). *Cultural change in family firms.* San Francisco: Jossey-Bass.

Eden, C., Jones, S., Sims, D., & Smithin, T. (1981). The intersubjectivity of issues and issues of intersubjectivity. *Journal of Management Studies, 18,* 37-47.

Eden, D., & Leviatan, U. (1975). Implicit leadership theory as a determinant of the factor structure underlying supervisory behavioral scales. *Journal of Applied Psychology, 60,* 736-741.

Eigen, L. D., & Siegel, J. P. (1989). *The manager's book of quotations.* New York: American Management Association.

Eisenhardt, K. M. (1989). Building theories from case study research. *Academy of Management Review, 14,* 532-550.

Eisenstadt, S. N. (Ed.) (1968). *Max Weber: On charisma and institution building.* Chicago: University of Chicago Press.

Eldredge, N., & Gould, S. J. (1972). Punctuated equilibria: An alternative to phyletic gradualism. In T. J. Schopf (Ed.), *Models in paleobiology* (pp. 82-115). San Francisco: Freeman, Cooper.

Emery, F. B., & Trist, E. L. (1973). *Towards a social ecology.* New York: Plenum.

Emmett, D. C., & Melcher, A. J. (1978). *Dynamic analysis: A framework for analyzing organizations.* Unpublished manuscript, Department of Administrative Science, Kent State University,

England, G. W. (1967). Personal value systems of American managers. *Academy of Management Journal, 10,* 53-68.

England, G. W., & Lee, R. (1974). The relationships between managerial values and managerial successes in the United States, Japan, India, and Australia. *Journal of Applied Psychology, 59,* 411-419.

England, G. W., Negandhi, A., & Wilpert, G. (1979). *Organizational functioning in a cross-cultural perspective.* Kent, OH: Comparative Administration Research Institute.

Etzioni, A. (1975). *A comparative analysis of complex organizations.* New York: Free Press.

Evan, W. M. (1976). Organization theory and organizational effectiveness: An exploratory analysis. In S. L. Spray (Ed.), *Organizational effectiveness: Theory, research, utilization.* Kent, OH: Kent State University Press.

Evans, L. N. (1976). A psycho-temporal theory of personality: A study of the relationship between temporal orientation, affect, and personality type. *Dissertation Abstracts International, 37,* 1985B. (University Microfilms No. 76-22, 381).

Evered, R., & Louis, M. R. (1981). Alternative perspectives on the organizational sciences: "Inquiry from the inside" and "inquiry from the outside." *Academy of Management Review, 6,* 385-395.

Evered, R.D. (1973). Conceptualizing the future: Implications for strategic management in a turbulent environment. *Dissertation Abstracts International, 34,* 3625A-3626A. (University Microfilms No. 73-32, 663)

Executive Knowledgeworks (1986). *Executive education in corporate America.* Palatine, IL: Anthony J. Fresina.

Fahey, L., & Narayanan, V. K. (1986). Organizational beliefs and strategic adaptation. In *Academy of Management Best Paper Proceedings 1986* (pp. 7-11). Chicago: Academy of Management.

Fayol, H. (1949). *General industrial management.* London: Pitman. (Original work published 1916)

Feldman, D. C. (1988). *Managing careers in organizations.* Glenview, IL: Scott, Foresman,

Feldman, J. (1986). On the difficulty of learning from experience. In H. P. Sims, Jr., & D. A. Gioia (Eds.), *The thinking organization* (pp. 263-292). San Francisco: Jossey-Bass.

Fetterman, D. M. (1989). *Ethnography: Step by step.* Newbury Park, CA: Sage.

Fiedler, F. E., & Chemers, M. M. (1974). *Leadership and effective management.* Glenview, IL: Scott, Foresman.

Fiedler, F. E., & Garcia, J. E. (1987). *New approaches to effective leadership.* New York: Wiley.

Fielding, N. G., & Fielding, J. L. (1986). *Linking data.* Newbury Park, CA: Sage.

Finney, M., & Mitroff, I. I. (1986). Strategic plan failures. In H. P. Sims, Jr., & D. A. Gioia (Eds.), *The thinking organization* (pp. 317-335). San Francisco: Jossey-Bass.

Fisher, J. L. (1984). *Power of the presidency.* New York: Macmillan.

Fiske, S. T., & Linville, P. N. (1980). What does the schema concept buy us? *Personality and Social Psychology Bulletin, 6,* 543-552.

Fiske, S. T., & Taylor, S. E. (1984). *Social cognition.* Reading, MA: Addison-Wesley.

Flanagan, J. C. (1954). The critical incident technique. *Psychological Bulletin, 51,* 327-358.

Flavell, J. H. (1970). Cognitive changes in adulthood. In L. R. Goulet & P. B. Baltes (Eds.), *Lifespan development psychology* (pp. 247-253). New York: Academic Press.

Fleishman, E. A. (1953). The description of supervisory behavior. *Personnel Psychology, 37,* 1-6.

Fong, G. T., & Markus, H. (1982). Self-schema and judgments about others. *Social Cognition, 1,* 191-205.

Ford, J. D., & Hegarty, W. H. (1984). Decision makers' beliefs about the causes and effects of structure: An exploratory study. *Academy of Management Journal, 27,* 271-291.

Franklin, J. L. (1975). Down the organization: Influence processes across levels of hierarchy. *Administrative Science Quarterly, 20,* 153-164.

French, D. P. (1987). Milestones in naval leadership development past, present and future. In L. Atwater & R. Penn (Eds.), *Military leadership: Traditions and future trends* (pp. 115-121). Annapolis, MD: U.S. Naval Academy.

Fromkin, H. L., & Streufert, S. (1976). Laboratory experimentation. In M. D. Dunnette (Ed.), *Handbook of industrial and organizational psychology* (pp. 415-465). Chicago: Rand McNally.

Fromm, E. (1966). *The heart of man.* London: Routledge and Kegan Paul.

Frost, P. J., Moore, L. F., Louis, M. R., Lundberg, C., & Martin, J. (Eds.). (1985). *Organizational culture.* Newbury Park, CA: Sage.

Fry, R. E., & Pasmore, W. A. (1983). Strengthening management education. In S. Srivastva (Ed.), *The executive mind* (pp. 269-296). San Francisco: Jossey-Bass.

Gabarro, J. J. (1988). Executive leadership and succession: The process of taking charge. In D. C. Hambrick (Ed.), *The executive effect: Concepts and methods for studying top managers (pp. 237-268)*. Greenwich, CT: JAI Press.

Gagliardi, P. (1986). The creation and change of organizations: A conceptual framework. *Organizational Studies, 7,* 118-133.

Ganster, D. C., Hennesey, H. W., & Luthans, F. (1983). Social desirability response effects: Three alternative models. *Academy of Management Journal, 26,* 321-331.

Gardner, H. (1985). *The mind's new science.* New York: Basic Books.

Geertz, C. (1973). *Local knowledge.* New York: Basic Books.

Gioia, D. A., & Manz, C. C. (1985). Linking cognition and behavior: A script processing interpretation of vicarious learning. *Academy of Management Review, 10,* 527-539.

Gioia, D. A., & Sims, H. P., Jr. (1985). On avoiding the influence of implicit leadership theories in leader behavior descriptions. *Educational and Psychological Measurements, 45,* 217-232.

Glaser, B. G., & Strauss, A. L. (1967). *The discovery of grounded theory: Strategies for qualitative research.* New York: Aldine.

Gleick, J. (1987). *Chaos: Making a new science.* New York: Viking.

Glick, W. H. (1985). Conceptualizing and measuring organizational and psychological climate: Pitfalls in multi-level research. *Academy of Management Review, 10,* 601-616.

Glick, W. H. (1988). Response; Organizations are not central tendencies: Shadowboxing in the dark, round 2. *Academy of Management Review, 13,* 133-137.

Glueck, W. F., & Jauch, L. R. (1984). *Business policy and strategic management* (4th ed.). New York: McGraw-Hill.

Goffman, E. (1974). *Frame analysis.* New York: Harper & Row.

Goodstein, C. (1981, Summer). Commentary: Do American theories apply abroad? *Organizational Dynamics,* 49-54.

Goodwin, V. L., Wofford, J. C., & Harrison, D. (1990, August). *Measuring cognitive complexity in the organizational domain.* Paper presented at 50th annual meeting of the Academy of Management, San Francisco.

Gordon, G. G. (1985). The relationship of corporate culture to industry sector and corporate performance. In R. H. Kilmann, M. J. Saxton, R. Serpa et al. (Eds.), *Gaining control of the corporate culture.* San Francisco: Jossey-Bass.

Gough, H. (1969). A leadership index on the California Psychological Inventory. *Journal of Counseling Psychology, 16,* 283-289.

Graen, G., & Cashman, J. F. (1975). A role-making model of leadership in formal organizations. In J. G. Hunt & L. L. Larson (Eds.), *Leadership frontiers* (pp. 143-166). Kent, OH: Kent State University Press.

Graen, G. B., & Scandura, T. A. (1987). Toward psychology of dyadic organizing. In L. L. Cummings & B. M. Staw (Eds.), *Research in organizational behavior* (Vol. 9, pp. 175-208). Greenwich, CT: JAI Press.

Greenwood, R., & Hinings, C. R. (1988). Organizational design types, tracks and the dynamics of strategic change. *Organization Studies, 9,* 293-316.

Gregory, K. L. (1983). Native-view paradigms—multiple cultures and conflicts in organizations, *Administrative Science Quarterly, 28,* 359-376.

Gregory, R. A. (1987). Leadership training at the U.S. Air Force Academy. In L. Atwater & R. Penn (Eds.), *Military leadership: Traditions and future trends* (pp. 98-108). Annapolis, MD: U.S. Naval Academy.

Greiner, L. E. (1972). Evolution and revolution as organizations grow. *Harvard Business Review, 50,* 37-46.

Gupta, A. K. (1988). Contingency perspectives on strategic leadership: Current knowledge and future research directions. In D. C. Hambrick (Ed.), *The executive effect: Concepts and methods for studying top managers* (pp. 141-178). Greenwich, CT: JAI Press.

Hales, C. (1986). What do managers do? A critical review of the evidence. *Journal of Management Studies, 23*(1), 88-115.

Hales, C. (1988). *Management processes, management divisions of labour, and managerial work: Towards a synthesis* (paper presented at the Workshop on the Study of Managerial Labour Processes). Brussels: European Institute for Advanced Studies in Management.

Hall, D. T. (1976). *Careers in organizations.* Pacific Palisades, CA: Goodyear.

Hall, R. I. (1984). The natural logic of management policy making: Its implications for the survival of an organization. *Management Science, 30,* 905-927.

Hambrick, D. C., & Brandon, G. L. (1988). Executive values. In D. C. Hambrick (Ed.), *The executive effect* (pp. 3-34). Greenwich, CT: JAI Press.

Hambrick, D. C., & Finkelstein, S. (1987). Managerial discretion: A bridge between polar views of organizational outcomes. In L. L. Cummings & B. M. Staw (Eds.), *Research in organizational behavior* (Vol. 9, pp. 369-406). Greenwich, CT: JAI Press.

Hambrick, D. C., & Mason, P. A. (1984). Upper echelons: The organization as a reflection of its top managers. *Academy of Management Review, 9,* 193-206.

Hanneman, R. A. (1988). *Computer assisted theory building: Modeling dynamic social systems.* Newbury Park, CA: Sage.

Harris, M. (1976). History and significance of the emic/etic distinction. *Annual Review of Anthropology, 5,* 329-350.

Harris, M. M., & Schaubroeck, J. S. (1990). Confirmatory modeling in organizational behavior/human resource management: Issues and applications. *Yearly Review of Management of the Journal of Management, 16,* 337-360.

Harrison, D. F., & Lawrence, G. (1985). Psychological type and time orientation of middle school students: Do middle school students differ in projecting their personal futures? *Journal of Psychological Type, 9,* 10-15.

Hartl, D. L. (1981). *The primer of population genetics.* Sunderland, MA: Sinauer Associates.

Hastie, R. (1981). Schematic principles of human memory. In E. T. Higgins, C. A. Herman, & M. P. Zana (Eds.), *Social cognition: The Ontario Symposium* (Vol. 1). Hillsdale, NJ: Lawrence Erlbaum.

Hater, J. J., & Bass, B. M. (1988). Supervisors' evaluations and subordinates' perceptions of transformational and transactional leadership. *Journal of Applied Psychology, 73,* 695-702.

Hays, R. H., & Abernathy, W. J. (1980). Managing our way to economic decline. *Harvard Business Review, 58*(4), 67-77.

Heisler, W. J., & Benham, P. O. (in press). The challenge of management development in North America in the 1990s. *Journal of Management Development.*

Heller, F. A. (1984). The role of longitudinal method in management decision-making studies. In J. G. Hunt, D. M. Hosking, C. A. Schriesheim, & R. Stewart (Eds.), *Leaders and managers* (pp. 283-302). Elmsford, NY: Pergamon.

Heller, F. A., Drenth, P., Koopman, P., & Rus, V. (1988). *Decisions in organizations*. London: Sage.

Hellriegel, D., & Slocum, J. W., Jr. (1974). Organizational climate: Measures, research and contingencies. *Academy of Management Journal*, pp. 255-280.

Hellriegel, D., Slocum, J. W., Jr., & Woodman, R. W. (1989). *Organizational behavior (5th ed.)*. St. Paul, MN: West.

Helmich, D. L., & Brown, W. B. (1972). Successor type and organizational change in the corporate enterprise. *Administrative Science Quarterly, 17,* 371-381.

Hersey, P., & Blanchard, K. H. (1988). *Management of organizational behavior* (5th ed.). Englewood Cliffs, NJ: Prentice-Hall.

Hines, T. (1987). Left brain/right brain mythology and implications for management and training. *Academy of Management Review, 12,* 600-606.

Hirschman, E. C. (1986). Humanistic inquiry in marketing research: Philosophy, method and criteria. *Journal of Marketing Research, 23,* 237-249.

Hodgkinson, C. (1983). *The philosophy of leadership*. New York: St. Martin's.

Hofstede, G. (1980). *Culture's consequences: International differences in work-related values*. Beverly Hills, CA: Sage.

Hofstede, G. (1983). Dimensions of national cultures in fifty countries and three regions. In J. Dergowski, D. Dzivrawiec, & R. Anuis (Eds.), *Explications in cross-cultural psychology* (pp. 335-355). Liste, Netherlands: Suets & Zeithnger.

Hofstede, G., & Bond, M. H. (1988). The Confucius connection: From cultural roots to economic growth. *Organizational Dynamics, 17,* 5-21.

Holbrook, M. (1989, December). Farewell address. *ACR Newsletter*, pp. 1-9.

Holden, P., Fish, L., & Smith, H. (1941). *Top management organization and control*. Palo Alto, CA: Stanford University Press.

Hollander, E. P. (1978). *Leadership dynamics*. New York: Free Press.

Hollander, E. P. (1985). Leadership and power. In G. Lindzey & E. Aronson (Eds.). *The handbook of social psychology* (3rd ed.). New York: Random House.

Hollings, C. S. (1976). Resilience and stability of ecosystems. In E. Jantsch & C. H. Waddington (Eds.), *Evolution and consciousness: Human systems in transaction*. Reading, MA: Addison-Wesley.

Hosking, D. M., & Morley, I. E. (1988). The skills of leadership. In J. G. Hunt, B. R. Baliga, H. P. Dachler, & C. A. Schrieshiem (Eds.), *Emerging leadership vistas* (pp. 89-106). Lexington, MA: Lexington Books.

House, R. J. (1977). A 1976 theory of charismatic leadership. In J. G. Hunt & L. L. Larson (Eds.), *Leadership: The cutting edge* (pp. 189-207). Carbondale: Southern Illinois University Press.

House, R. J. (1987). Review of Dansereau, Alutto, and Yammarino: "Theory testing in organizational behavior: The Varient approach." *Administrative Science Quarterly, 32,* 459-464.

House, R. J. (1988a). Leadership research: Some forgotten, ignored, or overlooked findings. In J. G. Hunt, B. R. Baliga, H. P. Dachler, & C. A. Schriesheim (Eds.), *Emerging leadership vistas* (pp. 245-260). Lexington, MA: Lexington Books.

House, R. J. (1988b). Power and personality in complex organizations. In L. L. Cummings & B. M. Staw (Eds.), *Research in organizational behavior* (Vol. 10, pp. 305-357). Greenwich, CT: JAI Press.

House R. J., & Baetz, M. L. (1979). Leadership: Some empirical generalizations and new research directions. In B. W. Staw (Ed.), *Research in organizational behavior* (Vol. 1, pp. 341-424). Greenwich, CT: JAI Press.

House, R. J., Howell, J. M., Shamir, B., Smith, B., & Spangler, W. D. (1990). *Charismatic leadership: A 1990 theory and seven empirical tests.* Unpublished manuscript, Wharton School of Management, University of Pennsylvania.

House, R. J., & Mitchell, T. R. (1974). Path-goal theory of leadership. *Journal of Contemporary Business, 3,* 81-97.

House, R. J., Spangler, W. D., & Woycke, J. (1990). Personality and charisma in the U.S. presidency: A psychological theory of leadership effectiveness. In *Academy of Management Best Paper Proceedings 1990.* Chicago: Academy of Management.

House, R. J., Woycke, J. & Fodor, E. M. (1988). Charismatic and noncharismatic leaders: Differences in behavior and effectiveness. In J. A. Conger & R. N. Kanungo (Eds.), *Charismatic leadership* (pp. 98-121). San Francisco: Jossey-Bass.

Howard, A., & Bray, D. W. (1988). *Managerial lives in transition.* New York: Guilford.

Howard, A., Shudo, K., & Umeshima, M. (1983). Motivation and values among Japanese and American managers. *Personnel Psychology, 36,* 883-898.

Howell, J. M. (1988). Two faces of charisma: Socialized and personalized leadership in organizations. In J. A. Conger & R. N. Kanungo (Eds.), *Charismatic leadership* (pp. 213-236). San Francisco: Jossey-Bass.

Huff, A. S. (Ed.). (1990). *Mapping strategic thought.* Chichester, UK: Wiley.

Hughes, M. A., Price, R. L., & Marrs, D. W. (1986). Linking theory construction and theory testing: Models with multiple indicators of latent variables. *Academy of Management Review, 11,* 128-144.

Hume, D. (1955). *An inquiry concerning human understanding.* New York: Liberal Arts. (Original work published 1748)

Hunsicker, J. Q. (1980). Can top managers be strategists? *Strategic Management Journal, 1,* 77-83.

Hunt, J. G. (1971). Leadership style effects at two managerial levels in a simulated organization. *Administrative Science Quarterly, 16,* 476-481.

Hunt, J. G. (1984a). *Leadership and managerial behavior.* Chicago: Science Research Associates.

Hunt, J. G. (1984b). Leadership: The state of the art and the future battlefield. In J. G. Hunt & J. D. Blair (Eds.), *Leadership on the future battlefield* (pp. 76-96). Washington, DC: Pergamon-Brassey's.

Hunt, J. G. (1985). Organizational leadership: The contingency paradigm and its challenges. In B. Kellerman (Ed.), *Leadership: Interdisciplinary perspectives* (pp. 114-138). Englewood Cliffs, NJ: Prentice-Hall.

Hunt, J. G., Baliga, B. R., Dachler, H. P., & Schriesheim, C. A. (Eds.). (1988). *Emerging leadership vistas.* Lexington, MA: Lexington Books.

Hunt, J. G., Baliga, B. R., & Peterson, M. F. (1988). Strategic apex leader scripts and an organizational life cycle approach to leadership and excellence. *Journal of Management Development, 7*(5), 61-83.

Hunt, J. G., & Blair, J. D. (Eds.). (1985). *Leadership on the future battlefield.* Washington: Pergamon-Brassey's.

Hunt, J. G., Boal, K. B., & Sorenson, R. L. (1990). Top management leadership: Inside the black box. *The Leadership Quarterly, 1,* 41-65.

Hunt, J. G., Hill, J. W., & Reaser, J. M. (1973). Correlates of leadership behavior at two managerial levels in a mental institution. *Journal of Applied Social Psychology, 3,* 174-185.

Hunt, J. G., Hosking, D. M., Schriesheim, C. A., & Stewart, R. (Eds.). (1984). *Leaders and managers.* Elmsford, NY: Pergamon.

Hunt, J. G., & Larson, L. L. (Eds.). (1975). *Leadership frontiers.* Kent, OH: Kent State University Press.

Hunt, J. G., & Liebscher, V. K. C. (1971, March). *Leadership behavior effects at multiple management levels in a highway department.* Paper presented at the Institute of Management Science, College on Organization, Washington, DC.

Hunt, J. G., Osborn, R. N., & Larson, L. L. (1975). Upper level technical orientation and first level leadership within a non-contingency and contingency framework. *Academy of Management Journal, 18,* 476-488.

Hunt, J. G., Osborn, R. N., & Martin, H. J. (1981). *A multiple influence model of leadership* (Technical Report #520). Alexandria, VA: U.S. Army Research Institute for the Behavioral and Social Sciences.

Hunt, J. G., & Phillips, R. L. (in press). Leadership in battle and garrison: A framework for understanding the difference and preparing for both. In R. Gal & A. D. Mangelsdorff (Eds.), *Handbook of military psychology.* Chichester, UK: Wiley.

Hunt, J. G., Sekaran, V., & Schriesheim, C. A. (Eds.). (1982). *Leadership: Beyond establishment views.* Carbondale: Southern Illinois University Press.

Hunt, R., Krzystofiak, F., Meindl, J., & Yousry, A. (1989). Cognitive style and decision making. *Organizational Behavior and Human Decision Processes, 44,* 436-453.

Hunt, S. D. (1989). Naturalistic, humanistic, and interpretive inquiry: Challenges and ultimate potential. In E. Hirschman (Ed.), *Interpretive consumer research.* Provo, UT: Association for Consumer Research.

Hunt, S. D. (1990). *Positivism and paradigm dominance in consumer research: Toward pluralism and rapprochement.* Unpublished manuscript, College of Business Administration, Texas Tech University.

Hunt, S. D. (1991). *Modern marketing theory: Critical issues in the philosophy of marketing science.* Cincinnati: South-Western.

Hurd, J., & Hunt, J. G. (1991). *Simulation and the study of process in leadership.* Unpublished manuscript, College of Business Administration, Texas Tech University.

Hurst, D., Rush, J. C., & White, R. E. (1989). Top management teams and organizational renewal. *Strategic Management Journal, 10,* 87-105.

Iacocca, L. (1984). *Iacocca: An autobiography.* New York: Bantam.

Ilgen, D. R., & Feldman, J. M. (1983). Performance appraisal: A process focus. In L. L. Cummings & B. M. Staw (Eds.), *Research in organizational behavior* (Vol. 5, pp. 141-197). Greenwich, CT: JAI Press.

Insko, C. A., Gilmore, R., Moehle, D., Lipsitz, A., Drenan, S., & Thibaut, J. W. (1982). Seniority in the generational transition of laboratory groups: The effects of social familiarity and task experience. *Journal of Experimental Social Psychology, 18,* 557-580.

Insko, C. A., Thibaut, J. W., Moehle, D., Wilson, M., Diamond, W. D., Gilmore, R., Solomon, M. R., & Lipsitz, A. (1980). Social evolution and the emergence of leadership. *Journal of Personality and Social Psychology, 39,* 431-448.

Isenberg, D. J. (1984). How senior managers think. *Harvard Business Review, 62*(6), 81-84.

Isenberg, D. J. (1985). Some hows and whys of managerial thinking: Implications for future army leaders. In J. G. Hunt & J. D. Blair (Eds.), *Leadership on the future battlefield* (pp. 32-46). Washington, DC: Pergamon-Brassey's.

Jackofsky, E. E., & Slocum, J. W., Jr. (1988). CEO roles across cultures. In D. C. Hambrick (Ed.), *The executive effect* (pp. 67-100). Greenwich, CT: JAI Press.

Jackson, J. (1990, January 28). [Interview with Jesse Jackson.] *Parade*, p. 5.

Jackson, S. E., Schuler, R. S., & Rivero, J. C. (1989). Organizational characteristics as predictors of personnel practices. *Personnel Psychology, 42*, 727-786.

Jacob, P. E., Flink, J. J., & Shuchman, H. L. (1962). Values and their function in decision-making. *American Behavioral Scientist, 5* (Supplement 9), 6-38.

Jacobs, R. C., & Campbell, D. T. (1961). The perpetuation of an arbitrary tradition through several generations of laboratory microculture. *Journal of Abnormal and Social Psychology, 62*, 649-658.

Jacobs, T. O., Clement, S., Rigby, C., & Jaques, E. (1985). Executive leadership. *Army Organizational Effectiveness Journal, 1*, 16-19.

Jacobs, T. O., & Jaques, E. (1987). Leadership in complex systems. In J. A. Zeidner (Ed.), *Human productivity enhancement* (Vol. 2, pp. 7-65). New York: Praeger.

Jacobs, T. O., & Jaques, E. (1990). Military executive leadership. In K. E. Clark & M. B. Clark (Eds.), *Measures of leadership* (pp. 281-295). West Orange, NJ: Leadership Library of America.

Jacobs, T. O., & Jaques, E. (in press). Executive leadership. In R. Gal & A. D. Mangelsdorff (Eds.), *Handbook of military psychology*. Chichester, UK: Wiley.

Jaffee, J. M. (1980). The relationship of Jungian psychological predispositions to the implementation of management by objectives: A sociotechnical perspective (Doctoral dissertation, University of Southern California). *Dissertation Abstracts International, 4*(11), 4833A.

Jago, A. G. (1982). Leadership: Perspectives in theory and research. *Management Science, 28*, 315-336.

James, L. R., & James, L. A. (1989). Causal modeling in organizational research. In C. L. Cooper & I. T. Robertson (Eds.), *International review of industrial and organizational psychology 1989* (pp. 372-404). Chichester, UK: Wiley.

James, L. R., & Jones, A. P. (1974). Organizational climate: A review of theory and research. *Psychological Bulletin, 81*, 1096-1112.

James, L. R., Joyce, W. F., & Slocum, J. W. (1988). Organizations do not cognize. *Academy of Management Review, 13*, 129-132.

Jaques, E. (1976). *A general theory of bureaucracy*. London: Heinemann.

Jaques, E. (1986). The development of intellectual capability: A discussion of stratified systems theory. *Journal of Applied Behavioral Science, 22*, 361-383.

Jaques, E. (1989). *Requisite organization*. Arlington, VA: Cason Hall.

Jaques, S. E., Clement, S., Rigby, C., & Jacobs, T. O. (1986). *Senior leadership performance requirements at the executive level* (Research report #1420). Alexandria, VA: U.S. Army Research Institute for the Behavioral and Social Sciences.

Jelinek, M., Smircich, L., & Hirsch, P. (1983). Introduction: A code of many colors. *Administrative Science Quarterly, 28*, 331-338.

Jermier, J., Slocum, J. W., Jr., Fry, L. W., & Gaines, J. (in press). Organizational subcultures in a soft bureaucracy: Resistance behind the myth and facade of an official culture. *Organization Science.*

Jöreskog, K. G., & Sörbom, D. (1985). LISREL VI: *Analysis of linear structural relationships by the method of maximum likelihood.* Chicago: National Educational Resources.

Joyce, W. F., & Slocum, J. W., Jr. (1979). Climates in organizations. In S. Kerr (Ed.), *Organizational behavior.* Columbus, OH: Grid.

Joyce, W. F., & Slocum, J. W., Jr. (1984). Collective climate: Agreement as a basis for defining aggregate climates in organizations. *Academy of Management Journal, 27,* 721-742.

Jung, C. G. (1971). Psychological types. In H. G. Barnes (Trans.) & R. F. C. Hull (Ed.), *The collected works of C. G. Jung* (Vol. 6). Princeton, NJ: Princeton University Press. (Original work published 1921)

Kaczka, E., & Kirk, R. V. (1967). Managerial climate, work groups and organizational performance. *Administrative Science Quarterly, 12,* 253-272.

Kahn, H., & Bruce-Briggs, B. (1973). *Things to come.* London: Macmillan.

Kanter, R. M. (1968). Commitment and social organizations: A study of commitment mechanisms in utopian communities. *American Sociological Review, 33,* 499-578.

Kanter, R. M. (1972). *Commitment and community.* Cambridge, MA: Harvard University Press.

Kanter, R. M. (1989). *When giants learn to dance.* New York: Simon & Shuster.

Karmel, B. (1978). Leadership: A challenge to traditional research methods and assumptions. *Academy of Management Review, 3,* 475-482.

Katz, D., & Kahn, R. L. (1966). *The social psychology of organizations* (1st ed.). New York: Wiley.

Katz, D., & Kahn, R. L. (1978). *The social psychology of organizations* (2nd ed.). New York: Wiley.

Katz, D. J. (1987). Leadership education and training at the U.S. Naval Academy. In L. Atwater & R. Penn (Eds.), *Military leadership: Traditions and future trends* (pp. 95-97). Annapolis, MD: U.S. Naval Academy.

Katz, R. L. (1955, January-February). Skills of an effective administrator. *Harvard Business Review,* pp. 33-42.

Katz, R. L. (1970). *Cases and concepts in corporate policy.* Englewood Cliffs, NJ: Prentice-Hall.

Kegan, R., & Lahey, L. L. (1984). Adult leadership and adult development: A constructionist view. In B. Kellerman (Ed.), *Leadership: Multidisciplinary perspectives* (pp. 199-230). Englewood Cliffs, NJ: Prentice-Hall.

Kelly, G. A. (1955). *The psychology of personal constructs, volume 1: A theory of personality.* New York: Norton.

Kelly, J. R., & McGrath, J. E. (1988). *On time and method.* Newbury Park, CA: Sage.

Kenny, D. A. (1979). *Correlation and causality.* New York: Wiley-Interscience.

Kerlinger, F. N. (1973). *Foundations of behavioral research* (2nd ed.). New York: Holt, Rinehart, & Winston.

Kerr, J. L., & Jackofsky, E. F. (1989). Aligning managers with strategies: Management development versus selection. *Strategic Management Journal, 10.*

Kerr, S., & Jermier, J. M. (1978). Substitutes for leadership: Their meaning and measurement. *Organizational Behavior and Human Performance, 22,* 375-403.

Kets de Vries, M. F. R., & Miller, D. (1986). Personality, culture and organization. *Academy of Management Review, 11,* 266-279.

Keys, B., & Wolfe, J. (1988). Management education and development: Current issues and emerging trends. *Yearly Review of Management of the Journal of Management, 14,* 205-230.

Keys, B., & Wolfe, J. (1990). The role of management games and simulations in education and research. *Yearly Review of Management of the Journal of Management, 16,* 307-336.

Khandwalla, P. N. (1976-1977). Some top management styles, their context and performance. *Organization and Administrative Sciences, 7,* 21-51.

Khandwalla, P. N. (1977). *The design of organizations.* New York: Harcourt Brace Jovanovich.

Khazanchi, D. (1990). *Subjective understanding of ill-structured problems: An information systems perspective.* Dissertation proposal, College of Business Administration, Texas Tech University.

Kilmann, R., Saxton, M. J., & Serpa, R. (1985). Introduction: Five key issues in understanding and changing culture. In R. Kilmann, M. J. Saxton, & R. Serpa, et al. (Eds.), *Gaining control of the corporate culture* (pp. 1-16). San Francisco: Jossey-Bass.

Kilmann, R. H. (1984). *Beyond the quick fix.* San Francisco: Jossey-Bass.

Kimberly, J. R., & Quinn, R. E. (1984). *Managing organizational transitions.* Homewood, IL: Irwin.

Kirk, J., & Miller, M. L. (1986). *Reliability and validity in qualitative research.* Newbury Park, CA: Sage.

Klemp, G. O., Jr. (1979). Identifying, measuring, and integrating competence. *New Directions for Experiential Learning, 3,* 41-52.

Klimoski, R., & Brickner, M. (1987). Why do assessment centers work? The puzzle of assessment center validity. *Personnel Psychology, 40,* 243-260.

Kolb, D. M. (1983). Problem management: Learning from experience. In S. Srivastva (Ed.), *The executive mind* (pp. 109-143). San Francisco: Jossey-Bass.

Kolb, D. M., Rubin, I. M., & McIntyre, J. M. (1984). *Organizational psychology: An experiential approach* (5th ed.). Englewood Cliffs, NJ: Prentice-Hall.

Korhonen, P. T., Santalainen, T., & Tainio, R. (1987). *Explaining variations in work performance.* Working Paper #168, Helsinki School of Economics.

Korukonda, A. R. (1989). Mixing levels of analysis in organizational research. *Canadian Journal of Administrative Sciences,* pp. 12-19.

Korukonda, A. R., & Hunt, J. G. (1987). *Management and leadership: Towards conceptual clarity.* Paper presented at ORSA/TIMS Joint National Meeting, St. Louis.

Korukonda, A. R., & Hunt, J. G. (1989). Pat on the back versus kick in the pants: An application of cognitive inference to the study of leader reward and punishment behaviors. *Group and Organization Studies, 14,* 299-324.

Kotter, J. P. (1982a). *The general managers.* New York: Free Press.

Kotter, J. P. (1982b, November-December) What effective general managers really do. *Harvard Business Review, 60,* 156-167.

Kotter, J. P. (1985). *Power and influence: Beyond final authority.* New York: Free Press.

Kotter, J. P. (1988). *The leadership factor.* New York: Free Press.

Kotter, J. P. (1990). *A force for change: How leadership differs from management.* New York: Free Press.

Kouzes, J. R., & Posner, B. F. (1987). *The leadership challenge: How to get extraordinary things done in organizations.* San Francisco: Jossey-Bass.

Kram, K. E. (1985). *Mentoring at work: Developmental relationships in organizational life.* Glenview, IL: Scott, Foresman.

Kuhn, T. S. (1962). *The structure of scientific revolutions.* Chicago: University of Chicago Press.

Kuhnert, K. W., & Lewis, P. (1987). Transactional and transformational leadership: A constructive/developmental analysis. *Academy of Management Review, 12,* 648-657.

Kurke, L. B. (1988). *Generational laboratory approaches to organizations and management.* Unpublished manuscript, Babcock Graduate School of Management, Wake Forest University.

Lammers, C. J., & Hickson, D. J. (1979). Towards a comparative sociology of organizations. In C. J. Lammers & D. J. Hickson (Eds.), *Organizations: Alike and unlike.* London: Routledge & Kegan Paul.

Langer, E. J. (1978). Rethinking the role of thought in social interaction. In J. H. Harvey, W. J. Ickes, & R. F. Kidd (Eds.), *New directions in attribution research* (Vol. 2). Hillsdale, NJ: Lawrence Erlbaum.

Latham, G. P. (1988). Human resource training and development. *Annual Review of Psychology, 39,* 545-582.

Laukkanen, M. (1989). *Understanding the formation of managers' cognitive maps.* Unpublished Ph.D. dissertation, Helsinki School of Economics and Business Administration, Helsinki, Finland.

Lawler, E. E., III. (1968). A correlation-causal analysis of the relationship between expectancy attitudes and job performance. *Journal of Applied Psychology, 52,* 462-468.

Lawler, E. E., III. (1984). Leadership in participative organizations. In J. G. Hunt, D. M. Hosking, C. A. Schriesheim, & R. Stewart (Eds.), *Leaders and managers* (pp. 316-332). Elmsford, NY: Pergamon.

Lawrence, B. S. (1984). Historical perspectives: Using the past to study the present. *Academy of Management Review, 9,* 307-312.

Lawrence, P. R., & Lorsch, J. W. (1967). *Organization and environment.* Boston: Harvard Business School.

Levin, D. P. (1989). *Irreconcilable differences: Ross Perot versus General Motors.* New York: Plume.

Levinson, D. J., Darrow, C. M., Klein, E. G., Levinson, M. H., & McKee, B. (1978). *The seasons of a man's life.* New York: Knopf.

Levy, A., & Merry, V. (1986). *Organizational transformation.* New York: Praeger.

Lewin, A. Y., & Huber, G. P. (Eds.). (1986). [Focused issue.] *Management Science, 32*(5).

Lippitt, G. L., Langseth, P., & Mossop, J. (1985). *Implementing organizational change.* San Francisco: Jossey-Bass.

Litterer, J. A. (1973). *The analysis of organizations* (2nd ed.). New York: Wiley.

Little, G. (1988). *Strong leadership.* Melbourne, Australia: Oxford University Press.

Locke, E. A. (1986). *Generalizing from laboratory to field settings.* Lexington, MA: Lexington Books.

Locke, E. A., Schweiger, D. M., & Latham, G. P. (1986, Winter). Participation in decision making: When should it be used. *Organizational Dynamics, 14,* 65-79.

Lockett, J., & Legge, K. (Eds.) (1989). Special issue: Managerial thinking in business environments. *Journal of Management Studies, 26* (4).

Lombardo, M. M., & McCall, M. W., Jr. (1982). Leaders on line: Observations from a simulation of managerial work. In J. G. Hunt, V. Sekaran, & C. A. Schriesheim (Eds.), *Leadership: Beyond establishment views* (pp. 50-67). Carbondale: Southern Illinois University Press.

Lombardo, M. M., McCall, M. W., Jr., Morrison, A. M., & White, R. P. (1983). Key events and learnings in the lives of executives. In M. Lombardo (Chair), *Key events and learnings in the lives of executives.* Symposium presented at the 43rd annual meeting of the Academy of Management, Dallas.

Lord, R. G. (1985). An information processing approach to social perceptions, leadership and behavioral measurement in organizations. In L. L. Cummings & B. M. Staw (Eds.), *Research in organizational behavior* (Vol. 7, pp. 87-128). Greenwich, CT: JAI Press.

Lord, R. G., Binning, J. F., Rush, M. C., & Thomas, J. C. (1978). The effect of performance cues and leader behavior on questionnaire ratings of leadership behavior. *Organizational Behavior and Human Performance, 21,* 27-39.

Lord, R. G., & Foti, R. J. (1986). Schema theories, information processing, and organizational behavior. In H. P. Sims, Jr., & D. A. Gioia (Eds.), *The thinking organization* (pp. 20-48). San Francisco: Jossey-Bass.

Lord, R. G., Foti, R. J., & Phillips, J. S. (1982). A theory of leadership categorization. In J. G. Hunt, U. Sekaran, & C. Schriesheim (Eds.), *Leadership: Beyond establishment views* (pp. 104-121). Carbondale: Southern Illinois University Press.

Lord, R. G., & Maher, K. J. (1989a). Cognitive processes in industrial and organizational psychology. In C. A. Cooper & I. I. Robertson (Eds.), *International review of industrial and organizational psychology* (pp. 49-92). Chichester, UK: Wiley.

Lord, R. G., & Maher, K. J. (1989b). Perceptions of leadership and their implications in organizations. In J. Carroll (Ed.), *Applied social psychology in business organizations.* IIillsdale, NJ: Lawrence Erlbaum.

Lord, R. G., & Maher, K. J. (in press). *Executive leadership and information processing: Linking perceptions and organizational performance.* Cambridge, MA: Unwin-Hyman.

Louis, M. R. (1981). A cultural perspective on organizations: The need for and consequences of viewing organizational culture-bearing milieux. *Human Systems Management,* pp. 346-358.

Louis, M. R. (1985). An investigator's guide to workplace culture. In P. J. Frost, L. L. Moore, M. R. Louis, C. C. Lundberg, & J. Martin, (Eds.), *Organizational culture.* Newbury Park, CA: Sage.

Luthans, F. (1982). Leadership: A proposal for a social learning theory base and observational and functional analysis techniques to measure leader behavior. In J. G. Hunt & L. L. Larson (Eds.), *Crosscurrents in leadership* (pp. 201-208). Carbondale: Southern Illinois University Press.

Luthans, F., Hodgetts, R. M., & Rosenkrantz, S. A. (1988). *Real managers.* Cambridge, MA: Ballinger.

Luthans, F., & Larsen, J. K. (1986). How managers really communicate. *Human Relations, 39,* 161-178.

Luthans, F., & Lockwood, D. L. (1984). Toward an observational system for measuring leader behavior in natural settings. In J. G. Hunt, D. M. Hosking, C. A. Schriesheim, & R. Stewart (Eds.), Leaders and managers (pp. 117-141). Elmsford, NY: Pergamon.

Luthans, F., Rosenkrantz, S., & Hennessey, H. (1985). What do successful managers really do? An observational study of managerial activities. Journal of Applied Behavioral Science, 21, 255-270.

Lyman, S. M., & Scott, M. B. (1970). A sociology of the absurd. New York: Appleton-Century-Crofts.

Macy, B. A., Izumi, R., & Smith, R. (in press). Organizational change: A meta-analysis of North American field experiments 1960-1990. In W. Pasmore & R. Woodman (Eds.), Research in organizational change and development. Greenwich, CT: JAI Press.

Madsen, D., & Snow, P. G. (1983). The dispersion of charisma. Comparative Political Studies, 16, 337-362.

Mann, F. C. (1965). Toward an understanding of the leadership role in formal organizations. In R. Dubin, G. C. Homans, F. C. Mann, & D. C. Miller (Eds.), Leadership and productivity (pp. 68-103). San Francisco: Chandler.

Manning, P. K. (1987). Semiotics and fieldwork. Newbury Park, CA: Sage.

Margerison, C., & Kakabadse, A. (1984). How American chief executives succeed. New York: American Management Association.

Markus, H. (1977). Self-schemata and processing information about the self. Journal of Personality and Social Psychology, 35, 63-78.

Markus, H., & Zajonc, R. B. (1985). The cognitive perspective in social psychology. In G. Lindzey & E. Aronson (Eds.) The handbook of social psychology (Vol. 1, 3rd ed., pp. 137-230). New York: Random House.

Marshall, C. (1985). Appropriate criteria of trustworthiness and goodness for qualitative research on education organizations. Quality and Quantity, 19, 353-373.

Martin, J., & Siehl, C. (1983, Autumn). Organizational culture and counterculture: An uneasy symbiosis. Organizational Dynamics, pp. 52-64.

Martinko, M. J., & Gardner, W. L. (1985). Beyond structured observation: Methodological issues and new directions. Academy of Management Review, 10, 676-695.

Maruyama, M. (1963). The second cybernetics: Deviation-amplifying mutual cause processes. American Scientist, 51, 164-179.

Maruyama, M. (1974). Paradigms and communication. Technological Forecasting and Social Change, 6, 3-32.

Mason, R. O., & Mitroff, I. T. (1981). Challenging strategic planning assumptions. New York: Wiley.

Masuch, M. (1985). Vicious circles in organizations. Administrative Science Quarterly, 30, 14-33.

Maturana, H., & Varela, F. (1980). Autopoiesis and cognition: The realization of the living. London: Reidel.

McCall, M. W., Jr., & Lombardo, M. M. (1982). Using simulation for leadership and management research: Through the looking glass. Management Science, 28, 533-549.

McCall, M. W., Jr., & Lombardo, M. M. (1983). What makes a top executive? Psychology Today, 26, 28-31.

References 319

McCall, M. W., Jr., Lombardo, M. M., & Morrison, A. M. (1988). *The lessons of experience.* Lexington, MA: Lexington Books.

McCall, M. W., Jr., & Segrist, C. A. (1980). *In pursuit of the manager's job: Building on Mintzberg* (Technical Report #14). Greensboro, NC: Center for Creative Leadership.

McCaskey, M. B. (1982). *The executive challenge: Managing change and ambiguity.* Boston: Pitman.

McCauley, C. D., & Lombardo, M. M. (1990). Benchmarks: An instrument for diagnosing managerial strengths and weaknesses. In K. E. Clark & M. B. Clark (Eds.), *Measures of leadership* (pp. 535-545). West Orange, NJ: Leadership Library of America.

McCauley, M. H. (1990). The Myers-Briggs type indicators and leadership. In K. E. Clark & M. B. Clark (Eds.), *Measures of leadership.* West Orange, NJ: Leadership Library of America.

McClelland, D. C. (1985). *Human motivation.* Glenview, IL: Scott, Foresman.

McGrath, J. E. (1964). Toward a theory of method for research on organizations. In W. W. Cooper, H. J. Leavitt, & M. W. Shelley, II, (Eds.), *New perspectives in organizational research* (pp. 533-556). New York: Wiley.

McGrath, J. E., & Kelly, J. R. (1986). *Time & human interaction: Toward a social psychology of time.* New York: Guilford.

McGuire, J. (1986). Management and research methodology. *Journal of Management, 12,* 5-17.

McKenney, J. L., & Keen, P. G. W. (1974, May-June). How managers' minds work. *Harvard Business Review,* pp. 79-90.

Meglino, B. M., Ravlin, E. C., & Adkin, S. C. L. (1989). A work values approach to corporate culture: A field test of value congruence process and its relationship to individual outcomes. *Journal of Applied Psychology, 74,* 424-432.

Meglino, B. M., Ravlin, E. C., & Adkin, S. C. L. (1990). *Value congruence and satisfaction with a leader: An examination of the role of interaction.* Unpublished manuscript, Riegel & Emory Human Resources Center, College of Business Administration, University of South Carolina, Columbia.

Meindl, J. R. (1988). *On the romanticized perception of charisma.* Unpublished manuscript, School of Management, State University of New York at Buffalo.

Meindl, J. R. (1990). On leadership: An alternative to conventional wisdom. In B. M. Staw & L. L. Cummings (Eds.), *Research in organizational behavior* (Vol. 12, pp. 159-204). Greenwich, CT: JAI Press.

Meindl, J. R., Ehrlich, S. B., & Dukerich, J. M. (1985). The romance of leadership. *Administrative Science Quarterly, 30,* 78-102.

Meindl, J. R., Tsai, C., & Lee, W. S. (1988). *The leader-manager distinction as a context for blaming.* Unpublished manuscript, School of Management, State University of New York at Buffalo.

Melcher, A. J. (1979). Leadership models and research approaches. In J. G. Hunt & L. L. Larsen (Eds.), *Leadership: The cutting edge* (pp. 94-108). Carbondale: Southern Illinois University Press.

Melcher, A. J., & Melcher, B. H. (1980). Toward a systems theory of policy analysis: Static versus dynamic analysis. *Academy of Management Review, 5,* 235-247.

Messick, S. (1984). The psychology of educational measurement. *Journal of Educational Measurement, 21,* 215-237.

Messick, S. (1988, Autumn). Testing for success: Implications of new developments in measurement and cognitive science. *Selections, 5*, 1-12.

Meyerson, D., & Martin, J. (1987). Cultural change: An integration of three different views. *Journal of Management Studies, 24*, 623-647.

Miles, M. B., & Huberman, A. M. (1984). *Qualitative data analysis: A sourcebook of new methods*. Newbury Park, CA: Sage.

Miles, M. C. (1949). *Middle management: The job of the junior administrator*. New York: Harper.

Miles, R., & Snow, C. G. (1978). *Organizational strategy, structure, and process*. New York: McGraw-Hill.

Miller, D. (1978). The role of multivariate Q-techniques in the study of organizations. *Academy of Management Review, 3*, 515-531.

Miller, D.. (1981). Toward a new contingency perspective: The search for organizational gestalts. *Journal of Management Studies, 18*, 1-26.

Miller, D. (1986). Configurations of strategy and structure. *Strategic Management Journal*, pp. 233-249.

Miller, D. (1987). The structural and environmental correlates of business strategy. *Strategic Management Journal*, pp. 55-76.

Miller, D., & Droöge, C. (1986). Psychological and traditional determinants of structure. *Administrative Science Quarterly, 31*, 539-560.

Miller, D., & Friesen, P. H. (1977). Strategy making in context: Ten empirical archetypes. *Journal of Management Studies, 14*, 259-280.

Miller, D., & Friesen, P. H. (1980). Archetypes of organizational transition. *Administrative Science Quarterly, 25*, 268-299.

Miller, D., & Friesen, P. H. (1982). The longitudinal analysis of organizations: A methodological perspective. *Management Science, 28*, 1013-1034.

Miller, D., & Friesen, P. H. (1984). *Organizations: A quantum view*. Englewood Cliffs, NJ: Prentice-Hall.

Miller, F. C. (1966). Problems of succession in Chippewa council. In M. J. Swartz & V. W. Turner (Eds.). *Political anthropology* (pp. 173-185). Chicago: Aldine.

Miner, J. B. (1980). Limited domain theories of organizational energy. In C. C. Pinder & L. F. Moore (Eds.), *Middle range theory and the study of organizations* (pp. 273-286). Boston: Martinus Nijhoff.

Mintzberg, H. (1976). Planning on the left and managing on the right. *Harvard Business Review, 54*(4), 49-58.

Mintzberg, H. (1979). *The structuring of organizations*. Englewood Cliffs, NJ: Prentice-Hall.

Mintzberg, H. (1980). *The nature of managerial work*. Englewood Cliffs, NJ: Prentice-Hall. (Original work published in 1973)

Mintzberg, H. (1983). *Power in and around organizations*. Englewood Cliffs, NJ: Prentice-Hall.

Misumi, J. & Peterson, M. F. (1985). *The behavioral science of leadership*. Ann Arbor: University of Michigan Press.

Misumi, J., & Peterson, M. F. (1987). Developing a performance-maintenance (PM) theory of leadership. *Bulletin of the Faculty of Human Sciences, Osaka University, 13*, 135-170.

Misumi, J., & Peterson, M. F. (in press). Performance-maintenance (PM) leadership theory: An interactionist perspective on leadership functions. *Communication Yearbook, 14*.

Mitchell, T. R., Green, S. G., & Wood, R. E. (1981). An attributional model of leadership and the poor performaning subordinate: Development and validation. In L. L. Cummings & B. M. Staw (Eds.), *Research in organizational behavior* (Vol. 3, pp. 197-234). Greenwich, CT: JAI Press.

Mitroff, I. I. (1978). Systematic problem solving. In M. W. McCall, Jr., & M. M. Lombardo (Eds.), *Leadership: Where else can we go?* (pp. 129-143). Durham, NC: Duke University Press.

Mitroff, I. I., & Kilmann, R. H. (1976). On organization stories: An approach to the design and analysis of organization through myths and stories. In R. H. Kilmann, L. R. Pondy, & D. P. Slevin (Eds.), *The management of organizational design* (Vol. 1). New York: Elsevier North-Holland.

Mohr, L. B. (1982). *Explaining organizational behavior.* San Francisco: Jossey-Bass.

Morey, N. C., & Luthans, F. (1985). Refining the displacement of culture and use of scenes and themes. *Academy of Management Review, 10*, 219-229.

Morgan, G. (1986). *Images of organization.* Beverly Hills, CA: Sage.

Morgan, G., & Smircich, L. (1980). The case for qualitative research. *Academy of Management Review, 5*, 491-500.

Morris, M. B. (1977). *An excursion into creative sociology.* New York: Columbia University Press.

Murray, A. (1989). Top management group heterogeneity and firm performance. *Strategic Management Journal, 10*, 125-141.

Murray, J. (1989, July 22). [Daily column.] *Lubbock Avalanche-Journal*, p. A8.

Myers, I. B. (1976). *Introduction to type.* Gainesville, FL: AMSA Foundation.

Myers, I. B., & McCaulley, M. H. (1985). *Manual: A guide to the development and use of the Myers-Briggs Type Indicator.* Palo-Alto, CA: Consulting Psychologists Press.

Nealey, S. M., & Fiedler, F. E. (1968). Leadership functions of middle managers. *Psychological Bulletin, 70*, 313-329.

Noblit, G. W., & Hare, R. D. (1988). *Meta-ethnography: Synthesizing qualitative studies.* Newbury Park, CA: Sage.

Nutt, P. C. (1986). Decision style and strategic decisions of top executives. *Technical Forecasting and Social Change, 30*, 39-62.

Oberg, W. (1972). Charisma, commitment and contemporary organization theory. *Business Topics, 20*, 18-32.

Olivia, T. A., Day, D. L., & MacMillan, I. C. (1988). A general model of competitive dynamics. *Academy of Management Review, 13*, 374-389.

Olmstead, J. A. (1973). *Working paper No. 2: Organizational structure and climate: Implications for agencies.* Washington, DC: Department of Health, Education, and Welfare.

Olmstead, J. A. (1974). Leader performance as organizational process: A study of organizational competence. In J. G. Hunt & L. L. Larson (Eds.), *Contingency approaches to leadership* (pp. 158-182). Carbondale: Southern Illinois University Press.

Olmstead, J. A., Christensen, H. E., & Lackey, L. L. (1973). *Components of organizational competence: Test of a conceptual framework* (Department of the Army, Technical Report No. 73-19). Alexandria, VA: Human Resources Research Organization.

Organizational Vision Project Team. (1990, August). *Organizational vision: Theory, research and practice.* Symposium presentation at national meeting of the Academy of Management, San Francisco.

Osborn, R. N. (1985). Research implications of army leadership doctrine. In J. G. Hunt & J. D. Blair (Eds.), *Leadership on the future battlefield* (pp. 99-118). Washington, DC: Pergamon-Brassey's.

Osborn, R. N., & Hunt, J. G. (1974a). An empirical investigation of lateral and vertical leadership at two organization levels. *Journal of Business Research, 2,* 209-221.

Osborn, R. N., & Hunt, J. G. (1974b). Environment and organizational effectiveness. *Administrative Science Quarterly, 19,* 231-246.

Osborn, R. N., Hunt, J. G., & Jauch, L. R. (1980). *Organization theory: An integrated approach.* New York: Wiley.

Osborn, R. N., Hunt, J. G., & Skaret, D. J. (1977). Managerial influence in a complex configuration with two unit heads. *Human Relations, 30,* 1025-1038.

Osborn, R. N., Morris, F. A., & O'Connor, P. E. (1984). Emerging technologies: The challenge to leadership theory. In J. G. Hunt, D. M. Hosking, C. A. Schrieshiem, & R. Stewart (Eds.), *Leaders and managers* (pp. 360-365). Elmsford, NY: Pergamon.

Osgood, C. E., Suci, G. J., & Tannenbaum, P. H. (1957). *The measurement of meaning.* Urbana: University of Illinois Press.

Osigweh, C. A. B. (1989). Concept fallibility in organization science. *Academy of Management Review, 14,* 579-594.

Ott, J. S. (1989). *The organizational culture perspective.* Monterey, CA: Brooks/Cole.

Ouchi, W. G., & Wilkins, A. L. (1985). Organizational culture. *Annual Review of Sociology, 11,* 457-483.

Paolillo, J. G. (1981). Role profile for managers at different hierarchical levels. *Academy of Management Proceedings,* pp. 91-94.

Par, O. S., Sims, H. P., Jr., & Motowidlo, S. J. (1986). Affect in organizations: How feelings and emotions influence managerial judgment. In H. P. Sims, Jr., & D. A. Gioia (Eds.), *The thinking organization* (pp. 215-237). San Francisco: Jossey-Bass.

Parsons, T. (1960). *Structure and process in modern societies.* New York: Free Press.

Pasmore, W. A. (1988). *Designing effective organizations.* New York: Wiley.

Pavett, C. M., & Lau, A. W. (1982). Managerial roles, skills and effective performance. *Academy of Management Proceedings,* pp. 95-99.

Pavett, C. M., & Lau, A. W. (1983). Managerial work: The influence of hierarchical level and functional specialty. *Academy of Management Journal, 26,* 170-178.

Payne, R., & Pugh, D. S. (1976). Organizational structure and climate. In M. D. Dunnette (Ed.), *Handbook of industrial and organizational psychology* (pp. 1125-1173). Chicago: Rand McNally.

People Express. (1983). [Management case.] Harvard Business School Case 9-483-103, Harvard Graduate School of Business Administration, Boston.

Perevia, D. F. (1987). *Factors associated with transformational leadership in an Indian engineering firm.* Unpublished manuscript, Lawson & Tubro, Bombay, India.

Perrow, C. (1961, December). The analysis of goals in complex organizations. *American Sociological Review,* pp. 854-866.

Peters, T. (1988, May). Restoring American competitiveness: Looking for new models of organizations. *Academy of Management Executive,* pp. 103-109.

Peters, T., & Waterman, R. (1982). *In search of excellence.* New York: Harper & Row.

Peterson, M. F. (1985). Experienced acceptability: Measuring perceptions of dysfunctional leadership. *Group & Organization Studies, 10*, 447-477.

Peterson, M. F., & Smith, P. B. (1988). Gleanings from a frustrated process analysis of leadership research stakeholders. In J. G. Hunt, B. R. Baliga, H. P. Dachler, & C. A. Schriesheim (Eds.), *Emerging leadership vistas* (pp. 183-200). Lexington, MA: Lexington Books.

Peterson, M. F., & Sorenson, R. (in press). Problem appropriate leadership. *Communication Yearbook, 14.*

Pettigrew, A. W. (1979). On studying organizational cultures. *Administrative Science Quarterly, 24*, 570-581.

Pettigrew, A. M. (Ed.). (1987). *The management of strategic change.* London: Basil Blackwell.

Pfeffer, J. (1977). The ambiguity of leadership. *Academy of Management Review, 2*, 104-112.

Pfeffer, J. (1981). Management as symbolic action: The creation and maintenance of organizational paradigms. In L. L. Cummings & B. M. Staw (Eds.) *Research in organizational behavior* (Vol. 3, pp. 1-52). Greenwich, CT: JAI Press.

Pfeffer, J., & Davis-Blake, A. (1986). Administrative succession and organizational performance: How administrator experience mediates the succession effect. *Academy of Management Journal, 29*, 72-83.

Pfeffer, J., & Salancik, G. (1978). *The external control of organizations.* New York: Harper & Row.

Pfiffner, J. M., & Sherwood, F. P. (1960). *Administrative organization.* Englewood Cliffs, NJ: Prentice-Hall.

Phillips, J. S. (1984). The accuracy of leadership ratings: A cognitive categorization perspective. *Organizational Behavior and Human Performance, 33*, 125-138.

Phillips, J. S., & Lord, R. G. (1982) Schematic information processing and perceptions of leadership in problem-solving groups. *Journal of Applied Psychology, 67*, 486-492.

Phillips, J. S., & Lord, R. G. (1986). Notes on the practical and theoretical consequences of implicit leadership theories for the future of leadership measurement. *Journal of Management, 12*(1), 31-41.

Phillips, R., & Hunt, J. G. (1989, May). *Impact of organizational policies and operating practices on organizational performance and leader development.* Contract with the U.S. Army Research Institute for the Behavioral and Social Sciences, Alexandria, VA.

Pinder, C. C. (1984). *Work motivation.* Glenview, IL: Scott, Foresman.

Podsakoff, P. M., Todor, W. D., Grover, R. A., & Huber, V. L. (1984). Situational moderators of leader reward and punishment behavior: Fact or fiction? *Organizational Behavior and Human Performance, 34*, 21-63.

Podsakoff, P. M., Todor, W. D., & Schuler, R. S. (1983). Leader expertise as a moderator of the effects of instrumental and supportive leader behaviors. *Journal of Management, 9*, 173-186.

Pondy, L. R. (1983). Union of rationality and intuition in management action. In S. Srivastva (Ed.), *The executive mind* (pp. 169-191). San Francisco: Jossey-Bass.

Pondy, L., & Boje, D. M. (1976). *Bringing mind back in: Paradigm development as a frontier problem in organization theory.* Unpublished manuscript, Department of Business Administration, University of Illinois, Urbana.

Pondy, L., Frost, P., Morgan, G., & Dandridge, T. C. (Eds.) (1983). *Organizational symbolism*. Greenwich, CT: JAI Press.

Pondy, L. R., & Rousseau, D. M. (1980). *Quantitative vs. qualitative methods: An issue of public and private methods*. OB/OD/OT doctoral consortium presentation, Academy of Management, Detroit.

Pool, R. (1989, February). Is it healthy to be chaotic? *Science, 243*, 604.

Porter, L. W., & McKibbin, L. (1988). *Management education and development*. New York: McGraw-Hill.

Porter, M. E. (1980). *Competitive strategy: Techniques for analyzing industries and competition*. New York: Free Press.

Posner, B. Z., & Kouzes, J. M. (1990). Leadership practices: An alternative to the psychological perspective. In K. E. Clark & M. B. Clark (Eds.), *Measures of leadership* (pp. 205-216). West Orange, NJ: Leadership Library of America.

Prince, H. T. (1987). Leader development at the U.S. Military Academy. In L. Atwater & R. Penn (Eds.), *Military leadership: Traditions and future trends* (pp. 109-111). Annapolis, MD: U.S. Naval Academy.

Quinn, J. B. (1978, Fall). Strategic change: Logical incrementalism. *Sloan Management Review, 20*(1), 7-21.

Quinn, J. B. (1981a). *Strategies of change: Logical incrementalism*. Homewood, IL: Irwin.

Quinn, J. B. (1981b, Winter). Formulating strategy one step at a time. *Journal of Business Strategy, 1*(3), 42-63.

Quinn, J. B., Mintzberg, H., & James, R. M. (1988). *The strategy process*. Englewood Cliffs, NJ: Prentice-Hall.

Quinn, R. E. (1988). *Beyond rational management*. San Francisco: Jossey-Bass.

Quinn, R. E., & Cameron, K. S. (1983). Organizational life cycles and shifting criteria of effectiveness: Some preliminary evidence. *Management Science*, pp. 33-51.

Quinn, R. E., & Cameron, K. S. (1988). *Paradox and transformation*. New York: Haper & Collins.

Quinn, R. E., Faerman, S. R., Thompson, M. P., & McGrath, M. R. (1990). *Becoming a master manager*. New York: Wiley.

Quinn, R. E., & Rohrbaugh, J. (1983). A spatial model of effectiveness criteria: Towards a competing values approach to organizational analysis. *Management Science*, pp. 363-377.

Ravlin, E. C., & Meglino, B. M. (1987). Effect of values perception and decision making: A study of alternative work values measures. *Journal of Applied Psychology, 72*, 666-673.

Rentsch, J. R. (1989). Climate and culture: An empirical investigation. In J. R. Rentsch (Chair), *Climate and culture: Concepts in conjunction*. Symposium presented at the annual meeting of the Southern Management Association, New Orleans, LA.

Ritti, R. R., & Funkhouser, G. R. (1987). *The ropes to skip and the ropes to know* (3rd ed.). New York: Wiley.

Rivera, J. (1990). *A look at stratified systems theory: Is it universally requisite?* Unpublished manuscript. College of Business Administration, Texas Tech University, Lubbock.

Robbins, S. P. (1990). *Organization theory: Structure, design and applications* (3rd ed.) Englewood Cliffs, NJ: Prentice-Hall.

Robbins, S. R., & Duncan, R. B. (1988). The role of the CEO and top management in the creation and implementation of strategic vision. In D. C. Hambrick (Ed.), *The executive effect: Concepts and methods for studying top managers* (pp. 205-236). Greenwich, CT: JAI Press.

Roberts, W. (1987). *Leadership secrets of Attila the Hun.* New York: Warner.

Roberts, N. C., & Bradley, R. T. (1988). Limits of charisma. In J. A. Conger & R. N. Kanungo (Eds.), *Charismatic leadership* (pp. 253-275). San Francisco: Jossey-Bass.

Robey, D. (1986). *Designing organizations* (2nd ed.). Homewood, IL: Irwin.

Robey, D., & Taggart, W. (1981). Measuring managers' minds: The assessment of style in human information processing. *Academy of Management Review, 6,* 375-383.

Robinson, W. S. (1950). Ecological correlations and the behavior of individuals. *American Sociological Review, 15,* 351-357.

Rohrbaugh, J. (1981). Operationalizing the competing values approach. *Public Productivity Review, 5,* 141-159.

Rokeach, M. (1973). *The nature of human values.* New York: Free Press.

Romanelli, E., & Tushman, M. L. (1988). Executive leadership and organizational outcomes: An evolutionary perspective. In D. C. Hambrick (Ed.), *The executive effect: Concepts and methods for studying top managers* (pp. 129-146). Greenwich, CT: JAI Press.

Ronen, S., & Shenkar, O. (1985). Clustering countries on attitudinal dimensions: A review and synthesis. *Academy of Management Review, 10,* 435-454.

Ropo, A. (1989). *Leadership and organizational change.* Acta Universitatis Tamperensis ser A/val 280. Tampere, Finland: University of Tampere.

Ropo, A., & Hunt, J. G. (1990a, August). *Dynamic case studies in organizational and management research.* Unpublished manuscript, College of Business Administration, Texas Tech University, Lubbock.

Ropo, A., & Hunt, J. G. (1990b, July). *Leadership and organizational change: A dynamic analysis.* Unpublished manuscript, College of Business Administration, Texas Tech University, Lubbock.

Ropo, E. (1989a, September). *Expert and novice English teaching: Differences in the lessons of experienced and novice English teachers.* Paper presented at the Third European Conference for Research on Learning and Instruction, Madrid.

Ropo, E. (1989b). Teachers' questions: Some differences between experienced and novice teachers. In H. Mandl, E. De Corte, S. N. Bennett, & H. F. Friedrich (Eds.), *Learning and instructing: European research in an international context (Vols. II & III).* Oxford, UK: Pergamon.

Ropo, E., & Jahnukainen, I. (1990). Business learning of an entrepreneur: A case study of the development in conceptions of business. *Administrative Studies, 8*(1), 2-23.

Rosenberg, A. (1988). *Philosophy of social science.* Boulder, CO: Westview.

Rousseau, D. M. (1985). Issues of level in organizational research: Multi-level and cross-level perspectives. In L. L. Cummings & B. M. Staw (Eds.), *Research in organizational behavior* (Vol. 7, pp. 1-37). Greenwich, CT: JAI Press.

Rousseau, D. M. (in press). Quantitative assessment of organizational culture: The case for multiple measures. In B. Schneider (Ed.), *Frontiers in industrial and organizational psychology* (Vol. 3). Lexington, MA: Lexington Books.

Rousseau, D. M., & Cooke, R. A. (1988). *Cultures of reliability and performance: A field study of the USS Carl Vinson*. Paper presented at Academy of Management Convention, Anaheim, CA.

Rowe, A. J., & Mason, R. O. (1987). *Managing with style*. San Francisco: Jossey-Bass.

Ruderman, M. N., Ohlott, P. J., & McCauley, C. D. (1990). Assessing opportunities for leadership development. In K. E. Clark & M. B. Clark (Eds.), *Measures of leadership* (pp. 547-562). West Orange, NJ: Leadership Library of America.

Rumelhart, D. E., & Ortony, A. (1977). The representation function of knowledge in memory. In R. C. Anderson, R. J. Spiro, & W. E. Montague (Eds.), *Schooling and the acquisition of knowledge*. Hillsdale, NJ: Lawrence Erlbaum.

Rush, M. C., Philips, J. S., & Lord, R. G. (1981). Effects of a temporal delay in rating on leader behavior descriptions: A laboratory investigation. *Journal of Applied Psychology, 66*, 442-450.

Rush, M. C., Thomas, J. C., & Lord, R. G. (1977). Implicit leadership theory: A potential threat to the internal validity of leader behavior questionnaires. *Organizational Behavior and Human Performance, 20*, 93-100.

Saari, L. M., Johnson, T. R., McLaughlin, S. D., & Zimmerle, D. M. (1988). A survey of management training and education practices in U.S. companies. *Personnel Psychology, 41*, 731-743.

The sad saga of Western Union's decline. (1987, December 14). *Business Week*, pp. 108-114.

Saffold, G. (1988). Culture traits, strength, and organizational performance: Moving beyond "strong" culture. *Academy of Management Review, 13*, 546-558.

Sanders, P. (1982). Phenomenology: A new way of viewing organizational research. *Academy of Management Review, 7*, 353-360.

Sashkin, M. (1984, Spring). Participative management is an ethical imperative. *Organizational Dynamics, 12*, 5-22.

Sashkin, M. (1986, Spring). Participative management remains an ethical imperative. *Organizational Dynamics, 14*, 62-78.

Sashkin, M. (1988). The visionary leader. In J. A. Conger & R. N. Kanungo (Eds.), *Charismatic leadership* (pp. 122-160). San Francisco: Jossey-Bass.

Sashkin, M. (1990). *Are competency models competent?* Unpublished manuscript, U.S. Department of Education, Washington, DC.

Sashkin, M., & Burke, W. W. (1990). Understanding and assessing organizational leadership. In K. E. Clark & M. B. Clark (Eds.), *Measures of leadership* (pp. 297-326). West Orange, NJ: Leadership Library of America.

Sashkin, M., & Fulmer, R. M. (1988). Toward an organizational leadership theory. In J. G. Hunt, B. R. Baliga, H. P. Dachler, & E. A. Schriesheim (Eds.). *Emerging leadership vistas* (pp. 51-65). Lexington, MA: Lexington Books.

Sashkin, S., & Sashkin, M. G. (1990, April). *Leadership and culture-building in schools: Quantitative and qualitative understandings*. Paper presented at meeting of the American Educational Research Association, Boston.

Sathe, V. (1985). *Culture and related corporate realities: Text, cases, and readings on organizational entry, establishment, and change*. Homewood, IL: Irwin.

Scarpello, V. G., & Ledvinka, J. (1988). *Personnel/human resources management*. Boston: PWS-Kent.

Schein, E. (1980). *Organizational psychology* (3rd ed.). Englewood Cliffs, NJ: Prentice-Hall.

Schein, E. H. (1983, Summer). The role of the founder in creating an organizational culture. *Organizational Dynamics*, pp. 13-28.

Schein, E. H. (1984, Winter). Coming to a new awareness of organizational culture. *Sloan Management Review*, pp. 33-15.

Schein, E. H. (1985). *Organizational culture and leadership*. San Francisco: Jossey-Bass.

Schein, E. H. (1986, Winter). A rejoinder to Sashkin and further clarification. *Academy of Management OD Newsletter*, pp. 6-7.

Schein, E. H. (1990). Organizational culture. *American Psychologist, 45*, 109-119.

Schermerhorn, J. R., Jr., Hunt, J. G., & Osborn, R. N. (1988). *Managing organizational behavior* (3rd ed.). New York: Wiley.

Schermerhorn, J. R., Jr., Hunt, J. G., & Osborn, R. N. (1991). *Managing organizational behavior* (4th ed.). New York: Wiley.

Schneider, B. (1975). Organizational climates: An essay. *Personnel Psychology, 28*, 447-479.

Schneider, B. (1985). *Annual Review of Psychology, 36*, 573-611.

Schneider, B. (1987). The people make the place. *Personnel Psychology, 40*, 437-453.

Schneider, B. (1989). Thoughts on leadership and management. In L. Atwater & R. Penn (Eds.), *Military leadership: Traditions and future trends* (pp. 30-33). Annapolis, MD: U.S. Naval Academy.

Schneider, B., & Gunnarson, S. (in press). Organizational climate and culture: The psychology of the workplace. In J. W. Jones, B. D. Steffy, & D. Bray (Eds.), *Applying psychology in business: The manager's handbook.* Lexington, MA: Lexington Books.

Schneider, B., & Rentsch, J. (1988). Managing climates and cultures: A futures perspective. In J. Hoge (Ed.), *Futures of organizations*. Lexington, MA: Lexington Books.

Schrank, R. E., & Abelson, R. P. (1977). *Scripts, plans, goals and understanding.* Hillsdale, NJ: Lawrence Erlbaum.

Schriesheim, C. A., Kinicki, A. J., & Schriesheim, J. F. (1979). The effect of leniency in leader behavior descriptions. *Organizational Behavior and Human Performance, 23*, 1-29.

Schroder, H. M., Driver, J. J., & Streufert, S. (1967). *Human information processing.* New York: Holt, Rinehart & Winston.

Schwartz, J. E., & Sprinzen, M. (1984). Structures of connectivity. *Social Networks, 6*, 103-140.

Scott, W. A. (1962). Cognitive structure and social structure: Some concepts and relationships. In N. F. Washburne (Ed.), *Decisions, values and groups*. Elmsford, NY: Pergamon.

Scott, W. A., Osgood, D. W., & Peterson, C. (1979). *Cognitive structure: Theory and measurement of individual differences.* New York: Wiley.

Scott, W. R. (1987). *Organizations: Rational, natural, and open systems.* Englewood Cliffs, NJ: Prentice-Hall.

Segal, D. R. (1981). Leadership and management: Organization theory. In J. H. Buck & L. J. Korb (Eds.), *Military leadership* (pp. 41-69). Newbury Park, CA: Sage.

Seiden, H. M. (1970). Time perspective and styles of consciousness. *Dissertation Abstracts International, 31*, 386B. (University Microfilms No. 70-11, 275).

Seiler, J. A. (1967). *Systems analysis in organizational behavior.* Homewood, IL: Irwin-Dorsey.

Shamir, B., House, R. J., & Arthur, M. (1990). *The transformational effects of charismatic leadership: A motivational theory.* Unpublished manuscript, Department of Sociology/Anthropology, Hebrew University, Israel.

Sheridan, J. E., Hogstel, M., & Fairchild, T. (1990). Organizational climate in nursing homes: Its impact on nursing leadership and patient care. In *Academy of Management Best Paper Proceedings 1990.* San Francisco: Academy of Management.

Shrivastava, P., & Mitroff, I. (1984). Enhancing organizational research utilization: The role of decision makers' assumptions. *Academy of Management Review, 9,* 18-26.

Shweder, R. A. (1975). How relevant is an individual differences theory of personality? *Journal of Personality, 43,* 455-484.

Shweder, R. A. (1982). Fact and artifact in trait perception: The systematic distortion hypothesis. *Progress in Experimental Personality Research, 1,* 65-100.

Siehl, C. (1985). After the founder: An opportunity to manage culture. In P. J. Frost, L. L. Moore, M. R. Louis, C. C. Lundberg, & J. Martin (Eds.), *Organizational culture.* Newbury Park, CA: Sage.

Silverstein, A., & Silverstein, V. (1980). *The genetics explosion:* New York: Four Winds.

Simon, H. (1977). *The new science of management decision* (3rd ed.). Englewood Cliffs, NJ: Prentice-Hall.

Simon, H. A. (1987, February). Making management decisions: The role of intuition and emotion. *Academy of Management Executive, 1,* 57-64.

Sims, H. P., Jr., & Gioia, D. A. (Eds.). (1986). *The thinking organization.* San Francisco: Jossey-Bass.

Smircich, L. (1983). Concepts of culture and organizational analysis. *Administrative Science Quarterly, 28,* 339-358.

Smircich, L., & Calas, M. B. (1987). Organizational culture: A critical assessment. In F. M. Jablin, L. L. Putnam, K. H. Roberts, & L. W. Porter (Eds.), *Handbook of organizational communication* (pp. 228-263). Newbury Park, CA: Sage.

Smircich, L., & Morgan, G. (1982). Leadership: The management of meaning. *Journal of Applied Behavioral Science, 18,* 257-273.

Smircich, L., & Stubbart, C. (1985). Strategic management in an enacted world. *Academy of Management Review, 10,* 724-736.

Smith, H, (1988). *The power game.* New York: Ballantine.

Smith, K. K. (1984). Rabbits, lynxes, and organizational transitions. In J. R. Kimberly & R. E. Quinn (Eds.), *Managing organizational transitions* (pp. 267-294). Homewood, IL: Irwin.

Smith, P. B., & Peterson, M. F. (1988). *Leadership, organizations and culture.* London: Sage.

Smith, P. B., & Tayeb, M. (1988). Organizational structure and processes. In M. H. Bond (Ed.), *The cross-cultural challenge to social psychology* (pp. 153-164). Newbury Park, CA: Sage.

Smithin, T. (1980). Maps of the mind: New pathways to decision-making. *Business Horizons, 23,* 24-28.

Snyder, N. H., & Wheelen, T. L. (1981). Managerial roles: Mintzberg and the management process theorists. *Proceedings of the Academy of Management,* pp. 249-253.

Sonnenfeld, J., & Kotter, J. P. (1982). The maturation of career theory. *Human Relations, 35,* 19-46.

Spector, P. E., Brannick, M. T., & Coovert, M. D. (1989). Job analysis. In C. L. Cooper & I. T. Robertson (Eds.), *International review of industrial and organizational psychology* (pp. 281-329). Chichester, UK: Wiley.

Speer, A. (1970). *Inside the Third Reich.* New York: Macmillan.

Sproull, L. S. (1981). Beliefs in organizations. In P. C. Nysrom & W. H. Starbuck (Eds.), *Handbook of organizational design* (pp. 203-224). Oxford, UK: Oxford University Press.

Srull, T. K. (1984). Methodological techniques for the study of person memory and social cognition. In R. S. Wyer & T. K. Srull (Eds.), *Handbook of social cognition* (Vol. 2). Hillsdale, NJ: Lawrence Erlbaum.

Stablein, R., & Nord, W. (1985). Practical and emancipatory interests in organizational symbolism: A review and evaluation. *Journal of Management, 11*(2), 13-28.

Stamp, G. (1978). Assessment of individual capacity. In E. Jaques, R. O Gibson, & D. J. Isaac (Eds.), *Levels of abstraction in logic and human action.* London: Heinemann.

Stamp, G. P. (1988, February). *Longitudinal research into methods of assessing managerial potential* (Technical Report DAJA45-86-C-0009). Alexandria, VA: U.S. Army Research Institute for the Behavioral and Social Sciences.

Sternberg, R. J. (1990). Intellectual styles. In K. E. Clark & M. B. Clark (Eds.), *Measures of leadership* (pp. 481-492). West Orange, NJ: Leadership Library of America.

Stewart, D., & Mickunas, A. (1974). *Exploring phenomenology.* Chicago: American Library Association.

Stewart, R. (1982a). *Choices for the manager.* Englewood Cliffs, NJ: Prentice-Hall.

Stewart, R. (1982b). The relevance of some studies of managerial work and behavior to leadership research. In J. G. Hunt, V. Sekaran, & C. A. Schriesheim (Eds.), *Leadership: Beyond establishment views* (pp. 11-30). Carbondale: Southern Illinois University Press.

Stewart, R. (1989). Studies of managerial jobs and behavior: The ways forward. *Journal of Management Studies, 26,* 1-10.

Stogdill, R. M. (1948). Personal factors associated with leadership: A survey of the literature. *Journal of Psychology, 25,* 35-71.

Stogdill, R. M. (1974). *Handbook of leadership: A survey of theory and research.* New York: Free Press.

Storm, P. H. (1977). Lateral and hierarchical leadership style congruence. In J. G. Hunt & L. L. Larson (Eds.), *Leadership: The cutting edge* (pp. 138-154). Carbondale: Southern Illinois University Press.

Streufert, S., & Nogami, G. (1989). Cognitive style and complexity: Implications for I/O psychology. In C. L. Cooper & I. Robertson (Eds.), *International review of industrial and organizational psychology* (pp. 93-143). Chichester, UK: Wiley.

Streufert, S., Pogash, R. M., & Piasecki, M. T. (1988). Simulation based assessment of managerial competence: Reliability and validity. *Personnel Psychology, 41,* 537-555.

Streufert, S., & Streufert, S. C. (1978). *Behavior in the complex environment.* Washington, DC: Winston.

Streufert, S., & Swezey, R. W. (1986). *Complexity, managers, and organizations.* Orlando, FL: Academic Press.

Suedfeld, P., & Rank, A. D. (1976). Revolutionary leaders: Long term success as a function of changes in conceptual complexity. *Journal of Personality and Social Psychology, 34,* 169-178.

Summey, J. H., & Bovinet, J. (1989). *The application of chaos theory to strategic market planning: A beginning.* Unpublished manuscript, Department of Marketing, Southern Illinois University at Carbondale.

Swezey, R. W., Davis, E. G., Baudhuin, E. S., Streufert, S., & Evans, R. (1980, September). *Organizational and systems theory: An integrated review* (Technical Report #595). Alexandria, VA: U.S. Army Research Institute for the Behavioral and Social Sciences.

Taggart, W. S., & Robey, D. (1981). Minds & managers: On the dual nature of human information processing and management. *Academy of Management Review, 6,* 187-195.

Tayeb, M. H. (1988). *Organizations and national culture.* London: Sage.

Taylor, S. E., & Crocker, N. (1981). Schematic bases of social information processing. In E. T. Hoggins, C. P. Herman, & M. P. Zana (Eds.), *Social cognition: The Ontario Symposium* (Vol. 1). Hillsdale, NJ: Lawrence Erlbaum.

Taylor, S. E., & Fiske, S. T. (1981). Getting inside the head: Methodologies for process analysis in attribution and social cognition. In J. H. Harvey, W. Ickes, & R. F. Kidd (Eds.), *New directions in attribution research* (Vol. 3, pp. 459-524). Hillsdale, NJ: Lawrence Erlbaum.

Terreberry, S. (1968). The evolution of organizational environments. *Administrative Science Quarterly, 12,* 550-613.

Thompson, J. D. (1967). *Organizations in action.* New York: McGraw-Hill.

Tichy, N. M. (1983). *Managing strategic change: Technical, political and cultural dynamics.* New York: Wiley-Interscience.

Tichy, N. M., & Devanna, M. A. (1986). *The transformational leader. New York: John Wiley.*

Tichy, N. M., & Ulrich, D. (1984a, Fall). The leadership challenge—a call for the transformational leader. *Sloan Management Review, 26,* 59-68.

Tichy, N. M., & Ulrich, D. (1984b). Revitalizing organizations: The leadership role. In J. R. Kimberly & R. E. Quinn (Eds.), *Managing organizational transitions* (pp. 240-264). Homewood, IL: Irwin.

Tierney, W. G. (1988). *The web of leadership: The presidency in higher education.* Greenwich, CT: JAI Press.

Todd, R., & Benbasat, I. (1987). Process tracing methods in decision support systems research: Exploring the black box. *MIS Quarterly,* pp. 493-512.

Tolman, E. C. (1948). Cognitive maps in rats and men. *Psychology Review, 55,* 189-209.

Trice, H. M., & Beyer, J. M. (1986). Charisma and its routinization in two social movement organizations. In B. M. Staw & L. L. Cummings (Eds.), *Research in organizational behavior* (Vol. 8, pp. 113-164). Greenwich, CT: JAI Press.

Tsoukas, H. (1989). The validity of idiographic research explanations. *Academy of Management Review, 14,* 551-561.

Tuelings, A. W. M. (1986). Managerial labour processes in organized capitalism: The power of corporate management and the powerlessness of the manager. In D. Knights & H. Willmott (Eds.), *Managing the labor process.* Cambridge, UK: Cambridge University Press.

Tully, S. (1990, June 4). The CEO who sees beyond budgets. *Fortune,* p. 186.

Tushman, M. J., Newman, W. H., & Romanelli, E. (1986, Fall). Convergence and upheaval: Managing the unsteady pace of organizational evolution. *California Management Review, 29,* 29-44.

Tushman, M. L., & Romanelli, E. (1985). Organizational evolution: A metamorphasis model of convergence and reorientation. In L. L. Cummings & B. M. Staw (Eds.), *Research in organizational behavior* (Vol. 7, pp. 171-222). Greenwich, CT: JAI Press.

Tversky, A., & Kahneman, D. (1974). Judgment under certainty: Heuristics and biases. *Science, 185,* 1124-1131.

U.S. Army Research Institute for the Behavioral and Social Sciences. (1989, May). *Impact of organizational policies and operating practices on organizational performance and leader development* (Request for Proposal MDA 903-89-R-0058).

U.S. Army War College (1988). *Special text: Executive leadership AY 88.* Carlisle Barracks, PA: Author.

Up up and away. (1985, November 25). *Business Week,* pp. 80-94.

Valerio, A. M. (1990). A study of the developmental experiences of managers. In K. E. Clark & M. B. Clark (Eds.), *Measures of leadership* (pp. 521-534). West Orange, NJ: Leadership Library of America.

Van de Ven, A., Ludwig, D., Oppenheim, L., & Davis, P. (1983). *An attempt to institutionalize an organization's culture.* Paper presented at Symposium on Organizational Culture at annual meeting of the Academy of Management, Dallas.

Van Maanen, J., & Barley, S. R. (1985). Cultural organization: Fragments of a theory. In P. J. Frost, L. L. Moore, M. R. Louis, C. C. Lundberg, & J. Martin (Eds.), *Organizational culture* (31-53). Newbury Park, CA: Sage.

Van Maanen, J. (1977). Experiencing organizations. In J. Van Maanen (Ed.), *Organizational careers: Some new perspectives* (pp. 15-45). New York: Wiley.

Van Maanen, J. (1978). People processing: Strategies of organizational socialization. *Organizational Dynamics, 7,* 18-36.

Vaughn, M. R., Kriner, R. E., & Reaser, J. M. (1973, June). *Military leadership in the seventies: Selected analyses* (Final Report, Human Resources Research Organization). Alexandria, VA: U.S. Army Research Institute for the Behavioral and Social Sciences.

Venkatraman, N. (1989). The concept of fit in strategy research: Toward verbal and statistical correspondence. *Academy of Management Review, 14,* 423-444.

Venkatraman, N., & Prescott, J. E. (in press). Environment-strategy coalignment: An empirical examination of its performance implications. *Strategic Management Journal.*

Voyer, J. J., & Faulkner, R. R. (1986). Cognition and leadership in an artistic organization. In J. A. Pierce, II, & R. B. Robinson, Jr. (Eds.), *Academy of Management Best Paper Proceedings 1986* (pp. 160-164). Columbia, SC: University of South Carolina.

Vroom, V. H., & Jago, A. G. (1988). *The new leadership.* Englewood Cliffs, NJ: Prentice-Hall.

Wagner, R. K., & Sternberg, R. J. (1990). Street smarts. In K. E. Clark & M. B. Clark (Eds.), *Measures of leadership* (pp. 493-504). West Orange, NJ: Leadership Library of America.

Wallendorf, M., & Belk, R. W. (1989). Assessing trustworthiness in naturalistic consumer research. In E. Hirschman (Ed.), *Interpretive consumer research.* Provo, UT: Association for Consumer Research.

Walsh, J. P. (1988). Selectivity and selective perception: An investigation of managers' belief stuctures and information processing. *Academy of Management Journal, 24,* 453-470.

Walsh, J. P. (1990). *Knowledge structures and the management of organizations: A research review and agenda*. Unpublished manuscript, Dartmouth College, Hanover, NH.

Walsh, J. P., & Fahey, L. (1986). The role of negotiated belief structures in strategy making. *Journal of Management, 12*, 325-338.

Walsh, J. P., Henderson, C. M., & Deighton, J. (1988). Negotiated belief structures and decision performance: An empirical investigation. *Organizational Behavior and Human Decision Processes, 42*, 194-216.

Warriner, C. K. (1965). The problem of organizational purpose. *Sociological Quarterly*, pp. 139-146.

Watson, D. (1982). The actor and the observer: How are their perceptions of causality divergent? *Psychological Bulletin, 92*, 682-700.

Weber, M. (1947). *The theory of social and economic organization* (A. M. Henderson & T. Parsons, Trans.; T. Parsons, Ed.). New York: Free Press. (Original work published 1924)

Wegner, D. M., & Vallacher, R. R. (1977). *Implicit psychology*. New York: Oxford University Press.

Weick, K. (1969). *The social psychology of organizing*. Reading, MA: Addison-Wesley.

Weick, K. E. (1979). *The social psychology of organizing (2nd ed.), Reading, MA: Addison-Wesley.*

Weick, K. E. (1983). Managerial thought in the context of action. In S. Srivastva (Ed.), *The executive mind* (pp. 221-242). San Francisco: Jossey-Bass.

Weick, K. E., & Bougan, M. G. (1986). Organizations as cognitive maps. In H. P. Sims, Jr., & D. A. Gioia (Eds), *The thinking organization* (pp. 102-135). San Francisco: Jossey-Bass.

Weick, K. E., & Gilfillan, D. P. (1971). Fate of arbitrary traditions in a laboratory microculture. *Journal of Personality and Social Psychology, 17*, 179-191.

Westley, F. R., & Mintzberg, H. (1988). Profiles of strategic vision: Levesque and Iacocca. In J. A. Conger & R. N. Kanungo (Eds.), *Charismatic leadership* (pp. 161-212). San Francisco: Jossey-Bass.

Westley, F. R., & Mintzberg, H. (1989). Visionary leadership and strategic management. *Strategic Management Journal, 10*, 17-32.

Wexler, M. N. (1983). Pragmatism, interactionism and dramatism: Interpreting the symbols in organizations. In L. Pondy, P. Frost, G. Morgan, & T. C. Dandridge (Eds.), *Organizational symbolism* (pp. 237-253). Greenwich, CT: JAI Press.

Wexley, K. N., & Baldwin, T. T. (1986). Management development. *Yearly Review of Management of the Journal of Management, 12*, 277-294.

Whetten, D. A., & Cameron, K. S. (1984). *Developing management skills*. Glenview, IL: Scott, Foresman.

White, R. (1959). Motivation reconsidered. The concept of competence. *Psychological Review, 66*, 297-333.

Whitely, W., & England, G. W. (1980). Variability in common dimensions of managerial values due to value orientation and country differences. *Personnel Psychology, 33*, 77-89.

Wiener, Y. (1988). Forms of value systems: A focus on organizational effectiveness and cultural change and maintenance. *Academy of Management Review, 13*, 534-545.

Wilden, A. (1980). *System and structure*. London: Tavistock.

Williams, L. J., & Podsakoff, P. M.(1989). Longitudinal field methods for studying reciprocal relationships in organizational behavior research: Toward improved causal analysis. In L. L. Cummings & B. M. Staw (Eds.), *Research in organizational behavior* (Vol. 11, pp. 247-292). Greenwich, CT: JAI Press.

Willner, A. R. (1984). *The spellbinders: Charismatic political leadership.* New Haven, CT: Yale University Press.

Wood, R., & Bandura, A. (1989). Social cognitive theory of organizational management. *Academy of Management Review, 14,* 361-384.

Wren, D. A. (1987). *The evolution of management thought (3rd ed.). New York: John Wiley.*

Wright, P. L., & Taylor, D. S. (1984). *Improving leadership performance.* London: Prentice-Hall International.

Wynne, B. E., & Hunsaker, P. L. (1975). A human information-processing approach to the study of leadership. In J. G. Hunt & L. L. Larson (Eds.), *Leadership frontiers* (pp. 7-26). Kent, OH: Kent State University Press.

Yammarino, F. J., & Bass, B. M. (1990). Long-term forecasting of transformational leadership and its effects among naval officers: Some preliminary findings. In K. E. Clark & M. B. Clark (Eds.), *Measures of leadership* (pp. 151-170). West Orange, NJ: Leadership Library of America.

Yang, A. I. (1981). Psychological temporality: A study of temporal orientation, attitude, mind states, and personality type (Doctoral dissertation, University of Hawaii, 1981). *Dissertation Abstracts International, 42*(04), 1677B.

Yin, R. K. (1989). *Case study research: Design and methods* (2nd ed.). Newbury Park, CA: Sage.

Yuchtman, E., & Seashore, S. (1967). A system resource approach to organizational effectiveness. *American Sociological Review,* pp. 891-903.

Yukl, G. A. (1981). *Leadership in organizations.* Englewood Cliffs, NJ: Prentice-Hall.

Yukl, G. A. (1987a, August). *A new taxonomy for integrating diverse perspectives on managerial behavior.* Paper presented at annual meeting of the American Psychological Association, New York.

Yukl, G. A. (1987b, May). *Development of a new measure of managerial behavior: Preliminary report on validation of the MPS.* Paper presented at the Eastern Academy of Management Meetings, Boston.

Yukl, G. A. (1989). *Leadership in organizations* (2nd ed.) Englewood Cliffs, NJ: Prentice-Hall.

Yukl, G. A., & Lepsinger, R. (1989). An integrating taxonomy of managerial behavior: Implications for improving managerial effectiveness. In J. W. Jones, B. D. Staffy, & D. W. Bray (Eds.), *Applying psychology in business: The manager's handbook.* Lexington, MA: Lexington Books.

Yukl, G. A., & Nemeroff, W. (1979). Identification and measurement of specifics of leadership behavior: A progress report. In J. G. Hunt & L. L. Larson (Eds.), *Crosscurrents in leadership* (pp. 164-200). Carbondale: Southern Illinois University Press.

Zajonc, R. B. (1960). The process of cognitive tuning in communication. *Journal of Abnormal and Social Psychology, 32,* 395-509.

Zalesnik, A. (1977, May-June). Managers and leaders: Are they different? *Harvard Business Review, 15,* 67-68.

Zalesnik, A. (1989). *The managerial mystique.* New York: Harper Collins.

Zalesnik, A., & Kets De Vries, M. (1975). *Power and the corporate mind*. Boston: Houghton Mifflin.

Zimmerman, D. H., & Wilson, T. P. (1973). *Prospects for experimental studies of meaning structures*. Paper presented at meeting of the American Sociological Association, New York.

Zohar, D. (1980). Safety climates in industrial organizations: Theoretical and applied implications. *Journal of Applied Psychology, 65,* 96-102.

Zucker, L. G. (1977). The role of institutionalization in cultural persistence. *American Sociological Review, 42,* 726-743.

Zuker, E. (1985). Leading edge workshop. *Success strategies.* New York: John Wiley.

Name Index

Subject Index

About the Author

James G. (Jerry) Hunt (Ph.D., University of Illinois) is Paul Whitfield Horn Professor of Management; Professor of Health Organization Management; Director, Program in Leadership, Institute for Management and Leadership Research; and former Department Chair of Management, Texas Tech University.

Coauthor of an organization theory text and an organizational behavior text (now in its fourth edition), he has authored or coauthored three leadership monographs. He founded the Leadership Symposia Series and has coedited the eight volumes based on the series. He coedited *Leadership on the Future Battlefield* in 1986 and also has coedited a proceedings volume and three special issues of journals. Professor Hunt has presented or had published more than 100 articles, papers, and book chapters.

He is former editor of the *Journal of Management* and is or has been on the editorial boards of a number of journals. He is an Academy of Management Fellow and has been chairperson of the Organizational Behavior Division and President of the Midwest Academy of Management and Southern Management Association.